BRITISH NOVELISTS SINCE 1900

**Georgia State
Literary Studies**
AMS Press
Editor, Volume One
Jack I. Biles
Series General Editor, Volume One
James D. Wilson
Series General Editor
Victor A. Kramer
Volume One: *British Novelists Since 1900*
Volume Two: *Harlem Renaissance Re-examined*
Volume Three: *The Cinematic Text: Contemporary Methods and Practice*
Volume Four: *Coleridge's Theory of the Imagination as Critical Method Today*

0884-8696.

BRITISH NOVELISTS SINCE 1900

Edited by

Jack I. Biles

AMS PRESS
NEW YORK

Library of Congress Cataloging-in-Publication Data

British novelists since 1900.

    (Georgia State literary studies; 1)
    Bibliography: p.
    Includes index.
    1. English fiction—20th century—History and criticism.
I. Biles, Jack I., 1920-   . II. Title.
III. Series.
PR883.B75 1986   823'.91'09   85-48000
ISBN 0-404-63201-7

Copyright © AMS Press, Inc., 1987

Manufactured in the United States of America

Contents

Prefatory Note

With this volume on twentieth-century British novelists, the Department of English at Georgia State University inaugurates *Literary Studies,* a series of books on literary topics of contemporary scholarly interest. The core of each volume in the series consists of essays selected and reprinted from back issues of *Studies in the Literary Imagination.* Authors of reprinted essays are given the opportunity to revise their initial work in light of new scholarship or altered perspectives. New essays, commissioned specifically for this project, are added to provide fuller coverage of the topic than was possible in the shorter journal issue, or to address points of scholarly controversy that have surfaced since the original *Studies* number appeared. Each new volume contains an index and a current bibliography. The whole is supervised by a member of the Graduate English faculty at Georgia State, who serves as Consulting Editor for the volume.

I should like to thank Gabe Hornstein, President of AMS Press, who encouraged us to reprint popular back issues now out-of-print and who has agreed to sponsor this new series. I should also like to thank Clyde Faulkner, Dean of the College of Arts and Sciences at Georgia State, whose continued financial support of *Studies in the Literary Imagination* and encouragement of professional research activity within our department have made this project possible.

JAMES D. WILSON
Series General Editor

Foreword

This opening volume of the Georgia State Literary Studies Series, *British Novelists Since 1900*, reflects the talents of its editor, the late Professor Jack I. Biles, always a reader who remained fascinated with England and its literature. During his years as a graduate professor at Georgia State Biles taught seminars in Modern British fiction and directed many theses and dissertations within this area revealing for several generations of students the depth and range of this fiction.

Through his sustained interest in modern British fiction Professor Biles came to be one of the significant consulting editors for the journal *Studies in the Literary Imagination* which published several issues edited by him. Because many essays included in this volume derive from *Studies*, this book not only provides a compendium about twentieth-century British fiction, but reflects the life and the scholarly career of Dr. Biles. Any successful teacher-scholar engages in many activities that nourish his total accomplishment, and such a volume as this one would never have taken the shape it possesses without Dr. Biles's spirited teaching and enthusiastic research.

One of Biles's favorite authors, and this is clear from this volume and the whole body of his scholarship, was William Golding whose work he early recognized as of a major stature. Serious questions about literature, human nature, and culture, raised by work such as Golding's fiction, are reflected in the scholarly inquiries which Biles and others have made as they have examined Goldling's work and that of other significant British novelists in the essays in this volume. These essays remind us that no easy answers about human nature or literature are forthcoming, yet by continuing to raise questions about fiction and its makers scholars such as Biles instruct, even entertain, so that readers can become better readers of all literature.

This volume should be recognized as a milestone in the history of the development of Graduate Studies in English at Georgia State. Succeeding volumes in the Series will, likewise, reflect the unique combinations of the contributors. Just as a teacher is never absolutely certain what may happen in any particular classroom meeting, no editor can completely control how an issue of a journal, or an edited collection in a book, will function; yet it is through the sustained interest and control of a scholar like Jack Biles that readers can more easily come to see the wonder of literature and life itself. As General Editor of the Series, I look forward to working with Georgia State University faculty editors who will edit volumes on a range of topics from early British to modern American literature.

Victor A. Kramer
General Editor
Literary Studies
Georgia State University

Introduction

JACK I. BILES

British Novelists Since 1900 concerns an arbitrarily chosen group of novelists taken from the uncounted total of such writers published in Great Britain during this century. The twenty-one essays in this volume treat seven male and nine female novelists; this sparse band is perhaps representative of the many, perhaps not.

I thought it desirable to feature novelists who have had relatively little scholarly or critical attention rather than to concentrate on the much-investigated, say Joyce or Lawrence. Such could not be the exclusive case, for one could scarcely talk of the century's novelists and ignore Virginia Woolf and Iris Murdoch, Joseph Conrad and William Golding. Topics have not been restricted to the authors as novelists nor to commentary altogether on their novels, a circumstance allowing for introductory exposition regarding the lesser-known writers.

An objective and logical organization for this collection of essays is the chronological, permitting a movement down the century and affording a natural ordering resting upon date of birth, ranging from Joseph Conrad (1857) to Dame Margaret Drabble (1939). A few minor difficulties arose: Ivy Compton-Burnett's birthdate is often not given at all or stated as 1892, but the correct date appears to be 5 June 1884; according to Diana Athill (Jean Rhys's editor at Andre Deutsch, Ltd.), Jean Rhys gave her birthdate as 1894, but an old passport gives 1890 and this was family tradition as well; Sybille Bedford's birthdate is 16 March 1911 and William Golding's is 19 September

1911, but because of the essay on Graham Greene (born 1904) and Golding, I have placed the Bedford essay nonchronologically after the Golding papers.

At my suggestion—although with some reservations as to the subject's potential—Frank Baldanza set upon and soon became absorbed in his inquiry regarding Joseph Conrad and opera as the extent of Conrad's interest and knowledge became evident. Professor Baldanza worked in the United States and in Europe, especially in Marseilles, and corresponded with Conradians in various parts of the world. From their uncertain beginning, his efforts resulted in his fine essays—thorough, perceptive, judicious, illuminating—an original and significant addition to Conrad scholarship.

William J. Scheick has written extensively about Wells's fiction of the 1920s and did a long, serious piece on *Apropos of Dolores* (1938). In 1980 Scheick published in *Studies in the Literary Imagination* an essay on Wells's *Brynhild* (1937), now incorporated into his *The Splintering Frame: The Later Fiction of H. G. Wells*. His contribution to this book, "Revisionary Artistry in Wells's *The Passionate Friends*," concerns a little-known novel which, surprisingly, has won the praise of Vladimir Nabokov and Graham Greene. (Wells's middle work has had indebtedness acknowledged by C. P. Snow, Kingsley Amis, and Jorge Luis Borges.) Scheick says that Henry James "hated" the novel. Scheick argues a case that *The Passionate Friends* achieves variations on "the popular novel of romance" [Marie Corelli?] and "conventional notions of passion, paternity, marriage and imperialism."

According to Avrom Fleishman, Ford's reputation "continues to hang on one book," *The Good Soldier,* despite all the haggling about it. Fleishman's view is that critical attention belongs "to Ford's actual performance of impressionist methods, to the novel's rich but unassayed verbal texture, and above all to its generic modes." Combining seriousness, wit, and banter, Fleishman takes issue with those who have deserted *The Good Soldier* as comic, and testifies to his pleasure in it, one of "the few great modern comic novels," and in John Dowell, "one of the great comic characters of literature." And he makes a trenchant case for both.

Norman Page, in an essay touching *The Good Soldier* but concentrated on *Parade's End,* shows how Ford's preoccupation with dictatorial upperclass social dogmas extending "from food and drink to morality and religion in order to restrict personal liberty" is subtly figured forth by the novelist's reiterated emphasis upon the word *convention* as a primary means of conveying the true subject of *Parade's End.* Ford chronicles the deterioration and collapse of the fashionably approved ritual in a tetralogy dominated by a Tolstoyan radical loneliness and despair of a woman who has always been outside the pale of ordinary respectability, tinged with a defiant determination not to let defenses down, not to give an inch of advantage to the enemy in spite of poverty and hopelessness."

Victoria Mary Sackville-West of Knole, "Vita" to most who know of her, is Virginia Woolf's Orlando; she also is somewhat notorious because of her son's revelations about his parents and his publication of some of her private writings. In her article, Carole Ames develops her examination of fundamental concepts in Sackville-West's work (the interdependence of man and nature and the sense of stewardship) through an investigation not only of the novels but also of the nonfiction, the gardening articles, the poetry, letters, and other private writings. Ames does Sackville-West a service—and justice—by showing her as of interest for a great deal more than merely her association with Virginia Woolf.

John Atkins provides a provocative article juxtaposing views of life to be derived from the writings of William Golding and Graham Greene. Mr. Atkins asserts of Golding that "the most fruitful comparison will always be with Graham Greene, who has been equally determined to expose the hollowness of man's illusions about his nature." Atkins goes on to make that comparison and reaches a conclusion favorable to Greene.

Cecil Davies' brief commentary in 1968 is to this date, so far as I have been able to determine in rather extensive bibliographic researches on Golding's work, the only published consideration of the 1934 *Poems*. That study seventeen years ago by Mr. Davies prompted my request that he treat the poetry and its connections to the novels rather more fully than he had previously done. The careful and perceptive execution of this task, and his minute examination of the *oeuvre*, culminated in his identification of fundamentally significant images from recesses of Golding's life, images which kindle the poet. Davies has given us an enlightening and valuable account of the necessity of an ignited poetic imagination to Golding's best work.

In "Golding and the Voice of Chapel," Jack Biles has written a detailed examination of William Golding's treatment of matters sexual in his fiction. In this regard, Golding characteristically exhibits captivation with the subject and, as by instinct, simultaneously recoils. He frequently associates sexual activity with infraction of religous and/or moral imperatives. But, despite his uneasiness with the motif, Golding scatters variations upon the sexual thickly throughout his work.

In his essay Richard Bradford pursues the facts in the strange case of

William Golding and the 1983 Nobel Prize for Literature. The unseemly
protests and ill-natured posturing of Artur Lundkvist before the Nobel
Committee and the world, together with the curious silence or milk-and-
water quasi-statements of the British press have cast an atmosphere of
murkiest fog over literary Britain's response, such as it was. And Britain's last
prize was Churchill's in ancient 1953. For his determined pursuit, Bradford
found that there was no controversy in Britain at the choice of Golding, only
an unaccountable limpness on the part of the press and of British authors. So,
in the absence of substantial repercussions, Bradford rightly devotes part of
his article to an assessment of the Golding canon at the time of the decision in
Stockholm.

Leaving out of account the recognition brought her by her outsize biography of Aldous Huxley, Sybille Bedford is perhaps the least known of the
novelists considered here. Further, Bedford has the smallest output: only
three novels, "not much," says Robert Evans, "for a writer for whom I am
about to claim serious stature." In an effort to rectify what he sees as the injustice of her having been so neglected, Evans argues a heartfelt case for
Bedford; a novelist, he declares, "of absolute integrity bent on telling her
readers the truth."

Margaret Drabble voices, in a charming personal essay, her admiration for
Angus Wilson's fiction and simultaneously provides a shrewd critique of it.
She finds him "a writer who is never satisfied with the simple, or with the
already achieved. He moves . . . restlessly enquiring, balancing and reassessing, extending his range with each new work." She discusses his development from a "merciless" and "savage" comic and satirical writer to the
compassionate writer of enlarged sympathies who, having turned from traditional social realism, produced in *No Laughing Matter* the innovative novel
which may prove his masterpiece. She pays tribute to his "immense store of
sheer information" and to his nourished literary imagination. Margaret
Drabble's shining essay establishes a point of departure for future studies of
this genuine nonpareil.

A very fine writer and an oddly ignored one, even in Britain, the late Olivia
Manning has a smallish, highly enthusiastic following. (She is all but unknown in the United States.) Of her numerous books, the *chef-d'oeuvre* is un-
questionably *Fortunes of War,* a six-volume novel sequence separated into *The
Balkan Trilogy* and *The Levant Trilogy.* Early in American recognition of Miss
Manning, Robert K. Morris discussed *The Balkan Trilogy* in his *Continuance
and Change: The Contemporary British Novel Sequence* (1972). Here, Prof. Morris

assesses the entire *Fortunes of War,* "one of the most remarkable books published in the past twenty-five years," taking into account metaphor, irony, action, theme, "the original paradox that furnishes the groundwork for the series," and more. Morris's range of knowledge and appreciation, buttressed by his fine, sometimes brilliant, insights make his essay both enjoyable and illuminating.

Robert Evans places the dystopias of Anthony Burgess in a tradition by describing their relations to the French *nouveau roman* and the Russian dystopias. He then specifies Burgess's failure in four novels to observe the conventions of that tradition: all dystopias since the Russian Revolution, says Evans, "are calculated to give their readers a warning . . . of what may happen if we do not pay attention to the way in which our social and political institutions develop." In *A Clockwork Orange,* for instance, the "climate of violence" possibly is a manifestation of "man's nature," which "in conjunction with his institutions" has brought about the circumstances giving rise to the hoodlumism and savagery of Alex and his fellows in near-future Britain. In any event, Burgess sounds no warnings, notes no "consequences of political action."

Utopian and dystopian fictions, with or without explicit warnings, do incline toward satire (at least they are analytical of the contemporary) and toward some display of the degenerated society or the coming nightmare. Evans assigns *A Clockwork Orange* and *The Wanting Seed* to the convention of Zamyatin's *We;* so he also assigns *1985* and *The End of the World News,* although these later works exhibit "a somewhat different focus." Hence, Burgess, even when he nominally adheres to a convention, remains unconventional. To illustrate his idiosyncracies from his professional life: he once reviewed one of his own novels published under the pseudonym of Joseph Kell; he wrote his own jacket blurb for *The End of the World News* (1983), saying that the three elements—a life of Freud, a Broadway musical about Trotsky, and the destruction of the earth—"are all the same story: they are all about the end of history as man has known it."

Jay L. Halio has cleared away much of the underbrush of ambiguity and confounding complication that, upon occasion, stands between the reader and the trickily fluctuating comedy of Muriel Spark. The essay is precisely titled, for the novelist's "sense of wonder" equates with "the childhood vision of life," which makes "games of life" and allows self-dramatization. Central to the writer's sense of wonder are the fascinating interrelations between fiction and reality—for life imitates art, as art imitates life—and the "self-reflexiveness" "persisting theme of conformity and its decline," such artifices to have little place in the postwar Tietjens world.

In an uncommonly pleasing and edifying essay, Angus Wilson traces the "always strong but strangely varied hold" of Virginia Woolf upon him from his youthful "first acquaintance with her work" to her "abiding presence" beside him as the "established novelist" whenever he writes. His essay offers shrewd insights into both Wilson and Mrs. Woolf, and his critical observations about her work are discerning and admiring. Wilson's remarks doubly reward the reader, for they are cogently revealing of one whom many regard as the principal female novelist of the century and of another whom many regard as in the first rank of male novelists of the present day.

Philippa Tristram characterizes Ivy Compton-Burnett as a novelist "much admired but little read" and undertakes to explain why in an informative analysis of the strengths and weaknesses of the novels. Among the elements explanatory of the infrequent reading, Tristram notes that in Compton-Burnett's books the essence is not a matter of "poetic justice, but of injustice made aesthetic." Her novels thus can offend the sentimental or stock-response reader, a circumstance which reduces readership. And novels written mainly in dialogue can be difficult reading. Tristram finds that Compton-Burnett "has stripped the novel of all but its essentials," another nonconcession to a popular following. Many would find her unattractive because she is *passée,* not contemporary: "Far from succeeding Lawrence and Virginia Woolf, Ivy Compton-Burnett in many senses precedes them. Her novels deliberately detach the reader from twentieth-century expectations; they are not only set in the nineteenth century, but conceived in its terms."

The resurgence of Jean Rhys, coming after the publication of *Wide Sargasso Sea* (1966), compensates somewhat for the decades of oblivion she has not deserved but had. Two critical essays are devoted to Rhys: in the first, Todd Bender examines her techniques; in the second, Frank Baldanza examines her themes. Both critics associate her with impressive company: Bender places Rhys with Conrad and Ford; Baldanza links her with Dostoevsky and "the lady diarists of Heian Japan." Bender provides a useful discussion of impressionism as well as of Rhys's work, especially *Wide Sargasso Sea,* which "deserves to stand with impressionist masterpieces like *Heart of Darkness, Lord Jim,* and *The Good Soldier.*" Observing that "the financially, socially, and mentally secure middle-class reader may have difficulty understanding the point" of many anecdotes in Jean Rhys, Baldanza supplies valuable aids to the reader. He describes the "thematic core" of Rhys's writings as "the evocation of the of "the process of composition itself." Prof. Halio makes a case for *The Mandel-baum Gate* (1965) as Spark's "most ambitious" work and provides an admirable analysis of it, a book he sees as "a watershed" in her work.

In 1973, Iris Murdoch published *The Black Prince*. At various times, she has identified her subject for fiction as love; and *The Black Prince* is "A Celebration of Love." Not only is it thus a characteristic Murdoch novel, but it also is one of her finest books, the view of a consensus of novelists and critics. Peter Wolfe, with his article about *The Black Prince*, returns after a long absence to critical analysis—as distinguished from reviewing—of a Murdoch novel. Wolfe is one of the early serious critics of Murdoch's work, his *The Disciplined Heart* having appeared in 1966. He analyzes and assesses *The Black Prince* with his customary acumen.

In the interview, Iris Murdoch comments interestingly and significantly upon a diversity of subjects, some of which she has not previously talked about for publication. The topics include: how she plans and writes a novel; how she sees herself as philosopher and novelist; herself as dramatist; herself as male narrator in the first-person novels; "women's lib"; Christianity, Existentialism, and moral bankruptcy in our time; the contemporary novel; her literary antecedents; her estimate of her own work; and metaphor and symbol in her novels.

Since 1964, Margaret Drabble has published numerous remarkable novels and various other books. Her consistent artistic development over these years and the sustained quality of her fiction indicate that she is an important novelist. Joan Manheimer has written an estimable survey-analysis of the first seven novels. She says that women, as traditionally presented in novels, are "dependent on each other for identity" and "shackled by an inverse double"; "to achieve autonomy, they must discover ways to dissolve that bond." Drabble wants to cope with the problem, and Manheimer specifies successes and failure in the novels. Manheimer terms *The Needle's Eye* (1972) in "many ways Drabble's strongest novel," but she thinks *The Realms of Gold* (1975) "describes a world difficult to credit" and marks a falling-off from *The Waterfall* (1969) and *The Needle's Eye.*

Like Dame Margaret's paper on Sir Angus Wilson, all those here, taken together, seem to me extraordinarily interesting and clarifying. Much is given in a small compass. For which my contributors are due credit.

Opera in Conrad: "More Real Than Anything in Life"

FRANK BALDANZA

I

In Part V of *The Rescue*, Mrs. Travers, the pampered wife of a millionaire, accompanies "King Tom" Lingard, the rough-hewn, burly adventurer who is the single most powerful force in this area of Borneo, to a conference with the native chief Daman in an attempt to free her husband and Mr. d'Alcacer, who were captured by the tribe when strolling near their accidentally grounded yacht. In chatting with Lingard after the conference, which was conducted in Malay, she remarks that the whole ceremony reminded her of a gorgeously costumed opera. When she launches on an explanation of opera, Tom interrupts her in a wholly unexpected manner:

> "You can't possibly guess how unreal all this seemed, and how artificial I felt myself. An opera, you know. . . ."
>
> "I know. I was a gold digger at one time. Some of us used to come down to Melbourne with our pockets full of money. I daresay it was poor enough to what you must have seen, but once I went to a show like that. It was a story acted to music. All the people went singing through it right to the very end."
>
> "How it must have jarred on your sense of reality," said Mrs. Travers, still not looking at him. "You don't remember the name of the opera?"
>
> "No. I never troubled my head about it. We—our lot never did."
>
> "I won't ask you what the story was like. It must have appeared to you

like the very defiance of all truth. Would real people go singing through
their life anywhere except in a fairy tale?"

"These people didn't always sing for joy," said Lingard, simply. "I
don't know much about fairy tales. . . . Fairy tales are for children, I
believe," he said. "But that story with music I am telling you of, Mrs.
Travers, was not a tale for children. I assure you that of the few shows I
have seen that one was the most real to me. More real than anything in
life."

Mrs. Travers, remembering the fatal inanity of most opera librettos,
was touched by these words as if there had been something pathetic in this
readiness of response; as if she had heard a starved man talking of the
delight of a crust of dry bread.[1]

This speech of Lingard's is the most direct and deeply felt defense of opera in
all of Conrad, and it comes from a reclusive, adventurous man of action who
has seen one performance in his life.

Indeed, the average Conrad reader is usually astonished at the idea that this
author knew anything at all of opera. Even friends who knew him well are in
distinct disagreement about his attitude toward music in general. Richard
Curle remarks, "I do not think that music came home to him with any sure
appeal." J. H. Retinger agrees, saying, "he discussed freely on art and literature, but he shared my myopia to music."[2] On the other hand, Gérard Jean-
Aubry argues that despite the few allusions to music or musicians in his fiction, he nourished a deep love of music in his heart and had "always un-
reservedly given it the foremost rank among the arts," adding the obligatory
quotation from the Preface to *The Nigger of the Narcissus*, in which Conrad calls
music "the art of arts."[3] M. Jean-Aubry attests to Conrad's strong love for
Chopin, adding that Conrad attended a Jean-Aubry lecture on "Verlaine et les
Musiciens" at Liverpool and that he had met and heard Ravel perform several
times and showed a strong interest in the man and his works; Conrad also met
Szymanowski and Paderewski.

However, it is certain that Conrad's interest in opera, within a circum-
scribed area, was vivid, even if the conditions of his life forbade very frequent
attendance at musical events. Donald C. Yelton remarks, "Such musical
preference as he evinced was for the more accessible reaches of the operatic
repertory."[4] It was the occasional subject of casual conversation: in *The Mirror
of the Sea*, he tells us that during a spell on the night watch on a docked ship in
Sydney, he conversed with an elderly Mr. Senior, sitting on the case of a piano
which Conrad's ship had carried—and one of the topics was operatic singers.[5]
Galsworthy tells us: "My first re-encounter with Conrad after that voyage was

a visit together to *Carmen* at Covent Garden Opera. *Carmen* was in the nature of a vice with him as with myself. It was already his fourteenth time of seeing that really dramatic opera" (Jean-Aubry, *Chesterian*). Conrad's son Borys says that his father's entire whistling repertoire consisted of airs from *Cavalleria Rusticana* and *Carmen*—especially the "Toreador Song."[6] Borys's dog, given him by Stephen Crane, was named "Escamillo," after the same toreador.[7] And Conrad's wife, Jessie, tells us he sang a few bars of *Carmen* in the bath. He enthusiastically took the family to a local performance when they were on holiday in Montpellier.

There are other, more casual, indications of a fairly close knowledge of opera in the pages of his writing. Early in *The Arrow of Gold* he describes the costume of a carnival reveler as resembling that of the operatic Faust in the third act; and he closes the same novel with an allusion to Doña Rita's hair ornament, the arrow of gold, as the golden beaker of the King of Thule, in the ballad that occurs both in Goethe's original play and in Gounod's opera. Also, in a letter to Mme. Poradowska, Conrad says, "I shall soon send you the last chapter [of *Almayer's Folly*]. It begins with a *trio*—Nina, Dain, Almayer— and ends with a long *solo* for Almayer which is almost as long as Tristan's in Wagner."[8] Notice that in both the *Faust* and the *Tristan* references, he has in mind a clear idea of the contents and the traditional costuming of the operas, sometimes by individual acts. In *A Personal Record* Conrad refers to Flaubert's handling of Donizetti's *Lucia di Lammermoor* in *Madame Bovary*.

We know that Conrad's most concentrated exposure to opera was during his sojourn in Marseilles, 1874–1878, and he could conceivably have seen opera in Australia, 1888–1890. In *The Sea Dreamer*, M. Jean-Aubry says it was Dominic Cervoni, the first mate of the *Saint Antoine*, a rabid opera fan, who initiated Conrad to performances at the Marseilles house: "It must have been this period that left the memories of Rossini, Verdi, and Meyerbeer operas and of Offenbach operettas that Conrad still used to recall with obvious pleasure toward the end of his life."[9] Elsewhere Jean-Aubry tells us that during seven or eight years of conversation,

> he often found delight in recalling the evenings he had spent in days gone by, about 1875, at the Marseilles Opera when staying in that town between two voyages to the West Indies on board a Franch sailing ship. Although 50 years, or very nearly, had elapsed since then, he had kept of that time most accurate recollections and he retained a very correct impression of Meyerbeer's or Verdi's operas, as well as of Offenbach's

operettas which were then in the fashion and which he had an opportunity
of hearing.

(Chesterian)

While we have no way of determining which specific performances Conrad
attended, we can at any rate narrow the possibilities to those operas which
were on the boards during his periods of residence in Marseilles between voy-
ages. In fact, a frequency count reveals that (aside from Gounod) those operas
most often performed were by Meyerbeer, Verdi, Rossini, and Offenbach,
thus confirming Jean-Aubry's recollections.[10] His favorite opera, *Carmen*, was
first performed on 12 April 1878, twelve days before his final departure, for
five performances to a lukewarm public, but to a very enthusiastic critical
reception.

His favorite composers are largely represented in the Marseilles repertoire
by historical costume pageants, with heavily melodramatic plots nearly always involving a conflict between patriotism and love; thus Conrad's own
typical historical fiction may have had unconscious genesis in the kinds of
operas he enjoyed as a young man.

Meyerbeer, then in his heyday, offered *Robert-le-Diable*, a legend of
medieval supernatural struggles; *Les Huguenots*, a complex historical drama
culminating in the St. Bartholomew's Day Massacre; *Le Prophéte*, a similar
treatment of John of Leyden's sixteenth-century Anabaptist seizure of Muns-
ter; and *L'Africaine*. The last work must have been especially interesting to a
young sailor for its romantic handling of the career of Vasco da Gama, the plot
involving exotic milieux, an interracial love affair (in which Selika, the
African maid of the title, considers herself abandoned by her European lover,
much like Jewel in *Lord Jim*), and a grand act, one of the most scenically
elaborate in all of opera, featuring an on-stage storm at sea, a shipwreck, and a
native boarding party that massacres nearly all those on board. Local concerts
also included fantasias based on *L'Étoile du Nord* and *Le Pardon de Ploërmel*.

Offenbach's *La Périchole*, after *Aida* the most often-performed work of this
period, makes hilarious comic intrigue out of the Viceroy of Peru's sexual
philanderings and of a minor comic "revolution" when a deceived lower-class
husband exposes the Viceroy's corruption to the assembled court. It is possible
that *La Périchole* might have had some tangential, subliminal influence on
comic, and even on serious, elements in *Nostromo*, though the question is more
likely one of general ambiance rather than specific parallels. For example, the
Viceroy's name is "Ribeira" and the dictator of Sulaco is "Ribiera," but since
these are common Spanish names, such parallels are probably accidental. As

to the parallels based on general ambiance, there is a ballad at the beginning of the operetta in which a Spanish conqueror seduces an Indian maiden—in this case a wryly comic version of the Jim and Jewel situation—on assurances of his high good intentions. When the girl produces an illegitimate child, her family console themselves by saying the child will flourish because he's really Spanish. The refrain from this ballad—*il grandira car il est Espagnol*—constitutes the finale to Acts I and III, an ironic view of sexual exploitation in colonialism such as occurs frequently enough in Conrad's Borneo.

At any rate, this operetta offered Conrad the example of extended use of South American material. Other standard Offenbach works like *La Belle Hélène*, *La Vie Parisienne*, and *Orphée aux Enfers* must have appealed to Conrad's famous relish for irony. Other Offenbach offerings included *La Grande Duchesse de Gérolstein* and *La Boulangère a des Écus*, as well as concert excerpts called "Offenbachiana." In addition, the composer himself attended a local concert devoted to his works.

Gioacchino Rossini's adaptation of *Le Barbière de Seville* was always popular in Marseilles—a contemporary newspaper carried ads for hair and beard dye called "Eau Figaro." This opera, as we shall see, provides a veiled allusion in *Nostromo*. Rossini was otherwise popular for heavy historical romances: *Moïse*, a biblical work, and his very grand grand opera *Guillaume Tell*. Concerts featured selections from *Le Siège de Corinth* and *Tancred*.

Verdi's *Le Trouvère* (*Il Trovatore*) was a perennial Marseilles favorite (to the chagrin of at least one local music critic, who pleaded that it be replaced by a work then unknown in Marseilles, *La Flute Enchantée*), and it seems to have filled the house regularly in these years. *Aida* was presented in an extremely popular run of twenty-five performances, in a sumptuous production which was also the first one in French. *Rigoletto* and *Violetta* (*La Traviata*) were performed less often, though they also appeared in concert fantasias, along with excerpts from *Ernani*, based on Victor Hugo's romantic drama; *I Lombardi*, a Crusader epic; and *Les Vêpres Siciliennes*, concerning a thirteenth-century revolt against the French occupation of Sicily. The Verdi allusions in Conrad's fiction are to *Il Trovatore* and *Aida*.

Perhaps it is germane to point out that all of Conrad's favorite composers—Mayerbeer, Offenbach, Verdi, and Rossini—conquered Paris with enormous financial and artistic rewards, though all were born abroad. He might have been emboldened by these examples of cosmopolitan success when he undertook a writing career as a transplanted Pole in London.

Apart from those of his stated favorites, the most popular Marseilles operas were those of Gounod—*Faust*; *Cinq-Mars*, a richly costumed historical work; and *Roméo et Juliette* . Also high on the list were *La Juive* of Halévy, based on Goethe's *Wilhelm Meister*. Other popular Shakespearean operas included Thomas's *Hamlet* and *Un Songe d'une Nuit d'Été*. Donizetti provided *La Favorite, Lucie de Lammermoor*, and *Don Pasquale*. The only work of Bellini was *La Somnambule*.

In ranking Conrad's tastes, it seems fairly clear that after his passion for *Carmen*, the operas of Meyerbeer drew his greatest enthusiasm. In a letter of 1910 to Galsworthy, Conrad remarked, "I suppose that I am now the only human being in these Isles who thinks Meyerbeer a great composer; and I am an alien at that and not to be wholly trusted."[11]

Conrad's attitude toward Wagner may be problematical if we trust Galsworthy's remark that "the blare of Wagner left him as cold as it leaves me" (Jean-Aubry, *Chesterian*). This opinion would seem to be reinforced by a remark of the narrator in Ford and Conrad's *The Nature of a Crime*, who says of *Tristan und Isolde* that "There are passages in that thing as intolerable as anything in any of the Germanic master's scores"—though this may reflect Ford's view rather than Conrad's. [12] On the other hand, we have Conrad's own word in a letter to William Blackwood of 1902 that he saw himself in the same light as Wagner: "I am *modern*, and I would rather recall Wagner the musician and Rodin the sculptor who both had to starve a little in their day—and Whistler the painter who made Ruskin the critic foam at the mouth with scorn and indignation. They too have arrived. They had to suffer for being 'new.' And I too hope to find my place in the rear of my betters."[13] We have already noticed a favorable comparison between the ending of *Almayer's Folly* and Tristan's long third-act solo. In *A Personal Record*, after describing a fiendishly rigorous examination in seamanship in which he was presented with every imaginable peril possible on the seas, he remarked that he would gladly change places with the Flying Dutchman. He also alludes to this opera in *The Shadow Line*. Wagner also has the distinction of being the only operatic composer whose works are actually performed by a major character in Conrad's fiction: Freya of the Seven Isles plays some unspecified Wagner on the piano—although this reference may reinforce Galsworthy's remark about the "blare of Wagner," since Freya is apparently trying at least in part to drown out the sound of tropical storms!

If we look more closely at parallels between operas and his fictions, we might decide that *Carmen* had a peculiar personal appeal; the plot outline (except for the ending) is remarkably close to *The Arrow of Gold*, and therefore similar to the version of his Marseilles experience that he gave to the public: a naive, unworldly young man falls obsessively in love with a richly seductive, somewhat fickle beauty of humble origins who persuades him to become a smuggler and for whom he fights a duel.

In somewhat broader parallels with Verdi, Meyerbeer, and Halévy, Conrad's handling of historical fiction in *Suspense*, *Romance*, *The Rover*, "The Duel," and "The Warrior's Soul" recalls the general approach of many an operatic costume piece. A work like "The Inn of the Two Witchs" has even closer echoes in the cauldron-stirring crones that resemble the Verdian witches Azucena (*Il Trovatore*) and Ulrica (*Un Ballo in Maschera*); and the inn where casual travelers are murdered reminds one of *Rigoletto*. The poisoned ring of *The Nature of a Crime* parallels Leonora's ring in *Trovatore*. If Conrad found Verdi and Meyerbeer especially congenial, it is because, certainly on the literary side, they shared the narrative conventions of nineteenth-century romanticism, many operatic works being derived from Scott, Hugo, and Scribe. And the man who wrote "Prince Roman" would certainly be stirred by Verdi's Risorgimento patriotism, a topic Conrad treats at some length in *Nostromo*.

Conrad also shares with these composers a technical plot gimmick somewhat like O. Henry's, playing cat-and-mouse with the audience over a secret which is revealed only at the very end of the work, though attentive readers/auditors could guess it from earlier hints. Conrad uses this device with Captain Whalley's blindness in "The End of the Tether" and with Mr. Bunter's dyed hair in "The Black Mate." Similar devices occur in Verdi's *Il Trovatore*, Meyerbeer's *Les Huguenots*, and Halévy's *La Juive*: in each case, a harsh revenger is tricked into killing his own brother or daughter by especially heinous means (burning, a cauldron of hot oil, a point-blank shot); only after he has begun to exult in his revenge is the unfortunate villain informed of what he has done, as the last line of the opera. A similar ending occurs in *Rigoletto*.

Before turning to a closer analysis of his fiction, let us look briefly at Conrad's attitude toward possible operatic versions of his own works. M. Jean-Aubry tells us Conrad requested a copy of the libretto to *Carmen* because "he expressed to me his desire that one of his books should form the subject-matter of a lyrical drama and we then frequently spoke of this idea" (*Chesterian*). Conrad himself favored *Nostromo* for operatic treatment, though Jean-Aubry thought the work "by reason of its exuberance to go beyond any musical interpretation," recommending *The Rescue* for its "evocative line" and for the possibilities of a duet between Mrs. Travers and Lingard; he also spoke in favor of adapting *Almayer's Folly*.

Around 1910, an American pianist and composer, John Powell, asked
Conrad for a libretto to "Heart of Darkness," and Conrad flushed and left the
room; several years later, when Powell again opened this topic, Conrad
remarked that the emotional tone of "Heart of Darkness" suited operatic treatment, but that he doubted it could be encompassed in that form, suggesting a
symphonic poem in its stead—which Powell wrote and dedicated to Conrad.
The force of Conrad's feelings about operatic adaptation are indicated by his
response to Powell's later inquiry about why he had left the room when the
subject was first mentioned. "Why, my dear fellow, I was not annoyed at
all—how could you think I was annoyed? . . . Ever since I began to write, it
has been my highest ambition to have one of my stories made into an opera,
and when you suggested that use for 'Heart of Darkness,' I was so moved I
could not speak, and had to leave the room to gain my self-possession."[14]

Conrad's desire for operatic adaptation has been justified in later years.
Among relatively recent settings, an opera on _Lord Jim_ by the Polish composer
Romuald Twardowski won the Prince Pierre de Monaco Prize for the best
opera of 1973. Another Polish composer, Tadeusz Baird, has adapted the
story "Tomorrow" (_Jutro_) for an opera which pianist Malcolm Frager described
as "very moving and highly intense" when he heard a recent performance in
Poznan.[15] A South African composer, John Joubert, composed a work on
Under Western Eyes which was performed at the Camden Festival in London in
1969; and Englishman Richard Rodney Bennett's opera on _Victory_ had its
premiere at Covent Garden in 1970 and was subsequently taken to Berlin.
The latter two works were heavily publicized at the time of their performance,
though neither has been revived since.

II

Allusions to opera in the works themselves function in a variety of ways. One
would not expect opera references in the South Sea adventure tales, and when
they do appear they have a startling effect. Rajah Lakamba in Chapter Six of
Almayer's Folly orders his prime minister Babalatchi, after a tense council of
state, to get out the music box given him by the white captain. The playing of

the "Miserere" from Verdi's *Il Trovatore* in the backwaters of Borneo functions on the surface as purely comic, though on reflection one might find a more sinister meaning, in that the Rajah has just ordered the death of Almayer, and in the operatic selection, as Conrad informs us, the hero the hero Manirico is bidding farewell to his beloved Leonora from his prison cell before his execution.

In one sense, opera itself, the refined and artificial European art form, thus serves as a kind of reverse exoticism. In Chapter Seven of Part One of *Nostromo*, an absolutely corrupt South American provincial official interrupts an important business conversation with Charles Gould to exclaim on the beauties of selections from *Lucia di Lammermoor* and Mozart which are being rendered outdoors by a military band. Here, an exaggeratedly precious, pretended enthusiasm for opera brands the official as a pretentious fool. It is very probable that Conrad chose these musical selections for their vapidity. In discussing Flaubert's handling of Donizetti's *Lucia*, Conrad refers to it as a "light" setting of the Scott novel, and we must remember, as W.H. Auden reminds us in his poem "Metalogue to *The Magic Flute*," that Mozart was taken as a light, if not a frivolous, composer during the nineteenth and early twentieth centuries.

Further along in *Nostromo*, there is a distinct possibility of a parodic allusion to Rossini's *Il Barbiere di Siviglia*. Although we usually think of the opera as a piece of comic fluff, the original play on which it was based was considered a dangerous political piece when it was first presented, in that the wily servant-protagonist proves himself resourceful, efficient, and dependably superior to the effete aristocracy, the same relation Nostromo has to the European colony of Sulaco. If we consider the relation of Nostromo to Sulaco and that of Figaro to the aristocrats of Seville as respectively tragic and comic refractions of the same theme, then a passage in Chapter Eight of Part Three of *Nostromo* takes on added significance.

Nostromo, after swimming back from Great Isabel and the burying of the silver, gloomily summarizes the emptiness of a career motivated largely by the vanity of being well regarded; Conrad gives him words that form a remarkable parallel to the famous "Largo al factotum" aria from Act I of Rossini's opera (when Conrad refers to particular numbers, it is nearly always to the obviously popular ones—the "Toreador Song" from *Carmen*, the "Miserere" from *Trovatore*, and the "Intermezzo" from *Cavalleria*):

Nostromo	*Il Barbiere di Siviglia*
What did he care about their politics?	*Pronto a far tutto*
Nothing at all. And at the end of it	*le notte e il giorno . . .*

all—Nostromo here and Nostromo there—work all day and ride all night—behold! he found himself a marked Ribierist . . .

Figaro! Son qua.
Ehi—Figaro! Son qua.
Figaro qua, Figaro la,
Figaro su, Figaro giù
pronto prontissimo . . .[16]

III

Most previous critical comment on the relation of opera to Conrad's fiction is confined entirely to very vague parallels with Wagner. We have no way of knowing when Conrad might have attended performances of Wagner's works, though they were done frequently at Covent Garden when he was living in England; he does show an acquaintance with *Tristan* and *The Flying Dutchman*, and I would guess he knew something of *Rheingold*. At any rate, I maintain that previous speculation has been too broad and haphazard, and that careful attention to details will place the Wagner references in sharper focus.

Paul L. Wiley and Donald C. Yelton suggest some relation between the curse on the silver in *Nostromo* and the evil consequences of coveting gold in *Der Ring des Nibelungen*; Wiley also compares the "perverse fascination" of several Conrad women to a Wagnerian love potion. John L. DiGaetani seconds these suggestions as well as the *Parsifal* parallels I shall discuss shortly. So broad are these cited parallels that they are less substantive analyses than rhetorical flourishes by the critics.[17]

A set of supposed *Parsifal* parallels, however, calls for closer investigation. Wiley makes a parallel between Almayer's decline and the sufferings of Amfortas, carrying the comparison further in equating Dain Maroola with a Parsifal who succumbs to Nina's Kundrian wiles. But this seems to me a careless reading, since a Parsifal who falls is thereby not a Parsifal but another Amfortas.

Edward W. Said joins Wiley in viewing Alice of "A Smile of Fortune" as a Kundry figure in relation to the narrator as Parsifal, Wiley also seeing her ship-chandler father Jacobus as a Klingsor type of evil magician.[18] The source for such speculation is, of course, the luxuriant tropical garden in which the nearly savage, untaught Alice is imprisoned. However, the parallel is not convincing. To be sure, the strikingly schizoid nature of Kundry in the opera—the wild-haired, almost truculent but saintly figure from Acts I and III, as contrasted to the voluptuous seductress of Act II— has some echo in the story, but there is no suggestion in Conrad that Alice's wild sulkings are expiation for a past sin, such as Kundry's having laughed at Christ's agonies in the crucifixion. Said believes the climactic kiss in the Conrad story echoes the famous kiss in the second act of the opera. But in Wagner, Kundry is a relentlessly aggressive seductress who builds up to the climactic kiss singlemindedly, whereas in Conrad's story, it is the narrator who kisses Alice repeatedly before eventually receiving the fleeting, mis-aimed brush of the lips, which hardly qualifies as a Kundrian technique. Wiley's carrying the parallel to the length of an analogy between Jacobus and Klingsor is the least persuasive of his points. In the opera, Parsifal, by his innocent horror at Kundry's intimate blandishments, disarms the evil magician and destroys his castle, whereas Jacobus in the story forces the narrator to accept a cargo of potatoes which he is to trade for personal profit, an act which the narrator considers contrary to high ethical standards. Therefore, it is the supposed Klingsor figure who corrupts the innocent, rather than the reverse situation of the opera.

Most of these speculations take their start from the image of the seductress in the garden, but when the further parallels are elaborated, one is drawn entirely away from the religious aura of the opera with its strong concentration on spiritual redemption. As a matter of fact, if one is looking for the archetype Conrad had in mind, in *Chance* he refers to the Armida of Tasso's *Jerusalem Delivered* as a general type for the voluptuous seductress in a garden.

The same kind of luxuriant garden in "Freya of the Seven Isles," a story from the same collection as "A Smile of Fortune," leads Said to suggest a general Wagnerian atmosphere. But no critic has observed the obvious import of the heroine's name. Freyia is a Germanic fertility goddess whose incarnation as Freia in *Das Rheingold*, the first opera of Wagner's Ring Cycle, functions as a guarantor of youth, beauty, and love. In the opera, she is taken hostage by a pair of giants until Wotan grants them a treasure hoard of gold, which he stole from the dwarf Alberich, to pay for their having built his castle, Valhalla. George Bernard Shaw in *The Perfect Wagnerite* (and critics like Wiley, who apply his insight to Conrad) emphasizes that one must renounce love if one wishes to control wealth and the power it confers; but he does not underline the fact that those men who renounce love do not do so for greed—both the dwarf Alberich, who originally cursed the gold, and the giant Fasolt, renounce love only after their intense sex drive is foiled by mocking, violent revulsion on the part of the women they pursue, the Rhinemaidens and Freia. Here we have the kernel of Conrad's story as well, since Freya mockingly rejects and humiliates the choleric Dutch naval captain Heemskirk, who has already been threatening economic sanctions against her father and who destroys the ship, and the livelihood, of her preferred lover, Jasper Allen.

Conrad's Freya, as we have seen, is the only character in his works who actually performs operatic music; especially during storms, ". . . Freya would sit down to the piano and play fierce Wagner music in the flicker of blinding flashes, with thunderbolts falling all around, enough to make your hair stand on end. . . ." But she also does so to annoy Heemskirk.[19]

When she is twenty-one, Freya plans to run off secretly with Jasper, the owner of a trim, sleek old ship which he has rejuvenated with loving care; he cherishes the ship equally with Freya: "His feelings for the brig and for the girl were as indissolubly united in his heart as you may fuse two precious metals together in one crucible" (158). We are told that the restored ship, "like some fair women of adventurous life famous in history, seemed to have the secret of perpetual youth" (157), a touch that ties in nicely with Wagner's Freia, whose magic golden apples assure the gods' youthfulness—when she is kidnapped by the giants, the gods turn instantly old and gray. The identification of Conrad's Freya with Wagner's seems further certified by Heemskirk's referring to her as a "goddess" several times, once specifying "Freya . . . Hey! You Scandinavian Goddess of Love! . . . That's what you are—of love" (163, 195).

Freya's father could easily be a Wotan figure in his desire to hold on to his island real estate at any cost, thus making his tobacco plantation similar to Valhalla; Heemskirk, in his violent, sputtering rage of sexual frustration, which Freya's father mistakes for facial neuralgia, would be an amalgamation of the two physically repellent foiled lovers in Wagner, Alberich and Fasolt, both of whom turn to gold only after their rejection.

One final Wagnerian parallel, also mentioned by Wiley (92), has escaped much detailed critical attention, though it informs the structure of the work and is made quite explicitly. The narrator of "Falk" concludes a ghastly tale of cannibalism aboard a ship adrift in southern latitudes with an observation about "that story before which . . . the fable of the *Flying Dutchman* with its convention of crime and its sentimental retribution fades like a graceful wreath, like a wisp of white mist."[20] The legend itself, which has several variants, concerns a Dutch captain who swears, when rounding the Cape of Good Hope in a gale, that he will succeed even at the cost of damnation, if it takes until Judgment Day, or that he will prevail against Hell. The devil (in some versions, there is a pact involved) condemns the Dutchman to a perpetual voyage with a crew of dead men, with the stipulation that he can put into port once every seven years where, if he can earn the love of a good woman, he will be released from this bondage. Wagner's early romantic opera on this subject, based in part on Heine, along with Captain Marryat's novel *The Phantom Ship*, did much to popularize the subject.

Conrad makes the explicit allusion only in the story within the story, that of Falk's having eaten human flesh. However, the fable has much broader implications for the story as a whole.

The Falk of Conrad's tale is the captain of a tug in an Eastern seaport who works with an exclusive, singleminded compulsion; he leaves his boat so seldom that he is compared to a centaur, a "man-boat." This is an obvious parallel to the Dutchman's compulsive sailing. When Falk was adrift, he also could be said to have had a crew of dead men, or ones close to death, as Falk was the only survivor. The clinching parallel is that Falk has been lured away from his boat for only two periods, both of them for a dogged pursuit of virtuous European women; on each occasion, however, he simply sat in the woman's presence, unable to bring himself to an overt proposal. We learn on the second of these occasions that his strange inarticulateness is based on the moral dilemma Conrad enunciates in the "Author's Note" to *Typhoon*: that of a rough man who combines "a perfect natural ruthlessness with a certain amount of moral delicacy" (x). Falk cannot marry a woman whose family does not know he has eaten human flesh, but he cannot bring himself to tell them so. In the second instance, it is through the agency of Conrad's narrator that Falk manages to convey this horrendous information and thereby ultimately gains redemption in the adoring, pitying eyes of Captain Hermann's voluptuously cushioned niece. I think the narrator of this tale is ill-advised in making his deprecatory reference to the "sentimental retribution" of the legend, since the tale has the identical conclusion.

I can offer no incontrovertible evidence that Conrad had the famous Wagner opera in mind in making this reference, though I think the likelihood is even stronger than the Freya-*Rheingold* analogue. He italicizes "Flying Dutchman" as if he were referring to the title of a specific version. And there are several convincing internal parallels between Conrad and Wagner. Conrad states in the "Author's Note" that the subject of the story is not the cannibalism, but "Falk's attempt to get married" (x), thus putting the emphasis exactly where Wagner does, on the protagonist's redemption by a good woman (though of course the opera has a tragic twist at the end—even if the libretto calls for a final tableau of the Dutchman and Senta slowly mounting to heaven in an eternal embrace). Wagner got the idea of redemption by a good woman from Heine (though the theme pervades *Tannhäuser, Lohengrin, Tristan, Siegfried,* and *Götterdämmerung*), but it does not occur in the Marryat novel, so we can rule out his *Phantom Ship* as an exclusive source. Second, the operatic Dutchman is fabulously rich, displaying only one of many chests full of pearls and precious jewels; Daland, the heroine Senta's father, a covetous man, immediately agrees to a union with such a wealthy suitor. In Conrad, Falk is also assumed to be very rich because he has an exclusive monopoly on tug service in this port, and he charges exorbitant rates; Captain Hermann, on learning of Falk's request for his niece's hand, overcomes an initial revulsion out of a covetousness even meaner than Daland's—by marrying his niece to Falk, he will save the cost of a separate stateroom on the family's impending return to Germany. The Conrad narrator, who is mistakenly taken as a rival suitor for the niece's hand, serves only as a very vague parallel to the more ardent Erik in Wagner.

IV

In summary, we are certain that Conrad's love of opera—as evinced by Tom Lingard's simple but strong defense of the medium against Mrs. Travers' refined skepticism—was based on a thorough knowledge of the "mainline" popular work of his youth in Marseilles. As with Lingard, who perhaps idealized the one performance he ever saw as more real than anything in life (whereas Mrs. Travers, who saw much opera, admits she was never imaginatively caught up in a performance), Conrad retained all his life a vivid romantic attachment to these French and Italian works. Since these operas, aside from Offenbach's, were almost exclusively romantic historical melodramas, the probability of their influence on Conrad's historical fiction is strong. His actual allusions to these works are sparing, but in a just proportion to the general culture of his characters and their environments.

However, it is anomalous that Conrad's most thoroughgoing use of opera as structural metaphor—for "Freya of the Seven Isles" and "Falk"—draws on two Wagnerian works, *Das Rheingold* and *The Flying Dutchman*. I have discovered no concrete evidence that Conrad attended a Wagnerian performance, though these operas were plentifully produced at Covent Garden during the time of his residence in England and he could easily have seen them then. Galsworthy suggested Conrad felt antipathy to Wagner, which was also apparently shared by Ford Madox Ford, though Conrad's own comments are at worst neutral, and in comparing his own artistic career to Wagner's in the letter to Blackwood, he might even have seen the composer as a model.

APPENDIX

The following operas were presented most frequently during Conrad's periods of residence in Marseilles (see note 10, above):

Verdi, *Aida*	25
Offenbach, *La Périchole*	22
Gounod, *Faust*	16
Verdi, *Le Trouvère*	15
Offenbach, *La Vie Parisienne*	12
Meyerbeer, *Les Huguenots*	11
Gounod, *Cinq-Mars*	11
Guiraud, *Piccolino*	10
Meyerbeer, *L'Africaine*	10
Rossini, *Le Barbière de Seville*	9
Halévy, *La Juive*	9
von Flotow, *Martha*	9
Gounod, *Roméo et Juliette*	9
Thomas, *Mignon*	8
Rossini, *Moïse*	8
Rossini, *Guillaume Tell*	7
Meyerbeer, *Le Prophète*	7
Harold, *Le Pré aux Clercs*	6
von Flotow, *L'Ombre*	6
Meyerbeer, *Robert-le-Diable*	6
Maillard, *Les Dragons de Villars*	5
Verdi, *Violetta*	5
Donizetti, *Le Favorite*	5
Donizetti, *Lucie de Lammermoor*	5
Thomas, *Hamlet*	5
Bizet, *Carmen*	4
Adam, *Si J'étais Roi*	4
Donizetti, *La Fille du Régiment*	4
Bellini, *La Somnambule*	4
Auber, *Le Domino Noir*	4
Verdi, *Rigoletto*	4

NOTES

1. Kent Edition (Garden City, N.Y.: Doubleday, Page & Co., 1926), 300–301. In *An Outcast of the Islands*, Lingard confirms that he sought gold in Victoria in the early days of the rush, which began in 1851. Vincenzo Bellini's *Norma* was the first opera presented in Melbourne in 1852. It would be interesting to know if Conrad had this opera in mind, because the story, which is decidedly not for children, involves love affairs between Pollione, a Roman Pro-Consul, and several Druid priestesses during the Roman occupation of Britain. It might well have suggested the remarks of Marlow in the frame narration of "Heart of Darkness." Although most of the fictional Tom Lingard's characteristics are drawn from a real-life namesake, the details of Australian gold prospecting are based on a Captain John Dill Ross whom Conrad knew. See Jerry Allen, *The Sea Years of Joseph Conrad* (Garden City, N.Y.: Doubleday, 1965), 205–10.

2. Richard Curle, *The Last Twelve Years of Joseph Conrad* (London: Sampson Low, Marston & Co., 1928), 128; and J. H. Retinger, *Conrad and His Contemporaries* (New York: Roy, 1943), 78.

3. "Joseph Conrad and Music," *The Chesterian*, 6: 42 (1924), 37–42.

4. *Mimesis and Metaphor* (The Hague: Mouton, 1967), 54.

5. Kent Edition (New York: Harper, 1906), 207.

6. He may have whistled the Mascagni with relish, but in a letter to Edward Garnett announcing the completion of *An Outcast of the Islands*, he says he finished off Willems "while the sun shone joyously and the barrel organ sang on the pavement the abominable Intermezzo of the ghastly Cavalleria." *Letters from Joseph Conrad 1895–1924*, ed. Edward Garnett (Indianapolis: Bobbs, Merrill, 1928), 39.

7. *My Father: Joseph Conrad* (London: Calder and Boyars, 1970), 32.

8. *Letters of Joseph Conrad to Marguerite Poradowska 1890–1920*, trans. and ed. John A. Gee and Paul J. Sturm (New Haven: Yale Univ. Press, 1940), 68.

9. Trans. Helen Sebba (Garden City, N.Y.: Doubleday, 1957), 67.

10. Conrad was in Marseilles during the following periods: October to 11 December 1874; 23 May to 25 June 1875; c. 1 January to 8 July 1876; and 15 February 1877 to 24 April 1878. The information about operas presented in Marseilles during this time comes from the following sources: "Nouvelles des Théâtres Lyriques," *Revue et Gazette Musicale de Paris*, 41–43 (selected numbers); V. Combarnous, *Notes et Souvenirs; l'Histoire du Grand-Théâtre de Marseille* (Marseille Imprimerie Meridionale, 1927); and daily issues of *Le Sémaphore de Marseille* for this period. See Appendix.

11. G. Jean-Aubry, *Joseph Conrad: Life and Letters*, 2 vols.(Garden City, N.Y.: Doubleday, 1927), II, 110.

12. (London: Duckworth, 1924), 45.

13. *Letters to William Blackwood and David S. Meldrum*, ed. William Blackburn (Durham: Duke Univ. Press, 1958), 155.

14. Dale B. Randall, *Joseph Conrad and Warrington Dawson: The Record of a Friendship* (Durham: Duke Univ. Press, 1968), 6ln.

15. Letter from Malcolm Frager, 23 October 1978.

16.   Ready for everything
                                by night or by day
                                Figaro! I am here!
                                Ho, Figaro! I am here!
                                Figaro here, Figaro there.
                                Figaro up, Figaro down.
                                Faster and faster . . .

17. Paul L. Wiley, *Conrad's Measure of Man* (Madison: Univ. of Wisconsin Press, 1954), 99,
    134; Yelton, *Mimesis*; John L. DiGaetani, *Richard Wagner and the Modern British Novel*
    (Rutherford, N.J.: Fairleigh Dickinson Univ. Press, 1978), 23-56.

18. Wiley, 137–138; Said, *Joseph Conrad and the Fiction of Autobiography* (Cambridge, Mass.:
    Harvard Univ. Press, 1966), 158.

19. *'Twixt Land and Sea*, Kent Edition (Garden City, N.Y.: Doubleday, Page & Co., 1926),
    152. Lightning and thunder occur occasionally in Wagner's stage directions for the Ring.

20. *Typhoon and Other Stories*, Kent Edition (Garden City, N.Y.: Doubleday, Page & Co.,
    1926), 234–235.

Revisionary Artistry in Wells's
The Passionate Friends

WILLIAM J. SCHEICK

H G. Wells is certainly not a neglected writer, but we tend to think of him in terms of his early science-fiction romances. With few exceptions[1] contemporary literary critics have dismissed Wells's middle and late fiction, in spite of the fact that in his later years Wells specifically devalued his early work in favor of the sociological fiction of his middle and late years. Interestingly, however, such contemporary authors as C. P. Snow, Kingsley Amis, and Jorge Luis Borges, among others, have indicated their indebtedness to the literary example of Wells's middle and late work. This recognized importance of Wells's sociological novels to a community of contemporary writers of fiction should urge us to review and reevaluate these Wellsian works. *The Passionate Friends* (1913) is a good example. In 1966, Vladimir Nabokov acknowledged that Wells, "a great artist," was an important influence on Nabokov's works and that *The Passionate Friends* and a few other of Wells's stories "are far better than anything Bennett, or Conrad, or, in fact, any of Wells's contemporaries would produce."[2] Lest we dismiss Nabokov's remark as an eccentricity or a joke, there is more recently Graham Greene's sobering observation that Wells was one of the most interesting of the Edwardian novelists in such books as *Ann Veronica* (1909) and *The Passionate Friends*.[3] The latter work is not the book most people recall when they think about Wells, if indeed they ever heard of it at all. So Nabokov and Greene, neither of whom elaborates upon his remarks, have left us with teasingly suggestive references to this book, which I too had hitherto barely noticed in spite of my extensive previous work on Wells's fiction.[4]

In its year of publication the novel was noticed, but not very well received on the whole. While a few readers praised the book for its convincing, complex characterization[5] and for its sensitivity[6]—one reviewer in fact claiming that it ranked among the leading novels of that year[7]—most complained of unrealistic characterization,[8] authorial self-delusion,[9] and narrative dullness.[10] One reviewer ventured the thought that Wells had been too subtle in the book.[11] Indeed, read carefully, *The Passionate Friends* reveals subtlety in Wells's artistic craft, especially in his correlation of the social conventions of imperialism, marriage, paternity, passion, and the romance type of popular fiction. In revising these traditions for the purpose of emphasizing the ultimate value of the art of language in the improving of the "art" of the reader's life, *The Passionate Friends* is transformed from a conventional novel of romance into an interesting experiment in self-reflexive fictional artistry.

Since *The Passionate Friends* is so little read today, a summary of its plot might be helpful. The book is a first-person narrative written by Stephen Stratton, who at middle age is reflecting upon the implications of his life experiences and recording his thoughts for the eventual benefit of his son, presently six years of age. Stratton's story concerns his youthful love for Mary Christian, who loves Stratton too but who marries a man named Justin, who has promised to make no sexual demands on her and who provides her with social position and wealth, permitting her the sort of life she thinks she requires. Dejected, Stratton goes to South Africa, where for five years he participates in the Boer War. When Stratton returns he and Mary resume their passionate love affair, which is discovered by Justin, who suddenly takes his unfaithful wife to Ireland. After some time of searching for her, Stratton gets an interview with Mary, who is ill and psychologically broken. She tells him that she has promised Justin never to see him again. For a number of years Stratton travels abroad, and with an American friend he publishes books designed to advance civilization toward a World State. He also marries Rachel More, who eventually bears him a son and two daughters. After a period of years Stratton and Mary exchange long letters, but after two and a half years the correspondence ends; and he does not see her again until a chance encounter years later, by which time Mary has two children and her relationship with Justin is particularly strained. Managing to escape Mary's companion, they spend a day together engaged in a passionate exchange of ideas without physical affection. Justin learns of their meeting, suspects the worst, and seeks a divorce. Mary, already miserable and now also worried that the divorce scandal will harm Stratton's effort to bring about the World State, tells Stratton that she can prevent the divorce and its scandal; and so she commits suicide in a way suggesting an accidental overdose of a drug. After her death Stratton meets briefly with Justin, who acknowledges his role in Mary's death and who learns the truth about Stratton's chance meeting with Mary. The novel then ends with an emphasis on Mary's "symbolical value" representing a quality of beauty in life that remains "entangled and stifled and unable to free [itself] from the ancient limiting jealousies which law and custom embody."[12]

A quality of beauty: throughout *The Passionate Friends* Stratton associates this ideal of life's potential beauty not only with Mary, who has special intimations of this beauty (64, 91, 335), but also (as if she were a muse) with the human mind and imagination, which is imaged in the novel as a light or a fire.[13] Mary yearns for contact with the latent beauty of life: "I *want* to live again—out of [the] body . . . and all that it carries with it," she tells Stephen, "to be free—as beautiful things are free" (353). The human body with its material demands is presented in the novel as a form of imprisonment,[14] preventing the imagination from sustainingly realizing life's beauty. Because the "sexual, egotistical, passionate side" of humanity obscures the human capacity to be "creative and unselfish" (317), the imagination's "creative forces must inevitably spend themselves very largely in blind alleys, futile rushes, and destructive conflicts" (228). "Sweet and beautiful possibilities," Stratton explains, are "caught in the net of animal jealousies and thoughtless motives and ancient rigid institutions" (382).

Egotistical jealousies, thoughtless motives, and rigid conventions are, in Stratton's account, informing characteristics of conventional imperialistic policies. In his youth Stratton supports the colonial program of his homeland, and in an early letter to Mary he remarks that imperialism is less an expression of aggression than an impulse toward the establishment of peace and order throughout the world; he says as well that Britain should remain in its acquired territories "only to raise their peoples ultimately to an equal citizenship with ourselves" (67). Stratton even participates in the Boer War. Later in life Stratton realizes how far conventional imperialism remains from the goals of peace and equality. He then advocates an imperialism beyond specific national interests, an imperialism which would transcend its current egotistical jealousies, thoughtless motives, and rigid conventions, and would unselfishly and creatively eventuate in a beautiful World State.[15]

Stratton perceives that the problems with current imperialistic policies apply as well to the conventions of marriage. For Stratton, a typical marriage

of his day is a mode of the imperialistic impulse, whereby spouses claim such
exclusive rights to each other that their creative capacities become entrapped
by egotistical jealousy, thoughtless motives, and rigid convention. Justin's
"vast passion of jealousy" (183) is aroused by Stephen's friendship with Mary,
and Mary is miserable as a result. "Jealousy for what we esteem our possessions, jealousy for those upon whom we have set the heavy fetters of our love"
(257), underlies the imperialism of conventional marriage. Stratton is not ex-
empt from such motives; contemplating Mary's suicide he confesses, "In Mary
. . . I found what many have dreamt of, love and friendship freely given, and I
could do nothing but clutch at her to make her my possession" (382). Because
her love and friendship were *freely* given, they were beautiful; and ideally a
proper marriage, like a proper imperialism, ought to be unselfish and creative—that is, free—so that beauty in life may emerge.

The same entanglement and stifling of the creative impulse by "the ancient
limiting jealousies which law and custom embody" (383-384) in conventional
imperialism and conventional marriage inform, in Stratton's view, typical
notions of paternity. Like imperialistic rulers and despotic husbands, fathers
tend to reign over their children in ways derived from egotistical jealousies,
thoughtless motives, and rigid conventions. On several occasions Stratton
evokes an image of the succession of fathers that suggests a rigidity and confinement opposed to the free expression of a son's creative impulse. When
Stratton, for instance, tells his son about the time he sat by the dead body of
his father, he recalls "the flatly painted portrait of his father, my grandfather
[i.e., his son's great-grandfather], hanging there in the stillness above the
coffin"; in this portrait Stratton's grandfather looks "out on the world he had
left with steady . . . blue eyes that followed one about the room" (7). This
memory suggests a paternal continuity between every father and every son, a
conventional continuity which can be as restrictive as the traditional attitudes
behind imperialism and behind marriage.

However, Stratton believes, the conventions of imperialism, marriage, and
paternity can evolve in ways permitting a greater and greater emergence of
life's beauty. This evolution requires the steady ascendancy of mind over
body—for example, the revision of typical romantic love, or passion, with its
absorbing emphasis on sex, toward a more sisterly or brotherly friendship
between the sexes (160, 303, 383). This evolution is difficult to discern
because life is essentially repetition, as evidenced, for instance, in the heritage
of fathers and sons: "Such moments . . . happened to me times enough, to my
dead father, to that grandfather of the portrait which is now in my study, to

his father and his, and so on through long series of Strattons" (11). The creative impulse in humanity, however, vies with this repetition, and as humanity becomes more conscious of the creative impulse (288), slight evolutionary variations occur within life's repetition, including the repetitive social conventions of imperialism, marriage, paternity, and passion. "Each one of us," Stratton tells his son, "was but a variation, an experiment upon the Stratton theme" (7): "The servitude of sex and the servitude of labour are the twin conditions upon which human society rests today, the two limitations upon its progress towards a greater social order, to that greater community, those uplands of light and happy freedom, towards which that Being who was my father yesterday, who thinks in myself to-day, and who will be you tomorrow and your sons after you, by his very nature urges and must continue to urge the life of mankind" (162). The urge behind this evolution is the creative impulse of the human mind and imagination, the impulse toward freedom and beauty.

If this higher evolution is to be realized, humanity must become increasingly conscious of it, and in Wells's system the vehicle for this consciousness is a product of the mind and imagination: words. Each generation, for instance, ought to leave a written record of its thoughts for the succeeding generation. "Because I wanted so greatly some such book from [my father]," Stratton explains to his son, "I am now writing this" (4): "I want to write my story not indeed to the child you are now, but to the man you are going to be" (3). Stratton wants to improve upon his son's expected inheritance of "the merest hints and vestiges . . . casual and fragmentary, of . . . obliterated repetitions" (7)—precisely all Stratton inherited from his father, who inherited a still more silent portrait from *his* father. If the human creative impulse is to be realized in freedom and beauty, humanity must become more self-aware, more articulate; and thereby it will no longer leave "so much of the tale untold" (7), as do the personal effects of his dead father and the portrait of his dead grandfather: "Why must we all repeat things done, and come again very bitterly to wisdom our fathers have achieved before us?" (7).

Words, however, are a two-edged sword. On the one hand, they can imprison when, for instance, they are used to reinforce the egotistical spirit in conventional imperialism, marriage, paternity, and passion. Mary rightly worries that the words of scandal likely to derive from her divorce proceedings might ruin Stephen's chance to continue to use language to awaken humanity to the dawn of a World State. On the other hand, words (in Wells's view) possess an intrinsic potential for transforming harmony in spite of itself. "Self-expression is . . . almost an instinct with many of us" (8), Stratton writes: "It is not reason but a deep-seated instinct that draws our intelligence towards explanations, that sets us perpetually seeking laws, seeking statements that will fit the infinite, incessantly interweaving complexities, and be true to them all" (236). Through this instinct expressed in language humanity stumbles, as if by some internal fate, toward truth. One of the subtleties of *The Passionate Friends* concerns language typified by the evolution of a higher meaning of the word *passionate*, which early in the novel refers conventionally to sexually active lovers but which late in the novel refers unconventionally to the passionate spiritual bond of a brotherly/sisterly friendship between Mary and Stephen.

The evolution of the meaning of specific words such as *passionate* and, more important, the contingent evolution of the human mind through a self-conscious use of words is neither a simple nor an orderly process. It involves trial and error, doubt, and plenty of near-futile repetition. But, Stratton maintains, this repetition evinces slight, albeit real, variations on a theme, like the plants Mary sees outside her window: "They aren't scattered evenly . . . but in little clusters and groups that die away and begin again, like the repetitions of an air in some musical composition" (336). Stratton's book, as it evolves from traditional meanings of passions, paternity, marriage, and imperialism to new ones, dies away and begins again. Its accretive structure includes fragments of language from letters he wrote, from telegrams and letters he received, and from letters he composed in his mind. Stratton's narrative incorporates bits of recalled information that give hints and clues of the life he lived, odd bits similar to the "significant litter" his father left behind: letters, scraps of newspaper, tokens, relics, a medal, a photograph (6). In the course of writing this book Stratton feels as if he were sitting "among a pile of memories that are now all disordered and mixed up together, their proper sequences and connections lost" (165).

Stratton's account remains very much a work in progress. There are numerous reminders that the story must be resumed, that notes are being used, that much has been forgotten. Not only does the fate of the work remain uncertain—"if ultimately I decide that it [this manuscript] shall reach your hands" (292)—but the work has been much less successful than Stratton had hoped: "before me is the pile of manuscript that has grown here. . . . I had meant it to be the story of my life, but how little of my life is in it! It gives, at most, certain acute points, certain salient aspects. I begin to realize for the first time how thin and suggestive and sketchy a thing any novel or biography must be. How we must simplify!" (379). One can never capture the whole of life in language, for "life is so much fuller than any book can be" (379). Also there is the problem of doubt derived from the fearful "sense of life as of an abysmal flood, full of cruelty, densely futile, blackly aimless" (343). And then there is an endless struggle: "to struggle out of our pit is this life, there is no individual life but that . . . and there comes no escape here, no end to that effort, until the release of death" (279).

The fullness of life is not capturable in language, but language drawing upon weak memory does convey something of that life, and in the process language combats despair and supports us in our struggle to live, the struggle for freedom and beauty. Because language derives from "a deep-seated instinct that draws our intelligence towards explanations" and because this instinct resides in the human mind and imagination, whence freedom and beauty are to arise through the "creative impulse" (255), Stratton's use of words, whatever its admitted shortcoming in capturing the fullness of life, is a better legacy than the miscellaneous personal effects of his father or the portrait of his grandfather. What Stratton hopes to leave his son is a somewhat clearer view of life than Stratton had at the same age received from his own father. Whatever language's limitations and however processive it must remain, it does, in Stratton's view, make more lucid the dark confusions of life: "I feel that the toil of writing and reconsideration may help to clear and fix many things that remain a little uncertain in my thoughts because they have never been fully stated" (3). Indeed, in terms of the evolving human mind, it is through language that man "ceases to be a creature and becomes a creator, he turns upon the powers that made him and subdues them to his service" (292). Man possesses a Logos power to speak into existence a higher mode of life. This belief underlies Stratton's career as a publisher who plans to produce encyclopaedias, guide books, gazetteers, dictionaries, textbooks, reference books, as well as world-wide translations and reprints—in short "so comprehensive . . . [a] choice of books, excluding nothing . . . on account of any inferiority of quality, obscurity of subject, or narrowness of demand, that in the long run anybody, anywhere, desiring to read anything would turn naturally and inevitably to . . . [his] lists" (298). This collection of words, so accessible, will (Stratton believes) represent clarifying variations on human themes that, through the intrinsic Logos power of language, will steadily advance future humanity toward a World State.

So Stratton's book, admittedly inadequate, remains processive. It clarifies life somewhat by using language to achieve variations on the conventional

notions of passions, paternity, marriage, and imperialism. The language of
the book also achieves a variation on the plot of the popular novel of romance,
a genre of literature (in Stratton's opinion) as replete with egotistical jealousies, thoughtless motives, and rigid conventions as are traditional attitudes
toward imperialism, marriage, paternity, and passion. The plot of *The Passionate Friends* is hardly innovative, and more than one reviewer expressed discontent with it. Wells, however, meant his plot to be somewhat trite because
in his novel he was attempting a variation, a subtle evolutionary revision of
the formulaic language of the novel of romance typified by the writings of
Marriott Watson:

> Now here it may seem to you that we are on the very verge of romance.
> Here is a beautiful lady carried off and held prisoner in a wild old place,
> standing out half cut off from the mainland among the wintry breakers of
> the west coast of Ireland. Here is the lover, baffled but insistent. Here are
> the fierce brothers and the stern dragon husband, and you have but to
> make out that the marriage was compulsory, irregular, and, on the
> ground of that irregularity, finally dissoluble, to furnish forth a theme for
> Marriott Watson in his most admirable and adventurous vein. You can
> imagine the happy chances that would have guided me to the hiding-
> place, the trusty friend who would have come with me and told the story,
> the grim siege of the place—all as it were *sotto voce* for fear of scandal—the
> fight with Guy in the little cave. . . . My siege of Mirk makes a very
> different story from that. (188–189)

As Stratton says elsewhere: "In . . . romances one goes from such a parting in
a splendid dignity of gloom. But I am no hero, and I went down the big
staircase of Tarville's house the empty shuck of an abandoned desire" (209).
Indeed, instead of Stephen rescuing the heroine, Mary dies by her own hand in
an effort to "rescue" Stephen from imminent bad publicity which could ruin
his career and thereby threaten the emergence of a World State.

   The Passionate Friends, then, was intended by Wells, through Stratton, to
be a variation of the conventional plot of the novel of romance, a variation
representing in his mind a slight evolution of the genre that makes the genre
more appropriate to contemporary reality: "it seems to me more and more as I
live longer, that . . . most literature . . . is discordant with the vastness and
variety, the reserves and resources and recuperations of life as we live it today.
It is the expression of life under cruder and more rigid conditions than ours,
lived by people who loved and hated more naively. . . . Solitary persons and
single events dominated them as they do not dominate us. We range wider,
last longer, and escape more and more from intensity towards understanding"

(380). From intensity to understanding: Wells wanted to transform the novel of romance from its emphasis on the intense individual and on physical passion to a newly evolved emphasis on the understanding of the human "collective will" (250) and on spiritual friendship between humans. This revision of the novel of romance, with Mary sacrificing her individual life for the collective will, made it a suitable vehicle for Wells's attempt in the book to transform the egotistical attitudes behind the social conventions of imperialism, marriage, paternity, and passion.

Moreover, Wells's wish to transform the novel of romance (with its implicit social conventions) from its old emphasis on a "still savage individuality" to a new stress on "the interests of the species" (24) required that *The Passionate Friends* become self-reflexive; that is, the novel calls attention to itself as an arbitrary and artificial construction of language, a mere work in progress whose language is never adequate for (and so fictionalizes) the narrated life "so much fuller than any book can be." Such self-reflexivity denies a particular lasting (egotistical) identity for the novel as an artistic artifact, as a finished and polished work of art and the sort Henry James would admire; James, in fact, hated *The Passionate Friends*.[16] By Stratton's own admission his book is "sketchy" (379), a scaffolding: "It is not [a] glorious work, I know, as the work of great artists . . . is glorious, but it is what I find best suits my gifts and my want of gifts. Greater men will come at last to build within my scaffolding" (313). Finally Stratton's book concerns less its author or itself as art (both of which would be features of egotism) than its audience, Stratton's son and all other readers of the book who are urged to build mentally within Stratton's scaffolding.

In other words, the self-reflexivity of *The Passionate Friends*, its tendency time and again to call attention to itself as an inadequate and artificial work in progress (scaffoldings) encourages dissatisfaction in the reader in a way designed to make the reader self-aware, first, of himself as a reader and, second, of himself as his own book. The latter effect is particularly reinforced not only by the fact that Stratton's work is an autobiography, but also by similes and metaphors equating life and books. When the narrator of the novel speaks of "the page of history" (223), of "reading [his] present life as one reads in a book," of "the page of [his] life before him" (309), and of "holding the realities of our lives before us as though they were little sorry tales written in books upon our knees" (355), the reader's thoughts are directed away from the specific book in hand to the book in progress that is his or her own life. In this way, Stratton's autobiography of mind merges with the reader's. This merging is particularly appropriate for a work designed to advance a tradition of the popular novel that commonly stressed the individual artist, character, and artwork in a way manifesting egotistical jealousy, thoughtless motive, and rigid convention—and advance this tradition toward a new emphasis on the collective will of the species (the readers) with a revised understanding of imperialism, marriage, paternity, passion, and popular romance fiction. This literary focus on the collective will of all humanity as readers-authors of the book of life represented, in Wells's mind, an evolutionary advance in literature, an advance which transformed *The Passionate Friends* from a typical novel of romance into a suitable vehicle for Wells's revisionist artistry.

Perhaps Nabokov and Greene, when they praised *The Passionate Friends*, recalled something of these subtle qualities of Wells's novel. Perhaps they particularly appreciated Wells's valuation of language in the book—Greene possibly sensitive to Wells's nervous, revisionist faith in the processive redemption of man within a fallen world and to his vision of language as a matrix for this redemption; Nabokov possibly sensitive to Wells's playful response to the romance novel as an exhausted literary form and to his use of self-reflexivity to correlate the art of fiction and the art of life as well as to break down the barriers between reader, author, and character. We may never know precisely why Nabokov and Greene thought so highly of *The Passionate Friends*, but by calling our attention to this novel they have encouraged us to reassess it. *The Passionate Friends* indeed reveals subtlety in Wells's artistic consciousness. In this novel the typical social notions of imperialism, marriage, paternity, passion, and popular novels of romance are revised in a way which emphasizes the ultimate value of the art of language in the improvement of the "art" of each reader's life. In terms of this revisionary artistry, *The Passionate Friends* was an interesting, even innovative experiment in the art of fiction in 1913.[17]

NOTES

1. For example, Richard Hauer Costa, "Edwardian Intimations of the Shape of Fiction to Come: Mr. Britling/Job Huss as Wellsian Central Intelligences," *English Literature in Transition*, 18 (1975), 229–242; Robert Bloom, *Anatomies of Egotism: A Reading of the Last Novels of H.G. Wells* (Lincoln: Univ. of Nebraska Press, 1977); and Robert Philmus, "Revisions of His Past: H.G. Wells's *Anatomy of Frustration*," *Texas Studies in Literature and Language*, 20 (1978), 249–266.
2. Vladimir Nabokov, *Strong Opinions* (New York: McGraw-Hill, 1973), 103–104.

3. As reported in a review of Anthony West's *H.G. Wells: Aspects of a Life*, in *Newsweek* (28 May, 1984), 83.

4. Most recently in *The Splintering Frame: The Later Fiction of H. G. Wells* (Victoria, British Columbia: Univ. of Victoria, 1984).

5. "Fiction," *Athenaeum*, 4481 (13 September 1913), 248–249.

6. Edwin Francis Edgett, "H. G. Wells the Iconoclast," *Boston Evening Transcript* (5 November 1913), 24; "Mr. Wells, the Wanderer," *Nation* (London) 13 (27 September 1913), 959–960.

7. Louise M. Field, "H. G. Wells," *New York Times Book Review*, (2 November 1913), 593.

8. Robert Lynd, "The World, the Flesh, and Mr. Wells," *Daily News and Leader* (London) (12 September 1913), 2; "Mr. Wells's New Novel," *New Statesman,* 1 (20 September 1913),760–761; "Novels," *Saturday Review* (London), 116 (13 September 1913), 339; "*The Passionate Friends*," *Times Literary Supplement* (London) (18 September 1913), 387. These reviews are echoed in Alfred Borrello, *H. G. Wells: Author in Agony* (Carbondale: Southern Illinois Univ. Press, 1972), 46–47.

9. "Current Fiction," *Nation* (New York), 97 (4 December 1913), 537.

10. Richard Curle, "H. G. Wells," *Bookman* (London), 45 (October 1913), 58.

11. B. S., "A New Novel by Mr. Wells," *Manchester Guardian*, (12 September 1913), 5.

12. *The Works of H. G. Wells* (New York: Charles Scribner's Sons, 1926), 18: 383–384. Subsequent quotations from *The Passionate Friends* are taken from this edition, and page numbers are included parenthetically in the text.

13. This imagery remained consistent for Wells at least from 1906 to 1919; see my "The Thing That Is and the Speculative If: The Pattern of Several Motifs in Three Novels by H. G. Wells," *English Literature in Transition*, 11 (1968), 67–78.

14. This sense of the body is most recently remarked in John R. Reed's *The Natural History of H. G. Wells* (Athens: Ohio Univ. Press, 1982), 56–57. The very personal elements of the novel for Wells himself are noted in Gordon N. Ray's *H. G. Wells and Rebecca West* (New Haven: Yale Univ. Press, 1974) and in Anthony West's *H. G. Wells: Aspects of a Life* (New York: Random House, 1984).

15. For Wells's notion of a World State, see Warren Wagar, *H. G. Wells and the World State* (New Haven: Yale Univ. Press, 1961).

16. On the disagreement between them, see Leon Edel and Gordon N. Ray, eds., *Henry James and H. G. Wells* (Urbana: Univ. of Illinois Press, 1958).

17. I would like to acknowledge my indebtedness to Dean Robert King and Professor William Sutherland for a special research assignment which permitted me free time to write this and other essays.

The Genre of *The Good Soldier:* Ford's Comic Mastery

AVROM FLEISHMAN

> It may strike you, silent listener, as being
> funny if you happen to be European.
> —JOHN DOWELL[1]

The "rediscovery" of Ford Madox Ford which took place in the early sixties—witness a dozen books and numberless articles—could not long be sustained at its high pace but seems to have done its work.[2] Ford is now squarely positioned among the modern masters—if not quite at the level of his cronies, Conrad or Pound, at least at an intersection between them and the wider field of modern letters. Yet his reputation, despite repeated scholarly rehearsals of the canon, continues to hang on one book—and that book deeply scarred by critical cuts and thrusts. The fierce and roughly even combat among *The Good Soldier's* interpreters over the unreliability of its narrator has turned to speculation about Ford's creative reliability. Skirting the question of whether the novel is a triumph or a failure of inadvertence, doubts have been raised about its thematic coherence, narrational consistency, and stylistic integrity.[3] The more cautious studies have shifted attention where it has all along belonged, to Ford's actual performance with impressionist methods, to the novel's rich but unassayed verbal texture, and above all to its generic modes.

Mark Schorer it was who started that hare, among others. In the essay which became the preface to the popular edition of the novel,[4] Schorer not only assumed that it was a comic work but produced a number of modal terms

41

to characterize its kind of comedy. Discussion has since turned from the comedic to such lame canards as "potential tragedy," medievalist romance, and ironic melodrama, until it now seems that no one finds the book funny. At the risk of taking the stance of Charles Addams's chuckling ghoul amid a weeping theater audience, I must testify to my immense pleasure in reading and laughing over Dowell's narrative. In order to put the issue beyond consideration of affective fallacies and psychological idiosyncrasies, we may review the genre alternatives.

Schorer gives only one comic mode a declarative statement—"*The Good Soldier* is a comedy of humor, and the humor is phlegm" (xiii)—but other phrases suggest the alternatives: "Irony . . . can thus enjoy the advantage of many ambiguities of meaning"; "grotesquely comic metaphors"; "a mode of comic revelation"; "wonderfully comic events"; "absurd anticlimaxes"; "incessant wit, of style and statement"; "habitually comic solemnity." The curious thing about these seemingly diffuse observations or casual encomia is that they are all demonstrably applicable to the text; Schorer merely begins the job of accounting their lovely appearances. What remains evasive is an awareness of the kind or level of comedy that could account for their co-presence in any one work. We recall that only certain plays of Shakespeare can accept infusions of humors, irony, ambiguity, grotesquerie, revelation, the wonderful, the absurd, incessant wit, and habitual solemnity. If Ford had achieved so much and no more, he would take his place in the great tradition of English comedy that comes down from Chaucer, yet finds few adequate modern exemplars. It is in that tradition that Ford's genius flowered: if *The Good Soldier* is not to be ranked with *Ulysses* as consummate artistry, it may stand with it among the few great modern comic novels.

Documenting the evidence of comedy bears all the inherent disadvantages of explaining a joke, yet in the somber atmosphere of Ford studies something must be done to break the ice. Following Schorer's listing, a few examples may suffice:

(a) *humors:* "He saw himself as the victim of the law. I don't mean to say that he saw himself as a kind of Dreyfus. The law, practically, was quite kind to him. It stated that in its view Captain Ashburnham had been misled by an ill-placed desire to comfort a member of the opposite sex [Miss Kilsyte] and it fined him five shillings for his want of tact, or of knowledge of the world. But Edward maintained that it had put ideas into his head" (157).

(b) *irony/ambiguity:* "Beati Immaculati" (epigraph, from Psalm 119).[5]

(c) *grotesquerie:* Maisie Maidan "had died so grotesquely that her little body had fallen forward into the trunk, and it had closed upon her, like the jaws of a gigantic alligator. The key was in her hand. Her dark hair, like the hair of a Japanese, had come down and covered her body and her face. Leonora lifted her up—she was the merest featherweight—and laid her on the bed with her hair about her. She was smiling, as if she had just scored a goal in a hockey match" (75–76)

(d) *revelation:* "Edward ought, I suppose, to have gone to the Boer War. It would have done him a great deal of good to get killed" (170).

(e) *the wonderful:* "The death of Mrs. Maidan occured on the 4th of August 1904. And then nothing happened until the 4th of August 1913. There is a curious coincidence of dates, but I do not know whether that is one of those sinister, as if half-jocular and altogether merciless proceedings on the part of a cruel Providence that we call a coincidence. Because it may just as well have been the superstitious mind of Florence that forced her to certain acts, as if she had been hypnotized. It is, however, certain that the 4th of August always proved a significant date for her. To begin with, she was born on the 4th of August. Then on that date, in the year 1899, she set out with her uncle for the tour round the world in company with a young man called Jimmy. . . . Then on the 4th of August 1900, she yielded to an action that certainly coloured her whole life—as well as mine. . . . On the 4th of August 1901, she married me, and set sail for Europe in a great gale of wind—the gale that affected her heart" (77–78).

(f) *the absurd: ad libitum.*

(g) *wit:* "the profusion of his cases, all of pigskin and stamped with his initials, E.F.A. There were guncases, and collar cases, and shirt cases, and letter cases, and cases each containing four bottles of medicine; and hat cases and helmet cases. It must have needed a whole herd of the Gadarene swine to make up his outfit" (26).

(h) *post-lapsarian solemnity:* "Is there then any terrestrial paradise where, amidst the whispering of the olive-leaves, people can be with whom they like and have what they like and take their ease in shadows and in coolness? Or are all men's lives like the lives of us good people—like the lives of the Ashburnhams, of the Dowells, of the Ruffords—broken, tumultuous, agonized, and un-romantic lives, periods punctuated by screams, by imbecilities, by deaths, by agonies: Who the devil knows?" (237–238)

To this listing may be added other comic modes:

(i) *social satire:* "She wanted her husband to have a English accent, an income of fifty thousand dollars a year from real estate and no ambitions to increase that income. . . . She gave out this information in floods of bright talk—she would pop a little bit of it into comments over a view of the Rialto, Venice, and whilst she was brightly describing Balmoral Castle, she would say that her ideal husband would be one who could get her received at the British court" (79).

(j) *situation-comedy:* "Her room door was locked because she was nervous about thieves. . . . And I was provided with an axe—an axe!—great gods, with which to break down her door in case she ever failed to answer my knock" (89).

(k) *burlesque:* "'Why,' La Dolciquita answered, 'I may just as well have the ten thousand dollars as the tables. I will go with you to Antibes for a week for that sum." Edward grunted: 'Five.' She tried to get seven thousand five hundred; but he stuck to his five thousand and the hotel expenses at Antibes" (163).

(l) *vulgarity:* "I suppose that, during all that time, I was a deceived husband and that Leonora was pimping for Edward. . . . And Leonora would treat [Florence] like the whore she was" (69,71).

(m) *literary parody:* "And then Florence said: 'And so the whole round table is begun'" (33); or: "She made him out like a cross between Lohengrin and the Chevalier Bayard. . . . 'Well,' I said, 'then he must really be Lohengrin and the Cid in one body'" (95–96); or: "'*Thou hast conquered, O pale Galilean.*' It was like his sentimentality to quote Swinburne" (251).

This melange of low-mimetic realism, reductive humors, displaced heroic models, paradisal yearnings, bedroom farce, monologist's one-liners, sops to entertain the groundlings, finer morsels for the quality, and self-reflexive awareness of the literary tradition makes up the comic world of *The Good Soldier.* But how should Ford have made it from his scanty personal store of comic vision?

Critics have sharply divided on the question of Ford's artistic control—roughly along the lines which have formed their debate about the novel's narrator. Those who credit Dowell with at least some powers of sympathy and insight, or who discover him improving in those virtues as he proceeds with his tale, or who find his very inadequacies testimony to a pervasive condition of fallibility and darkness in the modern condition, or in the human condition, are also likely to be found attesting to Ford's ironic control of the narration and to his successful practice of the theory of Impressionism. Those who find Dowell incoherent as witness and raconteur also tend to find Ford an incompetent artist whose inadequacies are unconsciously projected or skillfully displaced onto Dowell.

With such a hung jury, the record of Ford's personal life at the time of writing can be read either way: his biographers[6] have treated the breakdown of his marriage and friendships, the scandals of law courts and newspapers, his domestic turmoil and dire financial straits, together with the indications of mental imbalance at the time of writing, either as evidence of his artistic triumph in wordly adversity or as the source of the novel's incoherence, according to their lights. Nor is the singular place of *The Good Soldier* in the Ford canon indisputable proof either of his mastery or of a happy accident in creating it. A garrulous but only partly conscious craftsman, who disdained his own decisive breakthrough into the modern narrative mode (the multiple interior monologues in the final volume of *Parade's End, The Last Post*), Ford may yet have been in intuitive control of his art in the earlier as in the later work. The proper place to view his craftsmanly awareness must lie, not in the notoriously unreliable recollections that spin from the later grand old man of modernism, but in an essay written as *The Good Soldier* was being composed: "On Impressionism," published in two parts in June and December, 1914.[7]

Ford begins with the well-known canons of impression-psychology ("the impression of a moment"), of artistic abstraction ("the impression of the whole thing . . . in a few phrases"), and of the new mimesis ("one tries to produce an illusion of reality"), which he was later to elaborate as the fruit of his association with Conrad. Although inconsistencies are rife within this essay (blurring the impressions of men in general, of readers, of authors, and of characters), the chief interest of "On Impressionism" lies not so much in its theory as in the practical maxims on how to write (or how I write) which follow. Taking up the objection of a "futurist friend" that "A story is a story; why not just tell it any how?" (46), Ford responds with surprising sympathy:

> There is a good deal to be said for this point of view. Writing up to my own standards is such an intolerable labor and such a thankless job, since it can't give me the one thing in the world that I desire—that for my part I am determined to drop creative writing for good and all. . . .
>
> This adieu, like Herrick's to poesy, may seem to be a digression. Indeed it is; and indeed it isn't. It is, that is to say, a digression in the sense that it is a statement not immediately germane to the argument that I am carrying on. But it is none the less an insertion fully in accord with the canons of Impressionism as I understand it. For the first business of Impressionism is to produce an impression, and the only way in literature to produce an impression is to awaken interest. And, in a sustained argument, you can only keep interest awakened by keeping alive, by whatever means you may have at your disposal, the surprise of your reader. You must state your argument; you must illustrate it, and then you must stick

in something that appears to have nothing whatever to do with either subject or illustration, so that the reader will exclaim: "What the devil is the fellow driving at?" And then you must go on in the same way—arguing, illustrating and startling and arguing, startling and illustrating—until at the very end your contentions will appear like a ravelled skein. And then, in the last few lines, you will draw towards you the master-string of that seeming confusion, and the whole pattern of the carpet, the whole design of the net-work will be apparent. (46–48)

That this passage is to be taken with some seriousness is dictated by its confirmation of Ford's later prefatory statement that he intended *The Good Soldier* to be his last novel. What may have been "the one thing in the world that I desire" we may well wonder, but it did not remain absolutely necessary to the working novelist, who went on to produce a couple of dozen more works of fiction.

More to the point here are the ensuing digressions on digression and the declaration of their full "accord with the canons of Impressionism." By a mind-bending logic, Ford leads us up to the last rung of impressionist method—the "master-string of the seeming confusion"—and then drops us. This digressive method is quite an accurate description of the way Ford's narrator operates in *The Good Soldier,* and his esthetic aims are indicated by the plan for a closing gesture of psychic integration, formal resolution, and determinate meaning—if that is what the Jamesian metaphors of "the whole pattern of the carpet, the whole design of the net-work" are intended to convey. It is just this closing gesture that is missing from the novel, as witnessed by the history of its criticism: the failure to reach a consensus in reading this maddening book is sufficient testimony to the absence of a "master-string."

One current school of literary theorists might argue that all narrative—perhaps all literature—exhibits the same meandering, ambiguity, or ultimate openness as *The Good Soldier;* that, in Ford's theoretical statement, the age-old metaphors of the text as texture, the tale-teller as weaver of a fabric, and the narrator or his audience as followers of a thread of meaning toward a patterned design, are all marks of a narrative tradition that confesses its inevitable failure to tie down loose ends.[8]

Yet surely the characteristic practices of narrative art from Homer down are not so much typified as parodied by Ford's performance, or by Dowell's. There have been other alternatives to the opportunistic variety which Ford goes on to prescribe:

And the whole of Impressionism comes to this: having realized that the audience to which you will address yourself must have this particular peasant intelligence, or, if you prefer it, this particular and virgin openness of mind, you will then figure to yourself an individual, a silent listener, who shall be to yourself the *homo bonae voluntatis*—man of good will. To him, then, you will address your picture, your poem, your prose story, or your argument. You will seek to capture his interest; you will seek to hold his interest. You will do this by methods of surprise, of fatigue, by passages of sweetness in your language, by passages suggesting the sudden and brutal shock of suicide. You will give him passages of dulness, so that your bright effects may seem more bright; you will alternate, you will dwell for a long time upon an intimate point; you will seek to exasperate so that you may the better enchant. You will, in short, employ all the devices of the prostitute. (53–54)

Here we find the *ars poetica* of *The Good Soldier;* it has the virtue, if not of general application either to narrative or to Ford's practice at large, of specific application to a particular work of art. No stylistic critic has better characterized the novel's disparate techniques, no affective critic better expressed its readers' varied responses, no post-structuralist critic more surely anticipated its numerous falls into bathos.

In face of such a statement of intention—and particularly when imbued with the flavor of the prose by which it is conveyed—one is led to conclude that this master of Impressionism was incapable of calculating the impression his *ars poetica* would make upon a fastidious reader (unless a virgin peasant of precise design). Yet *The Good Soldier* unites its readers in a conviction of its pleasurable excellence, despite their inability to agree on anything else. How account for such unlooked-for unanimity? The source of this paradox, as of so many others, lies with the astonishing narrator. One will have detected him lurking in Ford's own prose, ogling his "silent listener," committing a number of sexual indiscretions (merely verbal, to be sure), and succeeding all too well in his design to surprise, fatigue, sweeten, shock, bore, brighten, exasperate, and enchant his audience. Before my ensuing remarks are taken to be yet another exposure of Dowell as unreliable narrator, Fordian persona, or emasculated poltroon, let me attest my conviction that he is one of the great comic characters of literature—on a level with Trimalchio, the Pardoner, and Leopold Bloom. As in the earlier consideration of the novel's modes, our business with him is to determine his peculiar comic power.

Dowell repeatedly tells us that he's naively deceived, and if he's at all reliable in this, we must take his other statements to be those of a fool, foolish. If, of course, we discount his self-estimation and find wisdom or validity in his report, we take this initial premise, at least, as unreliable. Bertrand Russell, faced with a similar quandary—the contemplation of a sheet on each side of which is written, "The statement on the other side of this paper is false"—suffered a mental breakdown. How are we to avoid this logical trap? There is no point in weighing the instances of Dowell's purported insight against the number of his manifest errors. Whether in trying and failing to establish a consistent chronology by his four summaries (4, 77–78, 98, and 222),[9] or in distinguishing between his earlier ignorance and his later, "informed" version of the same events,[10] or in describing the moral or even the literal situations before him, he reveals himself not merely as an inaccurate witness but a confusing and confused writer-reporter. It proves nothing against him to make this case, for the purported virtue of such a narrator is his enactment of the modern drama of blindness and discovery amid epistemological shadows, in which he stands as our avatar. It requires, however, a more profound, more bitter, indeed a comic self-recognition to identify ourselves not merely with his difficulties but with his absurdities.

One encouragement of comic identification lies in the novel's consistent caricature of its literary models, which encourages us to see Dowell as creature of a master parodist. Like the authoritative narrator of tradition, Dowell begins self-consciously by explaining his motives for writing: "You may well ask why I write. And yet my reasons are quite many. For it is not too unusual in human beings who have witnessed the sack of a city or the falling to pieces of people to desire to set down what they have witnessed for the benefit of unknown heirs or of generations infinitely remote; or, if you please, just to get the sight out of their heads. . . . Someone has said that the death of a mouse from cancer is the whole sack of Rome by the Goths. . . ." (5) If one could discover the source of that astonishing citation, one might be in a position to name the model of historiography from which the preceding paragraph takes off. The motive of recording the sack of a city, Rome or another, for posterity to recall and be admonished by is as old as the classical historians, but it is usually more modestly announced by writers of *personal* histories. Whether or not any domestic situation, even one ending in suicide and madness, can claim to exemplify "the falling to pieces of people," Dowell strikes here the first in a series of literary postures: pseudo-historian.

Dowell's next stance is that of amateur epistemologist: "If for nine years I have possessed a goodly apple that is rotten at the core and discover its rottenness only in nine years and six months less four days, isn't it true to say that for nine years I possessed a goodly apple?" (7). The answer to such rhetorical

questions usually takes the form—no, you've possessed an apple tart—but
one need not quibble with Dowell as an exponent of philosophic subjectivism
(or solipsism). For he immediately adopts another philosophic position, radical skepticism: "I know nothing—nothing in the world—of the hearts of
men. I only know that I am alone—horribly alone" (7). And for five pages, he
treats us to an extended rhapsody on the themes "no," "know," and "don't
know."

Perhaps most striking in his inflated rhetoric is the concluding sentence:
"It is all a darkness" (12). This seems to place the bawling, skeptical child on
the doorstep of his father, Joseph Conrad, and there are other indications of
the provenience of Dowell's inquest in Marlow's penetration of the Congo: the
repetition of the last-quoted sentence (164), Florence's cultural-imperialist
notion that she was "clearing up one of the dark places of the earth" (40), and
the persistent formulation of the heart patients' condition in foregrounded
phrases, for example, Mr. Hurlbird "wasn't obtrusive about his heart. You
wouldn't have known he had one" (19). So to Dowell's other models for his
posturing we may add the Conradian narrator, as he echoes the famous Preface
to *The Nigger of the "Narcissus"*: "But [Edward] talked like a cheap
novelist.—Or like a very good novelist for the matter of that, if it's the business of a novelist to make you see things clearly" (109).

Not content with a bathetic espousal of a number of philosophic and
literary positions, Dowell proceeds to parody Impressionism itself:

> It is very difficult to give an all-round impression of any man. I wonder
> how far I have succeeded with Edward Ashburnham. I dare say I haven't
> succeeded at all. . . .
> And have I, I wonder, given the due impression of how his life was
> portioned and his time laid out? Because, until the very last, the amount
> of time taken up by his various passions was relatively small. . . . But I
> guess I have made it hard for you, O silent listener, to get that impres-
> sion. . . .
> That question of first impressions has always bothered me a good
> deal—but quite academically. I mean that, from time to time, I have
> wondered whether it were or were not best to trust to one's first im-
> pressions in dealing with people. . . . And, as far as waiters and
> chambermaids were concerned, I have generally found that my first im-
> pressions were correct enough. (151–152)

And as he rambles on, about his first impressions on returning to America
(153), his impression of Philadelphia (154), etc., Dowell aptly characterizes
his mind as a field of shifting impressions, "so that the whole world for me is

like spots of colour in an immense canvas" (14).

Beyond being a bundle of impressions, Dowell claims to be an Impressionist in his narrative method:

> I have, I am aware, told this story in a very rambling way so that it may
> be difficult for any to find his path through what may be a sort of maze. I
> cannot help it. . . . [W]hen one discusses an affair—a long, sad
> affair—one goes back, one goes forward. One remembers points that one
> has forgotten and one explains them all the more minutely since one
> recognizes that one has forgotten to mention them in their proper places
> and that one may have given, by omitting them, a false impression. I
> console myself with thinking that this is a real story and that, after all,
> real stories are probably told best in the way a person telling a story would
> tell them. They will then seem most real. (183)

The plodding simplicity of these adages should not blind one (not Dowell's
omnipresent "one") to the fact that this is not a "real" story (although Ford
claimed to have it from "Edward Ashburnham himself" [xx]). For Dowell,
from his point of view, to adopt the moves of Impressionism to tell a "real"
story amounts to an estheticizing act: he makes a plain tale *artfully like* reality.
Instead of an artistic mimesis of "real" storytelling, however, his narration
adds complexity to complication, refinement to rarity, so that it emerges as
one of the most artificial tales ever told. There is a low-mimetic core of passion, deception, and ignorance in *The Good Soldier,* but Dowell has elaborated
it into a would-be minor epic. For this *reductio ad absurdum* of Conradian and
Jamesian narrative method, we have Ford's comic sense to thank.

A number of Dowell's stances as narrator more directly imitate the *histors* of
those Fordian masters. He proceeds to claim the authority of a perspectivist
multiple narration:

> I mean that I have explained everything that went before Maisie's death
> from the several points of view that were necessary—from Leonora's, from
> Edward's, and, to some extent, from my own. You have the facts for the
> trouble of finding them; you have the points of view as far as I could
> ascertain or put them. . . . Let us consider Leonora's point of view with
> regard to Florence; Edward's, of course, I cannot give you for Edward
> naturally never spoke of his affair with my wife. (I may, in what follows,
> be a little hard on Florence. . . .) (184)

Although it bravely tries to muster a variety of viewpoints for its synthetic
claims, the passage indicates that Edward's views are indirectly obtained,
since Dowell cannot communicate with him on the key subject, and that

Florence's views will be misrepresented, because of Dowell's bitterness in recollecting her infidelity to him. Beyond this, I believe, distortion is accountable to the same source as the strengths of Dowell's interpretation: since he saw nothing—not his wife's and friend's relations, not Leonora's awareness of the seduction from its inception during the trip to Marburg, neither Florence's motives for nor her method of suicide—all this information comes to him from Leonora. We are, in fact, informed of just so much as Leonora deems Dowell worthy of knowing; even the events at Branshaw Teleragh are largely concluded by the time Dowell arrives on the scene, so that most of the action of Part IV is also told him by Leonora (he does directly witness Edward's torment and Nancy's madness).[11] The *histor's* sifting of competing evidence and interpretation turns out to be a parody of perspectivism—the single-minded narrator coming slowly to realize his victimization, although still controlled by one of his deceivers.

Another novelist model whom Ford uses Dowell to parody is the Jamesian American, innocent abroad. There is something about Dowell that we should have recognized from the very first word, but it is only at page 47 that he identifies himself as the little man who writes those letters in the Paris edition of the Herald Tribune protesting about connections of the Belgian railways. His mode of travelling through some of the most beautiful landscape in Europe is characteristic:

> . . .the incident of the cow was a real joy to me. I chuckled over it from time to time for the whole rest of the day. Because it does look very funny, you know, to see a black and white cow land on its back in the middle of a stream. It is so just exactly what one doesn't expect of a cow.
>
> I suppose I ought to have pitied the poor animal; but I just didn't. I was out for enjoyment. And I just enjoyed myself. It is so pleasant to be drawn along in front of the spectacular towns with the peaked castle and the many double spires. (42)

Ford risks reducing his creature so far below the level of *homme moyen sensual* as to shift the comic mode from literary parody to topical burlesque, but such shifts are normal throughout the text. The final pages of Dowell's narration put side by side his self-estimation as "that absurd figure, an American millionaire" (254), last seen trotting off to Leonora with Nancy's telegram, and his absurdist theory of personality: ". . . I love [Edward] because he was just myself. If I had had the courage and the virility and possibly also the physique of Edward Asburnham I should, I fancy, have done much what he did" (253).

Ford's achievement in *The Good Soldier*, then, goes beyond the creation of a

great comic work, even beyond the comic peripety of turning the disorder of
his own fictional theory and practice against itself so as to convert its liabilities
into strengths. By some subtle yet probably inchoate intuition, Ford saw
through the codes of his intellectual milieu to discover the comic dimension of
modern fictional technique. The infinite complexities and ultimate ambiguities of James's later works, the elaborate self-consciousness and epistemological uncertainty of Conrad's narrators, became in his hands the materials of
verbal parody and eventually the basis of intellectual satire. For Ford's discovery cuts to the heart of modern literary practice, and not only in the fictional realm. The comedy of ubiquitous but fragmented knowledge, which is
only now beginning to emerge from our more relaxed, less shocked reading of
The Waste Land and *The Cantos*—and as it is found preeminently in *Ulysses* and
Finnegans Wake—was grasped by Ford in the midst of the emergence of
modernism. It is not enough to find *The Good Soldier* anticipating much of
what passes for black humor these days. This is the first novel to display the
modern comedy of infinitely questioning but inveterately self-defeating
speculation. As some Eastern European dissidents have said of their situation,
it is a condition that is critical but not serious. [12]

NOTES

1. All quotations are from Ford Madox Ford, *The Good Soldier: A Tale of Passion* (New York:
Knopf, 1951). This edition includes "An Interpretation" by Mark Schorer (first published
as an article in two places cited in a note) and the "Dedicatory Letter to Stella Ford" (from
the 1927 reissue of the novel).

2. Despite the passage of time and the appearance of more books and articles, Joseph
Wiesenfarth's summary of the critical situation remains fairly applicable to the present
state of affairs: "Criticism and the Semiosis of *The Good Soldier*," *Modern Fiction Studies*, 9
(1963), 39-49; the entire issue is a Ford special number.

3. For these lines of judgment, see: Grover Smith, *Ford Madox Ford* (New York: Columbia
Modern Writers Series, 1976), 26–33; Ann S. Johnson, "Narrative Form in *The Good
Soldier*," *Critique*, 11 (1968-69), 70–80; and William P. Peirce, "The Epistemological
Style of Ford's *The Good Soldier*," *Language and Style*, 8: 1 (1975), 34–46.

4. "An Interpretation," xiii-xv.

5. For the full Latin text and a commentary, see Wiesenfarth, 43.

6. See Frank MacShane, *The Life and Work of Ford Madox Ford* (New York: Horizon Press,
1965); Arthur Mizener, *The Saddest Story: A Biography of Ford Madox Ford* New York:
World Publishing Co., 1971); Thomas C. Moser, *The Life in the Fiction of Ford Madox Ford*
(Princeton: Princeton Univ. Press, 1980).

7. In *Critical Writings of Ford Madox Ford,* ed. Frank MacShane (Lincoln: Univ. of Nebraska Press, 1964), 33–55; quotations below are cited parenthetically. The essay appeared originally in *Poetry and Drama,* II, 161–175, 323–334.

8. See, for example, J. Hillis Miller, "Ariadne's Thread: Repetition and the Narrative Line,"*Critical Inquiry,* 3 (1976).

9. For detailed (but incomplete) analysis of the chronological inconsistencies, see Richard W. Lid, *Ford Madox Ford: The Essence of His Art* (Berkeley: Univ. of California Press, 1964), 52–64. For another attempt to justify the discrepancies, see Patricia McFate and Bruce Golden, *"The Good Soldier:* A Tragedy of Self-Deception," *Modern Fiction Studies,* 9 (1963), 50–60.

10. For this analysis, see Johnson, 73–76.

11. As Dowell claims to have part of his story from Edward, it is worth specifying the limits of that source. Near the beginning of his narration of the final events, Dowell proclaims portentously, "And that evening Edward spoke to me" (202). He goes on to relate "what in the interval [before his arrival] had happened," but the point of view for his evidence is Leonora's: "Upon her return from Nauheim Leonora had completely broken down—because she knew she could trust Edward" (202 ff.). If Dowell's story continues to be a redaction of the "trememdously long conversations full of worldly wisdom that Leonora has reported to me since their deaths" (8), what information has Edward contributed: Probably nothing more than an account of his love for Nancy; his speaking to Dowell on the evening of the telegram inviting Nancy out to India follows directly from a confession of his love: "'I am so desperately in love with Nancy Rufford that I am dying of it.' Poor devil—he hadn't meant to speak of it. But I guess he just had to speak to somebody and I appeared to be like a woman or a solicitor. He talked all night" (250). It is this emotional effusion that enables Dowell to perform his one bit of synthetic narration, the story of the Ashburnhams and Nancy at Nauheim: "What had actually happened had been this. I pieced it together afterwards" (109). Everything else is straight from Leonora's explanations, punctuated by Dowell's self-flagellating reflections on his obliviousness of the *presumed* facts. But are they facts, or only Leonora's version of them? We may well ask. When the bemused Dowell, who doesn't know that he is being used as Leonora's mouthpiece, thinks he is switching to her point of view for a spell, he suggests her narratorial power: "And now, I suppose I must give you Leonora's side of the case. . . . That is very difficult. For Leonora, if she preserved an unchanged front, changed very frequently her point of view" (177). It is *she* who renders the varied motivations and limited perspectives of the participants, and Dowell who merely *reports* them from her. The hidden protagonist—the covert narrator—of *The Good Soldier* may have yet to find her full acknowledgment.

12. Some recent books confirm the presence of other Addamsians in the audience: Ann Barr Snitow's *Ford Madox Ford and the Voice of Uncertainty* (Baton Rouge: LSU Press, 1984) attests to the novel's "comic irony"; while Robert Green's *Ford Madox Ford: Prose and Politics* (Cambridge: Cambridge Univ. Press, 1981) lends credence to the view that the novel is characteristic of, but also calls into question, the assumptions not only of traditional but of modernist historiography, narrative method, and ideology (88 ff.).

Living as Ritual in *Parade's End*

NORMAN PAGE

C ertain novelists, in common with many of us who are not novelists, betray an addiction, usually unconscious, to certain words or turns of phrase; and in them, as in us, the reiteration may be more than a trivial mannerism—may, indeed, offer an insight, through a tiny verbal crack in the fence, into central preoccupations or obsessions. I do not think, for example, that any of Arnold Bennett's critics has pointed to his fondness for two words, one of them very unusual and the two of them in conjunction highly suggestive as to his individual vision and method as a writer of fiction. *Dailiness* seems to convey a sense of boring but reassuring routine, of the pattern or ritual of repeated actions which make up an individual life; *mystical* (somewhat loosely used by Bennett), a contrasting and complementary sense of life's unpredictability, of the unguessed-at lurking just behind the humdrum. Less readily accounted for, but no less striking, is D. H. Lawrence's repeated use of *vague, vaguely, vagueness,* and (what seems to be related) the adverb *rather.* From a small verbal fulcrum of this kind we may venture to weigh the novelist's world.

With Ford Madox Ford, such a word is *convention,* and I shall try to show in this essay how the word and the idea dominate his tetralogy *Parade's End* without being at all confined to that work. But we may note first that some of his critics have been infected by Ford's fondness for the word and its near-synonyms. Mark Schorer tells us that *The Good Soldier* "is about the difference between convention and fact" and that the narrator discovers he has "mistaken the conventions of social behavior for the actual human fact"; while Arthur

Mizener sees the same novel as depicting "a society in which the life of men's feelings no longer flows into the beautiful, refined *ritual* of the society's most cultivated life" [italics mine].[1] The antitheses suggested here are also fruitful in relation to *Parade's End. The Good Soldier* may be allowed to detain us a little longer, however, in order to show that Ford's concern with the place of convention or ritual in individual and social life antedates the tetralogy, in which nevertheless this theme was to receive much more extensive treatment. In the earlier novel Ashburnham is introduced in terms which imply an extreme, even caricatural, conventionality in the sense of unquestioning adherence to the traditional way of life of a particular social class and an almost religious absorption in the material details of its prescribed life-style:

> His hair was fair, extraordinarily ordered in a wave, running from the left temple to the right; his face was a light brick-red, perfectly uniform in tint up to the roots of the hair itself; his yellow moustache was as stiff as a toothbrush and I verily believe that he had his black smoking jacket thickened a little over the shoulder-blades so as to give himself the air of the slightest possible stoop. It would be like him to do that; that was the sort of thing he thought about. Martingales, Chiffney bits, boots; where you got the best soap, the best brandy, the name of the chap who rode a plater down the Khyber cliffs; the spreading power of number three shot before a charge of number four powder . . . by heavens, I hardly ever heard him talk of anything else.
>
> (I, 32–33)[2]

This is very skillfully done: the tone is casual, but every detail tells, and the suggestion of simulation and calculation is not accidental (the "perfectly uniform" face, masklike rather than of human flesh; the moustache resembling a toothbrush rather than hair). Not only Ashburnham's clothes and habits but his physical features and complexion imply a self-conscious deference to a mode of life acknowledged as appropriate to a member of the British upper classes. And what at first appears to be a genuine concern with quality ("where you got the best soap . . .") is quickly shown to be a limitation of human freedom:

> The given proposition was, that we were all 'good people.' We took for granted that we all liked beef underdone but not too underdone; that both men preferred a good liqueur brandy after lunch; that both women drank a very light Rhine qualified with Fachingen water—that sort of thing.
>
> (I, 40)

"That sort of thing" is seen, in a moment of ironic rebellion or humorous disillusion on the part of the narrator, to be:

. . . an almost unreasonably high standard. For it is really nauseating, when you detest it, to have to eat every day several slices of thin, tepid, pink india rubber, and it is disagreeable to have to drink brandy when you would prefer to be cheered up by a warm, sweet Kummel. And it is nasty to have to take a cold bath in the morning when what you want is really a hot one at night. And it stirs a little of the faith of your fathers that is deep down within you to have it taken for granted that you are an Episcopalian when really you are an old-fashioned Philadelphia Quaker.

But these things have to be done: it is the cock that the whole of this society owes to Aesculapius.

(I, 42)

"These things have to be done": the class which appears to enjoy the greatest freedom, an enviable leisure and privilege and affluence, is constrained in matters great and small by the exactly ordained rituals of tradition. As we shall see, the subject of *Parade's End* is the death throes of that tradition. In *The Good Soldier,* the antithesis of the conformity that is unquestioned by everyone except the narrator (who is in every sense an outsider) is Ashburnham's helpless infatuations: his romantic and sexual impulses constitute a rebellion against the demands of a society shown as tyrannically working through conventions at all levels from food and drink to morality and religion in order to restrict personal liberty. Much later in the book, when Nancy Rufford is "exported to India," we are told:

It was the conventional line; it was in tune with the tradition of Edward's house. I daresay it worked out for the greatest good of the body politic. Conventions and traditions, I suppose, work blindly but surely for the preservation of the normal type; for the extinction of proud, resolute and unusual individuals.

(I, 205)

At a moment of moral crisis, convention and tradition are the substitutes for individual judgment and decision, and they work in the interests of a social Darwinism with the elimination of individuality as its goal. The struggle in *The Good Soldier* is between passion and convention, but the big battalions are on the side of the latter.

This antithesis is developed further in *Parade's End.* In *The Good Soldier,* convention is tyrannical but makes for social cohesion: stability is purchased at the price of variety, spontaneity, eccentricity, and unpredictability. Within the limits of this short novel the drama can only be shown as operating in the arena of private lives. In the tetralogy, the cohesion and stability of society are devastated by the upheaval of the Great War, and much of the action takes place on or near the battlefield; yet the historical cataclysm only dramatizes on a vast scale the upheaval in the Tietjens family caused by the unconventionality of Christopher. That quality is shown in the opening scene of the first novel, *Some Do Not,* the very title of which hints, of course, in one of its meanings, at Christopher Tietjens's nonconformity. Almost every detail of the description of Tietjens and Macmaster in the "perfectly appointed railway carriage" works to convey the profound antithesis beneath their superficial similarity—the one man's eager obedience to society's rules (conformity being the price of worldly success), the other's disregard for them. Both belong to "the English public official class," a common educational background (as a fact of social history) going far to neutralize the difference in their social origins. It is the class that "administered the world," yet very quickly the point is made that Macmaster is readier than Tietjens to operate the machinery of ruling-class influence, to resort to the "nonchalant" yet authoritative Balliol voice or a letter to *The Times*. Macmaster's appearance recalls the conscious conformity of Ashburnham's, but Tietjens "could not remember what colored tie he had on." As the first-class carriage runs smoothly and symbolically along the tracks, Macmaster reads the proofs of his belletristic efforts (for man of letters is one of the roles he plays)—and the detection of errors and lapses and their firm rectification is an entirely appropriate activity: his ambition, to pursue the metaphor, is to live his life as if it were a text beyond criticism.

This long chapter ends with the first appearance of the title phrase; it has begun with a suggestion of resemblance, almost uniformity, between the two men, but now it ambiguously foreshadows Tietjens's experience which is to be traced through four novels; for it is Macmaster, starting out with considerably less than Tietjens's advantages of birth, who becomes a "squire," acquires a title, and is accorded the public respect that eludes his friend. Tietjens's failure in worldly terms must in large part be laid at the door of his scant regard for convention; yet the antithesis between the man indifferent to society's dictates and the man enslaved by them is not oversimplified, for Tietjens himself is shown as cased in conventional reactions—in responses determined, that is to say, by what is prescribed and expected in a given case rather than by what proceeds from the special pleading of the mind or heart. Thus at the outset he is prepared to take back Sylvia, knowing her infidelity and suspecting that her child is not his, whereas Macmaster urges him to "drag the woman through the mud." That a gentleman does not initiate divorce proceedings is an article of faith with Tietjens; he is concerned with honor, Macmaster with honors. And this provides a solution to the apparent paradox: Tietjens, unlike Macmaster in both respects, is indifferent to conventionalities of surface but deeply conventional, even against his own interests, where honor is at stake. I borrow that last phrase from the lines of Hamlet that come to mind as apposite:

> Rightly to be great
> Is not to stir without great argument,
> But greatly to find quarrel in a straw
> When honor's at the stake.[3]

This reading of the two characters is confirmed by the similar contrast to be found (more dramatically heightened, however) between the two major women characters of the tetralogy. Sylvia's conventionality—she is a woman who is photographed for the society magazines, with all that this implies of conformity of appearance and social conduct—is a cloak for destructive malignity; Valentine Wannop is as unconventional as she can well be in her time, a sort of latter-day Sue Bridehead in her epicene appearance and her militant feminism, only much more attractive than Hardy's exasperating heroine and much more clearly enjoying the author's moral assent. Christopher and Valentine meet for the first time on a golf course, the scene, scrupulously kept as to appearances, of a highly ritualized and mainly masculine and upper-class game (the early Auden was to use "the golf-house quick one" as shorthand for a whole way of life); Valentine's behavior there is intrusive, maverick, rocking the boat of complacent privilege, and she is abetted by Christopher.

If there is something *voulu* in Valentine's defiance of convention, however, Christopher's unconventionality sometimes has the air of innocence, a total absence of calculation of effects. This does not prevent the conventional world from thinking the worst of him, and one of the most powerful elements in the whole work is the appalling sense of society's readiness to believe evil of a good man who has proved unwillingly to respect its conventions far enough to play the hypocrite.

The word "convention" makes a significant multiple appearance in the important scene which ends Part One of *Some Do Not*:

> "Are you all right?" The cart might have knocked her down. He had, however, broken the convention. Her voice came from a great distance
> . . . .

His last thought came back to him. He had broken their convention:
he had exhibited concern: like any other man. . . . He said to himself:
"By God! Why not take a holiday: why not break all conventions?"
They erected themselves intangibly and irrefragably. He had not
known this young woman twenty-four hours: not to speak to: and already
the convention existed between them that he must play stiff and cold, she
warm and clinging. . . .
A convention of the most imbecile type. . . . Then break all conventions: with the young woman: with himself above all. For forty-eight
hours. . . .

(III, 163)

Note the delicate mirroring of Tietjens's shifting responses through slight
linguistic variations: "the convention," "their convention," "all conventions."
The escapade—escape from convention—ends in detection by the General "in
full tog" (III, 177), feathered and bemedalled. The grotesquely elaborate
uniform ("something like a scarlet and white cockatoo") epitomizes convention at its most strikingly visual; like any uniform, it announces the submission of the individual to the group and reproves Tietjens's impulsive behavior.
Indeed, the whole episode seems stage-managed by providence to instruct
him in the perils of defying convention. Yet he is not, or not yet, an instinctively unconventional man: he accepts the unwritten rules of his class, later
accepting the inevitability of his ruin when his cheques are dishonored (the
banker's term is felicitous), even though the fault is not his: not inner motive
but public event is decisive in accomplishing his dishonor (III, 243). In this
context, membership of his club becomes not just a matter of convenience but
a badge of his own sense of his social acceptability: he resigns, withdraws the
resignation, and then in an assertion of his own dignity resigns again the next
day (III, 353). To an outsider (the American narrator of *The Good Soldier*, for
instance) such actions might seem to constitute an absurd charade; to Tietjens
they are a profound moral drama.

Before the end of *Some Do Not*, Mark Tietjens, Christopher's brother, is
presented in terms which make plain his role: if Christopher vacillates
between conformity and rebellion at this stage, Mark is a paragon of conformity for whom outward forms, however apparently trivial, are everything:

Mark was considering that one of the folds of his umbrella was disarranged. He seriously debated with himself whether he should unfold it at
once and refold it—which was a great deal of trouble to take or whether he
should leave it till he got to his club, where he would tell the proter to
have it done at once. That would mean he would have to walk for a mile

and a quarter through London with a disarranged umbrella, which was disagreeable.

(III, 251–52)

As we shall see, Mark's role becomes a major one in *The Last Post* and the representative quality of the two brothers then becomes fully explicit. But *The Last Post* is set in the postwar period, its predecessor having ended with the Armistice; and the two inside novels of the tetralogy are novels of the war that went far towards shattering forever the social order depicted in *Some Do Not*. *No More Parades* echoes in its title that of the whole tetralogy, *Parade's End*, and Ford surely intended the work to evoke not only (more obviously) the secondary, military sense of *parade* but the primary meaning (from *parare*, to adorn) of "show, display, ostentation," which both as noun and verb has a close semantic relationship to his use of "convention." The sweep of the tetralogy—its action brief in years, profound in irrevocable change to a whole civilization—records the death-throes of that world in which "parade," whether manifested in dress, in social behavior, or in public morality, had been erected into a principle of existence by a tiny but enormously powerful minority. (Not that the extinction was complete, of course, as any observer of the contemporary British scene can confirm: forty years after Ford's death the Eton and Harrow match, mentioned in *Some Do Not*, is still an annual ritual; certain shops in Piccadilly are devoted to furnishing the expensive and improbable impedimenta of an Edwardian lifestyle; and London clubs like the one Mark Tietjens belonged to still exist in order to persuade their members that the nineteenth century has not ended. But the exception in these cases proves the rule).

The Last Post, variously viewed as an integral part of the work and a superfluous afterthought, is of considerable interest in relation to the persisting theme of conformity and its decline as the century advances. Mark Tietjens has been shown as an almost parodically conventional creature, dressed like a foreigner's or cartoonist's stereotype of the English gentleman, even his vices regularized into unvarying and unquestioned habits: he visits his French mistress twice a week (with an equally regular interruption for his annual holiday), and for twenty years she has cooked him the same dinner. In *The Last Post* bowler and umbrella are abandoned, and he no longer sits down to his prescribed dinner of two mutton chops and two floury potatoes, for he has become an invalid who refuses to speak: the abandonment of the rituals which have hitherto composed his life in the period in which he now finds himself living. Before the war he had consciously incorporated ritual into his life:

Mark's response to the loss of this ritual (manifested, for example, in the brotherhood of the trenches) is to abdicate from life in as thoroughgoing a way as is possible, short of suicide. By a more abrupt and dramatic route, a more patently symbolic gesture, he has reached a conclusion not unlike his brother's.

Groby, the ancestral home in the north of England, dominates *The Last Post* not as a dramatic setting but as a constant point of reference. Its existence is coextensive with that of the Tietjens family and of Groby Great Tree, which has overshadowed the house and darkened the schoolroom and the children's wing. The fate of tree and house in this final novel gives us, by a kind of shorthand, a version of the fate of the family. The American tenant-usurper, Mrs. de Bray Pape, essays to preserve the rituals of the past: she has a sentimental, snobbish fondness for powdered footmen and forelock-tugging peasants, but of course these rituals are empty and meaningless. The tree is uprooted, as a contribution to progress and modern improvement, and brings down with it part of the building, including the rooms associated with Christopher's childhood. The symbolism is, to modern tastes, a little crude, and in any case superfluous, for the end of the Tietjens tradition has already been rendered, more subtly, through the postwar fates of Christopher and Mark.[4]

Like Forster's *Howards End*, *The Last Post* has an epilogue which asserts renewal and continuity after destruction. The child of Christopher and Valentine embarks on a life freed from the heavy hand of tradition and its limitations on personal freedom (of the self and of others). Convention and artifice have been dissolved—a point neatly made in a final image. *Some Do Not* has opened in a railway compartment in an atmosphere of newly varnished wood, and for Ford, as for Dickens in *Little Dorrit*, the varnish may well carry a metaphorical meaning. At the end of *The Last Post* Christopher holds in his hand a piece of wood from Groby Great Tree, as plain and unvarnished as Ford's symbolism, one is tempted to say. He has travelled from the first-class carriage to a rural retreat in which he will pursue a William Morris-like simple life (again, the path traced resembles that of Forster's remarkable prewar novel). It is a way of life in which convention and ritual will have no place.

NOTES

1. Mark Schorer, *The World We Imagine; Selected Essays* (New York: Farrar, Straus and Giroux, 1968), 99; Arthur Mizener, *The Saddest Story: A Biography of Ford Madox Ford* (New York: World Publishing Co., 1971), 254.

2. This and subsequent page references are to *The Bodley Head Ford Madox Ford*, 5 vols. (London: The Bodley Head, 1962–1963).

3. *Hamlet,* IV, iv, 53–56.

4. John A. Meixner has some good comments on the symbolism of Ford's settings in *Ford Madox Ford's Novels: A Critical Study* (Minneapolis: Univ. of Minnesota Press, 1962), 216–218.

The Always-Changing Impact
of Virginia Woolf

ANGUS WILSON

Virginia Woolf—not only her work but herself—has now been so anatomized and dissected and reshaped to fit in to academic studies, to take her place in the literary phenomenon of modernistic or social phenomenon, so peculiar in English life, of the cultural elitism conveniently labelled Bloomsbury, that it may seem and probably is reactionary, retrogressive to seek a clue to her greatness as writer by a return to her first impact on readers and to the reactions of subsequent generations in the decades before she found academic embalmment. But that is what I propose shortly to do in this article by tracing her impact, her very powerful but always-changing impact, upon another creative writer, myself, from my first acquaintance with her work in my teens to her abiding presence beside me whenever I seek now, as an established novelist, to begin to shape a new narrative, or organize a change of scene, or move from an inner vision to an outer vision, or merge the abstract and the particular in any scene I write. To chronicle this always strong but strangely varied hold that Virginia Woolf had and has upon another literary imagination may suggest her excellences and her defects in a way that will be fresh to students, who usually approach her as already embalmed and to be dissected only by approved university surgical techniques.

I came to Virginia Woolf from Katherine Mansfield about 1929 or 1930, when I was sixteen or seventeen. Katherine Mansfield's stories had been given to me by one of my sophisticated older brothers—a young man who in *his* twenties in *the* twenties had known very much the same sort of middle-class, bohemian, economically insecure London life that Katherine Mansfield had known when she came to London from New Zealand over a decade earlier. In the Mansfield stories my brother found and he showed me the feckless, class-conscious, financially rickety world that we had both grown up in portrayed both realistically (in dialogue, exactness of scene and objects) and with a poetry of language, a dimension of relation to absolutes that belonged essentially to her very urgent use of words. To find that our own rather sordid family world could claim this further dimension was inevitably both exciting and comforting. To see it thus, while all that was sordid remained palpably there also, made it convincing.

Katherine Mansfield, too, had the rather bitter wit which my brothers were wont to use to assuage their despair. She had, also, but I did not see it then, a stream of sugary sentimentalism that often runs through such bitter wit. And, often, even at her best, she was too consciously clever, almost "smart" as we should say now. But it was what I called for at sixteen, true to life's cheapness as I knew it and yet declaring that deeper values survived. One particular story about a failed concert singer, a "lady" by class, being driven by poverty to prostitute herself in approaching middle age seemed to me the height of truth, the probable story did I but know it of the many rather blowzy ladies who dined and breakfasted at the little tables in the rather cheap private hotel where we lived. I remember to my shame that I read the story aloud to one or two of these ladies, hoping that some hysterics or a fainting fit would prove my sixteen-year-old insight to be correct. But nothing happened. All the same, Katherine Mansfield was *real*.

As Virgina Woolf was not, my brother told me, when he gave me *To the Lighthouse* and *Mrs. Dalloway* to read. This was *"fine"* literature, in which real life such as there was (and to us Mrs. Dalloway's party and Mrs. Ramsay's *boeuf en daube* were, in any case, remote, wealthy, vaguely aristocratic oddities) had been rarefied into some poetry that left one exalted and bemused and, if this were not a contradiction, also a little bit flat, for it was all so very ethereal and clever, but not witty and "smart" and down-to-earth like Katherine Mansfield. We knew about young men in bed-sitting rooms who wanted to be artists—and we knew what sordid financial devices their pretensions forced them into. We knew about ladies who lived on the borderline of respectability and of the terrors that genteel poverty gave them in the night. Katherine Mansfield had helped us with her words to invest this life with poetry. And now here was Virginia Woolf, using words in the same manner although more magically, but the lives that she transformed meant almost nothing to us—philosophers who desperately could not go beyond the letter Q (Mr. Ramsay); painters whose scene would not come right (Lily Briscoe); grand ladies finding comfort at grand parties, when the fear of death attacked them, by contemplating the regularity with which an old woman went upstairs to bed (Clarissa Dalloway). It lacked the common touch. And when the authoress tried to put it in by describing ordinary people in crowds awestruck as the Prime Minister's car passed or old Cockney women mused, "it's been a hard life. . . . What hadn't she given to it? Roses; figure; her feet too," it seemed all wrong and condescending, and ununderstanding as though a reel of Movietone News of the London streets had been run through the work to give it life.

What I could not, of course, know was that Mrs. Woolf often felt exactly the same. So that when Katherine Mansfield died, she recorded the events as follows in her journal:

> Katherine has been dead a week, & how far am I obeying her "do not quite forget Katherine" which I read in one of her old letters. . . . Nelly [the maid] said in her sensational way at breakfast on Friday "Mrs. Murry's dead! It says so in the papers!" At that one feels—what? A shock of relief?—a rival the less? Then confusion at feeling so little—then, gradually, blankness & disappointment; then a depression. . . . When I began to write, it seemed to me there was no point in writing. Katherine wont read it. Katherine's my rival no longer. More generously I felt, But though I can do this better than she could, where is she, who could do what I can't! . . . I was jealous of her writing—the only writing I have ever been jealous of. [1]

I think this jealousy may seem very strange today, but it would not have seemed strange to me at sixteen, for I should have judged that in "Bliss" or in "Prelude" Katherine Mansfield was weaving the same patterns of feeling and seeing, of past and present, of external appearance and interior thought in the same complex entwining as Mrs. Woolf, but that her stories were often laced with a rawness of poverty, a sexual harshness and sexual passion experienced, a total personal precariousness. The world in short that, through my family, I knew as an adolescent. And that Mrs. Woolf's radiance (even her sorrow and fear) was a sort of virginity cutting her off from our sordid world.

I did not then know of Katherine Mansfield's hand-to-mouth life as a chorus girl after her wealthy New Zealand childhood nor of her sexual liaisons, her illegitimate child. But I should not have been surprised. As to what we now know of the sexual strangeness of Virginia Woolf's childhood, her adult cousin's playing with her girlhood, the advances of her brother-in-law—all of this would have seemed to me merely the disordered living of the upper classes. Just as Katherine Mansfield's long tubercular illness would have seemed more palpable to me then than Mrs. Woolf's periodic insanities. I had long years of growing up before me in such matters; all the same the ladylikeness which must seem so historic now, and perhaps to an American audience only a facet of Englishness, was a trouble then to those of us who found her insight and her vision transforming, for it undercut the reality of her vision and undermined the liberalism of her sympathy. It was ever present to someone more financially assured than she was, a prince of rentiers—E. M. Forster, so that he is forced to say of her snobbery "there is an admirable hardness here, so far as a hardness can be admirable." And I, like a very great number of other younger readers, could not stomach the patronage that seemed to go with the compassion that she tried to show for the poor and the derelict of London's streets in *Mrs. Dalloway*, and less still could accommodate her failure to depict the financial desperation that I felt would surely have hung around the furnished rooms where Septimus Warren Smith's mad visions brought him to suicide, a grubby sordidness that Katherine Mansfield would have known and shown.

At Oxford, I left behind for some years my family's genteel insecurity and flourished on an inheritance as a young cultured aesthete. I *"read"* history as my academic subject, but I also read all the fashionable books that mattered. One, of course, was *The Waves*. I bought a second-hand copy of the first edition, read and approved it. Here was a piece of beauty created, made out of the interplay of six characters and their growth, and by the intercutting of passages descriptive of natural scene. As an aesthete, it was just what I was looking for: "a pure work of art." That Rhoda committed suicide and Louis worked in a bank, these intrusions of real life did not disturb me, for they appeared so transiently and bejewelled with so many images. Here was a world of people who lived for the interplay of each with the other, for the nuances of immediate sensations, for the worship a little mockingly of physical strength and beauty in the athlete Percival and the expectation a little delightedly that, like all physical beauty, he would die suddenly and young.

The book was all that my university aesthetic vision demanded of literature, which was, in any case, not my serious study but my graceful pursuit. If there was a lack of the "real," the "raw," that I had felt in my early adolescence, this did not now matter, for my chosen subject of study—political and economic history—gave me all that and to spare. My understanding of *The Waves* was, therefore, superficial and elegant—and so the book was seen by very many young contemporaries. If I sensed something more intense, more profound in the wonderfully woven reunion of the six in middle age at Hampton Court or something more terrible, more splendid in the sleazy Bernard's final defiance of Death, I did not let it trouble me; *"The Waves* is an *enchanting* book," we all piped.

I still have (a rarely preserved possession of my earlier years in my much-traveled life) a copy of the first edition of *The Waves;* it says in the flyleaf Angus Frank Johnstone-Wilson, Oxford 1934. Above my name is crossed out a previous owner: Richard Rumbold, a young writer who was to try to follow in Ronald Firbank's footsteps, with some success. He committed suicide in the 1950s as Virginia Woolf had in 1941. It is rather an ominous beautiful book. But when I came down from Oxford in 1935 there was no time for beauty, ominous or otherwise. Everything was protest marches against Hitler, against Mosley, against Guernica, and marching with a sickening sense of the inevitability of war, the inevitability, as my generation then believed, that we should die at best by bombing, at worst with our guts spewed out from poison gas.

Mrs. Woolf was very low in my estimation then. I did not, of course, have any connection with the literary world, so that I did not know that the younger generation of poets were remonstrating her for not identifying herself more closely with the anti-Fascist Front. But I did know the poems and plays of Auden and Spender; they were "our writers." What I did not need was her very dignified and sensible defense, "A Letter to John." She took her stand on the values that had carried them all (Bloomsbury) through the First War with dignity, that had led them when Keynes persuaded Lloyd George to buy Degas paintings from the French Government for the Tate Gallery to send him a telegram, "Your sins are forgiven you" (meaning his war service at the Treasury).

She loathed and feared all that the Nazis stood for—how much we were to know when her posthumous novel *Between the Acts,* with its terrible images of rape in the barracks and the snake swallowing the toad, was to be published in the War—but she would not join protests and march in processions; that was "The Big Bow Wow Noise," which the private values of Bloomsbury, the concern for personal relationships and the contemplation of beauty, had always despised. She stood by her pacifist guns. And to my generation she lost all our sympathy by doing so. I still have a slight return of my impatience with her when I read her vague words, "Aldous is a pacifist and so I suppose am I." But for the duration of the war, at any rate, we proposed to put Mrs. Woolf out of our minds.

Or so we supposed. I now vividly remember travelling up to London for my war work; the journey was as usual endless, for two time bombs had been dropped upon the line in the previous night's raid and we had to go miles out of our way to reach Liverpool Street. It was midwinter, too, and there was no heat. And then I read in *The Times* of her suicide, and all the war and my intelligence work seemed as nothing. This was Hitler's triumph. I think it hit me more intensely, for I had grown up in those marshlands of the Sussex river where she drowned herself, and I knew their bleak bitterness in winter and the shallowness of the Sussex Ouse River and I sensed the terribleness of her death, its despair. I did not, of course, then know of her self-sacrifice, of her determination not to impose her madness again upon her loving husband and at such a time. But it seemed all the same the blackest moment of the war.

Yet that glimpse of what her work really meant to me was forgotten once more in the late forties, when I first started to write my short stories; one of my chief satirical targets was the cultured middle-class lady of high sensibility, innate snobbery, and indomitable possessiveness. Such was a principal figure of satire, Mrs. Craddock, in my first novel, *Hemlock and After*. And such middle-class ladies had too often modelled themselves upon an inadequate, self-extolling reading of Virginia Woolf's novels.

Indeed, in 1950, I was asked to give my first talk on BBC Radio (Third Programme). I chose to make Virginia Woolf my target of attack in a talk called "Sense and Sensibility." Even then I recognized how deeply I had been influenced by reading her novels, for I announced brashly "that it was always necessary for a new generation of writers to bite the hand that fed it." But I was against Mrs. Woolf on two grounds: the first one, that her sort of elitist middle-class sensibility or at any rate that of her imitators had been one of the deepest complacencies that had brought England near to destruction. I think it a very gross exaggeration now even of the poor cultured ladies who tried to model themselves on their feeble comprehension of Mrs. Ramsay or Mrs. Dalloway or Susan or Jinnie—and of Virginia Woolf, who was so much more than her creations it was cruelly laughable.

I remember that it led Leonard Woolf to write me a letter which seemed to me then to be charming reasonableness but was really, I think, patient disgust. However, the talk was very popular, especially the parody I made of the kind of Virginia Woolf lady I was attacking. It seems to me now crude, but here is some of it:

> Now please look at Mrs. Green—for so we will call her—her good
> tweeds, her untidy grey hair, her interesting beauty—for to her friends
> and indeed to herself she has always "interesting" beauty. She is think-
> ing—for we may transgress so much as to probe her thoughts—of the
> changing seasons, of the funny hat that her father used to wear at the
> seaside so many years ago, of the pleasure it gives her to hear her daughter
> so happy at the flute—Scarlatti is it? or Mozart? She can never quite re-
> member—and of Mrs. Green, who is enjoying a mathematical prob-
> lem—the square root of pi—she can't help visualizing it as the strange
> square-shaped root of the oak that fell last autumn—and then she watches
> with pleasure Ada, dear beloved Ada, emptying the ashes—only Ada's
> niece wears terrible shiny flesh-coloured stockings—and no! it is no
> good, whatever they say, she can not forgive people who have the wireless
> at full blast all day and prefer pilchards and canned beans—but now the
> square root of pi is not doing its part and Mrs. Green is frowning, pray
> Heaven! the risotto will be perfect—but it will be, it could not be other-
> wise while the clouds are making those lovely patterns and the polyanthus
> is still that delicate shade (for it is spring now). But then Mrs. Green hears
> the aeroplane overhead and she remembers old Mr. Crowfoot in the vill-
> age with his rheumatoid-arthritis and the snake slowly and deliberately
> swallowing the toad.

It is all there—the patronage to male activities, to the arts, to the lower
classes—the refinement, the blurs, and the sudden recital of sickness and evil.
But it doesn't for a moment, I think, touch Virginia Woolf's achievement. It
is cheek. But it was liked at the same time (1950).

My other charge was that her technique had disintegrated the novel's form.
This arose, I think, because of my anger at the incomprehension of Virginia
Woolf and E. M. Forster before Charles Dickens's intricate weaving of plot-
narrative and symbolic ballet. It was part of their anti-Victorianism—as indeed was her refusal to be sentimental about the poor. And my attack on this
incomprehension allowed me (mistakenly) to associate myself with the battle
for a return to the traditional novel being waged by C. P. Snow and his
followers. It was not the traditional novel I sought to defend but Dickens and
Dostoevsky, which was quite another point. However, in my defense of
Dickens, attack on Mrs. Woolf's technique was an easy weapon to hand.

And yet seven or eight years later I was composing *The Middle Age of Mrs.
Eliot,* which owes everything in conception although nothing in form to *Mrs.
Dalloway,* so deep was the haunting presence of Virginia Woolf's work
although I sought to ignore it. Critics praised the book, saw it as an attempt

to wed Woolf with Arnold Bennett. With reservations, I like it, too. But it was my last book written in the traditional form . And by the time I came to compose what I think is my finest novel, *No Laughing Matter,* in the late sixties, I was thoroughly conscious that my teacher to whom (after Dickens and Dostoevsky) I owed most was Mrs. Woolf herself; it was she who showed me how to preserve narration with disregard for unity of scene or time sequence or angle of vision or formal plot.

She is, I believe, the master of twentieth-century narrative technique. That I had come to realize it arose in the sixties, when I began to teach for the first time in my life at the newly founded University of Easy Anglia. I organized a Bloomsbury seminar, with four Forster and four Woolf novels for study. I began with reverence for Forster and sharp criticism for Woolf. I ended deeply disillusioned with all Forster's novels save *A Passage to India* and a worshipper to Mrs. Woolf's four novels—especially *The Waves* and *Mrs. Dalloway.*

What is it that is so miraculous in her narrative powers? We have only to sketch the organization of *Mrs. Dalloway* to see it.

We begin straight with Clarissa Dalloway's state of exaltation at the prospect of another day of life: "What a morning—fresh as if issued to children on a beach. What a lark! What a plunge!" And here, as nowhere else in English fiction we are taken straight into delight at the city *and* the countryside, at adult life *and* remembered childhood. For "issued to children on a beach" takes us to Virginia Woolf's own Cornish childhood paradise—to the Cornwall disguised as Scotland of *To the Lighthouse,* which also begins "up with the lark" (the pervasiveness of birds for good and evil in her work is a subject for study but not for a killing thesis). But the morning also takes Clarissa back to the countryside to her youth, to Bourton.

And then, as though one might fear the rural English romantic regression to childhood and flight to rural bliss, London is emphasized. Big Ben strikes. "Heaven only knows why one loves it so. . . ." And what she loves is "life; London; this moment of June." This passionate affirmation of the values of the city is almost unique from Clarissa Harlowe's failure to recognize drugged milk, because she thinks it is the bitter taste of London milk, through the trivializing arrival of the London Crawfords to Mansfield Park on to most modern novels: London is suspect; the country values are the good ones. Even that great Londoner Dickens capitulated to a sort of Cockney uniformed rustic delight, as we see in *Oliver Twist.*

But in Virginia Woolf's work we get an adult statement of the conflicting values and deficits of city and country, typified in *The Waves* by the opposition

of Jinnie and Susan, deep in her own passion for London parties and the grand
social life interspersed with the retreat of Rodmell. It is a most salutary note
and it is struck early in *Mrs. Dalloway,* where from the impact of London and
the evoked memories of Bourton we are taken at once to the central thesis of
the book, the social glitter of Clarissa, apparently so shallow and hard, yet at
the same time so vital and creative. And opposed to it we get her memories of
Peter Walsh, whom she had loved at Bourton—Peter who thought always of
the state of the world, of the state of her soul, of Wagner, of people's
characters; whereas she simply responded to life, lived it on a few twigs of
knowledge. Yet she knows very well that to Peter she appears the perfect social hostess: cold, hard, a prude. But Peter's love of causes makes her think of
Miss Kilman, the embittered, impoverished, religious governess of her
daughter. And again the Clarissa whom so many think cold and worldly says
to herself religion and causes make people callous, to consider Miss Kilman's
bitter religion makes her think of "hooves planted down in the depths of that
leaf-encumbered forest, the soul . . . the brute . . . stirring . . . a monster
grubbing at the roots." We have reached that buried evil horror of the world
that is to drive Septimus Warren Smith to suicide, that Louis in *The Waves*
hears when only a boy as "the great beast stamping."

   And so on in a very few pages of *Mrs. Dalloway* Virginia Woolf has presented the under battle that lies at the depth of her story and from there on she
continues by one brilliant device after another—the reactions of many to a car
backfiring, the gazing of the crowd at an aeroplane issuing smoke adver-
tisement, a cloud passing overhead—to take us round every aspect of her
theme, every contrast that lies in the diverse stories of Clarissa Dalloway and
Peter Walsh and Septimus Warren Smith until at last we have the resolution,
after suicide and brutality and worldly triviality, of the enduring power of a
love that was never communicated—for the book ends: with Peter Walsh,
recalling that Clarissa's breaking with him had ruined his life; and then, seeing her triumphant after her party, "'What is this terror? What is this ectasy?'
he thought to himself. 'What is it that fills me with extraordinary excitement? / It is Clarissa,' he said. / For there she was."

   It is the most completely successful, I think, of all her novels, for despite
many failures of social observation, snobberies, mistakes in reality, empty
involvements of language, the line is so perfectly held across so many scenes,
through so much memory, and among so many different characters. It is a
kind of *A La Recherche* in lyric form. *To the Lighthouse,* of course, manages
much of it, but the sense of anti-Victorianism, of being rid of her parents (as

she confesses in her journal) gives it a sort of *déjà vu* look, a sense of being her version of *The Way of All Flesh* or *The Longest Journey*. And the central section of the deserted house and Mrs. McNab the cleaner is horribly marred by the self-consciousness of the sentences in brackets portentously telling us of the fates of the characters in these intervening years: [Mrs. Ramsay having died rather suddenly the night before], [Twenty or thirty young men were blown up in France, among them Andrew Ramsay], and so on. The apparent casualness is too self-conscious, too much of a device. And even at the end, one feels that there is no need to give the novel an artificial encasement in an invented work of art, by coming to a final rest in Lily Briscoe painting her picture. Mr. Ramsay and James united in arriving at the lighthouse is more prosaic but enough.

The Waves certainly comes nearer to *Mrs. Dalloway* in its perfection, but there is a curious imbalance between the three women characters whom we can accept almost as allegories, and the three men who are littered with little particularities—an Australian accent, an unbrushed coat, a door open through which the deceived lover never comes. There seems some dichotomy between the three women drained out of the deepest essences of herself and the men drawn from her husband (?), Lytton Strachey (?), Desmond McCarthy; it is hard to say, but from observed individuals. Perhaps *Between the Acts* would have rivalled *Mrs. Dalloway* had it been revised. But I doubt it, for the scenes from the historical pageant have the clever parlor game feeling of parodies written at a Bloomsbury party. And here the encasement of the novel is a work of art; Miss LaTrobe's failed pageant is destroyed by the imposition of a Lawrencian ending most out of key with Virginia Woolf's linguistic range—"From that embrace another life might be born. But first they must fight, as the dog fox fights with the vixen, in the heart of darkness, in the fields of night."

All four are among England's most splendid twentieth-century novels, but only in *Mrs. Dalloway* do we proceed upon a strange pilgrimage of words, a complicated maze that seems at times to be leading nowhere, but which is always assuredly under the control of the author's mind, which is taking the reader exactly where she wishes him to go.

NOTES

1. *The Diary of Virginia Woolf*, Volume II: 1920–1924, ed. Anne Oliver Bell (London: Hogarth Press, 1978), 225–227.

Ivy Compton-Burnett: An Embalmer's Art

PHILIPPA TRISTRAM

The twenty novels of Ivy Compton-Burnett have been much admired but little read. On the one hand, it is no surprise to find her chosen, in Arnold Kettle's *Introduction to the English Novel,* as the sole female writer to represent the second quarter of this century, along with Huxley, Greene, Cary, and Green. On the other, she is less likely than all to find her way to a voluntary paperback readership. An American admirer, Blake Nevius, regards her as "one of the most interesting and original novelists of our century," but launches his monograph by prognosticating that "the day may never come when Ivy Compton-Burnett has the audience in the United States that she deserves."[1]

At first sight, it may seem that the fate of her work as "unread masterpiece" is easily explicable. Her scope is austerely restricted to the English landed gentry at the turn of the century, who are impervious to almost all claims save those of their estates. "The limitations are so obvious as to be scarcely worth emphasizing," Kettle comments,[2] but limitation may sometimes appear as a perverse alienation of her readership. She makes no effort, for the uninitiated, to give substance to her country houses or their inhabitants. Her characters talk a great deal, but no access is given to their thoughts. Their physical presence rarely conjures up an image, for it emphasizes a type rather than an individual, while the author provides only such additional information as would make it possible to construct a genealogy—age and descent, the latter possibly erroneous. Clothes are infrequently mentioned, and chiefly when they signify something else—poverty, for example, or poor taste. Furniture, rooms, houses, and estates are generic, for as settings their interest is purely extrinsic: if shabby, they connote precarious gentility; if cramped, they suggest restricted and probably dependent means. The writer seems determined to conflate one novel with another, not only in their titles (*Brothers and Sisters, Daughters and Sons*), but by the repetition of certain incidents—from unwitting incest, concealed illegitimacy, and the destruction of wills to the opening of letters and the dropping of tell-tale envelopes. If it is difficult to distinguish one novel from another; it is as hard to assign correctly the speeches of which they are largely composed, as the many printer's errors make evident.

This refusal to compromise with the reader's frailty has its own interest, but it may disguise the fact that problems in her novels exist at levels less obvious and more significant. Apart from the disowned *Dolores* (published in 1911), the period of her writing extends from *Pastors and Masters* (1925) to *The Last and the First*, which appeared, aptly titled, in 1971, two years after her death. Her stated reluctance to meddle with any period other than that of her earliest years (she was born in 1885), has often been quoted: "I do not feel that I have any real organic knowledge of life later than about 1910. I should not write of later times with enough grasp or confidence. I think this is why many writers tend to write of the past. When an age is ended you see it as it is. And I have a dislike, which I cannot explain, of dealing with modern machinery and inventions. When war casts its shadow, I find that I recoil."[3] The first part of this statement has attracted more attention, but the last is more revealing. Retrospect in such novels as *Middlemarch* and *Shirley* does not imply that a period has "ended"; it is the continuities of the past with their present which attracts both writers. In Ivy Compton-Burnett, despite the claims of some of her critics, no such continuities are felt. Once war has cast its shadow she does indeed recoil. The gap in her writing life coincides with that period, and the loss of a beloved brother and two sisters; as a consequence, perhaps, of these tragedies, the artist who came into her own in the postwar years is as detached as the person from the second quarter of the century. "It may be an old-fashioned view," she once said, "but I am surprised by some of these modern books, which have no structure at all."[4] The confident structures of nineteenth-century fiction certainly collapsed with the First World War, as did those of English society; the protean form of *Women in Love* or *To the Lighthouse* are responses to the moral and social instabilities of their time. The symmetry of Ivy Compton-Burnett's novels is, on the contrary, a rigorous forcing of pattern and order to the surface: "Real life seems to have no plots. And as I think plot desirable and almost necessary I have this extra grudge against life. But I do think there are signs that strange things happen, though they do not emerge."[5]

Far from succeeding Lawrence and Virginia Woolf, Ivy Compton-Burnett in many senses precedes them. Her novels deliberately detach the reader from twentieth-century expectations; they are not only set in the nineteenth century but conceived in its terms. It is no accident that her work should recall Jane Austen from the century's beginning, both by its confined canvas and the homogeneity of the novels, which seem facets of a single crystal. At the century's end her dialogue is often reminiscent of Chekhov, a dramatist she predictably admired; voices float in Chekhov, and reverberate; in Ivy Compton-Burnett they echo and intertwine. *Dolores* apart, however, "indebtedness" is no more the word for her writing than it is for Eliot's *The Waste Land*. If a nineteenth-century literary presence is felt in her work, it is there for comment, not as imitation. Her novels are *fin de siècle* in the decadent sense, not advanced or daring as Shaw and Wilde once seemed, but concerned with decay in art, in society, and in the individual life. It would not have been possible to write these novels in a period of Edwardian complacence. Retrospect affords her the ultimate chill of objectivity: she composes the corpse of the nineteenth century for burial. The nature of her contribution to the English novel may therefore be best understood as the decisive severance of certain threads traceable through nineteenth-century fiction.

In her early novels the high incidence of crimes, punishable in law, makes a formidable list. Murder and attempted murder are frequent occurrences; sexual offences—homosexuality, but more particularly incest—even more so. Crimes against property extend from the destruction of wills to the theft of puddings and pocketknives. Suicide is frequently contemplated, and blackmail is a concomitant of close family existence: "'I suppose a good deal happens in daily life,' said Charlotte. 'We have only to look at what is near to us, to find the drama of existence. It seems such a pity that that is so.'"[6] Since her two small sons have come near to murdering their father that morning, and her servant, in default of his own suicide, has repeated that attempt that afternoon, one may see her point. "What an event to break the daily life of a household!" (XI, 206) is a comment one might find in Jane Austen, though one would expect it to refer to a sore throat rather than a murder.

More lurid incidents are not, however, infrequent in nineteenth-century fiction. Rochester's mad wife and attempted bigamy, Heathcliff's vendetta against the Lintons and Earnshaws, have their root in similarly closed situations of birth and inheritance. If murder is largely associated with poverty in Mrs. Gaskell, Dickens, and Hardy, it is often connected with property in George Eliot. Bulstrode's need to dispose of Raffles, Gwendolen's suspicion of her own complicity in Grandcourt's death, originate in that excessive concern with possessions which overrides other fidelities. Where Hetty and Felix (whose motives are less calculating) fall into the hands of the law as is proper to the poor, Bulstrode is prosecuted only by public opinion, and Gwendolen merely by her conscience.

The operations of the law have as little place in the novels of Ivy Compton-Burnett. She would allow, as one of her characters does, that "poverty is a test few people can stand,"[7] but she has little interest in the poor, servants apart; and their offences are, perforce, on a scale inferior to those of their masters: ". . . we all do wrong . . . to yield to temptation may be as bad in one case as another, though the issues involved may be less great" (*Manservant and Maidservant*, XII, 216). No policeman or detective ever enters these apparently decorous houses; no arrests are made, charges preferred, or cases brought to court:

> "Everyone is sad sometimes," said Henry. "But they don't do what you did. Will you be put in prison?"
> "No, of course I shall not."
> "I thought that to kill yourself was against the law."
> "There is no need to use such words. This was not much more than a mistake."[8]

Henry is eight, and suffers from a child's *naiveté*. Such families may privately compose differences on a scale larger than suicide, and exact silence as retribution for murder. When Matthew murders his mother in *Men and Wives*, the family doctor prescribes: "You must take shelter behind that falsehood and spend your life in its cover. . . . You will do no more harm, Matthew. You will fall in with what is best for other people, and its being best for you will not prevent you."[9] Sybil Edgeworth, another murderer, is welcomed back to the bosom of the family whose heir she has gassed when (and because) she inherits a fortune. Her father views her offence as a "girl's early stumble," while her husband observes: "My natural affection is asserting itself. Or I am imagining it is, because affection seems so much better than avarice."[10] Anna Domme may remark that she feels "a sort of prisoner in the dock" being "arraigned by . . . relations,"[11] but there is no doubt that sentences passed by the family are mild compared with those of the law: "in future I will commit errors base enough to be hushed up,"[12] Grant concludes in *Parents and Children.*

Solicitors exist, but as the expositors, and occasionally manipulators, of those family secrets to which they have professional access. Though they may batten on the houses they serve, as Spong does in *Men and Wives*, they never acquire the powers of a Tulkinghorn. Sir Michael's view of the profession in *A God and His Gifts*, as "Something between ourselves and human good . . . that brings trouble and anxiety to innocent people,"[13] might stand for a general verdict. The same might of course be said not only of Tulkinghorn, but of law as a whole in *Bleak House*, but "human good" in Sir Michael's case means the liberty to exceed one's income and "innocence" the capacity to ignore one's creditors. Skimpole's analogous attitudes are exceptional in *Bleak House*, and they are not condoned; whereas Sir Michael, insofar as anyone does, becomes a moral arbiter, who finds it hard to exonerate totally the multiple adulteries of his son, the gift horse: "But I can't go the whole length. I feel we should keep our human laws" (*A God and His Gifts*, XII, 170).

Such comments are, however, rare in Ivy Compton-Burnett; imperviousness to any claims save those of the family is the general rule and class characteristic. As such it may seem remote from those subtleties of conscience displayed by Lydgate, Gwendolen, or even Bulstrode. But Ivy Compton-Burnett is quite as interested as George Eliot in that shadowy area where "spots of commonness," the habit of venality, merge into major crimes. For the latter, however, this continuity emphasizes the significance of little sins; for the former, it robs the great ones of importance. When the children, Jasper and Marcus, fail to warn their father that the bridge he is about to cross has become unsafe, they wonder themselves at the ease of their omission:

> "Why did we not tell him?" said Marcus, as though he wanted an answer to the question.
> "He walked away so quickly; there was not much time."
> "Why did we not run after him? We could have caught him up."
> "He might have been cross," said Jasper. "It startles him to be overtaken, and you know what he is like when he is startled."
> "It is better to be startled than killed."
> (*Manservant and Maidservant*, IX, 172–173)

Adult acts of commission seem as spontaneous and inevitable. When Josephine Napier assists her delirious daughter-in-law to leave her bed, thus destroying the latter's chance of recovery, her action, like Bulstrode's der of the brandy to Mrs. Abel, is a momentary impulse, prompted by the victim's own wishes. But the death of Raffles proves momentous for Bulstrode, exposing him to the sentence of public opinion. Josephine's action is witnessed by Miss Rosetti, but silence is preserved: "But it does no good to talk about it. We may be in danger from our memories." Miss Rosetti trades secret for secret: ". . . you and I have each looked at the other's hidden side, and looked away; and that is much." Josephine is enabled to conclude: "I have seldom met an experience that has not been grist to my mill."[14]

In George Eliot's view crime clearly does not pay; in Ivy Compton-Burnett's it does, as she once confirmed: "I don't think guilty people meet punishment in life. I think that the evidence tends to show that crime on the whole pays."[15] In art, her characters share her opinions: "It is not true that wickedness never prospers. Any little wickedness of mine has always prospered. And it is the same with small things and great."[16] Possibly reflecting that last insight, her later novels contain few spectacular crimes; murder is eliminated, incest foreseen and avoided. But the connection between venial and mortal offences continues to interest her; it is the theme of *Two Worlds and Their Ways* (1949), where children cheating at school are heavily punished while the adult sins of theft and adultery are quickly concealed. Such offences are still on a scale different from that of Emma's rudeness at the Box Hill picnic, but equivalent depravities lurk in Jane Austen's margins. On the one hand, Frank Churchill has much in common with Emma; on the other, he is the literary blood relation of Henry Crawford. Ivy Compton-Burnett not only drags the nineteenth century's skeletons from their cupboards; she remorselessly articulates them.

It is not that her predecessors refused to see what Ivy Compton-Burnett felt forced to face; their moral vision is far more searching than hers. But their insight is sustained by that connection of social with religious morality, which, in her world, had ceased to exist. The Edwardians might not have thought that of themselves, but those who survived their war had reason to think it. In Jane Austen the church is not only acceptable socially as a convenient destination for younger sons; despite clerical sycophants, such as Mr. Collins, younger sons like Edmund take their vocation seriously. George Eliot's clergymen may regret their choice of profession, but their views, if often worldly, are no disgrace to their cloth; more important, religious idealism is often her key to the highest of human motives. In Ivy Compton-Burnett younger sons do not enter the church; the clergy are incidental, often ludicrous, figures, while religious idealism is clearly bankrupt:

"We have not settled on the best thing in life," said Lavinia. . . .

"Real achievement?" said Selina.

"But we don't know a case of it," said Lavinia. "So we can't ask if it is the best. And anyhow no one would dare to answer."

"It depends on what kind of achievement you mean," said Teresa.

"Not service to humanity," said Hugo. "No one could feel that the best."

"Some people might," said Lavinia. "Those who could give it."

"People with religion," said Egbert. "Who feel they will be rewarded in the end."

"That might be a good thing," said Hugo. "But from what is said of it, I hardly think the best."

"Real achievement would be independent of reward," said Ninian. "The reward would be in itself."

"I knew there was some drawback," said Hugo. "Fancy having to provide the reward as well as earn it!"[17]

Social morality is at best sceptically treated. When, in *A God and His Gifts*, Reuben asserts that "There must be some moral standard in human life," he invites the retort "Standards seem to be based on the likelihood of their being violated" (XII, 164). Biblical resonances are not infrequent, but their note is ironic: when the mighty fall they inherit the earth, while the last becomes first because she is left a fortune. God has dwindled to an inexpensive member of the nursery staff: Selina Middleton "had no religion herself, but feared to let her grandchildren do without it": they are encouraged to believe in "an All-seeing Eye" since "no ordinary eye could embrace their purposes" (*The Mighty and Their Fall*, I, 21; IV, 72).

In the adult world nonbelievers form a majority, whose sceptical view of humanity is a source of strength. The good are either enfeebled, like the first Mrs. Edgeworth (*A House and Its Head*), or are notable chiefly for *naiveté* and tactlessness, as Justine (*A Family and a Fortune* [1939]) and Faith are:

"Our true selves should not be anything to be ashamed of," said Faith.

"I don't think it would be nice not to be ashamed of them," said Hope.

(*Parents and Children*, IV, 114–115)

Concepts with a religious connection, like truth, duty, temptation, and self-sacrifice, are submitted to an unremittingly sceptical scrutiny. Despite the price they exacted, these for Dolores were still mandatory; her successor, Emily Herrick in *Pastors and Masters*, is not so inconvenienced: "The sight of duty does make one shiver. . . . The actual doing of it would kill one, I think." Her preference, as she says, is for "wickedness and penetration."[18]

Concepts which flourished in 1911 have no authority in 1925.

Struggles against temptation are a necessary part of fiction, but where "success" in the nineteenth century lies in resistance or at least remorse, Ivy Compton-Burnett views it rather as the ability to make crime pay, or at least to outface one's accusers. It seems, in a version of Blake, that those who restrain desire are deficient in it. "Temptation is too much for us," observes Selina Middleton. "We are not always unwilling for it to be" (*The Mighty and Their Fall*, VII, 121). As the author herself once remarked: "wickedness . . . is not punished, and that is why it is natural to be guilty of it."[19] "Temptation" is more often seen as the attraction to virtue than to vice; thus, a character who preserves her "heart of hatred at the end" successfully resists it: "I am glad she died as she lived. The temptations of a death bed might have been too much" (*A House and Its Head*, XIX, 251).

There is much in the novels to suggest the dangers of guilty secrets, but even more to imply the hazards of honesty. In *A God and His Gifts*, Salomon, who narrowly escaped an incestuous union, not unnaturally protests: "But these secrets should not be. They lie beneath our life to escape and shatter it. They must be revealed and ended." But the danger here is to the victims, not to the perpetrator, Hereward, who retorts: "Do as you will. Expose it in this house and the other. Let two families be shocked and saddened" (XIII, 186). Where secret guilt consumes the life of Mrs. Transome and Lady Dedlock, whose sole relief is confession, no matter the price, the multiple adulteries of Salomon's father do not seem to cost him a single uneasy hour. He does feel impelled to prevent his son from transforming his daughter into his daughter-in-law, but makes light indeed of his own part in the proceedings: "She is what she might naturally be. It is simply what might have been" (XIII, 188). Far from feeling remorse, he is disposed on such occasions to charge his accusers with a lack of Christian charity: "Should a stumble be so hardly forgiven? (XIII, 170). Unusual persistence in crime can arouse admiration. Sophia's son, Robin, views it as a "dishonour" for his mother to be buried by the ordinarily moral parson, Edward: "Could Edward have locked up a will for twenty-eight years? And then unlocked it? That is the climax! Sophia and he were of a different stuff."[20]

Secrets must of course come to light for the good of the story, but not necessarily (as they do in *Bleak House* or *Felix Holt*) for the good of the characters. In *Mother and Son* Miranda dies reproaching her husband, Julius, for revealing at her deathbed that his supposed nephews and nieces are in fact his own children: "But I thank God that I have not dealt with you, as you have with me" (*Mother and Son*, VI, 128) are her final words. When Julius discovers subsequently that their supposed son is hers but not his, he is naturally irritated: "And she turned to me and said that! And she had done more wrong, the greater wrong that women do" (VII, 158–59). But Miranda's last words don't refer to sexual offences; his transgression is telling the truth. "She was a brave woman" in preserving her secret, as the son protests. Those who conceal guilt may do less damage than those who proclaim it:

> "Openness may indeed prevent distortion," said Alice.
> "And may also result in it," said Mrs. Spruce. "The human mind working as is known." . . .
>
> "Well, we see the harm in secret lives," said Alice.
> "I wish there was as little harm in many open ones," said Mrs. Spruce.
> "The word can have its meanings."[21]

Just as those who restrain desire have little to control, those who are characteristically truthful have almost shamefully little to hide. When in *North and South* Mr. Hale prefers honesty not only to his living, but perhaps to the life of his wife, Mrs. Gaskell does not question his preference, nor does she imply that Margaret and Thorton are unreasonable, when a necessary lie torments the conscience of one and alienates the affections of the other. In Ivy Compton-Burnett only the very naive can assert, as Justin does, that "truth is truth,"[22] or believe, like Mildred Hallam, that confession restores innocence:

> "I would not face you with anything on my conscience."
> "I face people with everything on mine," said Anne. "And I believe it is more than you would think. I like to believe it."
> "I get anything off mine, before I face them," said Mildred.
> "You mean you reveal it," said Sir Ransom. "Why does that take it off people's consciences? I never know the reason."
> (*Darkness and Day*, I, 15)

The more intelligent characters are agreed that ". . . there is horror in every heart, and a resolve never to be honest with anyone else" (*Elders and Betters*, XIV, 223). That resolve is necessary for self-protection: "And it is not true that people have nothing to fear, if they speak the truth. They have everything to fear. That is the reason of falsehood."[23] But reticence protects others as well as the self. Honest talk "means all sorts of risk. . . . Dishonest talk is far better" (*A Heritage and Its History*, III, 70). Since "Very few minds invite inspection" it is as well that in consequence ". . . most of them are not laid open to it."[24]

When only the stupid respond to moral imperatives, one may ask what code directs the intelligent, for they have shared assumptions, if not agreed ethical standards. The salient claims appear to be those of "property," attached chiefly to the estates, and secondarily to those financial resources which sustain them. To preserve and pass on the house of one's forefathers with its traditional life is allowed to be of paramount importance, even by those who are not themselves heirs, and who long to escape from their dependent status. For few *but* the heirs benefit from this traditional life; the estate is no longer a center of cultivation as Mansfield Park, for example, is felt to be. If the confidence of property damages the Bertram family, the qualities which property enables nurture Fanny, in sharp contrast with the defective environment of the house at Portsmouth. While the tree continues to flourish, there seems no need to suspect a radical infection, and a sign of this is continual "improvement," an occupation considered proper to a lifetime. For those who take its responsibilites seriously, the estate is a generator of moral quality: Elizabeth must curb her prejudice before she is fit to adorn the pride of Pemberley; Mr. Knightly must educate Emma as the future mistress of Donwell.

No such potential is felt in Ivy Compton-Burnett's estates; the tree has begun to wither, and a radical infection is everywhere apparent. The houses themselves tend to be shabby and in need of repair, while the land which should sustain them is either mortgaged or partially sold off: "The old house in question was large and beautiful and shabby, but only the last to any unusual degree. . . . The land about it stretched to a fair distance, and in the past had provided its support" (*A God and His Gifts*, II, 12). Marriage into these estates no longer emancipates a woman; it enslaves her. She is sought for biological rather than moral capacity: "I do want to marry. I want to have descendants. I want to hand down my name" (I, 5). She may also be sought for money, in which case the decaying estate will soon devour it. In *A Heritage and Its History*, Julia, as its mistress, acknowledges traditional sanctities: "It is the one house I know, where the present has not ousted the past. Everything is as it has been and will be" (XL, 215). Far from fostering virtue, the estate and all it involves can generate vice, even to murder: "Sybil has been through emotional strain, in a life in which succession had loomed too large. She never had a normal moral sense, and she was not in a normal place" (*A House and Its Head*, XIX, 267).

The Victorians harbored suspicions about great houses which were unusual in the Regency. Chesney Wold casts a blight upon the lives of its occupants, partly because Dickens digs down to the infected root. Where Jane Austen sees no need to analyze the West Indian fortune which sustains Mansfield Park, Dickens has questions to ask about the money and the mores which support the Dedlock place in Lincolnshire, just as Ivy Compton-Burnett assesses the human price at which her crumbling walls are buttressed. Yet Chesney Wold retains a radiant potential, glimpsed in Esther's first view of it: "The house, with gable and chimney, and tower, and turret, and dark door-way, and broad terrace-walk, twining among the balustrades of which, and lying heaped upon the vases, there was one great flush of roses, seeming scarcely real in its light solidity, and in the serene and peaceful hush that rested on all around it."[25] If that other Esther in *Felix Holt* escapes the Transome fate by resigning the Transome heritage, the restoration of the Court itself is not impugned. Quality of life still relates to location, though houses of humbler kinds do equally well: the two Bleak Houses dissipate the fogs of Chancery which Chesney Wold intensifies, and the rigors of Malthouse Yard sustain a spirit which starves in the bodily ease of Transome Court. There are no satisfying alternatives to Ivy Compton-Burnett's great houses, and they have no vestigial potential; they are more like Chekhov's, but bereft even of nostalgia. The Cherry Orchard was old, but still capable of flowering. In *A Heritage and Its History* the heir longs to cut back the creeper and admit some light to the house; but when the generation the creeper symbolizes no longer stands between him and inheritance, he is content to perpetuate darkness. The axe in *The Cherry Orchard* sounds the old order's destruction; Simon's failure to take an axe to the creeper marks it perpetuation.

"It has had its times" (*A Heritage and Its History*, I, 8), Simon as a young man remarks of the creeper, thinking also of the two lives which stand between him and succession; that comment is even more true when he is near-ly an old man, but he is then disposed to cling to his rightful inheritance. Moribund institutions are sources of infection, like corpses. In their growth the country houses came to mean more than property; in their decline they are as meaningless (and as damaging) as the miser's unused coin. Miserliness is a frequent vice in the novels, one most fully exposed in the clinging to estate. For the absence of description is functional: it denies these houses' intrinsic claim on the imagination. In contrast with the poignant presence of James's Poynton, they are merely rapacious stomachs, which no seemly flesh is allowed to adorn. They devour fortunes, and sacrifice not only wives and children, but the bevy of governesses and tutors who attempt to qualify all but the heirs for self-support. The butlers model themselves upon their masters, and perpetuate in the servants' hall the tyranny of the drawing room. The vice

of eavesdropping is indulged above and below stairs, as a right where masters
and butlers are concerned, as a forbidden relish in the case of lesser servants or
family. If provisions are not liberal (this is why George steals the pudding),[26]
its dependents batten on the family secrets, just as the cook sucks the marrow
from the bones in Ibsen's *Ghosts*.

There is nothing left to be said for hereditary estates, and much therefore to
be said against them. Unfortunately, there is also nothing to put in their
place, and the suspicion that there is nowhere to escape to is powerfully felt.
The moral void itself precludes other destinations. When Lavinia seeks liberation from her father's house by marriage with his adopted brother Hugo, she
protests her "legal right" to the fortune that will enable it; but a legacy of his
own encourages Hugo to dispose of Lavinia, and allows her father to retain the
"moral" right he claims to both daughter and fortune (*The Mighty and Their
Fall*, X, 162). In her final novels, and particularly in her last, unadorned
money seems to Ivy Compton-Burnett the key to most motives. It even takes
on a character and life of its own: "Do I love capital? I suppose I do. It is
dreadful to love money. I did not know I did. But capital is so kind to us, I am
sure anyone would love it. And it is sad if it is sometimes killed. It makes me
love it more" (*A God and His Gifts*, II, 16). Money may not be "a live thing" as
one character protests; but it may as another rejoins "underlie" live things and
be "involved" with them.[27] In her own final years Ivy Compton-Burnett
admitted, "I do wish one could just ask people what their incomes are"
("Introduction," *The Last and the First*, p. 9). Perhaps she felt that, knowing
that, one knew all.

In one of its aspects the fiction of the century that preceded her (even Jane
Austen's) dramatizes a sustained struggle with the effects of capitalism, and
the only weapons against it are ethical: charity, honesty, duty, and justice.
The First World War made evident capital's victory, proving decisively that
the weapons of conscience had long been laid aside. But Ivy Compton-
Burnett's characters are not particularly happy either in this surrender or in
their consequent amorality. When Mortimer remarks that "really we deserve
so little; so few things are really wrong" (*Manservant and Maidservant*, X,
191), he refers to punishment, but he might as appositely have regretted reward. When the worst are not "sinks of iniquity," but "well-intentioned,
everyday sort of creatures," when the "bad things" harbored in the heart are
"not those that the world calls wrong" (*Elders and Betters*, XIV, 224; 223),
there is little satisfaction left in any sense. The few remaining taboos, of which
incest is foremost, come to seem irritatingly irrational: "this to avoid some-

thing that in some days would have been lawful and right!" (*A Heritage and Its History*, IX, 161). "Stumble" is recurrently used to describe every sort of offence, from white lies to murder. One may recall that this word in the Bible denotes transgressions of the law, and that the law was durably incised upon tablets of stone. The law in these novels has no such objective existence; there is no real reason against doing anything—always provided one can bring it off. It is impossible to do more than stumble in the sense of taking a false step:

> "The things you regret, would be mistakes rather than sins?"
> "It is those we do regret. They have done us harm. That is why they are mistakes. And our sins do us good. That is what they are meant for."
> "Well, of course, they are not meant for that."
> (*Darkness and Day*, XXI, 23–24)

What then, one may wonder, is Ivy Compton-Burnett's purpose in finding out the sins of her characters; for if her novels do not arrive at judgment, the author herself is as tenaciously cool in her investigation as Bucket is in *Bleak House*. Sybille Bedford, in a personal letter, praises the novelist for her concern with truth, evidenced in her desire to make it bare: "Whenever truth is out, it rights a balance, removes spokes from wheels, restores a pattern, and leaves a basis to go forward on. The point is that it should be out, no matter for how long or to how many, and this is the beauty and the subtlety of it."[28] The last sentence is one that Bucket might cherish; the first more aptly applies to such writers as Dickens and George Eliot. Their revelation of truth does restore a pattern and provide a necessary basis for the future. Investigation is a serious responsibility, almost at times amounting to religious imperative. It is the way in which characters achieve self-knowledge—the key to happiness for Esther Lyon, for Lady Dedlock the road to redemption. For the novelist the detective form is a way of structuring a society grown increasingly impersonal and amorphous; it serves to establish those significant social connections which exist between Transome Court and Malthouse Yard, between Tom-all-Alone's and Chesney Wold. It is as necessary to individual as to social salvation that the secrets of the heart should be made plain.

Ivy Compton-Burnett's pursuit of truth is clearly less elevated, since she has no confidence in right as distinct from wrong, or in the existence of appropriate reward and punishment. She allows little more to her motive than curiosity, and her novels contain a host of minor characters who listen at doors or call at awkward times: "'We want to know the whole thing,' said Evelyn. 'Our curiosity is neither morbid nor ordinary. It is the kind known as devour-

ing. We want you to be completely satisfying. It is awful not to be satisfied'"
(*Daughters and Sons*, VIII, 202). Truths which are given so avid a reception
emerge more often by accident than design; they are not pursued, as in
Dickens and Eliot, because their revelation is necessary. Speech is directed to
concealing, not revealing, secrets:

> "I suppose I am too honest," said Anna. "I ought to edit myself more."
> "I expect you mean that you ought to edit yourself differently," said
> Terence. "You would think that we could choose our wrong impression."
> (*Elders and Betters*, XIV, 223)

Despite suspicions, Anna preserves her secret to the end, but verbal slips can
give others away. Hereward, incautiously expansive with words like the writer he is, thus reveals that his adopted son is his natural one: "No other has
been so much blood of my blood, so deeply derived from me" (*A God and His
Gifts*, IX, 126). One might argue that verbal slips, like the frequent preservation of incriminating letters and the dropping of tell-tale envelopes, are not in
fact pure chance, but belong in a *Psychopathology of Everyday Life*, as expressions of a repressed confessional instinct. As a means of revealing truth,
such stumbles are certainly more convincing than arbitrary coincidence, but
the author clearly has little interest in the psyche. She never discloses what
characters think to themselves, only what they are prepared to "edit" for
others.

When the truth is finally out, her conclusions offer no basis for advance; at
best they reestablish the *status quo ante*. At the end of *A Heritage and Its History*
Simon has succeeded to his inheritance, as he would always have done had he
not introduced obstacles himself. In *Two Worlds and Their Ways* the children
are restored to their first world of home, their expedition into the second, of
school, acknowledged as failure. Nor can one be confident that the truth
should be out: it causes the innocent to suffer rather than the guilty. Ivy
Compton-Burnett of course believed that this injustice was only true to life,
but she also felt that the emergence of truth was not: life's absence of plot was
her "extra grudge" against it. She defended the success of Anna Donne, from
the critics of *Elders and Betters* who "wanted wickedness to be punished,"[29] on
grounds of verisimilitude, but she admitted that her penchant for plot was the
need of an artist, not a realist: "But I think it is better for a novel to have a
plot. Otherwise it has no shape, and incidents that have no part in a formal
whole seem to have less significance."[30]

Symmetry and significance have only a limited meaning as the novels define them. It is not a case of poetic justice, but of injustice made aesthetic. The "shape," the "formal whole," are perfectly evident, but they satisfy only as a pattern does, a syllogism; and one may remember that the latter, in allusive usage, can mean subtle speech or poser of artifice. It is appropriate, however, to many of her plots: *A Heritage and Its History* could be described in this way—possession breeds envy, envy is corrosive, therefore possessions are corrosive—or *Two Worlds and Their Ways* in this—children reflect their parents, parents are dishonest, therefore children are dishonest. Probably all her novels are reducible to formulae, which is not to imply that the formula can substitute for the novel. Syllogism does, however, suggest the reader's sensation; the conclusion inheres in the premises, the end returns to the beginning, *huis clos*, there is no way out. What is true of the whole is equally true of the detail; when her characters converse, they cap each other's aphorisms, a game in which the cleverest always win:

> "My sister understands about the hidden things," said Egbert, "though she herself may not have them."
> "They would not remain hidden," said Lavinia, laughing. "In my case they would emerge."
> "They would not in mine," said Hugo. "They are far too securely hidden. I hardly dare to recognize them myself. I might betray them."
> "I know all mine. And I fear so do you all. I have not the gift of hiding them."
> "Fancy not having to cultivate it! I thought that became our second nature. I did not know we ever showed our first one."
> "You are patient with my family," said Ninian to his wife. "They love words for their own sake."
>
> (*The Mighty and Their Fall*, VI, 103)

Hugo's wit satisfies more by its form than its insight. Such aphorisms seem always to offer ideas, but they are pursued to sharpen wit rather than vision—as Ninian remarks to his wife. The logic of words, like the logic of acts, may be meaningless, and their "significance" no more than superficial in consequence. Whether dialogue elicits latent verbal symmetries, or plot discovers that relation of cause and effect which life conceals, such connections satisfy no more than the intellect. Plot makes evident the meaninglessness that life conceals; dialogue reveals that words are *flatuus voces*. The formal whole gives significance to the parts simply because it can't be assembled without them.

Ivy Compton-Burnett has stripped the novel of all but its barest essentials, in an effort to get down to "unaccommodated man." When his various

coverings are removed, little remains, as little indeed as in Beckett's *Godot* or
Endgame. Voices are raised merely to fill the vacancy—"that was a good little
canter"—while the speakers wait for nemesis to descend. Anachronism can
work in both directions: if Ivy Compton-Burnett is deliberately retrospective,
one might argue that she is prophetic too. Beckett's fundamental distrust of
significance is the result of two world wars, hers of only one. Her "bare forked
animal" is a cadaver: her embalmer's art both suggests the life that once inhab-
ited it, and as mockingly reduces that life to inanity.

NOTES

1. *Ivy Compton-Burnett*, Columbia Essays on Modern Writers (New York: Columbia Univ. Press, 1970), 3.
2. *An Introduction to the English Novel* (London: Hutchinson Univ. Library, 1953), II, 193.
3. Conversation with Margaret Jourdain, quoted by Elizabeth Sprigge, *The Life of Ivy Compton-Burnett* (London: Gollancz, 1973), 115.
4. Quoted by Nevius, 11.
5. Conversation with Margaret Jourdain, quoted by Pamela Hansford-Johnson, *I. Compton-Burnett*, British Council Bibliographical Series (London: Longmans, Green & Co., 1951), 36.
6. Ivy Compton-Burnett, *Manservant and Maidservant* (London: Gollancz, 1947), Chapter XI, 206. This novel was published in the USA as *Bullivant and the Lambs*. Throughout this essay initial references to novels by Ivy Compton-Burnett will appear parenthetically in the text of the essay. In all instances, chapter and page references are provided for the convenience of readers who have access only to American editions of the novels; on occasion the text of the American editions differs slightly from the text of the British editions.
7. *A Heritage and Its History* (London: Gollancz, 1959), Chapter VIII, 138.
8. *The Present and the Past* (1953; rpt. London: Gollancz, 1960), Chapter XI, 163.
9. *Men and Wives* (London: Gollancz, 1931), Chapter XXV, 245–246.
10. *A House and Its Head* (London: Gollancz, 1935), Chapter XIX, 246 and 267.
11. *Elders and Betters* (London: Gollancz, 1944), Chapter IX, 138–139.
12. *Parents and Children* (London: Gollancz, 1941), Chapter XII, 291.
13. *A God and His Gifts* (London: Gollancz, 1963), Chapter II, 14.
14. *More Women than Men* (1933; rpt. London: Eyre and Spottiswoode, 1951), Chapter XV, 160; Chapter XX, 195–196.
15. Ivy Compton-Burnett, as quoted by Nevius, 26.
16. *Mother and Son* (London: Gollancz, 1955), Chapter XI, 233.
17. *The Mighty and Their Fall* (London: Gollancz, 1961), Chapter VI, 100.
18. *Pastors and Masters* (London: Gollancz, 1925), Chapter II, 17; Chapter VI, 78.
19. Ivy Compton-Burnett, quoted by Nevius, 26. Cf. conversation with Margaret Jourdain,

quoted by Sprigge, 116–117: ". . . I think that life makes great demands on people's characters, and gives them great opportunity to serve their own ends by the sacrifice of other people. Such ill-doing may meet with little retribution, may indeed be hardly recognized, and I cannot feel so surprised if people yield to it."

20. *Brothers and Sisters* (London: Gollancz, 1929), Chapter IX, 241–242.

21. *Darkness and Day* (London: Gollancz, 1951), Chapter VII, 227 and 229.

22. *A Family and a Fortune* (1939; rpt. London: Gollancz, 1967), Chapter I, 14.

23. *Two Worlds and Their Ways* (London: Gollancz, 1949), Chapter II, 46.

24. *A Father and His Fate* (London: Gollancz, 1957), Chapter IV, 61.

25. Charles Dickens, *Bleak House*, 2 vols. (London: Chapman and Hall, 1911), II, 299.

26. In *Manservant and Maidservant*. George attempts his master's life as well as the pudding, which leads Charlotte to comment: "Horace takes an attempt on his life better than one on his household goods. I suppose George is too old to take things to eat, but no one is too old to take a life" (IX, 205–206).

27. *The Last and the First* (London: Gollancz, 1971), Chapter X, 123.

28. Sybille Bedford, quoted by Sprigge, 136.

29. Her reaction to a review in *The New Statesman*, quoted by Nevius, 26.

30. Conversation with Margaret Jourdain, quoted by Sprigge, 114.

Jean Rhys and the
Genius of Impressionism

TODD K. BENDER

Although Ford Madox Ford was deeply troubled in 1924 by the financial collapse of his international literary magazine *transatlantic review* and by Conrad's death, followed by the attack of Jessie Conrad on Ford's memoir of his friend, he was at the height of his creative power, engaged in writing the Tietjens Tetralogy. Living rather extravagantly with Stella Bowen in Paris, he met the beautiful young actress and author Jean Rhys. Jean Rhys had grown up in the West Indies, daughter of a Creole mother and Welsh doctor. Ford and Stella asked Jean to live with them, so that Ford could help her with her literary work. The relationship between Jean Rhys and Ford soon became intimate, "entangling" in his eyes, and Stella and Ford arranged for Jean to leave Paris to work as a translator in the south of France.

What was a casual episode in Ford's generally untidy life was far more painful for the impoverished young woman. If we can take her fiction as a reasonable representation of the affair, Jean Rhys records in *Postures* (later titled *Quartet*) and *After Leaving Mr. Mackenzie* a very unsavory picture of her former friends, Ford and Stella. If after all those years she still felt wounded, it must have been some gratification for her to be hailed by *The New York Times* as the greatest living novelist on the occasion of the publication of *Wide Sargasso Sea* (1966), an evaluation that could not have been made of Ford himself, except perhaps in an autobiographical vein. And yet, *Wide Sargasso Sea* owes much to Ford and his fellow impressionists and deserves to stand with impressionist masterpieces like *Heart of Darkness*, *Lord Jim*, and *The Good Soldier*.

Wide Sargasso Sea originates in Charlotte Brontë's *Jane Eyre* (1847). Jane is prevented from marrying Rochester because he has hidden away a mad West Indian wife, called Antoinette or Bertha, who finally perishes in the fire which she sets, burning down Rochester's ancestral home and blinding him. Only after the conflagration can Jane and Rochester be united. It is easy to see why Jean Rhys, a poor alien, feeling betrayed by the English and apparently wealthy (or at least middle class) Stella and Ford, might find her personal anxieties embedded in Charlotte Brontë's work, so that she casts herself vaguely in the role of the alien West Indian woman deprived of her man's love. The contemporary reader may smile at the idea of Ford Madox Ford playing the role of Rochester, but for Jean Rhys it was no joke. In *Jane Eyre* the West Indian wife is shown entirely from the exterior, and she lurks as a fearsome dark presence in Rochester's house. Seen mainly through his eyes or those of the English rival, she naturally takes on a hideousness altogether unbearable. In these words Rochester reveals her existence (in chapter XVI): "Bertha Mason is mad; and she came of a mad family;—idiots and maniacs through three generations! Her mother, the Creole, was both a mad woman and a drunkard!—as I found out after I had wed the daughter: for they were silent on the family secrets before. Bertha, like a dutiful child, copied her parents in both points." When Jane looks on the madwoman she sees: "In the deep shade, at the further end of the room, a figure runs backwards and forwards. What it was, whether beast or human being, one could not, at first sight, tell: it grovelled, seemingly, on all fours; it snatched and growled like some strange wild animal: but it was covered with clothing; and a quantity of dark, grizzled hair, wild as a mane, hid its head and face." The "hyena" with "bloated features" attacks Rochester in this scene, biting his cheek before being subdued.

Wide Sargasso Sea is the sympathetic history of this madwoman from her youth in the West Indies until the moment when she takes her candle to fire Rochester's home. Much of the tale is told in the stream of consciousness technique, looking through the eyes of Antoinette. On the simplest level, we can imagine *Wide Sargasso Sea* as an attempt to render justice, to present the alien woman's point of view and plead her case, or to explain plausibly how she and her husband have got to the sorry state evident in *Jane Eyre*.

Part I of *Wide Sargasso Sea* is narrated by Antoinette, who was growing up in Jamaica shortly after the Emancipation Act was passed.[1] Rejected by both the black community and the white in a state where civil disorder and violence are common, she lives in isolation and constant fear, impoverished on the crumbling estate of her widowed mother. Her companion is Christophine, a Martinique obeah woman, a voodoo witch. Her mother remarries, to a Mr. Mason, and their fortunes improve temporarily until the blacks revolt, burning her beloved home, Coulibri, and killing her half-witted brother. In town, she goes to convent school, and a colored "cousin" Sandi protects her from more hostile blacks.

Part II of the tale shifts to young Rochester as narrator on the honeymoon trip to their country estate. Following the details of the fictive "reality" outlined by Charlotte Brontë, he reveals how his marriage to Antoinette was arranged for financial reasons. After a period of uneasy passion, Rochester receives a denunciation of Antoinette from another half-caste colored "cousin," Daniel Cosway, who accuses her of incipient madness and unchaste behavior with Sandi. As Rochester's doubts grow, Antoinette gets a love potion from Christophine. True to its nature, the charm works for one night only. Antoinette, her future now in Rochester's control and surrounded by hostility, is torn away from her native land, transported to England, to confinement, and to her suicidal act.

Clearly, Jean Rhys saw that Brontë's presentation of the evil madwoman and the completely dead love of Rochester demanded a more fully fleshed, more rounded treatment. Reading her work, we "see round" Antoinette in a new way. Our sympathy comes into play and we are much more aware of the limitations of Brontë's Rochester. Those shortcomings in Jane Eyre's future husband are curiously ignored in Brontë's novel. Bringing Jean Rhys's characterizations to bear on Brontë's not only develops the blank character Antoinette, but converts Rochester into a much more interesting, equivocal figure. It counteracts his flatness in Brontë's version and questions the nature of Jane's judgment. "Why is Jane so uncritical of Rochester?" we ask as we turn from *Wide Sargasso Sea* to *Jane Eyre*.

It is not unusual for a novelist to base his story on another writer's fiction. George MacDonald Fraser's *Flashman* (1970), for instance, purports to follow the career of the villain of *Tom Brown's Schooldays* (1856), showing that he is the veritable hero of Victorian Imperialism. T. H. White's *Mistress Masham's Repose,* altogether a charming story, does not alter our reading of *Gulliver's Travels* (1726). But once we have read *Wide Sargasso Sea*, we can never again read *Jane Eyre* in quite the same way. This power to reach into the past and *transform* the nature of a previous text is the mark of high critical power which

Wide Sargasso Sea derives from the theory of literary impressionism as practiced by Ford and Conrad in their best work.

Ford's memoir, *Joseph Conrad: A Personal Remembrance*, completed in some sixty days in late 1924, is bound to be misunderstood if the reader expects "historical accuracy." Like Ford's Fifth Queen Trilogy, *Joseph Conrad* is better seen as fiction with a historical setting. The reality of Henry VIII does not suffer in these novels, although Ford made up for him speeches which are clearly fictions. So, too, Conrad's real existence is independent of the obvious fictions in the memoir constructed by his devoted friend. The author who uses fiction to "bring to life" a character does homage to that figure, whether it be Henry VIII, Joseph Conrad, or Charlotte Brontë's Bertha Mason. When Ford claims that he and Conrad were the vanguard of literary impressionism in England, it does not entirely discredit his claim to show that much of *Joseph Conrad* is invented.

In any case, Ford's explanation of the nature of their art may illuminate our knowledge of their work. *Joseph Conrad* shows us how a character can be vitalized and at the same time tells us the nature of that creative process.

In *Joseph Conrad,* Ford depicts the act of creating impressionist fiction. Impressionist writers aim to record the way impressions impinge on consciousness to make that "shimmering haze" which is life, and they try to control and manipulate the constructive activity of their audience as it registers an impression of their work, much like a pointillist canvas by Seurat. The pointillist canvas actually is covered with separate dots of color; only the fusion on the retina of the observer's eye creates the color and shape of the picture. To accomplish such aims, impressionist fictions typically utilize an "affair" as plot, limited "unreliable" narration, and "psychological" structures of time and space, so as to require a constructive activity from each reader. This is the formula to which *Wide Sargasso Sea* is written.

The "affair" at the center of *Wide Sargasso Sea* is Antoinette's insane, suicidal conflagration, an event which has already "happened," like Jim's abandonment of the Patna in *Lord Jim*, the disintegration of the foursome in *The Good Soldier*, or the death of Kurtz in *Heart of Darkness*. The story progresses in widening circles of understanding as the reader sees the scene through the eyes of one or more witnesses and tries to judge what the "facts" of the case may be. In such stories the reader struggles with multiple, limited, unreliable narrations in order to deduce and judge the true state of affairs. The plot is open to multiple, contradictory interpretations. Was Antoinette guilty of unchaste acts with Sandi? Or is she mad and only imagining such scenes? Is the voodoo charm of Christophine "really" magic? Or is it, as Rochester thinks, just poison? When Rochester confronts Christophine and says, "I would give my eyes never to have seen this abominable place," is Christophine "really" a witch when she replies, "And that's the first damn word of truth you speak."[2] Is all of *Jane Eyre* nothing but the working out of a voodoo curse? A curse pronounced in another book?

Since the story is told in limited narration, it follows the psychological processes of the speaker—in Antoinette's case, the mental processes of an incipient madwoman. What is fictive reality, what demented vision? The story shifts freely from fictive reality to fantasy. For example, at the end of *Wide Sargasso Sea,* the madwoman Antoinette describes, in detail which corresponds point for point to Brontë's description, her setting fire to the house and perishing in the flames despite Rochester's efforts to save her. The reader has no reason to suspect that these paragraphs are not fictive reality until she says she "woke" to find her nurse, Grace Poole, watching her. She says, "I must have been dreaming" (190). But now she knows what she must do, and within a few lines she takes up the candle to enact, presumably, the vision she has just "dreamed." As in the fiction of Robert Coover, the unwary reader is soon entangled in a hopelessly confused web of shifting levels of "reality" in the tale.

The audience is forced into a constructive role in impressionism and becomes intensely involved in the work of art when the limited unreliable narrators give the audience such suggestive, tangled glimpses of the affair. This structure gives the author a tool for creating a very strong emotional response in his readers. The artist cannot represent all possible impressions and associations of the mind. He must choose to present some and to suppress others from his writing. Ford insists that the whole of art consists in this selection. The principles of selection are therefore what distinguishes art from chaos. The author must, of course, choose to render only those impressions which carry the story forward or interest the reader, but the most important principle for selection is to seek what Ford in *The March of Literature* calls the "unearned increment":

> Impressionism began with the—perhaps instinctive—discovery . . . that the juxtaposition of the composed renderings of two or more unexaggerated actions or situations may be used to establish, like the juxtaposition of vital word to vital word, a sort of frictional current of electric life that will extraordinarily galvanize the work of art in which the device is employed. . . . Let us put it more concretely by citing the algebraic truth

truth that $(a = b)^2$ equals not merely $a^2 - b^2$, but a^2 *plus an apparently unearned increment called 2ab* plus the expected b^2. . . . The point cannot be sufficiently labored, since the whole fabric of modern art depends on it.[3]

Through the structure of a past affair reported in the fictive present by limited, unreliable, dramatic speakers, the impressionist writer forces his audience into a constructive role, like a jury, building up the story in its own mind. But merely to use the word "unreliable" shows how the impressionist writer tricks us. In a courtroom a witness is called unreliable when his report does not match the event he describes, perhaps because he is dishonest or does not know the facts. But a fiction is different; there is no real event reported by its speakers. We could compare a reader of fiction to a jury in a schematic way and see that where a jury tries to find "reality," the reader of fiction is forced to construct a second, unstated fiction:

Real Event	*Real Reporter*	*Real Jury*
1. Real Accident	2. Witness	3. Decides whether witness's report matches event

Unstated Fiction	*Stated Fiction*	*Constructed Fiction*
1. Unstated fictional event, the "affair"	2. "Unreliable" narrator's report	3. Audience constructs what it imagines unstated fiction to be

In reality the jury's judgment that a report is unreliable means that it does not correspond to the real event. In fiction the "unreliable" report means a story so constructed as to force the reader into a constructive activity, perhaps because the fiction as stated has internal contradictions or seems incomplete. Some "unreliable" narrations can be "solved." Mystery stories often have a single, clear-cut answer. But many fictions defy solutions, and platoons of clever literary scholars feel called upon to construct conflicting versions of the basic meaning of the work.

Wide Sargasso Sea supplies the second term of a collage, creating what Ford calls on "unearned increment." Brontë's version of Antoinette and Rochester is a, Rhys's is b, but the two in conjunction are more signifcant than either separately. *Jane Eyre* is a "closed" fiction. The reader does not read it a second time with the same interest as at the first reading. We discover "who done it." The dark shape in Rochester's house is revealed and purged. Jane and Rochester are to live happily ever after. Contrast such a "closed" plot to that of an "open" fiction like *Villette*. In this instance, the second reading is of the same quality as the first, for the same questions remain. In *Wide Sargasso Sea* Jean Rhys has "opened" *Jane Eyre* by altering the reader's relationship to the text. *Wide Sargasso Sea* may be a misreading of *Jane Eyre*, but it creatively shifts the reader's activity in an important way, and this alteration is accomplished through the techniques of literary impressionism.

The general situation of Rochester's alien wife recurs frequently in Jean Rhys's works. For example, in *Good Morning, Midnight* one of Sashe Jansen's gentlemen friends tells her of an incident that happened when he was living in a room near Notting Hill Gate in London. Hearing an eerie cry in the passage outside his room, he finds a half-Negro woman lying weeping on the floor. She tells him she is from Martinique. She was living with an Englishman on the top floor of the house, but for two years she had not gone out of her room except after dark. She finally ventures forth and meets a little English girl on the stairs who says she is dirty, smells bad, and has no right to be in the house. The child says, "I hate you and I wish you were dead." The mulatto woman drinks a whole bottle of whiskey and falls drunk in the hallway. The hatred of the women of the house after that is unbearable. Another example: in the short story "Let Them Call It Jazz," the West Indian Selina lives at Notting Hill Gate until her money is stolen. Temporarily given shelter by a man in an ancient decaying house, she lives in isolation, until through the hostility of her English neighbors she is sent to prison for disorderly conduct. While in Holloway prison, she hears a woman confined to the punishment cells, high in a turret, sing the "Holloway Song," letting her fellow prisoners know that she is equal to the ordeal. When Selina is released, she sings the song for a musician who turns it into a trivial jazz tune. In such stories, an alien, half-white, West Indian woman is emotionally and financially dependent on an Englishman, who abandons her to the prejudice and hostility of English society. She is confined to a room in a Gothic structure, misunderstood, drinks heavily, and is goaded to a self-destructive activity.

Once we have defined a general pattern for works overtly similar to *Wide Sargasso Sea*, we can see that there is a basic similarity in *all* the fiction by Jean Rhys. She tells the same tale over and over, a powerful feminist plea. All of her stories are about the indignity, the personal damage, which flows from a woman's financial and emotional dependence on men in an alien world. In a society where she is systematically denied the right of self-sufficing employment, what can a woman do to maintain her freedom? Perhaps only symbolic gestures are possible. In *Good Morning, Midnight*, for example, Sasha Jansen

refuses to be bought by men and refuses to buy herself a gigolo. In the concluding scene, in order to avoid rape, she tells a man to take whatever money
she has from her dresser drawer and get out. When he has left, she finds that
he has not, in fact, taken all her money. As she lies alone in the darkness, in a
collage of hallucination and fictive reality, she imagines him returning to her
bed, and opens the door for him, only to receive the truly slimy man in a
dressing gown who lurks in the hotel corridor. It is a bitter ending for an
incredibly bitter book. It perhaps could be argued that the area of female
freedom is so narrow, so limited, that only such a choice seems to Jean Rhys
free from the taint of the marketplace in European society.

The main theme of her later fiction is stated in her first book, a collection of
impressionist sketches, *The Left Bank* (1927). Ford Madox Ford wrote in the
Preface to this work that he wanted to be associated with it because "hundreds
of years hence" when "her ashes are translated to the Pantheon, in the volumi-
nous pall . . . a grain or so of my scattered and forgotten dust may go in too,
in the folds."[4] Ironically, his prophecy may turn out to be more nearly true
than he expected in 1927. In these early stories, especially in such pieces as
"Mannequin," the central idea of Rhys's later fiction is virtually complete.
The female is given by society a limited number of roles to play. She is paid or
rewarded only when she plays these roles to perfection: each of the twelve
mannequins in the dress shop knows her type and keeps to it: "Babbette, the
gamine, the traditional blond enfant: Mona, tall and darkly beautiful, the
femme fatale, the wearer of sumptuous evening gowns. Georgette was the
garconne . . ." (163). At the conclusion of the story there is a surrealistic
tinge to the evening as all the mannequins come out of their shops and make
the pavements gay as beds of flowers before the girls are swallowed up in the
night of Paris. But if a story like "Mannequin" looks ahead to the theme of her
later fiction, it also looks back to the great dramatic poems of the Victorian
period, like Browning's *Men and Women*.

The formula that Browning exploits in his dramatic monologues is to
create a tension between the reader's sympathy and his judgment of a
character. Typically, Browning does so by taking a strongly stereotyped
character and giving us a view of inner feelings and motives which contradict
the stereotype. For this reason he is particularly fond of depicting churchmen
who have natural impulses at odds with their public roles, like the Bishop at
St. Praxed's, Fra Lippo Lippi, and Bishop Blougram. Bishop Blougram explains Browning's characterization when he asserts that he will always be interesting because he is an enigma, a man who knows about skepticism yet

believes with the faith of a true bishop. How can he exist within the confines
of his public role? He says such characters will eternally hold our interest:

> The honest thief, the tender murderer
> The superstitious atheist, demirep
> That loves and saves her soul in New French books—
> We watch while these in equilibrium keep
> The giddy line midway: one step aside,
> They're classed and done with. I, then, keep the line
> Before your sages,—just the men to shrink
> From gross weights, coarse scales and labels broad
> You offer their refinement. Fool or knave,
> Why needs a bishop be a fool or knave
> When there's a thousand diamond weights between?

All of Jean Rhys's fiction has as its central figure a strong female stereotype,
a mannequin of one kind or another, cast in some role thrust on woman by
society. Then, like Browning's monologues, her work lets us into the interior
of the character and sets up a contradictory, crossed purpose, showing us that
the stereotype is painful to play. For example, the short story "Illusion"
depicts Miss Bruce, tall, thin, a shining example of what "British character
and training" (151) can do for a woman. In Paris, surrounded by the cult of
beauty and love, she is always severe, sensibly dressed in "neat tweed costume
in winter, brown shoes with low heels and cotton stockings" (152). Miss
Bruce suddenly falls ill, and the narrator of the tale enters her flat to get some
necessities for her in hospital. When she opens Miss Bruce's wardrobe she
finds a "glow of colour, a riot of soft silks . . . everything that one did not
expect" (153). Evidently the clothes are never worn, but indicate that the
sensible Miss Bruce is afflicted "with the perpetual hunger to be beautiful and
that thirst to be loved which is the real curse of Eve" (154). Miss Bruce is
shown acutely embarrassed that her friend knows she collects clothes, and she
asserts at the conclusion of the story that she would never make such a fool of
herself as actually to wear them. The reader finds such characters fascinating
for the same reasons as he does Browning's churchmen. How can the Bishop at
St. Praxed's, with all his love of luxury and the pleasure of the senses, play the
role of the ascetic? How can Miss Bruce, with her streak of feminine longing
for soft, bright fabrics, play the role of the sensible British woman? The core
of such characters is repression. At what cost must Miss Bruce's love of clothes
be repressed? At what cost must Bishop Blougram combat his skeptical
thoughts or St. Praxed's Bishop his sensuality?

This is, of course, the pattern of Conrad's *Lord Jim* as well. Such characterization produces split figures, *Doppelgänger*. As in a morality play, the good or socially approved type struggles with a bad or disapproved tendency. One pole is the repressed type, the other is the freedom of personal inclination. Failure to repress the personality results in social ostracism, loss of affection, incarceration, madness. All of Jean Rhys's heroines are trying to be "good girls," but find it impossible to fit into the stereotype. They are forced to "misbehave" socially and sexually, to drink excessively, to commit all sorts of "excesses," until they are disgraced. Many readers will see in *Jane Eyre* a similar split in the central character. Jane herself is the heroine of repression, control, decency. Her dark twin lurking in Rochester's home is the mad, unrepressed, licentious West Indian. Only when the dark woman is burned out, can Jane unite with Rochester. Jane effects purgation through intense suffering and British schooling, elements which Jean Rhys shows as unacceptable to Antoinette. Rather than killing the dark, sensual, loose shadow in order to become the prim governess and wife, Antoinette overpowers the stereotype and rages destructively against the restraints of British customs. No reader doubts that Antoinette must be judged to fail in fitting into British expectations, but the real sympathy for her lies in her questioning the cultural assumptions on which the stereotypes of British female decency are built. In the light of Jean Rhys's fiction, the madwoman is the true heroine, not the submissive Jane Eyre.

Many of Jean Rhys's stories involve deviations from normal perception, such as hallucinations induced by extreme pain or suffering, drunkenness, or madness. Such scenes raise questions about what is normal, what is normative in the fiction. What are the bases for the reader's formation of judgments? For instance, in *Voyage in the Dark,* the heroine is a young West Indian who hates England and is forced to tour as a chorus girl to earn a pittance. An older, wealthy Englishman, Walter, keeps her as his mistress. A climax of the novel occurs when the heroine and Walter spend a weekend in the country with his friend Vincent, a sneering young man, and Vincent's girlfriend, Germaine. They reveal that Walter is about to leave for America for several months; then they ask how old the heroine is and where Walter met her. She replies that she was in a show in Southsea. Vincent jokingly asks Walter what he was doing on a pier in Southsea, and the three English people begin to laugh. The heroine does not understand what they are laughing at. The others ignore her when she asks them to explain the joke. Suddenly, she grinds her lighted cigarette into the back of Walter's hand. The act is as mad and destructive as Antoinette's blinding Rochester by fire. It is self-destructive as well; because, from that episode on, Walter is set on deserting her. But the act of burning Walter's hand seems crazy or antisocial only if we do not question the assumptions of the society, if we assume that the laughter of Walter, Vincent, and Gemaine is acceptable aggression; whereas, burning his hand is beyond the limits of reasonable action. The thrust of the story, however, is to question that normative framework. It is not so crazy to burn Walter's hand; it is not really incomprehensible that Antoinette burns Rochester's house, provided we are willing to see things from their side.

Many critics feel that a major value of literature lies in the exploration of human values embodied in social behavior. When the traditional roles and patterns of behavior available to individuals in a society seem unacceptable, fictions allow us to examine possible ways to fit our desires to traditional expectations. Many fictions present characters with a possible choice, such as marriage. We can ask three questions about the character's possible behavior: is it approved by society? is it profitable? is it desired by the individual? If the answer to all three questions is "yes," there is no need to write a novel. On the other hand, if the answer to one of the questions is "no," we have the formula for literally thousands of fictional works analyzing how to reconcile approved and profitable behavior with the desired. Both Jean Rhys and Charlotte Brontë personally lived through this kind of conflict between social roles available to them and their contrary desires. Both can claim to be more than ephemeral writers, because they give serious exploration in fiction to such conflict.

A frequent question about *Wide Sargasso Sea* is: does this novel work independently of *Jane Eyre* or does it simply cannibalize the work of Brontë? It would appear that no novel can be read entirely "independently" of a literary tradition. It is perhaps better to rephrase the question: can *Wide Sargasso Sea* be read profitably with reference to the general tradition of the nineteenth-century novel, rather than specifically with reference to *Jane Eyre*? The answer to this question is "yes," both on practical and theoretical grounds. Practically, I have worked with many young readers who respond favorably to Rhys's work without suspecting that it refers to Brontë's. Theoretically, we can see that such responses are possible because her work is in the general tradition of the novel of serious social criticism exploring the limitations of available social roles, especially of young women, in Western culture.

NOTES

1. By the Imperial Parliament in 1833. Slaves actually became free in 1838, after a time of "apprenticeship." [Ed.]

2. *Wide Sargasso Sea* (New York: Norton, 1966), 161.

3. Ford Madox Ford, *The March of Literature, from Confucius to Modern Times* (London: George Allen and Unwin, 1947), 734.

4. Ford Madox Ford, "Preface to Stories from *The Left Bank,*" rpt. in Jean Rhys, *Tigers Are Better-Looking, with a Selection from The Left Bank* (New York: Harper and Row, 1968), 150. Subsequent references to stories by Jean Rhys are to this edition.

Jean Rhys on Insult and Injury

FRANK BALDANZA

I

In discussing the seeming monotony of tone in the work of many distinguished literary figures, Alberto Moravia remarked that most major writers have only one string to their lute, so that the fundamental question ought not to be one of the variety of their effects, but of the complexity and intensity with which they do what they do well. Although few readers outside coteries would call Jean Rhys a major writer, Moravia's remark is nevertheless quite apposite to her fiction. Miss Rhys works, in terms of both theme and technique, in a severely limited range—but, since another essay in this collection discusses her Impressionist technique I shall concentrate on her thematic complexity and intensity and shall try to avoid, insofar as possible, analysis of method.

The "archetypal" career of the Rhys protagonist—which can be pieced together from glimpses of variously named characters at various phases of similar lives in her five novels and three collections of short stories—closely resembles the few scraps of biographical information now available about the author, though we have no warrant for a reverse extrapolation from fiction to life.[1] It is in the context of this career that we find her most deeply felt values and most typical thematic concerns.

We first encounter a sensitive, anti-social, reclusive — nearly misanthropic — West Indian girl whose severe alienation seems self-contained and *sui generis*, though many exterior factors reinforce her withdrawal. In the social sphere, she belongs neither to the stuffily rigid colonial society of her English father nor to the economically precarious but proudly exclusive circles of her Creole mother, a woman of marginal nervous stability. Her only instinctive alliance, and one her mother disapproves of, is with a black servant girl, an omen of her later adult alignment with "the insulted and injured" outcast in Europe. But even here, the general hostility of the subservient natives as a class is a constant source of tension for a girl uncertain of her social identity. In terms of pubescent sexual experience, the girl's passive acceptance of an elderly eccentric's salacious talk and furtive pawing convinces her that she is naturally bad and therefore outside the whole structure of conventional convent-taught morality. (In the deeply felt "Goodbye Marcus, Goodbye Rose," a recently published sketch, the girl bids farewell to her own two pretend-children about whom she and her classmates had heretofore fantasized.)

The apparent ease and simplicity of this self-judgment along with her unreflecting passivity, remain highly typical traits throughout her career—the epistemological sanction for most judgments of self and others is simply emotive, never discursively rational, sometimes barely conscious. This passive-emotive decision making reaches a frozen impasse when one protagonist decides on whether or not to go from France to England to visit an ailing mother by the chance of a taxi horn's blowing before she counts to three. And the most frequent charge against persons she dislikes is their incapacity to feel, their refusal, in effect, to experience emotion. Many characteristics of the protagonists' epistemology bear a remarkable resemblance to those illustrated in the second half of Dostoevsky's "Notes from Underground," in itself a *locus classicus* for tense moods of reclusive alienation. One of the Rhys protagonists, in fact, disagrees with her uncle in his facile dismissal of Dostoevsky's world view, in a scene that constitutes one of the author's most acute confrontations between the alienated and the solidly bourgeois.

After a convent education in the West Indies and a brief period at an English girls' school just before World War I, the girl decides on a stage career on the basis of several scraps of praise for her portrayal of Autolycus in a school production of *A Winter's Tale*. Typically, the girl includes in her performance words and phrases which some of the teachers wanted to censor. Already we sense the Rhys protagonist's virulent hostility to the ranks of the respectable.

The girl launches herself on an independent course, after a short period at the Royal Academy of Dramatic Art, with the partly grudging, partly relieved permission of distant relatives, by joining the chorus for the provincial tour of an English musical comedy. From this point on, the Rhys protagonist's career is fairly stable in its typicality and predictability, if rather unstable in terms of economic and emotional security. "Reckless, lazy, a vagabond by nature" (*Quartet*, 14), the girl seems to accept with a quiet passivity, after a brief initial revulsion, the attentions of well-off young bachelors; partly schooled by more experienced fellow chorines, partly induced by an insatiable delight in luxurious clothing and a need to feel protected, she goes from one fairly deep emotional involvement through a series of liaisons to a madcap marriage with a dashing, free-wheeling, pettily criminal young man whose appeal is his capacity to live entirely in the present moment. At this point, the early 1920s, she discovers in the Left Bank a more congenial *ambiance* than in the gray streets of London.

She may briefly attempt to work as a manicurist, an artist's model, a teacher of English, or a mannequin, but never for more than a few days at a time, since the slightest contact with middle-class regularity shatters her nerves. Essentially, her life, following the death of a baby and the departure of her husband after he has served a jail sentence, is that of a drifting mistress, sometimes kept for a period of time, sometimes dependent on casual street encounters. When she receives a windfall payment from a present or former lover, new clothes are the first concern; but she has also learned to live with hunger. This lust for new clothes is largely a matter of keeping up street appearances before the implacable phalanxes of the respectable; it recalls the machinations of Dostoevsky's underground man to obtain a new beaver collar for his coat when he plans to go out and jostle the elegant strollers on the Nevsky Prospect.

The tone of her experience becomes the sour, rebellious despair of an aging outcast in Europe, given to the false consolations of alcohol and veronal, occasionally begging from former lovers or disapproving relatives, but still retaining token independence and defiance, as her beauty wanes. The Rhys protagonist is giving a local habitation to the same concerns as Dostoevsky's underground man, who asks within his own context of experience whether a man who takes a perverse pleasure in his own humiliation can possibly retain any degree of self-respect. Much of the direct aim of Miss Rhys's writing, especially at this state of the protagonist's career, is to communicate the emotional states of a rudderless beggar-drifter in Paris—the depressing wallpaper of the cheap hotels, the care to avoid cafes where one has wept openly or made a scene, the spiritless encounters with casual men in which the woman depends on a gradually diminishing charm in order not to reveal too soon in the evening her desperately passive dependence on the man's gratuity—either to him or to herself.

The author aims cleanly and taciturnly at communication of emotion,
though various readers will respond to the presentation of these emotional
states in ways suggested by their own experience, education, and values:
Marxist, feminist, formalist, or clinically psychological readers will place dif-
fering emphases; feminist critics occasionally use the dilemma of the protagonist to illustrate assumptions that Rhys herself denies and that have no source in
the text. However, if there is a thematic core to the whole varied body of
work, it is the evocation of the radical loneliness and despair of a woman who
has always been outside the pale of ordinary respectability, tinged with a
defiant determination not to let defenses down, not to give an inch of advantage to the enemy in spite of poverty and hopelessness.

From a sociological viewpoint, Miss Rhys gives voice to a class and type of
person rarely heard in English writing since the eighteenth century, but her
works do not supply enough exterior detail to be hailed as documentary in any
sense. The closest analogue I can find for the peculiarly desperate, passive,
haunting, hopelessly melancholy loneliness of these pages is in the lady
diarists of Heian Japan—Lady Murasaki's *Tale of Genji* and Sei Shonagon's
Pillow Book, but most particularly The Mother of Michitsuna's *The Gossamer
Years (Kagero Nikki).* Both the Heian diarists and Miss Rhys present the impasse of a helpless woman entirely dependent on the casual whims of male
attention, who must maintain a mask of elegant indifference and unruffled
economic security as she desperately watches both her material means and her
personal beauty decline.

In this world, there are certain constants. Paris grants anonymity and even
the possibility of positive pleasure in youth, whereas England's cold climate
and darkly oppressive streets constitute an inferno for the Rhys woman. One
must have money to buttress respectability, which she early discovers to be
the single, massive, anathematic force in her experience. Meanly spying land-
ladies and policemen are the immediate agents of the hypocritically punc-
tilious, emotionlessly calculating, penny-pinching majority, who can kill
with a glance. The only escape from this dour army are the well-off bachelors
who are willing to support a mistress in lodgings and supply pretty clothes,
good times, and an occasional weekend in the country as long as their initial
passion lasts.

II

Miss Rhys's first publication, *The Left Bank, Sketches and Studies of Present-Day*

Bohemian Paris, includes a few West Indian vignettes along with Paris material, some of which show up in fuller form in later fiction—for example, the sketch "From a French Prison" parallels certain chapters of her first novel, *Quartet.* The most impressive piece is "La Grosse Fifi," detailing the narrator Roseau's observations of fat, vulgar Fifi's stormy amours with a young gigolo, who later murders her when she objects to his proposed marriage to a young girl. The refraction of Fifi's life through the mind of Roseau guarantees instant and implicit sympathy, since Roseau, despite her morose manner, is herself a similar (if quieter) outcast from respectability whom Fifi tries to resuscitate. In Roseau's allying with Fifi rather than with her snobbishly disapproving friends, the upright Olsens, Miss Rhys initiates a strategy that becomes familiar in later work—if the focus is not on the experience of the protagonist/narrator herself, it is frequently transferred to another derelict. In one of Miss Rhys's late sketches, "Night Out, 1925," Suzy overpays a pair of whores from the wallet of her stingy escort to compensate them for failing to interest the couple. When Suzy's escort abandons her, she drapes a medallion given her by one of the whores over a discarded red hat in the gutter. This image, by no means as sentimental as it may sound in summary, combines her sympathy for the unlucky whores with an extension to whoever lost the red hat in whatever sad circumstances.

Though slightly marred by explicit "description" of characters here and there, Miss Rhys's first long work, *Quartet,* presents the absolute confrontation between the outcast and the respectable in a taut domestic situation. Marya Zelli, without resources during the imprisonment of her husband for fraud in the sale of art works, is taken in by Hugh and Lois Heidler, rich dilettantes of the Left Bank who repeatedly "adopt" vagabonds and repeatedly quarrel with them. Although at first the offer is simply one of succor, it soon becomes evident that Hugh is overmastered by a passion for Marya, in which his wife, Lois, is prepared to acquiesce for his sake, though she extracts her price in insisting Marya show up at social functions to quell the gossip about the affair; she habitually practices mean little cruelties that would reduce Marya to the status of a family rag doll.

After a nasty domestic squabble, Hugh removes Marya to a cheap hotel as an occasional mistress. The Heidlers' attempt almost literally to enslave Marya is balked when she leaps from a taxi, after her husband's release from prison, in her determination to be with him despite the Heidlers' disapproval.

The epigraph to this work, a verse by R. C. Dunning, warns against having any doings with Good Samaritans, and despite Miss Rhys's taciturn cleanliness of narration, the deck is stacked fairly heavily against the Heidlers—Hugh wants passion, but not at the cost of breaking with Lois, the perfect snobbish party hostess; Lois thinks she wants Hugh to have his fling, but she erupts in crying spells and endless petty cruelties to Marya. The Heidlers want to dabble in Bohemia without renouncing one bit of respectability.

From all the evidence given in the text, Marya is a helpless victim: at each important early juncture in the relationship, she would prefer not to take up with Hugh and Lois, but their indomitable bossing, coupled with her imprisoned husband's advice to take advantage of their largesse, pushes her into the menage. Once committed, she develops a hopeless love for Hugh, though apparently despising his character throughout. Frequently, the Rhys woman's position as a guest at a bourgeois household or celebration (a weekend in the country with the Heidlers) is generally similar to that of Dostoevsky's underground man at the farewell dinner for Zverkov, the sulking, resentful, brooding intruder whose enraged eruptions and denunciations are simply dismissed by the irritated host. To be sure, Miss Rhys presents such situations with certain differences due to a feminine protagonist and a set of manners removed from nineteenth-century St. Petersburg. And Marya is also much more passively helpless than the underground man, to a degree that taxes my own sympathies: if one frequently behaves like a rag doll, one's right to complain about rag-doll treatment is therefore qualified.

In the two years that intervened before her next novel, Miss Rhys's art matured remarkably; *After Leaving Mr. Mackenzie* is a poignant, masterful evocation of her peculiar blend of desperation, loneliness, and defiance. There is even less emphasis on narrative trajectory than in the slight "story" of the first novel, in favor of a consequent emphasis on mood-moments and individual confrontations. Julia Martin, having broken with rich Mr. Mackenzie in Paris, is cut off from her weekly stipend by a lump payment, which she angrily tears up; at their next encounter, she taps his cheek with her gloves in a restaurant. The bulk of the rest of the novel concerns her return to London to visit her dying mother while maintaining an acquaintance with Mr. Horsfield, a tepid interim lover. Always just a pound or two away from total poverty, abandoned, rejected, and despised, Julia nevertheless maintains an admirably integral grittiness, an assertion of her own autonomy in the face of impossibly bleak prospects and outright hatred by smugly respectable relatives. Her virtues are, without much exaggeration, those that sustain people who keep dignity in the face of incurable illnesses or prison death sentences.

The presentation is one of subtle nuance, in which juxtaposition of extremely short scenes often serves an expressive function. For example, we know that before the opening of the novel, Julia made a loudly hysterical scene at the Restaurant Albert; we then observe her second encounter with Mr. Mackenzie, when she follows him to the same restaurant, he fearing a recurrence of the ugliness, but getting off more easily with a soft slap. At the conclusion of the novel, perhaps in unconscious gratitude for her restraint at the restaurant, he actually goes over to Julia in the street, after her return from London, congratulating himself on his liberality in even acknowledging her existence, and when she asks him for a small sum, he cavalierly hands her most of the change from his pocket.

The situational irony at this juncture is complex, because in the meantime Julia has in part sustained herself on handouts from Mr. Horsfield, the only man in the Restaurant Albert who observed the slap and who followed her that evening out of interest at her pluck. There is an interesting implicit contrast between Mackenzie and Horsfield in themselves: the former is a very upright, respectable businessman whose general probity carries him through in bourgeois circles, despite the minor weaknesses of having written a few poems and having indulged in the secret liaison with Julia; Horsfield, by contrast, had earlier felt the same kind of smug superiority, the same self-satisfaction in using and discarding unfortunate victims, until wartime experience obliterated his sense of the categorical difference between exploiter and victim. At an important juncture in their London meetings, Julia remarks that seeming benefactors often extract one's life story in lurid detail, and then take subtle pleasure in refusing to give one a penny. Horsfield responds that the pleasure is not so subtle—it is direct and brutal—but that he has learned it is also mistaken and cruel. Julia mentioned this kind of situation because she had just asked money of her uncle, who is even more summarily cruel than Mr. Mackenzie; after pumping her for details of her failed marriage, he refuses her absolutely, only relenting to the extent of one pound to pay her fare back to France. Perhaps the most trenchant focus for the oppositeness of Julia and her uncle is in his puzzled opacity in the face of her assertion that Dostoevsky saw man's condition clearly.

The Marya of *Quartet* was at a somewhat younger phase, when her physical appeal still gave her a minimal confidence; whereas Julia has begun to sense the onset of middle age—indeed, one agressive young Parisian pursues her vigorously until he catches a close look at her face in a good light and then departs muttering, *"Oh, la, la, . . . Ah, non, alors."* As she walks through the tawdry Halles quarter, she no longer feels a quick sympathy for tired horses or doorway drunks: Julia realizes that through an accumulation of troubles, she has ended up where most hard-hearted respectable people begin, with an impassive coldness toward the suffering of others. This sense of both physical and spiritual aging gives peculiarly painful poignancy to the closing lines, "The street was cool and full of grey shadows. Lights were beginning to come out in the cafes. It was the hour between dog and wolf, as they say" (191).

In her fourth work, *Voyage in the Dark,* Miss Rhys gives us her typical protagonist, now named Anna Morgan, at a much earlier stage in her career, two years after her arrival in England from the West Indies. The work teems with minor characters, complexity of perceived detail, and an increased emphasis on story line—altogether thicker in texture than any of the preceding novels. In addition, the psychological complexity of Anna's presentation is augmented by sudden recalls of fairly lurid, frightening details from her Caribbean childhood. The substance of the narration concerns Anna's loss of virginity during her chorus-girl phase, and the subsequent breakup of this first love attachment, followed by a brief period as manicurist to a masseuse and a series of brief liaisons and one-night encounters.

The previous novel treated in an elegiac tone the onset of middle age for a vagabond woman; now the author is looking back to a protagonist who recalls her first menstruation, undergoes sexual initiation and later disillusionment, culminating in a lonely, nightmarish, fear-ridden abortion. From the outset, Anna always instinctively turns toward others outside received society rather than to their respectable persecutors: as a child, she is obsessed by the very name of a slave in family estate records; she is only happy with the black cook Francine, and fervently wishes *she* could be black; perplexed by her first menstruation, she goes immediately to Francine, who reassures her gently, but her fears are revived in a subsequent talk with her mother. Even as an adult, when the forty-year-old masseuse takes her to a cinema in Camden Town, Anna sympathizes totally with Three-Fingered Kate, the burglaress, and feels the audience always applauds in the wrong places, as when the police arrive to arrest Kate. Rhys's implicit view of society shares many of the assumptions of Jean Genet.

As she makes her first encounter with the edges of English society, she shows little of the *savior-faire* of her more seasoned comrades and their playboy admirers, and despite their best efforts to initiate her, she persists in her own peculiar nonconformity. She frequently looks sad, withdrawn, and contemplative in situations where a chorine is uniformly expected to be chipper and sparkling, again like the underground man at Zverkov's banquet. She repulses the attentions of men who do not stimulate her romantically, but when she does find the right man, Walter Jeffries, she relates herself to him in terms of a loving equal, despite what all the pulp fiction, her fellow *artistes,* and even the playboys themselves tell her about the evanescence of the man's interest. Indeed, one of Walter's reasons for tiring of her is that Anna burdens him like a heavy stone, rather than taking vigorous advantage of his offer of singing lessons and professional contracts. Unlike her more astute friends, she never saves a penny, and when Walter breaks up with her, Anna impulsively refuses help (just as Julia tore up Mr. Mackenzie's parting check). This passive failure of the instinct of self-advancement again demonstrates that the Rhys protagonist hasn't a bourgeois bone in her body.

In Part Two, when Anna has come on desperate times, she is appropriated by the masseuse Ethel Matthews, who takes her up on the impressive strength of her owning a fur coat. But after an occasional success with men like a rich visiting American bussinessman, Anna's seeming lumpish passivity culminates in a pregnancy that is three months advanced before she seeks help. Ether abandons her in anger and exasperation.

In contrast to the narration itself, my summary runs the danger of moralizing, to the degree that it incorporates as explicit statement certain value-conclusions which are presented in the text as extremely subtle implicit meanings. Miss Rhys's own emphasis is on the reader's participatory sharing in Anna's sensibility, without generalization. The most masterful effects are in the juxtaposition of present emotional states and recalled childhood traumas, with the hallucinatory abortion at the end as a general recall of previous imagistic *leitmotifs.* In the flow of Anna's contemporary experience, the implicit meanings are carried by scraps of songs or conventional pictures on the walls, and especially by images of walls and streets associated with the stern, repressive grayness of English morality. The Caribbean memories, like that of the face of a noseless victim of yaws, tend toward drama and horror.

A morose verse of Emily Dickinson provides the title of Miss Rhys's fourth novel, *Good Morning, Midnight,* which takes us forward in the protagonist's career to 1937. This novel moves along on a rich flow of perceived detail, even fuller than in the preceeding novel, though the narrative progress is considerably less evident; indeed, this seems by far the most episodic of all her novels. In other works, there is a surface commitment to the detached moment, but one senses the steady flow of the story underneath—in *Voyage in the Dark,* for example, the stages in the initiation of a young girl. In this novel, seemingly random street encounters and lengthy reminiscences take up the first three parts. Sasha Jansen, the protagonist, is in Paris for a brief rest, financed by a London friend who wishes to rescue her from her immersion in alcohol. The novel ends, in Part Four, on Sasha's tense, dramatic, shattering confrontation with gigolo René—a devastating impasse which, even if it does seem to stem from the cliché comic encounter of a gigolo and a streetwalker, is handled with masterful power and gripping emotion that give it profound human significance.

On reaching this final scene, the reader senses a structural ambiguity in the work that may be either a weakness or a strength, perhaps depending on the depth of one's sympathy for Sasha's whole world view. One feels the final scene concentrates the essence of Sasha's whole experience, and yet the drifting, episodic character of much of the previous material does not encourage one to expect a definitive conclusion. In short, the loose structure may be an organic expression of living from moment to moment.

Part One sketches out situation and mood, along with preliminary recall of earlier passages in Sasha's life; Part Two is entirely taken up by an encounter with a subduedly disillusioned Russian who introduces her to an eccentric Dutch painter. Part Three consists of Sasha's memories of her earlier vagabond marriage to the ebullient Enno, and her loss of a baby. To be sure, Sasha first meets René at the end of Part One, but the reader barely distinguishes him from the texture of other random encounters.

What *may* serve to hold together the exceedingly disparate materials of the first three parts—and may even weld them to the climactic fourth part—is the common theme of down-and-outers, of people at the end of the tether, derelicts at the edge of desperation, like the tramp in a Halles-quarter *café* who tried to eat his glass to earn a drink. The material makes one think of the James Purdy of "63: Dream Palace" or *Eustace Chisholm and the Works.*

Sasha herself, in recalling her humiliating days as a receptionist at a *haute couture* establishment, dwells on her English employer's spite (the animus against the English is strong in all these novels): perhaps his type has the power to cut off one's legs at one blow, but should he then have the right to ridicule the cripple? She later recalls a grim period when she was living in a cheap hotel. On leaving a *café* with a casual escort, Sasha staggered from drunkenness, saying she'd not eaten in three weeks; as a result, the man slammed the taxi door in her face and raced off. A train of such incidents illustrates the hideous irony that the more desperate one is, the more cruelly people treat one; the more one needs help, the less one gets. As a capstone to this kind of reminiscence, the Dutch painter recalls finding a sobbing, drunken mulatto woman in his hallway during a London sojourn in Notting Hill Gate. She had lived for two years with a man she didn't love, who only tolerated her for her cooking. She almost never went outdoors because one time when she entered the street at twilight, a child had shouted, "I hate you and I wish you were dead."

This emphasis on the lacerating pain of such humiliations raises a central issue of interpretation and of value in Rhys. The financially, socially, and mentally secure middle-class reader may have difficulty understanding the point of such anecdotes. If one steps out of a suburban home and the child next door shouts such a remark, one either laughs it off or gives the parents the name of a good psychiatrist. It becomes obvious that the reference to Dostoevsky in *After Leaving Mr. Mackenzie* is not just window dressing: the narrator of "Notes from Underground" has the same open-wound sensitivity to slights like being jostled on the street. It would be too facile to dismiss both Dostoevsky and Rhys as chroniclers of a certain cast of neurotic sensibility (though the observation is true); the value of their art lies in its achievement in inducing readers to extend imaginative sympathy toward the insulted and injured.

But if we recall how Dostoevsky's protagonist got revenge for his many humiliations—by seeming to redeem a prostitute by genuine love, and then cruelly debasing her—the final section of this novel becomes clearer. Sasha indeed tells herself when she first meets René that his tales of service in the Foreign Legion are lies, but she will lead him on with the lure of her fur coat (the same bait that drew the masseuse in the preceding novel) into thinking her a lonely, rich woman and will then slap him down to get revenge for her own humiliations.

In Part Four, in the final confrontation in her room, Dostoevskian ironies proliferate. Sasha refuses René's overtures (though she has been ambivalent about his sexual appeal), and he threatens violence because, though an obvious gigolo, his male pride is piqued. Sasha offers him money from her purse if he will only leave, and when he discovers that this *is* all the money she has, he departs. There is a very subtle suggestion that each of the down-and-outers comes to see the other's wretchedness, though the multiple ambiguities leave open many paths of interpretation.[2]

But the *tone* of the ending is certainly not one of tender sympathy triumphant. In another Dostoevskian reversal, Sasha lies naked on her bed with the door open hoping against hope that René will return and take her passionately. Instead, the repellent traveling salesman from the next room, a man who has despised and vilified her, enters and takes her as she moans Molly-Bloom yeses.

Miss Rhys's latest novel, *Wide Sargasso Sea*, receives full treatment in Todd Bender's essay in this volume, so I shall simply remark that this attempt to right Charlotte Brontë's apparent prejudice against the West Indies in *Jane Eyre* carries forward typical thematic interests. For one thing, the experience of the protagonist fits interestingly into the standard Rhys pattern of what Ford Madox Ford called her "underdog" sympathies.[3] The vindication of Rochester's mad wife, a bit like Anna Morgan's cheering on Three-Fingered Kate at the movies, does not express itself as partisan pleading or tourist brochure blurbs; by simply inducing the reader to share the experience of an outcast, Miss Rhys puts her faith, as she does in all her works, in the proverb *Tout comprendre, c'est tout pardonner.*

NOTES

1. I am aware that it is a precarious speculative venture to extract this general career from eight different books; but I think the pattern will be clear to anyone who reads the *oeuvre*. Miss Rhys has stated that her writing stems from personal experience and that it had its genesis in diary form. Her autobiographical reminiscences are collected as *Smile Please: An Unfinished Autobiography* (Berkeley: Donald Ellis/Creative Arts, 1979). And valuable biographical information appears in Thomas F. Staley, *Jean Rhys: A Critical Study* (Austin: Univ. of Texas Press, 1979), Chapter 1, "Art and Experience," 1–19. In the following list of Rhys's works, the date in parentheses is that of the currently available reprint by Andre Deutsch; all books were published in London. *The Left Bank, Sketches and Studies of Present-Day Bohemian Paris*, 1927; *Postures*, 1928 (the American title, *Quartet* [1969] was preferred by the author); *After Leaving Mr. Mackenzie*, 1931 (1969); *Voyage in the Dark*, 1934 (1967); *Good Morning, Midnight*, 1939 (1967); *Wide Sargasso Sea*, 1966; *Tigers Are Better-Looking; with a Selection from The Left Bank*, 1968; and *Sleep It Off, Lady*, 1976.

2. For literary archeologists, a careful comparison of this situation with the short sketch "The Chevalier of the Place Blanche," a freely adapted translation from Edouard de Neve in *Sleep It Off, Lady*, will show interesting parallels.

3. Ford Madox Ford, *The March of Literature, from Confucius to Modern Times* (London: George Allen and Unwin, 1947), 734.

Nature and Aristocracy
in V. Sackville-West

CAROL AMES

The unifying sensibility in Victoria Sackville-West's gardening articles, poetry, and fiction is her romantic concept of the aristocrat as the person most capable of achieving a continuing, nurturing harmony with the natural environment. She gradually softens her grievance against a society which excludes a woman from inheriting and caring for the land she loves. Vita Sackville-West comes to believe that a person who allows his inheritance to bind him to conventionality or to encourage a self-centeredness based on hereditary privilege is not a true aristocrat; he is destructive to himself and the society which has endured because of the energy, initiative, and creativity of the natural aristocrat who is in harmony with himself, with his inferiors, with his equals, and most important of all, with his land. Eventually, however, Sackville-West's novels show a realization that a jealous love of place can interfere with open, generous love and mutual respect between two people.

V. Sackville-West is now best known for the confession of a passionate affair with another woman which was published by her son Nigel Nicolson in *Portrait of a Marriage,* and as the model for Virginia Woolf's *Orlando.* People read letters she wrote to Harold Nicolson, her husband of forty-nine years, which are printed in the various volumes of his *Diaries and Letters*; the garden they created at Sissinghurst is visited by many people each year. She was, however, a prolific writer who deserves to be remembered for the merits of her writing. Her articles on gardening and essays on diverse subjects appeared in

newspapers and magazines; her novels and biographies were successful with
both critics and the general reader; for her poetry she received the Hawthorn-
den Prize for *The Land* in 1927 and the Heinemann Prize for *The Garden* in
1947.

Sackville-West's concept of aristocracy causes American readers difficulty.
There is evidence that she was aware of this problem, and she suggests her own
solution. In a letter to Nicolson responding to Edmund Wilson's article in
The New Yorker about H. N.'s writing she said: "where he goes wrong over
criticising you for so obviously belonging to a definite class, by birth, education, experience and consequent outlook, is that he ought to have stated it as a
fact and not as an adverse criticism. He is falling into a common error of
critics, which is to demand that a writer shall be something he is not. . . . I
think that both your merits and your shortcomings as a writer proceed from
things in your own character."[1] What most influences her own character is her
upbringing as a member of the upper nobility and her bitterness that English
law does not allow a woman to inherit land. Her amazing ability to create
strong, independent female characters and to convey the value of union with
nature stem from this background; the sense of isolation and of being essentially different from other people, which may be a limitation in her writing,
also originates in this background.

Sackville-West grew up loving Knole as the epitome of all that is good in
English life and English architecture. Records of Knole date back to 1281. In
1456 Knole was sold to the Archbishop of Canterbury and in 1566 Queen
Elizabeth granted it to Thomas Sackville.[2] Vita Sackville-West seems to value
Knole most for its gradual and organic development. She deplores houses
built all at once by a *nouveau riche* owner with pretensions to being country
gentry. In *English Country Houses* (1942) she says a real house "is essentially
part of the country, not only *in* the country, but part of it, a natural growth.
Irrespective of grandeur or modesty, it should agree with its landscape and
suggest the life of its inhabitants past or present; should never overwhelm its
surroundings."[3] She adds that "the charmed genius of our domestic architecture lay in its gradual and continuous development" (*Houses*, 10), and she
believes that Knole is a primary example of this genius:

> One of the largest houses in England, Knole may stand as representative
> of the enormous homes erected for themselves by the Elizabethan and
> Jacobean nobility. Yet here again we find that Knole grew, and that its
> gables (which give it so peculiarly Elizabethan a character) were added to
> an earlier structure. Once the palace of the Archbishops of Canterbury,

then a royal palace, Knole came to its fulfilment as the home of an English family in whose hands it has remained ever since 1566. It is an interesting example of a house which, although so vast in extent (being built round a system of seven courtyards and covering over five acres of ground), is yet perfectly subdued in its external parts.

(*Houses*, 24)

Thus, despite its size and lavishness, despite what seems to most people conspicuous consumption and the inequality of the feudal age, Knole represents the harmony with its surroundings of the gradual evolution that Sackville-West holds as a primary value.

Sackville-West maintains a feudal perspective, developed during her child-hood at Knole, as she watches the world change. During World War II, she wrote to Nicolson: "It is silly and selfish of me to say I mind the war, when so many people are suffering from it so infinitely more, but one does mind watching the downfall of all the things one cared about. . . ." (*War Years*, 158). At times she wished she could be more flexible: "I feel one ought to be able to adapt oneself, and not struggle to go back to, and live in, an obsolete tradition" (*War Years*, 420). Nevertheless, the thought that a bus route might run near Sissinghurst brings on an outburst: "I hate democracy, I hate *la populace*. I wish education had never been introduced. I don't like tyranny, but I like an intelligent oligarchy. . . . (It's rather what most men feel about most women!)" (*War Years*, 433). When Knole was damaged by bombs, she felt she should have been there to share its wounds (*War Years*, 350).

And when Knole had to be given to the National Trust in 1947, she wrote:

> . . . times when beauty and all that stands for culture make no more impact on men's ears than the unreality of a dead language—in such times it comes as a plumb luxury to indulge even for a moment in the contemplation of something so very different, something so unnecessary, so inordinate, prodigal, extravagant, and traditional, as the great houses of the past. Of the past they are indeed, not only in century but in spirit; anachronisms both in time and in tenure. Yet in their growth they were organic, and in their creation they involved the completion of many a human life, the life of the craftsman who laboured, the stone-mason, the carver, the carpenter, the builder of chimneys, and the life also of those who ordered and enjoyed. . . .

(*Knole*, 215)

Thus, like the cathedrals of the past, the house is the living monument to the lives of the entire community of people of various ranks and duties living under its roofs, and to the lives of the artists of an earlier time who are known by their works, not by their names. She wonders, "But what of those to whom these things belonged by birthright, and who belonged to the service of these things by tradition? Shall they weep over the passing, or shall they cultivate the philosophy that the old world must with cheerfulness relinquish its heritage into the hands of the new?" (*Knole*, 217). To Sackville-West "the service of these things" is as much a part of the feudal tradition as the privileges of ownership; one might call it stewardship rather than ownership. An aristocrat of the past held the house and the land in trust for future generations, a trust whose obligations only the national government now has resources to support.

But because she was born a woman, Vita Sackville-West can never become the steward of the buildings, lands, and gardens of Knole. Succession is to a male heir, her cousin. Her mother, the illegitimate daughter of a Sackville by the Spanish dancer Pepita, married her cousin, the heir, but for Vita Sackville-West marriage and her father's death mean exile from Knole. Nigel Nicolson tells of his mother's reaction to Virginia Woolf's *Orlando* (1928): "She loved it. Naturally she was flattered, but more than that, the novel identified her with Knole forever. Virginia by her genius had provided Vita a unique consolation for having been born a girl, for her exclusion from her inheritance, for her father's death earlier that year. The book, for her, was not simply a brilliant masque or pageant. It was a memorial mass."[4] Perhaps *Orlando* could console her for losing Knole, but it could not replace Knole in her heart.

She did not marry the landed heir of some other great family, because she felt that the aristocrats of her day were insipid and decadent, smothered by the weight of tradition and social convention. She believed that she had been saved from such insipidness by her passionate, creative, Spanish blood, which gave her the daring and energy that she identified with the true aristocrats of the feudal age.

She seems to have fallen in love with Harold Nicolson's energy, intelligence, and the sunny nature contrasting her own. In the confession in *Portrait of a Marriage*, she says: "The delay over my engagement began to irritate me, and one day I wrote to Harold saying we had perhaps better give up the idea. He sent me a despairing telegram in reply and then I scarcely know what happened inside my heart: something snapped, and I loved Harold from that day on; I think his energy in sending me a telegram impressed me, just as I was impressed when he came after me in an aeroplane when I ran away" (*Portrait*, 35). She also loved a childhood friend, Rosamund

Grosvenor, at the time of her marriage. She thought that love of Knole and love of a man are mutually exclusive, but not love of a man and love of a woman. Law separated her from the first great love of her life, Knole.

In the early years after the birth of her two sons, when her marriage does not yet seem to offer her a steadying continuity, she became embroiled in a passionate affair with Violet Trefusis, which she writes about so movingly in the autobiographical sections of *Portrait of a Marriage.* For the first time she agonizes about her love of women: "It never struck me as wrong that I should be more or less engaged to Harold, and at the same time very much in love with Rosamund" (*Portrait*, 33). She comes to see herself as a divided person: "But, as a sole justification, I separate my loves into two halves: Harold, who is unalterable, perennial, and *best*; there has never been anything but absolute purity in my love for Harold, just as there has never been anything but absolute bright purity in his nature. And on the other hand stands my perverted nature, which loved and tyrannized over Rosamund and ended by deserting her without one heart-pang, and which now is linked irremediably with Violet" (*Portrait*, 34). Though she eventually separated from Violet, she continued to have sporadic affairs with both women and men, and Harold had liaisons with men. The resolution of her difficulty once more stems from her aristocratic background: she makes a commitment to a continuing and permanent, an "unalterable, perennial" value—her marriage; her marriage, like an aristocrat's stewardship of his estate, allows, but outlasts, other interests or passions. Thus, her marriage and the continuing life and gardens she and Harold Nicolson built together embodied the feudal values of Knole and the Sackvilles.

Her articles on gardening and her poems *The Land* (1926) and *The Garden* (1946) advocate the same princples of stewardship, continuity, and union with nature's yearly cycle. Nigel Nicolson says of their garden at Sissinghurst: "When a season has produced its best, that part of the garden must be allowed to lie fallow for another year, since there is a cycle in nature that must not be disguised. It is eternally renewable, like a play with acts and scenes: there can be a change of cast, but the script remains the same. Permanence and mutation are the secrets of this garden" (*Portrait*, 224). Like the best of the old houses, a garden, according to Vita Sackville-West, should grow organically: "The owner, or tenant, is usually in a hurry to produce an immediate effect, which is humanly understandable but is bad gardening, since good gardening is a matter of infinite patience."[5] Besides patience, good gardening requires a sense of harmony and oneness with the natural world, as the titles of some of her gardening articles show: "Daylilies Are Obliging Plants"; "A Dignified and Comely Magnolia"; "A Hint from Nature"; and "Generous Old Roses." The plants can only be obliging, dignified, and generous if the gardener fulfills his obligations to nurture, care for, weed, trim, and transplant.

The same concerns found in her articles on gardening are obvious in her poetry. In the opening lines of *The Land* she says:

> I sing the cycle of my country's year,
> I sing the tillage, and the reaping sing,
> Classic monotony, that modes and wars
> Leave undisturbed, unbettered, for their best
> Was born immediate, of expediency.
> The sickle sought no art; the axe, the share
> Draped no superfluous beauty round their steel.[6]

The aristocratic houses such as Knole developed slowly, as did the traditional farming practices and tools, in response to felt need. And stewardship of such a house or such land or such a garden does not imply romantic indolence but active participation and hard work:

> But I, like him, who strive
> Closely with earth, and know her grudging mind,
> Will sing no songs of bounty, for I see
> Only the battle between man and earth,
> The sweat, the weariness, the care, the balk;
> . . . .
> Husbands alone force fruitfulness and tilth;
> Strange lovers, man and earth! their love and hate
> Braided in mutual need; and of their strife
> A tired contentment born.
>
> (*Land*, 21)

Man and nature are interdependent.

Any superiority of man over nature requires superior duty, as the aristocrat's superiority demands superior duty toward the land and people under his care. In "Moral Tangles," a gardening article about digging up a spadeful of earth to transplant and therefore rescue one particular plant, she writes: "All a living tangle underground, struggling together, and me the superior human with my sharp weapon, prising up the chosen plant I wanted, destroying all that other scrambling and wrestling, which might have come to completion had I not interfered" (*Gardening*, 27-28). But any kind of tilling and any kind of growth imply such destruction and such value judgments.

As Michael Stevens says, "The idea, and particularly the title, of *The Land*, which V S-W probably began writing in 1923, should be regarded to some extent as an answer to *The Waste Land* (1922)."[7] For V. Sackville-West, duty to onself and to nature involves "forcing fruitfulness" from the soil.

While believing that her creativity belonged to the wild, Mediterranean side of her nature, she also believed that art came from her approaching her material with the same careful craftsmanship and husbandry as she approached her gardening. She says, "The poet like the artisan / Works lonely with his tools . . ." (*Land*, 87). Like good gardening, writing demands patience, hard work, and a sensitivity to the needs of the material:

> All craftsmen share a knowledge. They have held
>   Reality down fluttering to a bench;
> Cut wood to their own purposes; compelled
> The growth of pattern with the patient shuttle;
>   Drained acres to a trench.
>   Control is theirs. . . .
>
> (*Land*, 86)

Precision of detail and observed experience make the poems informative and the gardening articles poetic. Sackville-West reports that Virginia Woolf read *The Land*: "She was disappointed, but very sweet about it. She says it is a contribution to English literature, and is a solid fact against which one can lean up without fear of its giving way. She also says it is one of the few *interesting* poems—I mean the information part" (*Portrait*, 208). Vita wrote Harold Nicolson another of Virginia's comments: "She asks if there is something in me which does not vibrate, a 'something reserved, muted. . . . The thing I call "central transparency" sometimes fails you in your writing.' Damn the woman, she has put her finger on it. There *is* something muted. What is it, Hadji? Something that doesn't come alive. I brood and brood, feel I am groping in a dark tunnel. It makes everything I write a little unreal; gives the effect of having been done from outside" (*Portrait*, 212). I believe that the sense of writing from the outside comes from the same source as many of the greatest virtues in her writing—from her sense of herself as being aristocratic and therefore different in some essential way from other people. While she can convey the nuances of harmony between an individual and nature, her depictions of relationships between two people are less subtle, except perhaps when the two relate through their separate though congruent love of a house, estate, or garden.

This sense of an essential difference in background and in sensibility probably accounts for her being dismissed by many of the members of the Bloomsbury group. It probably also accounts for the sense of strangeness one feels in some of her later works when she isolated herself more and more from society to write and cultivate her garden at Sissinghurst, where the family moved in 1930. Nicolson visited Sissinghurst on weekends, and they kept in touch through numerous letters rather than in daily, intimate conversations. In several of her novels published in this period, love of place and the definition of aristocracy are central preoccupations. At Sissinghurst, as she made fewer attempts to overcome her sense of her own difference from most people, her novels show characters more and more cut off from any sense of a community of interest or feeling except perhaps with one person. The one chosen person empathizes with a character's sense of place, and after a prolonged test is allowed to glimpse his or her secret, interior life.

In *The Edwardians* (1930), Sackville-West begins to question the degree of freedom available to both the male heir and the daughter of Chevron, a large estate resembling Knole. Her tentative conclusion is that the restriction against the girl's inheriting the land may actually force her to become creative and daring, approximating the writer's ideal of the Renaissance aristocrats; in contrast, the son, who is subjected to fewer restrictions, may be tempted to succumb to the lure of "playing the part" of aristocrat. Only a revitalizing influence might save him.

As always, Sackville-West does not sympathize with those who fear others' opinions of them. Of the fashionable society of Sebastian and Viola's mother, she says, "The code was rigid. Within the closed circle of their own set, anybody might do as they pleased, but no scandal must leak out to the uninitiated. Appearances must be respected, though morals might be neglected."[8] People who follow the code may believe they have superior freedom because of their exalted positions, but they are deluding themselves, because they cannot act in harmony with their own desires.

The revitalizing force in this novel is Anquetil, the explorer and foreign traveler who feels that Sebastian can be saved from wasting his life. Anquetil tries to force Sebastian to examine his values. Early in the novel Sebastian senses that what Chevron represents is actually antithetical to what his mother's fashionable society represents: "He felt . . . that in the placid continuity of Chevron lay a vitality of an order different from the brilliant excitement of his mother's world" (*Edwardians*, 63). Anquetil thinks "they *ought* to rebel against the oppression of the past" (*Edwardians*, 69). Still, he realizes that all that is good in Sebastian comes into focus in his careful concern for and interest in estate matters. Anquetil's influence is insufficient to overcome the lures and pressures for a young man to fall into the accepted pattern. Sebastian has an affair with his mother's friend Lady Roehampton and seems destined for a life of superficial excitement.

Anquetil's influence is more effective with Viola, because she has always chafed at restrictions, perhaps because society imposes more restrictions on a girl than on a boy. She hates the fuss, the wasted time, and the restrictiveness of wearing dresses, having her hair done, and making polite conversation. She rebels openly: "Viola had rebelled; on one unforgettable evening at Chevron, after dinner, she had announced that she had taken a flat in London. 'You prevented me from going to Cambridge, Mother, but you can't prevent me from doing this. I'm of age.' That phrase had entered Lucy's soul as a dagger. She had never heard it before as applied to a girl . . ." (*Edwardians,* 281). Sebastian realizes that she has done what is right and necessary: "I wish I had her courage, and I envy it" (*Edwardians,* 283). He finds the role of Lord of the Manor too seductive, however. Dressed in the full grandeur of the robes of his caste, he participates in the coronation, which embodies all of the glamor and the weight of tradition, but which in this case also represents the end of an era. Afterwards when he bumps into Anquetil, he learns that the explorer and his sister will be married in three years when Anquetil returns from his next expedition. Sebastian goes with him, leaving the old era and the superficial, effete, decadent aristocracy behind him. Nevertheless, the novel is a kind of requiem for the probable passing of both the good and the bad in the feudal way of life.

All Passion Spent (1931) posits that it is never too late to free oneself by declaring oneself independent of society's pressures and expectations. At the death of Deborah's ninety-four-year-old husband, she is eighty-eight. She finally declares that she will satisfy her own needs. Her first step is to arrange to move into a little house she saw and liked many years before. She refuses to see her family, lives with her memories and associates only with "those who are nearer to their death than to their birth."[9] One consolation is that her belated acts of rebellion may serve as a model for one great-granddaughter.

When their old father dies, Deborah's children assume that she will allow them to arrange her life according to their ideas: "Mother had no will of her own; all her life long, gracious and gentle, she had been wholly submissive—an appendage" (*Passion,* 15). She at last finds the strength to claim her own life: "I have considered the eyes of the world for so long that I think it is time I had a little holiday from them. If one is not to please oneself in old age, when is one to please oneself? There is so little time left!" (*Passion*, 58). She wants to be only with the people such as old Mr. Bucktrout, who understands her feeling for the house which together they slowly transform into a place which belongs to her, unlike various embassies and mansions in which she has functioned as the viceroy's or ambassador's hostess, his legal possession.

Through Deborah's introspection and her memories we learn of the dreams she has sacrificed while no one has realized that she is not superbly satisfied. In her youth she wanted to be a painter and to be a boy so as not to be so restricted. When Henry courts her, he interprets her behavior in the way most flattering to him, and all the people around her seem to conspire to aid his courtship. She does not know how to resist, and once she is married, the only role she knows to play is "the good wife." She sacrifices her art: "It would not do if Henry were to return one evening and be met by a locked door. It would not do if Henry, short of ink or blotting paper, were to emerge irritably only to be told that Mrs. Holland was engaged with a model. It would not do, if Henry were appointed Governor to some distant colony, to tell him that the drawing master unfortunately lived in London . . ." (*Passion*, 156). She cannot resist the assumptions of husband, children, grandchildren, and society that she exists to satisfy their needs. When she rebels and refuses to see the grandchildren and great-grandchildren, she is saying that now she will satisfy her own needs. Ironically, she helps several people by helping herself.

She learns that besides sacrificing her art, her submission to convention has also lost her a deep and enduring love. A reticent friend of one of her sons obtains permission to visit her. He reveals that, as a young man he met her in India and recognized her dissatisfaction with life as vicereine, and that he fell in love with her. He has never married. When he dies he leaves her everything, which she promptly gives away because it will annoy her children and because she realizes that he is testing her to see if she is true to herself. Deborah's self-knowledge fulfills some of the young FitzGeorge's ancient dreams.

Deborah has some consolation for her wasted life when the great-granddaughter named after her visits her against her grandfather's wishes. She is engaged and Deborah sees the girl being molded by the same pressures which subdued her years before. When the girl breaks her engagement to pursue her career, the old lady is pleased: "She would form no estimates of Deborah's talents; that was beside the point. Achievement was good, but the spirit was better. To reckon by achievements was to make a concession to the prevailing system of the world" (*Passion*, 285). Deborah no longer makes such concessions, and her rebellion against familial and societal pressure may tip the balance to allow the young Deborah to live a life according to her desires. *All Passion Spent* says that, for women, breaking tradition and rebelling are necessary.

In *Family History* (1932) the themes of rebellion and social class are explored, but the focus is more on how men are affected. Mr. Jarrold, who made his fortune in coal, is proud that he has been made a peer and that he is able to send his grandson Dan to Eton and give him all the advantages aristocratic children receive. Jarrold's son was killed in World War I shortly after his marriage; Evelyn remains a dutiful daughter-in-law and her rather weak son allows her to intercede with his grandfather and explain that he dislikes hunting and that he is unhappy at Eton. Evelyn hopes that an eccentric young landowner, Miles Vane-Merrick, will be a more spirited model for her son than his weak, debilitated uncles.

I6fthis novel, Miles Vane-Merrick is Sackville-West's type of the true aristocrat. Viola Anquetil and her husband reappear to represent people who live life true to their own needs. Viola tells Evelyn "Miles is a reversion to type. Your Englishman of birth and education wasn't always the cautious, repressed creature he is today. There was a time when he was ashamed neither of his feelings nor of his culture. He was cruder and coarser then, in some ways—less gentlemanly, according to modern ideas, but *more* gentlemanly, as I see it . . . . Miles would have fitted into the Italian Renaissance."[10] Miles has rebelled, insisting that he leave Eton. He lives in a partially ruined house which resembles Sissinghurst and willingly defies convention to follow his own ideas.

Knowledge and expertise are two requirements that the contemporary effete Englishman lacks. Miles Vane-Merrick, however, is widely read, cultured, and an expert farmer. In many ways this ideal aristocrat is like the coal baron, Mr. Jarrold, who tells Dan: "I could make you a partner now, if I liked. But I won't. Not good for you. You'd better go into the shops when you leave Eton. Teach you things that Eton won't teach you. However, you must choose for yourself. But you must be something, boy; not an imitation of something" (*Family*, 83). Jarrold's own sons, including Dan's father, are feeble imitations of the feeble aristocracy. The true aristocrat must have the knowledge, skills, and spirit to mold his own life. But although Evelyn loves and admires Miles and hopes that her son will emulate him, she sacrifices her own desires to convention. Despite the Anquetils' efforts to persuade her to accept Miles, she dies without marrying him, because he is fifteen years her junior.

The Dark Island (1934) is probably the most violent of Sackville-West's novels. Sarah Ruth Watson groups it with the much earlier novels *Challenge* (1923) and *Seducers in Ecuador* (1925): "*The Dark Island* (1934), although it does not belong in date of publication to this period, does belong in spirit with the other novels. Indeed, we find in this novel the ultimate expression of the author's pessimism and of her deep concern over the origin of evil within man."[11] But *The Dark Island* is more understandable if seen as developing the themes that most concerned Sackville-West in the early 1930s. The novel says that shared love of a place could lead to the deepest, most passionate love possible between two people, but that love makes a person vulnerable.

As a child, Shirin learns to protect her secret passion for the island of Storn by assuming a mask of conventionality. Violence and destruction result when she and the heir to Storn, Venn Le Breton, who both love the island, are unable to develop this love into a mutual passion and trust, because of Venn's jealous possessiveness of the place. *The Dark Island* also speaks more directly of love between two women than any other work of Vita Sackville-West's except for that appearing after her death in *Portrait of a Marriage*. In the novel, Christina respects Shirin's reticence and does not insist on instant, absolute submission as a condition of love, as does Venn.

Shirin learns to protect her deepest feelings very early. With her blind, bitter, middle-class father, she shares a secret life of the imagination unguessed by anyone else. But her deepest love, her love for the island of Storn seen from the mainland every year during the family vacation, is kept entirely to herself. To her the island is the "symbol of all romance and of all escape from the humdrum weariness of life, from its meannesses, its falsity, and its pain. It was the secret, undetected refuge from her family, from Dulwich, from herself. It was the sanctuary she never desired to enter, save in spirit . . ."[12] She knows already that her secrecy leads to loneliness: "That inner knowledge which told you that life was cruel, told you also that life, just for mischief, might take away such things if it suspected that you loved them. Loneliness was not so very great a price to pay for such security; she would call it privacy rather than loneliness" (*Island*, 24). Of her mind, she believes, "Admission is by privilege, not by compulsion. Only to the person I love, if ever there is one . . . will that privilege of admission ever be granted" (*Island*, 42). But until she gives in to temptation, violates her childhood intuitions, and is therefore deeply hurt, her sweet appearance and her disciplined show of conventionality provide a bluff against the dangers of being wounded.

Venn Le Breton has many of the qualities associated with the ideal aristocrat in the earlier novels, but his love of Storn is also the source of his greatest flaws, his inability to empathize with others and his unwillingness to share Storn with Shirin. The adult Venn is described as being much like Miles Vane-Merrick, who appears offstage in this novel as Shirin's first husband: "Friends he [Venn] did not desire, nor women. His only friends were the fishermen and the people on his estates. With them he had a really close understanding. . . . Over his own realm he was king, and intended to remain a king, but apart from that he was self-sufficient and truly solitary, asking no better than to be left alone" (*Island*, 103). As a hereditary aristocrat, he must dominate the land he has inherited.

Venn's first impulse on meeting Shirin when they are teenagers is to subjugate her, to crush her spirit and extract her secrets. Angered by her presence in a mainland cove, he grabs her wrist to make her cry. Later, after she has broken her own resolve never to go to Storn, he instantly feels "that he did after all resent her presence there" (*Island*, 47). To intimidate her he shows her the place he calls Andromeda's Cave, which has iron rings in the stone walls. He tells her, "I should like to chain you up to them naked and beat you till you screamed" (*Island*, 51). But even years later when Christina sees them acting out his fantasy of dominance in the cave, Shirin does not submit to him and scream. Christina understands "that towards the people over whom he had been able naturally and legitimately to exercise domination he had proved a kindly and friendly master; but towards Shirin, who had resisted him, a devil and a sadist, morally and physically" (*Island*, 251). Even as Venn falls in love with her on their second meeting when she is twenty-six, his reaction is to wonder, "why did he feel such a savage desire to take her back to Storn, to isolate her from this world of London, and to make her suffer until he had broken her elusive spirit into irreparable fragments?" (*Island*, 99). Shirin's bluff against the hurt of the world makes her very being a challenge to the easy dominance Venn is accustomed to exercising over everyone on his estate and over people he meets who are naturally impressed by his social position. This easy dominance allows him to live without ever learning to empathize with others or to intuit their needs. As a teenager he is baffled by Shirin's apparent ability to read his mind. Her intuition is a form of power she has developed to protect herself against people who might hurt her.

When Venn asks Shirin to marry him, she momentarily allows herself to feel and believe that the world is less hostile than she has thought, and that possessing Storn in actuality will make her safe: "with an inner knowledge she now recognised, she had always known that Storn some day would be hers;

Storn was hers at last" (*Island*, 123). As they approach the coastline, "to her own surprise, she felt a rush of gratitude towards Venn for giving her a right to claim this beauty, this serenity, as now her own. She felt her trust in life revive, bringing with it a sense of being at a new beginning" (*Island*, 147-148), and as she steps onto Storn, "everything twisted and broken in life was straightened and healed; Venn did not exist; nothing but Storn existed; and Storn was hers. She had no wish to control it . . . she desired only the right to live there, to lose herself in its fantastic beauty . . . working her way through to some inward peace in which one might come at last to terms with life" (*Island*, 153). But her confidence that her love of this place will heal her is illusory.

She again violates her childhood precepts by revealing her love of Storn to Venn, telling him, "You can't be humanly jealous of such things as the sea and the trees, the only things I ever cared for" (*Island*, 170). She forgets his possessiveness, which years before she had recognized intuitively. He asserts, "Storn is mine not yours" (*Island*, 170). Since she feels he has murdered her new life in its infancy, her only defense is to return to her mask of superficiality by pretending it doesn't matter: "how well he and I could unite in our understanding of Storn and all that Storn stands for, keeping our personal independence always inviolate, respecting one another's separateness all the time, leaving our understanding implicit, unexpressed. . . . by what a narrow margin have we, Venn and I, missed the pure perfection offered us!" (*Island*, 173). He has violated the intimacy she allowed him. She will never let down her guard again, no matter how violent his efforts to extract a revelation from her become.

Only the sculptor Christina, who does not try to dominate and force admittance into Shirin's mind, is ever granted any love. As an artist, she realizes Shirin does not have art as an outlet, as a means of expressing her innermost self in such a way that the world cannot violate it. Like Shirin she can empathize with another and intuit what the other suffers without having to be told. She understands Shirin's character enough to warn her to reveal nothing she may regret, and thus by privilege rather than by compulsion, she is allowed to share Shirin's inner life. Tracey and Mrs. Jolly are two others who gain admittance through patience and merit, but Storn and Christina are Shirin's only loves.

Because he has been so shut out of Shirin's life, Venn becomes jealous of Christina as soon as she arrives on the island; though Shirin has never confided in him, he assumes that she has shared girlish confidences with Christina:

"Had she told Christina how, on the first night of their marriage, he had killed her soul in killing her love for Storn?" (*Island*, 210). Since he has no intuition, he does not realize that Christina can understand without being told. His jealousy of being excluded from Shirin's thoughts is so great that he murders Christina, and in doing so murders Shirin's soul a second time.

To avenge this second death, Shirin uses the only power she has as a woman, sex. And when Venn is dead, her son tells her that he won't share Storn with anyone, even his wife; he wants a wife like his mother who will not interfere with the man's dominance over the place. The boy's great-grandmother has claimed not to be a "foreigner" because she married her cousin the heir, but she has remained on the island as a hanger-on, not as the true master. Shirin will not lower herself: "I don't belong anywhere. I've never belonged anywhere" (*Island*, 306). This is one of Sackville-West's bitterest statements of women's rootlessness and lack of the identity that can develop through a lifetime possession and stewardship of one loved place. Shirin lets herself die, rather than recover from her illness and risk the possibility of the world cruelly murdering her soul a third time.

Unlike Shirin, V. Sackville-West does not allow herself to wither and die from the sorrow of not possessing her loved place, Knole. She struggles to develop beyond her bitterness. Later works, such as *The Easter Party* (1953), also show the limitations of love of place if it excludes or substitutes for a deep, mutual love and respect between two people, the ideal presented in *No Signpost in the Sea* (1961).

The Edwardians (1930), *All Passion Spent* (1931), *Family History* (1932), and *The Dark Island* (1934) show the variety, complexity, and richness with which V. Sackville-West elaborated one of her major themes: that the nurturing unity between the true aristocrat and nature can lead him to a broader love of the world, can become destructive through his selfishness, or can lead to a deep sense of displacement if, like a plant, he is torn from his native soil, as are women because they cannot inherit the land.

NOTES

1. Harold Nicolson, *The War Years 1939–1945:* Vol. II of *Diaries and Letters*, ed. Nigel Nicolson (New York: Atheneum, 1967), 351–352.

2. V. Sackville-West, *Knole and the Sackvilles*, 4th ed. (London: Ernest Benn, 1958), ix.

3. (London: Collins, 1942), 7–8.

4. *Portrait of a Marriage* (New York: Atheneum, 1973), 208.

5. *A Joy of Gardening*, ed. Hermine I. Popper (New York: Harper & Bros., 1958), 97.

6. V. Sackville-West, *The Land* (London: Heinemann, 1926).

7. *V. Sackville-West: A Critical Biography* (New York: Scribner's, 1974), 135.

8. *The Edwardians* (Garden City: Doubleday-Doran, 1930), 86.

9. *All Passion Spent* (Garden City: Doubleday-Doran, 1931), 59.

10. *Family History* (Garden City: Doubleday-Doran, 1932), 69.

11. Sarah Ruth Watson, *V. Sackville-West* (New York: Twayne, 1972), 97.

12. *The Dark Island* (Garden City: Doubleday-Doran, 1934), 22.

Two Views of Life: William Golding and Graham Greene

JOHN ATKINS

A t the outset of *Lord of the Flies* Ralph jerks his stockings "with an automatic gesture that made the jungle seem for a moment like the Home Counties."[1] Despite the jungle, we are invited to feel at home. He sees the inviting lagoon and in a moment is naked; it is the natural gesture of a boy on holiday, though the Home Counties would keep their underpants on. When he dresses again he finds it "strangely pleasing" (20). Then Jack and his choristers come marching down the beach. Again, all is well; religion and order are to be maintained. Piggy, representative of our civilization at a certain level, is intimidated by their uniformed superiority. When the boys choose a chief they vote, using a sophisticated mechanism which has become second nature to them. Ralph, Jack, and Simon go to explore the mountain. They are soon hot, dirty, and exhausted, but immensely happy. They are enjoying the primitive pleasure of release from restraint, which flowed from them with their sweat. Part of liberation from civilized restraint lies in killing without suffering afterwards. It is not easy, and their first attempt (on a pig) fails because they are squeamish. But this doesn't last long. Jack is "liberated from shame and self-consciousness" with the help of his mask, his painted face. His laughter becomes a "bloodthirsty snarling" (80). Later all the hunters paint themselves and become a tribe. They are "freed by the paint" (216).

Our acceptance of dualism easily picks out savagery on the one hand and civilization on the other. Piggy knows you must choose one or the other. As Jack says, "We've got to have rules and obey them. After all, we're not savages. We're English; and the English are best at everything" (55). Piggy and the world he comes from have not yet suffered from postwar loss of nerve. At the end the naval officer echoes Jack: "I should have thought that a pack of British boys . . . would have been able to put up a better show" (248). One can see his point of view. The Home Counties represent man's most successful attempt yet to repel Nature. Imperial success bred a self-confidence which lingered among the less sophisticated even through war and the political decline in its aftermath. Piggy represents intelligence, or what our culture regards as intelligence. He is contemptuous of those who cannot see how important it is to build shelters and keep a fire going. For Piggy it is never intelligent to take your clothes off unless the rules permit and advise it. He remembers such things when they are becoming faint in Ralph's bemused mind. Piggy clings desperately to "civilized values"; the choristers revert willingly, become hunters and then savages, which affirms what both Golding and Greene would probably accept, that the religious impulse is anticivilized.

These things are obvious. The in-between man is the unhappiest stratum of our civilization. He spoils the symmetry, and he is consequently resented. Ralph is neither a thoroughgoing savage, nor does he have a firm grasp on civilized values. He doesn't really like flicking his tangled hair out of his eyes or sleeping on leaves. He would like a bath and to clean his teeth with a toothbrush, but not as a matter of conviction. He likes comfort. He also survives, which is more than Piggy does. Perhaps he is too blurred to be killed off. The religious savages also survive, though they will probably be tamed. Doubtless Jack now teaches Maths at the University of Sussex.

This world of children without adult control must be interpreted in terms racial as well as individual. Ralph started biting his nails (like many characters in Greene) although it was a habit he had once been weaned of. He wondered if he would be sucking his thumb next. Simon, who was considered odd, loved solitude, and thought his own thoughts rather than those officially recommended, made a particularly arcane remark to Ralph: "You'll get back to where you came from" (137). Ralph, a born prefect, took this literally. At the end, he "wept for the end of innocence, the darkness of man's heart . . ." (248).

At this point we check to be sure we are reading Golding and not Greene. We certainly have been here before—the savage, primitive state which is in reality a form of childhood, more than is meant by the cliché "childhood of the race," a state very like that of the individual, undomesticated child. Greene saw it as a golden age of innocence. Golding has added a new dimension; it leaps with horror as the savages bound through the flames accompanied by their fluttering shadows.

Critics have tried to make much of Simon, and it has proved a Sisyphean task. Golding is an author of outstanding independence of mind, notably resistant to the pressures of fashion that make it increasingly difficult for anyone to write his own book rather than his milieu's book. But this is his first novel and there are flaws. Simon looks like a major flaw only after he has been inflated into a figure of immense significance. (Golding says he doesn't object to people's finding more in his work than he thought he put in; he is obviously polite and mystified about the matter.) Simon is a bare sketch and not an impressive one, perhaps a ritual bow towards Marlborough and Oxford. In fact, Simon's role is a muted one. One may deduce from it, as do Kinkead-Weekes and Gregor, that the fault lies not in Jack, or in a Beast of a Devil, but in man's inherent wickedness. Golding, some years later, saw man in these terms—but you have to squeeze the book hard to extract this particular juice. Although *Lord of the Flies* asserts that there is evil in all human beings, even those who seem eminently rational and civilized, it never comes near to asserting that the illness is of man's essence. May it not be an accident, produced by special circumstances (a sort of racial malady)? In other words, the Greene diagnosis.

The Inheritors is about two groups of true primitives, not lapsed citizens. One group is savage, in the sense of untamed and cruel. They are, significantly, our forefathers. The last Neanderthals, on the contrary, behave with a touching dignity which can provide no defense against Sapiens, us. It is an ironic contrast. Sapiens has learned how to get drunk, and this has released other qualities. Much, much later he will learn how to release sex (that is, to free it from ritual), and this will provide more freedom and define a new type of subservience for, say Pincher Martin. The Neanderthals are capable of only a fuzzy kind of thought, their sharpest experience is a picture (in an essay Golding tells how he experiences archaeology through pictures),[2] but even this can fade quickly to the sort of vagueness that increasingly overtakes Ralph. At first he knew what should be done, but by degrees sharpness of impression deserted him and he was left with a sense of loss and feeling that something should be done. Was Ralph a Neanderthaler? Are we to understand this term to specify something more in the nature of a phase in civilization than a genetically different race?

The new men carry weapons, make war, and kill as a matter of course and of social organization. The Neanderthalers eat meat reluctantly and only when the animal has been killed by a cat. Sapiens is drenched in blood. Neanderthal is engaged in a losing struggle for existence, Sapiens in a winning struggle for power. There is a strong allegorical element, for the Neanderthalers are true innocents, without evil in themselves and not understanding it in others. It is not the meek who inherit the earth, but the killers of the meek. The New Men are *fallen*. They have initiative and efficiency. The Neanderthalers have some qualities their supplanters lack, including abnormally active senses—particularly smell—and a power of communion whereby they share one another's pictures.

Lok and Fa watch a drunken orgy and comment, "Oa did not bring them out of her belly."[3] To them the New People are alien: "They are like a fire in the forest" (197), and fire was the major weapon in *Lord of the Flies*. In each book we see the same race, at the beginning of its travail and at its present end. A lot has happened in the meantime. Among other things, sex has been tamed and cerebration given a place of honor. But these are not matters to please Sapiens (his name was given him by a traitor). Violence and compulsion are at the root of their society; the old chief whips the people as they heave the log. They are driven by fear, both in prehistory and on the Pacific island. They destroy anyone different, especially one who might question their wisdom; hence, they destroy the Neanderthals and Piggy. One cannot imagine that Golding ever regarded Piggy as a satisfactory replacement for the Neanderthals, but he has the strain in him. Did Neanderthal and Sapiens miscegenate? Sapiens did carry off the baby and Neanderthals are rumored to exist in the deserts of Iraq.

Golding was not satisfied with his first draft: "he clearly felt he had only begun to see what his novel was about," write Mark Kinkead-Weekes and Ian Gregor.[4] This is a welcome insight, for Golding is a poet possessed by his own vision. He is not, except in a technical sense, the master. The first draft was concerned with the tragedy of the People and showed little concern for its implications. Was he horrified by his own conception? The first draft dealt mainly with the animus against man, derived from Golding's disgust and pessimism. Whatever the reasons for the addition of a final, more hopeful chapter, the original impulse was bleak. Yet such an interpretation is glib and says little for Golding's sensibility. It seems more likely that shame rather than horror caused second thoughts. As it stands, we are told that the New Men set off on their racial journey with a sense of love, which they somehow picked up from their victims. In the final chapter Tuami differentiates between good and evil, but only as self-awareness. He can distinguish; it is doubtful if he can put his findings to any pragmatic use. The main story of the succeeding novel is man's failure to make the best use of the loving impulse and his use of it for exploitation. A grain of it does survive—don't forget the ape-baby; it struggles to the surface in decent old Ralph and is parodied in absurd Piggy. But the passion is poured into the bloodletting.

At first view Pincher Martin, all guts and resolution, is repellent. Then we reflect that he gets things done, often things the rest of us appreciate. One remembers Orwell's sad comment that the worthwhile things done in India by the British would not have been performed by men of the Forster stamp. Golding is a resourceful author, for this tale of a contemporary man is set in an environment that makes him virtually a primitive. The situation has much in common with the earlier one, only the solitude is new. He is alone on a rock, pitting his strength and his intelligence against the hostile universe. At the same time he is aware of the link between his rock and the continents, although it exists beneath the sea. There is nothing hysterical about his situation. He retains his intelligence and his "pictures" bring relief. He is in fact a Neanderthal in his use of pictures. Whenever circumstances threaten, he resorts to them. During his return to consciousness (if it is a return) they come in a flood. Golding's descriptions of things seen (not pictured) by savages and men on the edge of consciousness resemble those attributed to babies—planes, surfaces, colors, angles, not yet organized into meaningful wholes.

For me the really fruitful comparison with *Lord of the Flies* was always *Robinson Crusoe*, not *The Coral Island*. The Crusoe theme is strong in *Pincher Martin* and the similarity is much greater. Conscious intelligence and stubborn will are comrade protagonists: he will not die, he will be rescued. He looks round the rock and says, "The first thing to do is to survey the estate."[5] He plans survival very much in Crusoe's style. The flaw in his make-up is libido. There is little opportunity to exercise it on the rock. He (his rock) has imperfections. He will overcome them by the exercise of intelligence. "Everything is predictable. I knew I shouldn't drown and I didn't. There was a rock. I knew I could live on it and I have. I have defeated the serpent in my body [sickness]. I knew I should suffer and I have. But I am winning" (166).

Did he survive? Did he win? My major criticism of Golding is that he doesn't play fair. He wraps key points in an unnecessary obscurity. The novelist has a duty to write plainly unless he is attempting to express the ineffable—and Golding is not. But here (as in *The Spire*), he muffles what he has to say. Near the beginning of the novel he tells us, if we are exceptionally aware, that Martin is already dead. Even a careful reader may miss the import of this the first time, which prompts me to ask whether novels are written for readers or researchers. If Golding's novels are primarily vehicles for researchers, they lose their universality and become arcane and esoteric.

Even when we spot Martin's death, nothing really tells us when it occurred. Perhaps Golding has been too clever. In a novel employing flashbacks it is exceedingly difficult to know the exact chronological sequence of events, unless it is clearly stated. The revelation about the seaboots, unpleasantly like a trick ending, could be adapted to at least two interpretations which accept Martin as having survived on the rock over a period of days. The clues planted to show unreality (the red lobster, the solid guano, the flying lizards) could be explained by madness, the stress of hanging on. In fact, at one point such an interpretation is suggested.

In the end we know he didn't survive. His story parallels that of the race which, after surmounting almost insurmountable obstacles, may yet founder in its self-confidence. "The solution lies in intelligence. This is what distinguishes us from the helpless animals that are caught in their patterns of behavior, both mental and physical" (173–174). Martin's situation is man's situation, his flaws are man's flaws: "beyond the muddle there will still be actuality and a poor mad creature clinging to a rock in the middle of the sea" (180).

I take the conclusion of *Free Fall* to be that we are forced to torture each other: "Once a human being has lost freedom there is no end to the coils of cruelty. I must I must I must."[6] We watch ourselves becoming automata. The most vulnerable are those we love. This is seen most starkly during the exercise of love. Beatrice was forced to torture Sammy; their imperfections forced them to torture each other. There was a more successful love affair, with Taffy. But the reason for success was unflattering: "The lovers demand far less but they achieve far more," as Kinkead-Weekes and Gregor put it (180). Golding now brings in memory as a factor additional to the molding of experience in his picture of man: "Man is not an instantaneous creature, nothing but a physical body and the reaction of the moment. He is an incredible bundle of miscellaneous memories and feelings, of fossils and coral growths. I am not a man who was a boy looking at a tree. I am a man who remembers being a boy looking at a tree" (46). Man is not simply a string of love affairs, sunsets, farewells, examinations, and beatings, but these plus their memories. At a stroke the comparison with early men and forefathers is wiped out or made minimal.

The longer the race lives, the more complicated becomes a man's situation and the less hope he has of solutions: "I welcomed the destruction that war entails, the deaths and terror. Let the world fall. There was anarchy in the mind where I lived and anarchy in the world at large . . ." (131). Nineteenth-century optimism (the optimism of Golding's father) had run out. The simple world of the rationalist was false; he had been pretending in an amoral and savage world. "There is no spirit, no absolute. Therefore right and wrong are a parliamentary decision like no betting slips or drinks after half-past ten" (226). But opinion veers according to which you are dealing with, the neat world of science or the world of revelation. Both are real, but there is no bridge between them.

None of this is new, of course. But from it Golding evolves a refusal to give reasons, which is something like a rude gesture to our received literary practice. Sammy is afraid of the dark. Why? I don't know, says Golding—it is part of his Being and cannot be explained in terms of environment or behavior. The belief that everything can be accounted for is part of the old rationalist conviction that modern psychology has swept aside, but psychology has not realized this. There is no valid reason for believing that there must be a circumstantial cause for everything; it is mere superstition to believe that the human creature is born without a single characteristic and then sets about acquiring them. And what is true of the individual is true of the race. We are not to explain ourselves by drawing attention to an event in the Mesozoic and another during the Enlightenment. All we can be sure of is that, as event succeeds event and memory is tangled with memory, we get further and further away from our own reality. Guilt cannot be localized in action but must be sought in Being. "Guilt comes before the crime and can cause it," writes Sammy Montjoy (232). There is, in addition, the will, exhibited so powerfully by Pincher Martin. The will can be put to use in the choice of an aspect of Being, and this is most likely to happen during adolescence (as in John Wain's *Strike the Father Dead*). All this is a long way from the noble arbitrament of soul man used to pride himself on.

Golding, as novelist, is not concerned with making a system for us, and it would be false for us to divine a system from the novels. The novelist works in hints and suggestions. Liberal Europe made all kinds of patterns through the eighteenth and nineteenth centuries, all satisfactory to their founders and unsatisfactory to us, the legatees. It became a habit, and it is now being broken—but painfully. Recalling his mother's lodger, Sammy suggests he had lung cancer because of the way he breathed, "and I notice with a certain wry amusement my instant effort to fit that uninformed guess into a pattern" (25). As a child he looked for people who could control his world. Once he felt sure that Evie could, for she seemed to have magical qualities, but when his belief in magic was lost, he lost his belief in control.

Throughout childhood Sammy was in a state of defiance and isolation, always against society. He came from the slums, he experimented with lewdness and communism, but not in deliberate efforts to disrupt. God wasn't much help, perhaps because of the way Miss Massey tried to teach Him. She "hit him on both sides of the head, precisely with either hand, a word and a blow":

> "God—"
> Smack!
> "—is"
> Smack!
> "—love!"
> Smack! Smack! Smack!
> (56)

The history of Christianity has seldom been written so succinctly.

In the previous year *The Brass Butterfly* had made a similar point. Euphrosyne said her god was the God of Love and of Battles. Here the issues are more clearly stated than in the novels, but with less subtlety. The theme of rejection and alienation is repeated. Euphrosyne's rejection of her would-be lover, Mamillius, is the product of the rejection of her brother. Man's instinct, when faced by something he cannot understand, is to strike and destroy it. Phanocles says he has asked for nothing more than goodwill and common sense but has received incomprehension and malice. "We build on the expectation of man's goodness and the foundations collapse under us."[7] The emperor asserts that there is nothing wrong with man's intelligence. Indeed, it is a very fine instrument, but who is to use it and to what end? "Any man can bring about a change—and yet change is the one thing no man can control," he adds (72).

The Spire with its central institution, the Church, itself one of the major human efforts at "control of the pattern," is certain to invite comparisons of Golding with Greene. In many ways the two seem to agree about the human dilemma, but Golding trusts in no supernatural power. If man's intelligence is insufficient to solve his problems, he will destroy himself. In certain situations there are gods (the naval officer in *Lord of the Flies,* for instance), but as a race man stands on his own.

One could imagine *The Spire* emanating from some Super Fictional Project, where it exists in counterpoint to, say, *A Burnt-Out Case.* Jocelin, the seer, is building without foundation (not using intelligence) and earns the distrust of all practical men. His attempt brings misery to everyone. Not even Jocelin reaps any happiness from his well-meant attempt. The godless builders live in violence and sin. (This is the Church's word, but then it is the Church's idea.) There is grave sexual scandal which infects even Jocelin until he finds the devil stretching his loins. We are reminded of Pincher Martin and Sammy Mountjoy and of the sexual fury of the New Men. Animal nature (which some consider the major barrier to realization of man's idealism) is seen here as aggressive sexual nature. Jocelin's failing is pride, but he cannot escape the virus which runs from flesh to flesh like an *ignis fatuus*. Perhaps the building of the spire is a self-erection, a substitute gratification for a need he would not recognize, an erect phallus.

In this novel there is no author. Everything is seen, sensed, understood, and misunderstood through Jocelin, a return to the method of *Pincher Martin,* but more engulfing. It is Golding's best writing to date, for at last he is involved, not acting merely as a critic. Lack of understanding, stressed in *Free Fall,* here becomes a dominant theme. Jocelin's aunt is a darling of the period, getting on in years but still restless in the awareness of her charm. She is not capable of understanding him. To her the Holy Nail is a nail. She may be right, but she fails to understand that it is possible to be wrong. Her mental state is a third force that simply does not comprehend. The two major forces are the spiritual and the material, which accept each other. Neither understands the other's nature but is aware of the other's existence. The builders accept the spiritual with all humility; Jocelin comes to accept the physical life of the builders with a degree of gratitude. But there is a Higher Misunderstanding, that of idealism. Jocelin says, "I thought I was chosen; a spiritual man, loving above all; and given specific work to do."[8] But he wasn't. He confused his egoism with a sense of election: "Imagine it. I thought I was doing a great work; and all I was doing was bringing ruin and breeding hate" (209). The tensions are the same as in Greene. The difference is that Greene accepts their reality while Golding sees it all as a colossal misunderstanding. This is seen (in a reminiscence of Sammy Mountjoy's view) when Jocelin asks

Anselm's forgiveness not for what he has done but for what he *is*. This strikes a new note in the European code of spiritual justice. Golding's own despair is echoed in Jocelin's outburst: *"How proud their hope of hell is. There is no innocent work. God knows where God may be"* (222). Man is irrational and absurd, therefore evil. In his great intelligence he is abysmally ignorant.

The writing in *The Spire* is spare and intense. Its feverishness parallels Jocelin's eagerness to build. The tension reflects his desire to hide something important, particularly from himself. "It reflects the way he has tended all along to see things and direct things only as he wanted to in terms of his obsession about the spire, blinding himself to the truth," Leighton Hodson writes.[9] We know that the whole truth is never accessible to any of us. The unthinking idealists are those who see no truth in themselves or in humanity.

The Pyramid is a more nearly conventional novel than Golding's others; thus, it paradoxically seems strange to the reader. Its only link with the distant past is its epigraph: "If thou be among people make for thyself love, the beginning and end of the heart."

Sex, which struck its jarring note in all the novels except the first, is here exorcised. When Olly finally gets Evie, peace descends: "I was aware of nothing but peace; peace in my blood and nerves, my bones, peace in my head and my deep breath and in my slowing heart. It was a good peace, that spread."[10] And yet it is delusive, it doesn't last. It is followed by fear of a baby and then of disease. It gives birth to anger. This is love in favorable circumstances, but consider other loves. Olly once lusted after the desirable, *soignée* Imogen; she represented a sexual goal, peace, but she married Claymore, and their love was revealed as like answering like, the stupid and the insensitive answering to the insensitive and the stupid. Thus love, like pride, blinds. We all know this in textbook fashion; yet we all have to learn. Intelligence does not seem to be enough.

Thinking of Miss Dawlish after visiting her grave, Olly is aware of a great truth, his creator puts it in italics and sets it in isolation: *"I was afraid of you, and so I hated you. It is as simple as that"* (214). This is the principle that runs through Golding's work: the destructive power of fear and hate. It is as simple as that. The best many of us can do is to come to a working arrangement, like Bounce and Henry. Bounce never got from Henry the love she wanted; Olly speaks of her "pathetic, horrible, unused body" lying two yards away, as he stands by her grave (213). But the mere expression of her need was a kind of fulfillment. Henry had her help in his business and he was kind to her. But the relationship was not allowed to develop, and love denied led to madness.

The same thing happened to Beatrice in *Free Fall*.

Golding is a writer with a strongly developed sense of tragedy. His love of mystification has had the effect he may have desired in a secret place of his being: the manipulation of symbols to produce significances that were not intended (and none of us ever intends all we are responsible for) muddles the optimum effect. In *The Spire*, for instance, there is an occasional masking of the action where it would benefit the reader to have no doubts. Probably Golding would reply that life is hedged with doubts. One is aware that Golding has read Wells and had taken from Wells his later pessimism, if nothing else. But he is outside the mainstream of the English tradition, and the most fruitful comparison will always be with Graham Greene, who has been equally determined to expose the hollowness of man's illusions about his nature. But, whereas Greene has a gift for realism, which allows the reader to see things clearly even where the normal aspect is uncertain, Golding has been more concerned with the invention of a new form of moral fable.

One gets the impression that Golding has been conducting his own voyage of discovery. Like a fifteenth-century sailor, he has never been quite sure where he has been going, with perhaps one exception, and a natural one at that. America can only be discovered once; all succeeding journeys are on the known map. *Lord of the Flies* may have started as a parody of *The Coral Island*, but Golding sailed further than he expected. The suggestion that Golding discovered the full implications of *The Inheritors* only after he had finished the first draft supports the idea that Golding is not quite sure where he's going. In "On the Crest of the Wave," Golding wrote that he is "by nature an optimist; but a defective logic—or a logic which I sometimes hope desperately is defective—makes a pessimist of me."[11] By *The Pyramid* he feels he can be more forthright, can make assertions with fewer qualifications. The result is, in spirit, unlike the Golding we have known; it is characterized by a lack of complexity.

Like many another writer, by the time he comes to write essays on his work and thought, he finds he has a philosophy that can be set out in confident propositions. Apart from anything else, critics and reviewers have given him a good idea of what his philosophy is. In an essay called "Fable," he says "man produces evil as a bee produces honey," writes of "the terrible disease of being human," then says he deliberately isolated this malady from *Lord of the Flies* by excluding sex and a possible Marxist exegesis.[12] It is very neat, good shorthand and would not arouse the slightest interest if the novel had not first stated something approaching this but in complex human terms and not in the form of "Notes on Life."

We may fudge out of Golding's fiction a circular process which serves as man's trap, or a spider's web from which he cannot escape. It would go like this: Man is doomed to fear. He reacts with hate and ritual defenses, leading to violence. He seeks salvation through love. But love is riddled with fear. He reacts with hate, etc.

Graham Greene, subject to the same misgivings as Golding, approaches the problem with greater clarity. This is not a field where clarity is necessarily to be trusted, but Greene has one advantage: he has faith and a philosophy ready-made. Although he is very critical of certain aspects of this philosophy, it provides him with a basis. In reading Greene we never experience the feeling (which comes to us while reading Golding) that the building is erected on sand. [13]

Apart from theology, the best introduction to Greene's views about man's situation is to be found in *Journey without Maps* (1936). He found Africa to be "a long journey backwards without maps." [14] Getting to the coast, after weeks in the jungle, Greene found himself welcoming civilization, but it was an emotion he regretted as he wrote. He would soon forget something experienced in the interior, "the finer taste, the finer pleasure, the finer terror on which one might have built" (279). He had experienced the gentleness and kindness of the African, whom he had been warned against: "A black will always do you down," they said on the Coast (93). It was useless to protest that he had not come up against one case of dishonesty. But it wasn't only the blacks; he also found communities of priests and nuns who practiced standards of gentleness and honesty equal to the native standard. English nuns he met were gentle, devout, childlike, and unselfish, superior to the rapacious people on the Coast. Had Africa brought them to better standards? Or was it religion? It is a measure of Greene's integrity that he asks this question instead of assuming (as Waugh would) that religion was responsible.

In Africa he felt moments of extraordinary happiness and a sense of being nearer to the racial source than he had ever been. He mused on the violence of Western society: "when one sees to what unhappiness, to what peril of extinction centuries of cerebration have brought us, one sometimes has a curiosity to discover if one can from what we have come, to recall at which point we went astray" (11).

The true primitive, he felt, was at Africa's back, not centuries away. "If they had taken the wrong road, they had only to retrace their steps a very little distance in space and not in time" (307). Some Europeans have felt the need to go back by this route (he mentions Rimbaud and Conrad while remaining unsure of Mungo Park, Livingstone, and Stanley). Fascination worked on these men despite the dirt, disease, barbarity, and unfamiliarity of Africa. Can we retrace the steps we have taken? "If one could get back to this bareness, simplicity, instinctive friendliness, feeling rather than thought, and start again . . . " (235).

Some places seemed certainly "bad" to Greene, who is not always clear when he tries to explain what he feels. His critical work is full of moments when he is trying to express something on the edge of feeling, and we are often left wondering whether the impression we get is really the one he was trying to impart. In this respect he is no better guide than Golding. For example, in one place he suggests equivocally that evil seemed to emanate not from the devil's power but from one's own mind: "It was not that I believed in the devil's power so much as in the power of my own mind. The suggestion of malice and evil here [Zigita] was so great that I could imagine it influencing my mind until I half believed, and a half-belief can be strong enough to affect the health" (171). One didn't experience evil in the Christian sense (he cites *The Turn of the Screw*) but as disembodied Power. His conclusion was that the African devil simply controlled power, like the creatures of one's early dreams (220). At least two distinct beliefs seem confused here, so that one cannot be sure whether evil comes from an independent source or is the product of one's own mind. When Greene turns to cruelty, however, the ambiguity disappears. We have exchanged supernatural cruelty for that of our own making. Our evil is our own product—we have chosen to make it. Were we wise?

Like Golding, Greene is not building a system. He makes his comments as and when they seem relevant, and we must make what we can of them. He is more direct and positive than Golding, and although he uses symbols he does not hide behind them. Golding gives the impression of cerebration (his characters, obsessed with will and intelligence, must derive partly from his own self-examination), with the result that if he often reaches similar truths it is by a different path, and less convincingly. Despite appearance, Greene is more subtle. His threefold division into the interior, the coast, and the chic gives a sample of the territory explored in his novels. Golding's jungle, rock, and spire are not so satisfyingly integrated into a single vision.

In *Brighton Rock* Greene tries to posit two worlds: that of Good and Evil and that of Right and Wrong. The attempt is unsuccessful, largely because his treatment of Ida Arnold is unbalanced. But he is right in his insistence that man has made a choice (although to Greene a wrong one). This belongs to the essence of Greene and is rarely touched by the foggy mysticism of some critics. The notion of a wrong choice is implicit in Golding and brings up the conception of the "alternative society." This notion is felt to be quite contemporary, but in its wider implications, it has been with us for a couple of generations in the sense of "alternative civilization." D. H. Lawerence, deploring the emphasis on will and intellect at the expense of instinct and spontaneity, is clearly one of Golding's mentors. Golding adds the idea of the flaw, expressed mainly though violence; there is a moral component, but man is hindered by his nature. Greene's contribution (taken from his religion) is opposed powers—one need not be a Manichaean to speak in terms of good and evil and therefore of good versus evil. One makes a choice and does it deliberately. One is naturally concerned with morality, but morality is in fact engulfed by power, not surprising in an age such as ours.

I have referred to the trap into which Golding feels man has fallen. In *The Heart of the Matter* Greene reveals the weight of the burden he and numberless others have taken upon themselves. He accepts the interpretations of a religion he finds difficult to defend and later gives up trying to defend. Scobie watches survivors being brought across the river and up the bank. He thinks, "It would need all Father Brule's ingenuity to explain that. Not that the child would die: that needed no explanation. Even the pagans realized that the love of God might mean an early death, though the reason they ascribed was different; but that the child should have been allowed to survive the forty days and nights in the open boat—that was the mystery, to reconcile that with the love of God."[15] In fact, only the nonexplanation can satisfy the enquirer.

Here Greene is faced with the inexplicable and admits it. Bit by bit, as Scobie becomes entangled in his theology, Greene becomes nonplussed by the tensions of an incredible interpretation. One is tempted to call it irrational until one remembers that *irrational* is a nonword where theology is concerned, but even this is only a half-truth. The perfect theology, or metaphysic, for which we seek will be perfectly rational. Twentieth-century man has turned to irrationality as to a miraculous philosophical hold-all, which will explain everything, from the Final Solution for the Jews to the mercy of God. Scobie can choose between receiving Holy Communion while in a state of sin or leaving the church, confessing, and returning another time to start again with a clear conscience "and a knowledge that he had pushed innocence back where it properly belonged—under the Atlantic surge. Innocence must die young if it isn't to kill the souls of men" (248–249). This expresses Greene's conviction, at that time, that innocence is ignorance of God's law rather than the more familiar view that it is a state where sin is unknown. The implications of this are extraordinary—that innocence is another name for guilt. Characteristic of Greene's habit of bullying sense and meaning into abnormal forms, it can be paralleled by Golding's conviction that man may be born guilty.

Greene implicitly contradicts this position in *A Burnt-Out Case*. Too much knowledge can defeat its own ends. Rycker, too well informed in spiritual matters, is alarmed by his wife's ignorance. In *The Heart of the Matter* ignorance, identified with innocence, is to be destroyed. There are senses in which both Rycker and his wife can be considered innocent: the one because he has not yet discovered good and the other because she has not yet discovered evil. Either is a state of unknowing. Marie Rycker's innocence kills Querry: "God preserve us from all innocence. At least the guilty know what they are about," he says to Mother Agnes.[16] Although the dangers of Rycker's knowledge and Marie's ignorance are convincingly demonstrated, it is difficult to derive a helpful conclusion from them. It is the clearest expression we have of Greene's defeatism and hopelessness. A cosmic sense of unfairness lies at the heart of things, even more strongly than is shown in *The Heart of the Matter*: survivors from torpedoing survive forty days of suffering, and then die; leprosy does not preclude other diseases.

In *The Comedians* Jones's deepest research into the meaning of life is summed up in the trite expression "One never knows. . . ."[17] One feels (it is no discredit to him) that Greene's own researches have taken him no further. He has probed much deeper than Jones, but has he come back with any valid proofs? The world-weariness and cynicism of his latest works suggest he has not. Brown (as narrator) says that as he approached the end of life only his sense of humor enabled him sometimes to believe in God. "Life was a comedy, not the tragedy for which I had been prepared, and it seemed to me that we were all . . . driven by an authoritative practical joker towards the extreme point of comedy" (28). Is this, then, all it comes to—humor alone, which the grave despise and which the apparently wise tend to dismiss as a defensive covering against harsh reality? Humor alone providing the gateway to the only possible deity? Greene approached this notion in *A Burnt-Out Case* with its intense ironies, as yet unfunny. And is it coincidence that *The Pyramid* is bathed in a humor previously absent from Golding's novels?

Greene's characters act like members of a pre-Columbian (ours is the only world) or a pre-Copernican (there are other worlds, but they go around us) fraternity. And Greene's excellence as a novelist is achieved because of and in spite of his Catholic religious framework. It helps him by giving resistance, and it provides a context which to the great mass of men is utterly unjustified as an interpretation of man and his condition, at times verging on the idiotic. We wait for the novelist who can write convincingly from a wider, more credible view of his framework; until we get him we shall remain grateful for the less credible. Golding works in a more credible area but his talent is smaller.

Greene's conceptions of God and of good and evil, shared with millions, are like the rules of a complex game sanctified by long tradition. The critic's duty is to view his work through a wider, though certainly vaguer, aspect. Anyone with a point of view can be definite—definite enough, in the last resort, to maim and kill and at any time to distort. Greene has a point of view which coarsens his vision, though not nearly so much as some critics suggest. He is the spokesman of a cult rather than the novelist of the human comedy. Greene points this out again and again, but still the critics judge him according to the "rules" and not according to man's known situation or even his limited wisdom.

Greene and Golding operate in a territory rarely explored by the secular writer. Therein lies Golding's oddity. It is much more usual for secular writers, when chance brings them into the neighborhood of metaphysical matters, to retreat in a hurry. Sometimes, however, they are caught and are compelled to declare themselves—and they declare their fear. Pamela Hansford Johnson, for example, writes like an agnostic but is tolerant of religious concerns. Her characters who profess religion do so superficially and rarely go beyond routine matters of worship. In *An Error of Judgement* the narrator, Vic Henrey, considers the damnation of a sordid little killer. He is appalled at the thought of Christian punishment. He realizes that tepid Christians think only of mercy; they turn away from the unpleasant aspects, taking what is agreeable from their religion. He wonders how the Christians face up to the horror of it all: "How many have the guts to take the lot? *But the whole lot must have been meant.* I clung to my own agnosticism as to a blessed spar in mid-Atlantic." Which brings us back to Pincher Martin, defying the cosmos of his rock. Vic Henrey is terrified. Pincher Martin is not. Vic sees his refusal to commit himself to a metaphysical standpoint as the only sensible course. Golding and Greene agree that Martin, at least, is a modern diplodocus who cannot survive.

NOTES

1. (London: Faber, 1954), 11.
2. "Digging for Pictures," *The Hot Gates and Other Occasional Pieces* (London: Faber, 1965), 61–70.
3. (London: Faber, 1955), 173.
4. *William Golding: A Critical Study* (London: Faber, 1967), 117.
5. (London: Faber, 1956), 77.
6. (London: Faber, 1959), 115.
7. (London: Faber, 1958), 55
8. (London: Faber, 1964), 194.
9. *William Golding* (Edinburgh: Oliver and Boyd, 1969), 88.
10. (London: Faber, 1967), 71.
11. *The Hot Gates,* 126.
12. Ibid., 87, 89.
13. But this must not be taken to mean that the foundations are necessarily secure.
14. (New York: Viking, 1961), 114.
15. (New York: Viking, 1963), 124–125.
16. *A Burnt-Out Case* (New York: Viking, 1967), 231.
17. (New York: Viking, 1970), 12.

"The Burning Bird":
Golding's *Poems* and the Novels

CECIL DAVIES

I n a slim volume bound in thin blue card, Macmillan published *Poems* by
W. G. Golding in 1934. Twenty years later, Faber published *Lord of the
Flies.* Before he retired from teaching, William Golding described himself as
"a citizen, a novelist, and a schoolmaster,"[1] but not as a poet, and he has
referred to the 1934 volume as "mummified juvenilia."[2] Nevertheless, many
themes and preoccupations of the novelist are foreshadowed in the poet.[3] And
the poet, like Golding's phoenix of the final poem of his early volume, rises
again in the novelist, "In splendour from grey ashes flashing."[4]

In spite of his tiny output of verse Golding may be regarded as belonging to
the small but very special group of novelists—like Emily Brontë and Thomas
Hardy—who, because of the characteristics of their imaginations, can be
described as poets. To see Golding in this light is to transcend some awkward
questions about his work; and if, as I believe, this approach is in harmony
with the essentials of Golding's genius, it can lead towards an evaluation of
the novels.

"The Eyes' Delight" is the opening poem, and the eyes' delight is a quality
which stands out in the twenty-nine uneven poems. "The painted Pegasus,"
"crawling wrinkles," "the pillow / Of moss and mandrake," "the flapping
fire," "dark wine blazing in the crystal cup," "nosing curs that prowl the
park," and "let the swerving plough jolt on"[5] are a few of the images that last,
though expressed in vocabulary and rhythms derived from poetic styles

already dead when Golding was born. Some of the best poems are based upon
one intensely seen picture; the hazel-catkins, for example,

> . . . tassel'd in the leafless trees,
> Before the world was waked and won,
> Flaunting among the spears of ice,
> Pale standards of the rebel sun. . . .
>
> (16)

or the old boat

> . . .with sail
> Over the dark of her low hull dreaming white,
> Moving slow by the slow wind under the veil
> Of sea-mist and the coming of the night.
>
> (30)

So, too, with a direct appeal to the eye and the other senses Golding made
his initial impact as a novelist: "The boy with fair hair lowered himself down
the last few feet of rock and began to pick his way towards the lagoon. . . .
Though he had taken off his school sweater and trailed it now from one hand,
his grey shirt stuck to him and his hair was plastered to his forehead. All
round him the long scar smashed into the jungle was a bath of heat. He was
clambering heavily among the creepers and broken trunks when a bird, a vision of red and yellow, flashed upwards with a witch-like cry; and this cry was
echoed by another."[6]

In *Lord of the Flies*, the picture of the environment and its new inhabitants is
broadened and developed with a precise attention to details, those "Minute
Particulars"[7] demanded by William Blake, to whom one of the poems pays
tribute. First, the immediate scene, where "the white surf flinked on a coral
reef . . ." (14) and "The beach . . . was a thin bow-stave . . ." (15); later, the
special features, the "great platform of pink granite" and the lagoon "clear to
the bottom and bright with the efflorescence of tropical weed and coral" (17);
and, finally, the exact topography of the island, "roughly boat-shaped," and
"where the island petered out in the water . . . another island" carefully established in preparation for the story's climax, "a rock, almost detached,
standing like a fort, facing them across the green with one bold, pink bastion"
(38). This topographical precision provides a foundation for the structure of
story, image, and myth: one of many things lost in the film version.

In *The Inheritors*, Golding's ability to use language to present precise sense
impressions, all the more clear because stripped of inessentials, becomes the

basis of a style created for this book. One reviewer called it "prose quite astounding in its poetic clarity."[8] What Golding had to invent was a language which could enable the reader to see each scene and follow a story through the eyes and minds of the Neanderthal people, a people with rudimentary language whose thought is prelogical and dependent upon "pictures," memories, and simple associations. The making of the log bridge is a fine example of the method.[9] It is not a matter of mere simplification of vocabulary and sentence structure, though this is how he writes the dialogue:

> "I have a picture. . . ."
> "Mal is not old but clinging to his mother's back. There is more water not only here but along the trail where we came. A man is wise. He makes men take a tree that has fallen. . . ."
> "I do not see this picture. . . ."
> "Find a tree that has fallen."

> (15–16)

Where the novelist narrates, however, he imposes no such limitation but uses a rich vocabulary to express unarticulated impressions received by the pre-man:

> Lok put his palms into the hollows of his eyes and rubbed them sleepily. Green spots from the pressure floated across the river. He blinked to the left where the waterfall thundered so monotonously that already he could no longer hear it. The wind moved on the water, hovered and then came strongly up from the forest and through the gap. The sharp line of the horizon blurred and the forest lightened. There was a cloud rising over the waterfall, mist streaking up from the sculptured basin, the pounded river water being thrown back by the wind. . . . Lok's nose opened automatically and sampled the complex of odors that came with the mist.

> (41–42)

The full vocabulary is needed to convey the complexity and intensity of the pre-man's sense impressions, but because for him events occur merely in sequence and logical connections are rarely made, the author uses very simple, usually short sentences, almost in the manner of *The Anglo-Saxon Chronicle,* avoiding periodicity and stating only facts. He avoids explanations beyond the comprehension of his characters. When the Neanderthalers first see the new people in broad daylight:

> Lok did not look immediately at their bodies; he was far too absorbed in the stuff round their eyes. A piece of white bone was placed under them, fitting close, and where the broad nostrils should have shown were narrow slits and between them the bone was drawn out to a point. . . .
> Chestnut-head . . . spoke sideways to the others in the boat out of his

slit; soft twittering speech; the whiteness quivered.
    Lok felt the shock of a man who has trusted to a bough that is not there.
He understood in a kind of upside-down sensation that there was no Mal
face, Fa face, Lok face concealed under the bone. It was skin.

(138-139)

Completely alienated from our own species we explore the human face from
without, through the eyes of Lok, the Neanderthaler.

No other book of Golding's is so dependent upon poetry, in the sense that
"primarily poetry is an exploration of the possibilities of language."[10] In
Pincher Martin too, Golding endows his protagonist with pictorial imagination. The greater part of the book consists of Christopher Martin's images of
his Promethean struggle for life upon Rockall. These images have the brilli-
ance of stage settings, for Christopher has been an actor. As in the theater we
find ourselves convinced of their reality and are shocked at hints that they are
scenes in his interior drama: "It was not really necessary to crawl but the background music underlined the heroism of a slow, undefeated advance against
odds."[11]

Martin is a magnificent re-creation of a kind of man who had caught Golding's imagination before. His sonnet "Baudelaire" sees the poet who celebrated *Les Fleurs du Mal* as a Luciferian figure "Proud as an angel, terrible as sin!"
who neither "counts the cost, nor fears the wrath of God!" but is also "Like a
tormented corpse foretasting hell" who "Swore like a mangy parrot till he fell /
Into the stinking limbo of the dark" (27).

The rock also is deeply rooted in the author's imagination. Not for nothing
did he begin with a desert-island story. The pink tail of the island of *Lord of the
Flies* is reimaged here: "Beyond the rock was a gap of shallow water, then
another smaller rock, another and another in a slightly curving line. Then
there was a rock that interrupted the pattern of the water and after that, the
steep climb of the sea up to the sky" (78). The Cornish-bred poet had seen in
childhood many such tails and diminishing rocky series off the headlands of
Cornwall. *Poems* includes the "The Lonely Isle," where

> . . . Night and Day
> Are tiny blows of the hammer of time
> Wearing the ancient rock away.
> Only once in a thousand years,
> From hanging cliffs and desolate streams,
> A crag falls into the moving sea
> And a sea-bird screams.

(28)

So, too, under the screaming gulls, Martin (with an echo of Ecclesiastes 12: 3) sees the rocks as teeth "being worn away in infinite slow motion. They were the grinders of old age, worn away. A lifetime of the world had blunted them, was reducing them as they ground what food rocks eat" (78).

Each of these novels, then, achieves its impact and is stamped upon the memory through the concrete image of a remote, isolated, simplified setting for events described with vivid exactitude as they appear to those involved—the schoolboys, the Neanderthal people, Pincher Martin. For each an appropriate language is devised. One is based in part upon the language of children, in part upon a reaction against R. M. Ballantyne; perhaps it also owes a little to the clear, understated descriptions of Richard Hughes's *A High Wind in Jamaica*.[12] The second, the most remarkable, is based upon the imagined limitations of speech and thought of Neanderthal man; and the third is colored by the theatricality of Martin, the actor-sailor. In each book the poet is creatively central, both as explorer of the possibilities of language, and, in a more Wordsworthian sense, as the man of imagination drawing upon the deeply founded impressions of childhood: the Cornish coast and *The Outline of History*, Wells's great book that influenced so strongly the thought and imagination of those who were children in the 1920s.

It is evident in the reading of *Poems* that some poems are more deeply felt than others. These are not always the best poems technically, for Golding had not learned to express his strongest feelings in controlled language. To be brought up where the sound of Atlantic waves breaking upon a granite coast never ceases is an ineradicable experience. Golding declares himself "Mazed with Breakers" (*mazed* is a Cornish dialect word for "maddened"). "The sea is roaring in my blood," he declares, and when he writes of the sea he writes out of his innermost being: "I can no more say 'nay' to her / Than the tide to the master-moon" (20). In "Song of the Flowers at the Land's End," he identifies himself with the flowers and expresses that sense of being young yet being part of what is old that is induced by the ancient headland

> Darkness hovers on the sea,
> The sun is set, the earth lies cold,
> And we are wild with mystery,
> So young we be, and oh! so old.
>
> (21)

Sunset over the sea, cries of gulls—these are focal centers of sight and sound for the coast dweller. Gazing into the night sky at Pegasus in "The Winged

Horse," Golding cries:

> Oh might I rise on his sunny wings for flight
> In fields of crimson above the sea's rich rim,
> Where day still wrestles with the angel of night!
>
> (23)

And he writes of the grave as a place "Where seagulls cry and tumbled waters rave" (9). No wonder that the horizon's rim and the moving sun dominate Pincher Martin on Rockall and that as he first crawls onto the rock "A seabird cried over him with a long sound descending down wind" (29). The book ends at sunset: "There was a wintry sunset behind her [the drifter] so that to the eyes on the beach she seemed soon a black shape from which the colour had all run away and been stirred into the low clouds that hung just above the horizon. There was a leaden tinge to the water except in the path of the drifter—a brighter valley of red and rose and black that led back to the dazzling horizon under the sun" (202). The drifter succeeds "The Old Boat," "old and foul as any boats that be," which had inspired a poem years before, the boat that almost

> . . . seemed the enchanted boat that bore
> Sir Launcelot to his vision of the grail
> Or Arthur darkward to the unknown shore.
>
> (30)

In the novel the picture is more somber: "the sun was going down—seemingly for ever" (206). Christopher Martin has suffered his two deaths, and the final image in the book is a fearful fusion of sinking ship and everlasting fire, the death and damnation of the protagonist: "Beyond the drifter the sun sank like a burning ship, went down, left nothing for a reminder but clouds like smoke" (208).

The seagulls of Rockall become for Martin flying reptiles, and as he comes in the end to realize that his experiences are only hallucination, he says, "A madman would see the gulls as flying lizards, he would connect the two things out of a book and it would come back to him when his brain turned no matter how long ago and forgotten the time when he read that . . ." (179). What book can this be but *The Outline of History*, with its drawing of pterodactyls and the like? That Martin is evoking a childhood memory is shown by the fact that he is at the same moment recalling his childhood fear of darkness and the terror of Death and the Old Woman in the cellar, the Old Woman he now identifies with his rock dwarf. This recreation of childhood terror gives the touch of intensity to Martin's nightmare. The motif of fear of the dark does not appear in the poems,[13] but its power here provides a suggestive basis. Certainly the night fears of the boys in *Lord of the Flies* are described too inwardly to be the mere outcome of schoolmasterly observation, and the motif occurs again in *Free Fall*.

The Inheritors remains throughout in the environment of river, waterfall, cliff, and island; in *Lord of the Flies* there are but a few flashbacks, slight and made to depend on a child's memory of detail—"that bright copper kettle and the plate with the little blue men" (139)—so that Golding can realize them with clarity; of *Pincher Martin* about one-fifth is flashback, partly to scenes and settings, such as those on board the destroyer, which Golding can recreate from experience. His ability to make the most in fewest words of isolated scenes is shown in "Vignette," in which "Demos, ruddy, round, and short, / Made bolder by the inky port," "Urges revolt," but is countered by "the squire, / Didactic by the flapping fire," who "Puts back the ticking clock of heaven / And keeps the world at half-past seven" (13). Other flashback settings in the novel are vague rooms, cars, theaters, of no importance as such and consequently drab and blurred.

Free Fall consists entirely of flashback, being Samuel Mountjoy's reflections upon his past as he seeks the place where he lost his freedom. Whether or not Golding wrote the novel, as Samuel Hynes suggests (33), as an answer to those who criticized the "narrowness and remoteness" of the world of *Pincher Martin,* the loss of that narrowness is tremendous. There is no one scene framing and projecting the whole action, but instead, there is a series of uninteresting settings which failed to stimulate Golding's imagination: schoolrooms, streets, hospitals. Occasionally a scene springs to life: the night scene in the general's garden on Paradise Hill with its echoes of Dante—"wild animals roamed those secluded acres"[14]; "Slowly the noises of people died down and our tremors died away with them so that the lions were forgotten. The high parapet of the house began to shine, a full moon lugged herself over the top and immediately the gardens were translated. There was a silver wink from the pool nearer the house, cypresses, tall and hugely still, turned one frosted side to her light. . . . Statues meditated against black deepnesses of evergreen and corners of the garden were swept by dashes of flowering trees that at that month were flowering nowhere else" (44). Night and the trespass endow the garden with remoteness, and Golding's imagination has been caught, so that when Mountjoy returns to visit Beatrice in "Paradise," now a mental hospital, he achieves that same quality of *peripeteia* that he achieved at the ends of his first two novels:[15] the transformation of the savage tribe into "A semi-circle of little boys, their bodies streaked with coloured clay, sharp sticks in their hands" (246), and that of Lok to a "red creature" (216), "a strange creature, smallish, and bowed" (218–19)

These startling payoffs, which reveal the meaning of all that has preceded, are possible because Golding has maintained consistently his viewpoint and the appropriate language. In *Pincher Martin* the peripeteia is less surely handled. First, there is the true peripeteia when Martin realizes that the seaboots are real and the Wagnerian scene on Rocknall imaginary: "The hands were resting one on either knee, above the seaboot stockings. Then there were seaboots, good and shiny and wet and solid. They made the rock behind them seem like cardboard, like a painted flat. . . . There was no background music now and no wind, nothing but black, shiny rubber" (195). Then, as if fearing his readers may miss the point, Golding adds another chapter, in which Martin is a drowned corpse, and Davidson speaks the final words: "He didn't even have time to kick off his seaboots" (208).

In *Free Fall* Golding attempts to use the method twice. Not content with the visit to Paradise Hill, where image, significance, and language are fused, he artificially withholds the explanation of the "thing . . . like an enormous dead slug" (181) in the lightless cupboard where Mountjoy is placed after interrogation by Halde, another narrow and—because locked and blacked out—remote environment that brings the author's imagination and language control to their highest pitch. The motif of childhood fear of the dark adds intensity. When we learn on the last page that the "thing" was merely a damp floor-cleaning cloth and realize that this paragraph was simply omitted from the beginning of Chapter 10, we feel tricked and, even more strongly than at the end of *Pincher Martin,* that revelation has been reduced to a gimmick.

A third limited environment in *Free Fall* that achieves glory and freshness is Rotten Row, seen through the eyes of a child, a world in itself, remote and narrow because the child knows nothing beyond it: "I crawled and tumbled in the narrow world of Rotten Row, empty as a soap bubble but with a rainbow of colour and excitement around me" (17). Even here, however, the touch is less certain than on the islands or in the primeval forest. Golding places Rotten Row "right in the heart of the Garden of England";[16] as Sammy says, "the hop gardens glowed round us" (22). But Sammy has already cast our minds to the far west and revealed himself, like his author, a man whose images spring from Cornwall by his phrase "They remind me of the druids on Brown Willie, or somewhere . . ." (13). Brown Willie, on Bodmin Moor, the highest point in Cornwall, is the first topographical name in the book, and you cannot escape its impact. Moreover, Golding has transferred to the Garden of England a type of clothesline almost universal west of Plymouth, but, I think, never seen elsewhere: "There were poles with cleats on and a variety of simple mechanisms for hoisting away the washing where it would catch the wind" (18). This book is Golding's first attempt to write a novelist's and not a poet's novel. The skill in handling language has not been lost, and Mountjoy is as surely a painter as Martin is an actor, but the central preoccupations of the book are meditative and didactic. Instead, remembering Golding's descriptions of himself, might we not say this is the schoolmaster's novel? And the schoolmaster provides the answer to its central question: "If you want something enough, you can always get it provided you are willing to make the appropriate sacrifice. Something, anything. But what you get is never quite what you thought; and sooner or later the sacrifice is always regretted" (235).

Both *Lord of the Flies* and *The Inheritors* had in part literary inspiration: they were reactions against *The Coral Island* and *The Outline of History,* personal springboards for the author. Full appreciation of the novels does not demand knowledge of the earlier works, though intellectual interest may be gained from that knowledge. In *Pincher Martin* the inspiration seems less specific. Golding has not used *Robinson Crusoe* or any other single book as his starting point, but, as Hynes says, "Golding has used the 'man-against-the-sea' conventions here just as he used the desert island conventions in *Lord of the Flies,* to provide a system of expectations against which to construct a personal and different version of the shape of things" (26). Yet we are not asked to relate the novel consciously and cerebrally to its antecedents.

Free Fall is different. The literary terms of reference are to Dante, and through allusions the whole book is made to depend on the reader's knowledge of *The Divine Comedy:* Paradise Hill, Beatrice, the wild animals, "up to the neck in the ice on Paradise Hill" (241). These references are fitful, however; unlike the earlier books, *Free Fall* is not a unified counter-image of its source. There are other allusions, too, chiefly biblical: "I have taken you up to a pinnacle of the temple and shown you the whole earth" (147); "Mr. Carew and Miss Manning were our Adam and Eve . . ." (229). Rotten Row itself, in the Garden of England, is for Sammy a prelapsarian Eden, and Ma, who "shared pleasure round like a wet-nurse's teat" (15), a kind of Oa, an earth goddess, "subnormal," "above morals or below them or outside them" (14), for as its title suggests, *Free Fall* is, like *Lord of the Flies* and *The Inheritors,* a lament for "the end of innocence, the darkness of man's heart" (*Lord of the Flies*, 248).

I have implied that in *Free Fall* Golding did not follow his true bent. Instead of centering the novel upon his poetic gifts, the exploration of language to articulate the eyes' delight in images rooted in childhood, he applied his talents peripherally to a meditative, moralizing, and didactic book that can only occasionally achieve visionary clarity. In *The Spire* he returned from this bypath, and his fifth novel is in direct line from the first three.

The central image of *The Spire* does not derive from Golding's childhood but from his teaching at Bishop Wordsworth's School, Salisbury. That the cathedral had long impressed itself upon his imagination, so that its image could join the sea and the seacoast among the deep sources of his inspiration, is already clear. Of the cathedral choir in *Lord of the Flies* Golding has said, "I chose deliberately the most highly organized, civilized, disciplined group of children it's possible to find anywhere—the cathedral choir school. It's only because of that civilized height that the fall is a tragedy."[17] This element from his adult experience fuses with those from earlier sources. But the cathedral is a world in itself, and when in *The Spire* it is also removed several centuries in time,[18] it acquires the isolation that seems more strongly than anything else to stimulate Golding's imagination and to challenge him to explore a new dimension of language. The language this time must be consistent with the medieval period and must be shaped by the mind of Jocelin, with its visions, its limited education, and its uncertain grasp of practicalities. The opening paragraph exemplifies the medieval spirit: "He was laughing, chin up, and shaking his head. God the Father was exploding in his face with a glory of sunlight through painted glass, a glory that moved with his movements to consume and exalt Abraham and Isaac and then God again. The tears of laughter in his eyes made additional spokes and wheels and rainbows."[19] This poetical splendor has another element in it, for the glory has physical causes and the seeds of the payoff are already planted, seeds that will flower bitterly when the angel is revealed as "a consumption of the back and spine" (218). Jocelin's simplicity and lack of understanding demand that Golding use nontechnical terms when describing the problems and solutions of the mason, so that we see them as the dean sees them: "He set dishes of water on the pavement, chocking them up with slivers of wood, and sighted at them. He made a scratch on the stone of each of the four pillars of the crossways and drew a chalk mark over each scratch. . . . He would stand . . . by a door in the south transept, and squint at each mark in turn, then look for their reflections in the dish of water. When the chalk dropped from a pillar, he marked it again" (74).

The technique breaks down in the important description of the octagons and wedges contrived to support the spire from within. The general idea is clear: "He'll slacken the cable little by little and let the octagons, or the members between them, stretch down. The whole thing'll hang, and hold the spire against the wind" (145). But it is probably impossible, from the words of the book, to visualize precisely the working of the device. We are left with Roger Mason's irritated "There aren't any names for bits of stone and wood. That thing fits on that thing, which'll fit on that thing—perhaps" (146). It is an isolated failure and, as such, a measure of Golding's success in the book as a whole: the digging of the pit, the raising of the walls, the welding of the iron band around the tower, the swaying height, the bending pillars. Once more Golding is writing from strength. The basic moral issue is again that of *Free Fall:* "Let it be so. Cost what you like" (35). But in this book the cost is not sought and found through meandering reflection, but manifested in unmistakable pictures. The spire is Jocelin's phallic aspiration, to which Goody is sacrificed: the innocent child seen as devil, married off to the impotent Pangall—himself also sacrificed to the spire—allowed to be seduced by the mason, and destroyed in childbirth; the mason himself corrupted and broken. It is all visible in the eye of writer and reader. So, too, the moment of peripeteia—derived to some extent from Hyde and Dorian Gray, but freshly re-created—is achieved through the eye: "Someone else was facing him. This creature was framed by the metal sheet that stood against the sky opposite him. For a moment he thought of exorcism, but when he lifted his hand, the figure raised one too. So he crawled across the boards on hands and knees and the figure crawled towards him. He knelt and peered in at the wild halo of hair, the skinny arms and legs that stuck out of a girt and dirty robe. . . . Well Jocelin, he said soundlessly to the kneeling image; well Jocelin, this is where we have come" (154–155). The dean has become devil. And we see it with our eyes. By no coincidence Jocelin realizes at this moment, as the Midsummer Night bonfires flicker, that Pangall was ritually murdered: "and at the crossways, the replaced paving stones were hot to his feet with all the fires of hell" (157).

If this were all, the novel would add a new image but little new meaning to Golding's works. It is not all. In *Free Fall* Golding attempted to suggest that through the experience in the dark cupboard Mountjoy became "a man resurrected . . . desiring nothing, accepting all things and giving all created

things away" (186). But the book as a whole does not convince us of his trans-
mutation. The effort to express a positive conclusion, in contrast to that of
Pincher Martin, is unconnected with the sacrifice of Beatrice Ifor, against
which it is to be set.

The spire, however, is an image capable of comprehending positives as well
as negatives. "Four hundred feet up in the sky," it exists before our eyes. It has
not the purity and perfection of the "invisible geometric lines that sketched
themselves automatically above the battlements of the crossways" (35) in
Jocelin's vision; instead it "leans a little, threatening the cloisters. It's im-
pacted into the parapet at the top of the tower. There's deal of broken stone"
(189). But it stands. A dead man walled into its foundations, built on moving
bog and hollow pillars, based, like Jocelin's career, on sin and corruption, it
stands: *"It's like the appletree!"* (223). Again, for his conclusion, Golding finds
not discourse but an image—the apple tree "bursting up with cloud and
scatter, laying hold of the earth and the air" (205). There is a charity, a
breadth and humanity in *The Spire* lacking in the earlier books. There is
complexity and subtlety of relationship and meaning far greater than in any of
them, but because Golding has returned to his sources of strength and laid
hold upon a more complex and positive image than any he previously found,
the book has the unity and force of *The Inheritors* while achieving something of
the humanity he attempted less successfully in *Free Fall.* The final tremor of
Jocelin's lips might be interpreted as *"God! God! God!"* but almost certainly is
"Goody! Goody! Goody!," a play upon sounds, a sort of serious pun, that allows
the closing sentence to be without sentimentality: "So of the charity to which
he had access, he laid the Host on the dead man's tongue" (223).[20]

The spire is the most clearly realized of Golding's major images; it is introduced on the first page and is central to the book. The sole reference to the
title image in *The Pyramid* is about forty pages from the end: "They also
vibrated in time to the crystal pyramid."[21] The significance is far from evident
until we recall the description of Bounce's tomb: "At the head was at least a
ton of marble rhomboid; and, finest touch of all, this rhomboid had been
carved with such a naturalistic representation of a harp, one might have
thought the marble strings were vibrating in sympathy with the organ"
161–162). A rhomboid is not quite a pyramid, and marble is not crystal, so it
is possible to read the book several times before realizing that Bounce's tomb
is the pyramid that gives the book its title, and that this tomb is an image of
the major themes: sexual frustration, the exploitation of persons, the snobbery
of small-town class structure, bourgeois philistinism, the ugly perversions

and hatreds underlying the humdrum pattern of life in Stilbourne, and the haunting fears of childhood (much the same as haunted Martin and Mountjoy). "That pathetic, horrible, unused body, with the stained frills and Chinese face" (213) which lies in the tomb is a victim, as Beatrice in *Free Fall* is a victim, both driven insane through exploitation and sexual unfulfillment. The weight of the marble and the cruel irony of the quotation of her father's words, "Heaven is Music," express the destruction of Bounce through the twin forces of her father's frustrated musical ambitions and Henry's econo-mico-emotional exploitation of her starved personality. And Bounce, the hated music teacher to whom the boy is always alleged to be "devoted," is an image, too, of Evie the exploited temptress, victim of Captain Wilmot's sadism and her father's incest, whom Oliver regards as "our local phenomenon," merely an "accessible" female, until years later he sees "a different picture of Evie in her life-long struggle to be clean and sweet. It was as if this object of frustration and desire had suddenly acquired the attributes of a person rather than a thing . . ." (111). These connections, however, are made intellectually and in retrospect. The pyramid lacks the numinous quality of the spire, of Oa, of the pig's head, or of the moonlit gardens on Paradise Hill. It is a symbol as solid and matter-of-fact as its own marble.

This is Golding's second attempt to write a novelistic novel. A great advance upon *Free Fall* in readability, it leaves an impression of lightness and triviality by no means justified when the underlying darkness has been un-covered; for covered it is, and a rapid reader can easily miss the horror of the Babbacombe and Dawlish households. It is as if Golding, trying to make his somber vision of the human condition more palatable to a popular audience, allowed his literary talents to displace his poetic genius. The comedy has been welcomed by some critics. There is riotous farce in the two-seater car that dumps Robert and Evie in the pond, but most of the comedy is too superficial to justify the expenditure of the time and energies of William Golding.

In this book Golding shows less imaginative grip upon place than in *Free Fall*. His village of Stilbourne (a dreadful pun?) is placed in an unsubstantial area vaguely compounded of an unvisualized South Devon (suggested by the names Babbacombe and Dawlish) and a casually introduced Trollopian world of Barchester and Omnium that contributes nothing but bookish unreality. So uncertain is the reader's picture of Stilbourne in the 1930s that when Oliver returns in 1963, we receive no shock that "That right hand side of the High Street, almost from the Old Bridge to the Square has been swallowed by concrete, plateglass, chrome" (158), because the old High Street has never been sharply presented.

For most of the book, Golding has cut himself off from the sources of his inspiration. Occasionally there is a flash of the intensity of his best work, as when the child Oliver is left in the lavatory: "I stayed where I was against the wall and the ice of that darkness and remoteness formed on my skin and in my hair. The stump of candle shortened itself" (170). It has not the power of similar passages in *Pincher Martin* or *Free Fall* but is of the same order. At a major climax of the book, when Oliver is so carried away by Evie's sensuality that he in his turn becomes a mere thing and cannot practice the *coitus interruptus* of his first intercourse with her, Golding, seeking expressive imagery, does call upon the sea, and for a few moments the words break into fire:

> She would not consent to any quick rhythm; only the long, deep ocean swell in which her man, her boy, was an object, no more: and this deep swell of an apparently boneless woman was accompanied by a turning away of the head, both eyes shut, forehead lined—a kind of anguished journey, concentrated on reaching a far spot, dark, agonizing and wicked. I was a small boat in a deep sea; and the sea itself was a moaning, private thing, full of contempt and disgust, a thing to which a partner was necessary but not welcome. I could no longer direct; and my boat was overwhelmed by waves, suddenly controlled by her, driven towards the rock, where a cry arose, loud and tortured, and I was among the breakers, shipwrecked. . . ."(79)

In *Lord of the Flies* "the end of innocence" has nothing to do with sex. In *The Pyramid* it has everything to do with it. Oliver's father has watched him and Evie through his binoculars:

> . . . suddenly, for all his professed but indifferent agnosticism the voice of generations of chapel burst out of him.
> "This man what d'you me call him—these books—cinema—papers— this sex—it's *wrong, wrong, wrong!*"
> I stood, a heap of dung, yearning desperately for some sewer up which I might crawl and reach my parents, kneel, be forgiven, so that the days of our innocence might return again. (100)

Sex is an essential element of the Fall in *The Inheritors, Pincher Martin,* and *The Spire,* but in none of these does Golding have to bring women into the foreground as people. The postlapsarian sexuality of the New People is seen by the Neanderthalers with objectivity: "The two people beneath the tree were making noises fiercely as though they were quarreling. In particular the fat woman had begun to hoot like an owl and Lok could hear Tuami gasping like a man who fights with an animal and does not think he will win. He looked down at them and saw Tuami was not only lying with the fat woman but eating her as well for there was black blood running from the lobe of her ear" (175). The women in *Pincher Martin* are seen only fitfully in flashback scenes; in *The Spire* the celibacy of Jocelin forms a kind of distancing glass through which even Goody Pangall is little more than a "long, sweet face" and "a glimpse of green dress as the grey cloak swung back" (11). But in *Free Fall* and *The Pyramid* women are brought into the foreground as objects and as persons.

In Golding's *Poems* about eight poems are addressed to or directly about women or girls. Some are among his most immature:

> I will not moan
> Nor rant of endless love or make-belief,
> For I have known
> In my few years a brimming meed of grief.
> (9)

Even so, adolescent truth rings in the couplet "And I could lie and close my eyes, / And cry for you as a child cries" (33). Some relate the girl to the world of nature, as if Golding were more at ease with images of natural objects than with the girl:

> Thunder that mutters,
> Brooklets that murmur
> Are words that she utters,
> And runes to confirm her.
> I will not rime thee—
> 'Twere to be ringing
> Cracked bells and crazen,
> When all the earth is singing.
> (14–15)

. . . .

> At noon the drowsy sun-winds brush
> A shadow from the swarted corn,
> At noon the linnet and the thrush
> Sing dirges for the light of morn,
> And oh! I think our world is dead
> So much is fallen, so much is fled.
> (33)

In others he has a more objective, lighter touch, the slightly Donne-ish quality of the "Non-Philosopher's Song," for instance: "Her sweet resemblance I do find / In the dim cavern of my mind" (17). This lightness is prepared in "Pish and Tush" to confirm "the rule / That brainless be the beautiful" (31). He writes of "the touch of your hands," "the softness of your tongue," "the shadows of your hair," "our larklike laughter," and "the swiftness of your feet" (18). Feet are in two poems the image for the whole woman: the "winking-white" feet of Helen in "Rondo" (6) and the dancer's feet that

> . . . make complete
> With wisdom of
> Their own the tale
> Her lips would love
> To speak—but fail.
>   (24)

Is there a recollection of this youthful fascination with girls' feet in Evie's "unquiet walk" in *The Pyramid* and the "tightrope poise" of Beatrice in *Free Fall?* The lightly satirical vein of "Pish and Tush" appears more strongly in "Long Division": "And then she'll feel soul-moist, and good, / As one who Grieved and Understood—" (11).

No girl in the *Poems* is clearly realized, and when Golding is faced, in *Free Fall* and *The Pyramid,* with the problem of realizing women he barely solves it. Never does he portray convincingly a satisfactory and lasting sex-love relationship. The first suggestion of one in the novels is that of Nathaniel and Mary in *Pincher Martin,* but it is only a hint. Taffy in *Free Fall* makes great impact when we first see her: "She was dark and vivid. She had the kind of face that always looks made-up, even in the bath—such black eyebrows, such a big, red mouth. She was the prettiest girl I ever saw, neat in profile, with soft cheeks and two dimples that were in stunning contrast with her tenor voice and scarifying language" (126). But this brilliant creature disappears into the background, and the happy and fulfilled married life of which Kenneth is jealous must be taken as read. Oliver's wife is not even granted a name, let alone a character. When he has to bring women into the foreground Golding must *distance* them in some way. It may be by age: Mountjoy's Ma and Oliver's mother are competently created "character parts." Eccentricity (a species of psychological distancing) also enables him to succeed—Miss Pringle, for instance, and above all, Bounce, his best and fullest portrayal. Beatrice Ifor and Evie Babbacombe are seen as their young seducers see them—as objects, and in each book the identity of the person hidden behind the object is but glimpsed. Every sexual act described by Golding is one of exploitation. Sex as expression of love is implied faintly in the background, but what is actualized, made real before the mind's eye from Tuami to Oliver, is sex as lust, as possession, sex of the serpent and the Fall. The wolf whistle given as a "stage direction" at the end of "Pish and Tush" echoes through the novels from the primeval jungles to the woods of Stilbourne. Whatever his personal attitude may be, Golding the novelist shows sex as dirt, "life's lavatory," and his novels repeat endlessly the cry of Oliver's father: "This sex—it's *wrong, wrong, wrong!*"

Love between the sexes did not evoke the best of Golding's youthful poetry; the "mate-less Beauty" of the phoenix was more powerful. Nor does it call out the best in the poet of prose fiction.[22] The remote in place and time, the burning bird in the desert sky, the sea, the island, the prehistoric world, the narrow life of the medieval monk, the forbidden garden by moonlight, the dark cupboard and childhood fear of the dark—these are the things which bring to Golding's imagination clear pictures, alive with "The glory and the freshness of a dream," and which arouse in him the ablity to communicate the pictures, "exploring the possibilities of language" to convey not only the picture but all its meanings and associations.

Twelve years divide *The Pyramid* from Golding's next full-length novel, *Darkness Visible*, whose title tells us that this time Milton provides the counter-image of hell and the encounter of "Thrones, Dominions, Princedoms, Virtues, Powers." In the very first paragraph the "cope of hell," "vaulted with fire,"[23] is evoked in a "kind of tent in the sky over London, which was composed of the faint white beams of searchlights." Hell is on earth, here in London. Or is it? For the fire caused by the bombs is described as "a burning bush,"[24] and out of a burning bush, as we know, will come not a devil but "the angel of the Lord."[25] "The figure was a child, drawing nearer. . . . He was naked and the miles of light hit him variously" (14). There is something miraculous about the apparition: "Nor do small children walk out of a fire that is melting lead and distorting iron" (13). Biblical associations flicker through the mind: "walking in the midst of the fire, and they have no hurt; and the form of the fourth is like the Son of God."[26]

The associations crystallize in Robert Southwell's "The Burning Babe." Not that this matters, except to the critical explorer, any more than *The Coral Island* or *The Outline of History* matter to the new reader, for Golding once more has created image and myth that exist independently of their counterparts. The phoenix of his early poem is transformed from burning bird to burning babe. "Toiling through the hot dumb sand / Bare-footed in the barren hills" of Australia, he is crucified and partly castrated by Harry Bummer, the corrupted aboriginal:

> Oh Phoenix! did they hear as I
> The agony, the lonely cry
> Of mateless, mateless, mateless Beauty,
> Echoing in the desert sky?
>
> (34)

Matty's beauty is not physical but spiritual. He is mateless *because of* his physical ugliness; yet his manner of coming and his nature recall "The Eyes' Delight":

> In what age of wonder came
> From nowhere to the earth and sky
> Such a flower and such a flame?
>
> (5)

Phoenix-like, Matty (Matthew, the first evangelist), born of flame, Milton's flame of "liquid fire" (I, 229)—"Somewhere a tank of something had exploded" (11–12)—dies in the same flame:

> The water ran into the burning tank, and instead of putting out the flames, sank down and pushed the petrol up. The burning petrol flooded out in a blazing tide. . . . In the chaos a strange man dressed as a soldier was able to carry a burden out of the school. . . . This man . . . ran as fast as he could towards the darkness of the trees. But the flaming tide made him take a curving run and as he did so, a strange thing happened in the fire. It seemed to organize itself into a shape of flame that rushed out of the garage doors and whirled round and round. It made as if on purpose for the man and his burden. It whirled round still and the only noise from it was that of burning. It came so close to the man and it was so monstrous he dropped the bundle and a boy leapt out of it and ran away. . . . The firemonster jigged and whirled. After a time it fell down; and after some more time it lay still.
>
> (248)

He has died as the elders told him he would die: "Now there is a great spirit that shall stand behind the being of the child you are guarding. That is what you are for. You are to be a burnt offering" (238). And in this book there are no seaboots, there is no wet floorcloth, no rationalist explanation. The mystery is unexplained.

So is the mystery of Sophy. Matty, the visionary, believes his destiny is determined by spirits. Sophy believes in the increase of entropy, in her own will, and in the proposition that "as soon as the future was comprehended it was inescapable" (108), like the death of the dabchick killed by her well-aimed and firmly-willed pebble. The path from the death of the dabchick to the bomb—"Sophy's idea worked perfectly" (248)—and the realization that she was capable of "the last outrage" (251) is then as "foreordained" as the curving flight of the pebble and the "scrap of fluff turning gently as the stream bore it out of sight" (109). In no earlier novel has Golding created so perfect an image of unregenerate Man, with no attempt at excuse or extenuation, and simultaneously for the first time he has created a real, fully imagined, completely convincing woman. He has done this by using again his extraordinary ability, revealed in *Lord of the Flies,* to portray children from within. Within ourselves we do not "grow up," we know the continuity between what we are as adults and what we were as children. Starting with the little girl and the dabchick, Golding follows from within, in terms of concrete, specific, usually visual imagery, her predestined growth to amoral criminality. The description of Sophy—after she has deliberately lost her virginity—washing out her womb and feeling with her fingers "the rounded shape of her own turd working down the coiled gut" (138) expresses, in a fearful poetry more intense than anything of the sort he has done before, Golding's sense of what in *The Pyramid* he called "life's lavatory" (91). At the same time and through the same character, he leads the reader down through the circles of hell of our own times, from the air-raids of the 1940s to the terrorism and kidnappings of the 1970s.

In Matty and Sophy are polarized the limits of Golding's poetic world, each, like pebble and dabchick, carried forward by a different kind of necessity, touching each other without comprehension through the "lost" engagement ring, yet both, the destroyer and the savior, terrifyingly and inexplicably essential aspects of an even more terrifying and inexplicable Oneness.

Through that brief contact with Sophy, Matty recovers the virility he thought he had completely lost and becomes again a complete human being: "I am a man I could have a son" (237). She comes to him in a dream "in terrible glory all in colours" (236) as the woman of the Apocalypse, but though she makes him "defile" himself, as he expresses it, "I could not either be *frightened or ashamed*. . . . Is she then disguised as an angel of light or is she a good spirit" (237). The "convergence of the twain" adumbrated in the pebble and the dabchick provides the novel with a structure firmer than any since *Pincher Martin* and one which images its meaning. Avoiding the "novelistic" pitfall, Golding has buried under his poetic sequence a story line that leads to the most powerful narrative climax he has yet achieved.

With the recovery of poetic imagery has come the recovery of the vivid

sense of place. The clarity of vision is uneven, but most of the many localities
are seen in firm detail and outline: Frankley's, with its now demolished
system of overhead communication; the Australian desert; the room in the
stables; the old, rotting barge on the canal, which recalls "The Old
Boat"—"She was old and foul as any boats that be" (30).

In the early part of the book there are some images which are perhaps not
essential to the central theme, though not discordant with it, as if after twelve
years of gestation Golding could not bring himself to discard some of the
isolated visions he had met on the way: Mr. Hanrahan's room of distorting
mirrors is an obvious example. But if a few new images could possibly be
trimmed away, those which can be traced back to the poems are always
organic parts of the whole: In the "Non-Philosopher's Song" we read:

> For when I tread with careful thought
> The tunnels that my brain has wrought
> Her sweet resemblance I do find
> In the dim cavern of my mind.
>
> (17)

Far from the sentimental world of the poem we find Sophy, as she reflects on
her own individuality, asking herself "how could the creature called Sophy
who sat there at the mouth of the tunnel behind her belong to anyone but
herself?" (123).

The notion of "the vacuity of your mind," instead of leading to the trite
conclusion of the poem, "That brainless be the beautiful" (31), leads to
Sophy's judgement on her twin sister, Toni: "But there's nothing there . . .
nothing at all. Just the minimum flesh and bones, nothing else, no one to
meet, no one to go with, be with, share with. Just ideas. Ghosts. Ideas and
emptiness, the perfect terrorist" (253).

As part of a coda, half of the last chapter is given to the pain and humiliation of Sim Goodchild as his participation in the "seance" is exposed to the
prurient and contemptuous public gaze. Leaving the courts, "he walked down
the side road to join Fleet Street and thus avoid the queue of those who were
still unable to get in" (255). "Queue at the Law Courts" is the title of a savage
little poem that compares those in the queue to "nosing curs" who

> Themselves too weak to sin or kill,
> Too weak for anger or for hate
> That red blood pulses out in spate—
> Must sidle here to lick the crust
> And leaving of another's lust.
>
> (25)

Reading this we may begin to understand how Golding is able to create Sophy and compel us to accept her. So vividly has he made "visible" the "darkness of man's heart," so far penetrated the underworld, that he stands in awe of his own apocalypse and in his epigraph appeals with Vergil and the gods whose empire is of souls, *Sit mihi fas audita loqui.* And as we close the book we know that it is indeed lawful for Golding to speak what he has heard, because he has had the courage and the honesty to write what he has found within himself, to expose the heights and depths of his soul to the fire of artistic creation.

Of the poet, Wordsworth said, "he has acquired a greater readiness and power in expressing what he thinks and feels and especially those thoughts and feelings which, by his own choice, or *from the structure of his own mind* arise in him without immediate external excitement"[27] [italics mine]. When Golding finds his subject matter in thoughts and feelings which arise spontaneously "from the structure of his own mind," the poet is brought to life, and when such thoughts and feelings are the center of a novel, then poetic power pervades the whole book. With other subject matter, the fire is not kindled, the imagination does not take wing, and he writes simply as a talented man of letters.

NOTES

1. Quoted by Samuel Hynes, *William Golding,* Columbia Essays on Modern Writers, No. 2 (New York: Columbia Univ. Press, 1964), 3. See also William Golding, "The Writer in His Age," *London Magazine,* May 1957, pp. 45–46. [Ed.]

2. In a personal letter to me, 27 January 1964.

3. Cecil W. Davies, "The Novels Foreshadowed: Some Recurring Themes in Early Poems by William Golding," *English,* 17 (Autumn 1968), 86–89.

4. W. G. Golding, *Poems* (London: Macmillan, 1934), 34.

5. Ibid., 6, 10, 10, 13, 19, 25, 34.

6. *Lord of the Flies* (London: Faber, 1954), 11.

7. William Blake, *Jerusalem,* "Foreword" by Geoffrey Keynes (London: Trianon Press for the William Blake Trust, 1952), plate 55, 1.51, 64.

8. Peter Green in *The Daily Telegraph.*

9. *The Inheritors* (London: Faber, 1955), 15–18.

10. Michael Roberts, ed., *The Faber Book of Modern Verse* (London: Faber, 1948), 3.

11. *Pincher Martin* (London: Faber, 1956), 164.

12. In an interview at Purdue University, 10 May 1962, Golding conceded that he had read *A High Wind in Jamaica,* but only *after* he had written *Lord of the Flies.* See James Keating, "Interview with William Golding," in *William Golding's "Lord of the Flies,"* Casebook ed., ed. James R. Baker and Arthur P. Ziegler, Jr. (New York: Putnam's, 1964), 194. [Ed.]

13. Unless the lines addressed from "Youth to Age" are relevant:

> . . . thy bed
> Is set in dark night
> Among the quiet dead.

(10)

14. *Free Fall* (London: Faber, 1959), 42.

15. I use the word *peripeteia* for the sudden reversal of viewpoint so frequent in Golding, which is similar in artistic effect to that sudden reversal of fortune that is the normal meaning of the word.

16. The counties of Kent and Worcester are both termed the "Garden of England." [Ed.]

17. Quoted by Ian Gregor in three pages of duplicated notes headed *William Golding,* January 1964.

18. Salisbury Cathedral itself had a squat tower and no spire until 1330. See G. H. Cook, *The English Cathedral through the Centuries* (London: Readers Union, Phoenix House, 1960), 107, *et passim.*

19. *The Spire* (London: Faber, 1964), 7.

20. A similar wordplay, that on the name of Rockall in *Pincher Martin*—"I call that name a near miss" (31)—is no mere vulgarism, for it is one of the earlier hints that this "Rockall" is nonexistent, nothing—in common parlance, "fuck-all." Golding has acknowledged that he intended the pun. See Jack I. Biles, *Talk: Conversations with William Golding,*74. [Ed.]

21. *The Pyramid* (London: Faber, 1967), 178.

22. Two quotations from *Free Fall* are relevant here. The speaker is, of course, Golding's creation Mountjoy:

> She did not make love, for *I take that to be* a passionate attempt to confirm that the wall which parted them is down [italics mine]. (14)

* * *

> A young man certain of nothing but salt sex; certain that if there was a positive value in living it was this undeniable pleasure. . . . Therefore the tickling pleasure, the little death shared or self-inflicted was neither irrelevant nor sinful but the altar of whatever shoddy temple was left to us. But there remained deep as an assessment of experience itself the knowledge that if this was everything it was a poor return for birth, for the shames and frustrations of growing up. (108)

23. John Milton, *Paradise Lost,* X, 460; I, 345; I, 298.

24. William Golding, *Darkness Visible* (London: Faber, 1979), 9.

25. Exodous 3: 2.

26. Daniel 3: 25.

27. *Preface to Lyrical Ballads* (1800).

Golding and the Voice of Chapel

JACK I. BILES

"This sex—it's *wrong, wrong, wrong!*"
—OLIVER'S FATHER

"You must offer up mariage, sex, love,
because, because, *because!*"
—MATTHEW SEPTIMUS WINDROVE

The great traumas of life have been identified as birth, marriage, and death. Marriage may strike one as a euphemism, dating from some more nearly innocent past, for sexual initiation. William Golding behaves uncertainly and exhibits in his writings both a fascination (slightly horrified) with the sexual trauma and a revulsion (again, slightly horrified) from it. Commentators, critics—especially writers at length, who have an obligation to notice such fundamental matters—ignore the subject consistently, but Golding does not leave it alone. For better or for worse, the attraction and the shrinking persistently recur.

To the remark that the Calvinism attributed to him seemed rather too rigid, Golding replied, "It might not be rigid for what I've written. . . . Now I don't think it's true I'm a Calvinist, but I'm willing to believe that my capacity for writing, such as it is, and my general make-up and my experience have made my books shape themselves so that Calvinism could be deduced from them."[1]

As a writer about sex, Golding is apt to display in the same passage a quasi-puritanical reticence and a self-conscious show of four-letter words; the combination suggests a sort of bashful exhibitionist, one who talks of "the rigid and burning root of the matter"—both metaphor and vulgarism—and is mindful of how dreadful it all is. And the metaphor is likely to be a figure for transgression of religious or moral dicta. Both the reticence and the compensatory indelicacy appear in the killing of the maternal sow in *Lord of the Flies*: "the hunters followed, wedded to her in lust, excited by the long chase and the dropped blood. . . . Jack was on top of the sow, stabbing downward with his knife. Roger found a lodgment for his point. . . . The sow collapsed under them and they were heavy and fulfilled upon her."[2] Although one may disagree with the Freudianizing of her death,[3] the slaughter of the sow is couched in obvious sexual imagery. In the quotation, "lust" is the only incontrovertibly sexual word, but practically every word or phrase is clearly sexual metaphorically; and few adult readers would not recognize that Jack's knife and Roger's spear are phalluses. Pincher Martin states the figure bluntly: "A sword is a phallus. . . . A phallus is a sword"[4]; another ready example is Captain Wilmot's "Fix bayonets!" in *The Pyramid*.[5] The coarseness is seen in Robert's ribaldry as Roger withdraws his spear: "Right up her ass!" (162). Golding pulls away from overt phrasing in *The Pyramid* when Oliver cannot maneuver his halberd up the stairway:

> "He couldn't get his halberd up the back passage. They'll never believe it."
> "What shall I do?"
> "You'll have to enter from in front, then, won't you?" (152)

The double entendre here serves a double function. It says what Robert says without saying it and it is funny, which Robert's words are not, no matter how much the prepubescent boys may laugh.

To treat sex humorously is to treat it figuratively, evasively; to refuse to call its name is to avoid calling spirits from the vasty deep, lest they come. Golding depends much upon humor as subterfuge to evade a discomforting sexuality. An especially funny instance is the offstage, distanced intercourse of Bobby Ewan and Evie Babbacombe:

> [Bobby]   "Not much room in these machines. Our young friend was sitting in the front seat and I took the boards out so that I could stand on the ground. Got it? Only we ran away—the old bus did. I must have sort of jerked the handbrake off with me arse, somehow."

Oliver asks why he didn't put the brake on.

> [Bobby]   "Have you ever tried running backwards down a slope with

your trousers round your ankles?"

[Oliver]   "Bloody girl, then. Why didn't *she* put on the brake?"

[Bobby]   "How could she, with her feet up on the windscreen? . . .
          Still—she's a really sporty girl, that young Babbacombe, I
          give her that."

[Oliver]   "Why?"

[Bobby]   "She tried to steer." (19–20)

When Golding does not avoid the dramatized, onstage account of a sexual encounter, he is prone to undercut the action with a farcical presentation. In *Rites of Passage*, Edmund Talbot's physical congress with Zenobia Brocklebank—even self-important, impercipient Edmund, who at least knows her for what she is, could not term it a seduction—is masked by burlesque, allusion, metaphor:

> . . . soon, sure enough, Miss Zenobia came tripping down to find perhaps a shawl against the tropic night! I was out of my hutch, had her by the wrist and jerked her back in with me before she could even pretend a startled cry! But there was noise enough from other places and noise enough from the blood pounding in my ears so that I pressed my suit with positive ardor! We wrestled for a moment by the bunk, she with a nicely calculated exertion of strength that only just failed to resist me, I with mounting passion. My sword was in my hand and I boarded her! She retired in disorder to the end of the hutch where the canvas basin awaited her in its iron hoop. I attacked once more and the hoop collapsed. The bookshelf tilted. *Moll Flanders* lay open on the deck, *Gil Blas* fell on her and my aunt's parting gift to me, Hervey's *Meditations among the Tombs* (MDCCLX) II vols London covered them both. I struck them all aside and Zenobia's tops'ls too. I called on her to yield, yet she maintained a brave if useless resistance that fired me even more. I bent for the *main course*. We flamed against the ruins of the canvas basin and among the trampled pages of my little library. We flamed upright. Ah—she did yield at last to my conquering arms, was overcome, rendered up all the tender spoils of war!
>
> However—if your lordship follows me—although it is our male privilege to *debellare* the *superbos*—the *superbas*, if you will—it is something of a duty I think to *parcere* the *subjectis*! In a sentence, having gained the favors of *Venus* I did not wish to inflict the pains of *Lucina*! Yet her abandonment was complete and passionate. I did not think female heat could increase—but as bad luck would have it, at that very critical moment there came from the deck above our heads the sound of a veritable explosion.[6]

Facetious and witty, the farce is rendered more penetrating by the skillful use of allusion. After the tilting of the bookshelf, "*Moll Flanders* lay open on the deck." As Moll was "Twelve Year a Whore" and participated in a variety of sexual activities throughout a substantial part of a long life, it seems fair enough to dub her an old whore; and, given Zenobia's ubiquitous fornicating, Moll seems an appropriate literary counterpart for her. One notes further that "to lay open on the deck" seems not only an obvious but a standard position for Zenobia literally and for Moll figuratively in the form of her autobiography. *Moll Flanders* is a celebrated near-picaresque story and Moll shows a virtue close to that of the picaro; *Gil Blas* is what Dickens would call "the genuine article," and the title character, like Lazarillo de Tormes, epitomizes the amoral rogue of the *gusto picaresco*. Like Tom Jones, fornicators all. Golding roguishly has the male book fall on the open female book, and most appropriately so, for *Moll Flanders*, *Gil Blas*, and Golding's scene are pornography in the literal sense—derived from the Greek for depiction of whores and prostitution.

Edmund's "little library" consists of three titles, two undoubtedly chosen by him and shamelessly cavorting on the deck; the third, his "aunt's parting gift," is James Hervey's *Meditations and Contemplations*, originally published in two volumes in 1746–47 and presented to him by his surely maiden aunt in a reprint of this much-handled book. This pious work stands in conspicuous contrast to the two impure books and the shopworn favors of Moll and Zenobia.

The wretched quality of Hervey's "false gallop of rhetoric" is described by Sir Leslie Stephen as "precisely of that kind which disgusts a cultivated reader, and passes with the half-educated for true eloquence."[7] That Gil has fallen upon Moll and that Hervey's tomes of piety and broodings upon death cover them both with sentimentality, enthusiasm, and "the religious unction of Wesleyanism" implies the fundamentalist connection of sex with sin and the scarlet woman of Revelation. One might also reasonably see reference to the familiar association of orgasm with a "little death,"[8] certainly since Hervey meditated in a graveyard. And "fired," "flamed," and "sexual heat" bring to mind in such a context not only sexual urgency, but also the blazes of hell.

The language of this passage has a burden of cliché and other trite formulaic expressions. This wretched language serves two consequential purposes: first, here is precisely the phrasing of vain, dull Edmund Talbot to the life; second, the author clearly relies upon the reader's recognition that this diction is used ironically as a major component of the humorous effect of the scene. Beyond suspension of disbelief is that the strumpet Zenobia could "come tripping," except affectedly, under any circumstances; however, one instantly knows the reality as Edmund, much conscious of his wit, writes his labored and leaden-footed irony about the "shawl against the tropic night!"—a would-be witticism needlessly emphasized by the exclamation mark. At this point, Golding, beyond his character's subtlety, has his narrator's jibe at Edmund for the reader's benefit by causing Edmund to write "had her by the wrist," when he has not had her, but in the nature of things assuredly is going to have her. Edmund recites his rosary of cliché: before "she could even pretend a startled cry!" his blood is "pounding" so that he "pressed my suit"—presumably double-breasted—with "positive ardor!" At this juncture, "We wrestled for a moment by the bunk, she with a nicely calculated exertion of strength that only just failed to resist me, I with mounting passion!" She sufficiently manages to hold Edmund off, but his passion mounts; what else could it do? *Mounting* is "the act of rising [indubitably phallic here] or getting up on something." Mounting is a virtual homophone of mountain, which directs us to *mons* (mountain) *veneris* (Venus or love, lust). Directly, therefore, "My sword was in my hand [like Oliver's in Evie's] and I boarded her!" Again, Pincher Martin has *le mot juste*: "A sword is a phallus. What a huge mountain-shaking joke! A phallus is a sword" (95–96). No wonder that Zenobia "retired in disorder" and "maintained a brave if useless resistance."

Pursuing his own special lingo of superiority, Edmund quotes from Virgil: "*Parcere subjectis et debellare superbos*," "to battle down the haughty, / To spare the meek."[9] Then, he parades what learning he has and makes the quotation more directly applicable by offering the substitution of the feminine "*superbas*, if you will." He forgets his exclamation mark, apparently.

Manipulation of language for purposes of humor, especially in sexual contexts, is not exclusive with Golding, but it is a customary usage, a sort of identification. So also is it a mode of evasion. Shortly before Oliver's first sexual success with Evie, Golding proffers some fairly typical adolescent maneuvering:

> I laughed and held up my bruised finger. She took it to examine the tip with her own white fingers; and the performance repeated itself as if we were something reproduced from a die or plate—the giggles and laughter, the change from pursued to pursuer, the lugging down into the darkness of the pier, the semisurrender face to face, denial, consent, denial, kiss and struggle, scent, three plums and a glimmering skin, vibration—
> "Don't you like me?"
> "'Course I do—no, Olly, you mustn't—"

"Aw come on—"

"You mustn't—it's not nice!"

I knew and accepted that it wasn't nice; knew too that as far as I was concerned, niceness wasn't the point.

(53–54)

This encounter is amusing, familiar, and ostensibly innocent; nonetheless, double entendre and sexual innuendo are present. In Golding, Shakespearean reference is so frequent as not to be ignored. The opening to-do about Oliver's finger may well reflect Lady Percy's sexually ambiguous effort to persuade Hotspur to remain at home; when he will not answer plainly, she threatens amorously:

> In faith, I'll break thy little finger, Harry,
> An if thou wilt not tell me all things true.
> (2.3.90–91)

The digit to which she alludes is neither finger, toe, nor number symbol. Hotspur is evasive, but reassures her with a glance at Ruth, 1.16: "Whither I go, thither shall you go too" (2.3.118). Golding's finger pun looks forward to Oliver's maiden intercourse with Evie, that results when "I took out the rigid and burning root of the matter and laid her unresisting hands on it" (71). There are other multimeaning words like "bruised." Oliver has hurt his finger on the piano: "There's a note—G natural—I have to hit it in passing with this finger, you see—" (48); it feels "as if the end of the bone had been bruised" (50). Because he suspects her promiscuity, Sergeant Babbacombe blackens Evie's left eye (24, 28, 45); Evie's mouth and eyes are described as "three plums," bruises are plum-colored, Evie and her father commit incest; thus, "finger," "bruise," and "eye" are images with sexual implication. Other comparable words are "tip," "performance," "repeated," "reproduced," as well as the more obvious "semisurrender," "denial," "consent," "kiss and struggle," "scent," "skin," "vibration."

A few pages earlier, this episode is prepared for by a first finger-pulling: "I held my right forefinger up close to her face. She took it in both hands and examined it, pulling it about . . . Evie pulled and pulled" (48). The effect of the second finger episode is intensified by the repetition of numerous words and phrases of sexual innuendo which occur in the initial incident: "held up," "She took it," "examined," "laughing," "giggles," "wrestled/struggled," "changed from pursued to pursuer," "struggle," "three black plums," "perfume/scent," "kisses," and others (48–49). Terminated by the striking of the church clock, this encounter leaves Oliver frustrated: "I got more kisses than I wanted. I didn't get anything else" (49); so does the second encounter, but it leads forward toward success.

Oliver "knew and accepted that it wasn't nice" (54); the iniquity *is* insisted upon; he "played with extravagant bravura, determining that somehow I would get Evie to a place where I might wreak my wicked will. I understood it to be wicked. Well, I was wicked. I swore a great oath of implacability and felt better" (56). The cliché statement, with its formulaic expressions from penny-dreadful melodrama, makes the teenage imaginary bedroom farce funny, a circumstance underscored by the excessive alliteration. Oliver, sitting at the piano, manages to bruise his finger again (57), a sort of eighteen-year-old immoderation. Subsequently, he holds up his newly reinjured "forefinger, in explanation [of his muffled piano playing] and invitation [to symbolic sexual activity]. But Evie glanced at it then away" (63).

In Golding's work there is little showing of love as spiritual communion between two people; almost invariably,[10] love is shown as physical—merely physical—joining. And the sexual union very frequently appears to constitute a transgression of religious or moral imperatives. Sex connects also to the will to power, notably and viciously in Pincher Martin's lust for Mary Lovell, "who was nothing but the intersection of influences from the cradle up." Mary, who "would fly to what was respectable," is incomprehensible to Pincher; her eyes, "large and wise," combined with all her prudishnesses, "made her a madness, not so much in the loins as in the pride, the need to assert and break, a blight in the growing point of life" (148). This plain statement points to Pincher's compulsive need for the ambivalent gratifications inherent in the subjugation of another, which is the madness "in the pride."[11]

However Golding depicts the sexual—even when he employs the ubiquitous Anglo-Saxon physiological monosyllables—he is given to evasion, is perhaps mindful of the interdicting voice of chapel. His mastery of language, his poetic style, is often the agency of evasion. In two studies of the relations between Golding's *Poems* and the novels, Cecil Davies found that "In each book the poet is creatively central, both as explorer of the possibilities of language and, in a more Wordsworthian sense, as the man of imagination drawing upon the deeply-founded impressions of childhood: the Cornish coast and sea ... ." Davies makes the case that when Golding "writes of the sea he writes out of his innermost being. . . ."[12]

In Oliver's first (and onanistic) intercourse with Evie, the physical conjunction is bypassed: Evie says, "Get on with it, then"; there is a break in the text; the text resumes with Oliver "aware of nothing but peace . . ." (71). Their second coupling is a different matter. Evie is in the "erotic woods" with Oliver when she hears the bell and shout of her father, the town crier:

> Evie caught her breath. Before my eyes, two buttonlike projections rose in the thin stuff over her breasts. She pushed against me, pawing, eyes shut. [13]
> "Take me, Olly! Now! Have me!"
>
> (78)

In this instance, Golding does not dodge the actual copulation, although he turns aside into the obliquity of metaphor:

> "Hurt me, Olly! *Hurt* me—"
> I did not know how to hurt her. As I beat my hasty tattoo in boyish eagerness, I was lost among the undulations, the contractings and stretchings of her body. She would not consent to any quick rhythm; only the long, deep ocean swell in which her man, her boy, was an object, no more: and this deep swell of an apparently boneless woman was accompanied by a turning away of the head, both eyes shut, forehead lined—a kind of anguished journey, concentrated on reaching a far spot, dark, agonizing and wicked. I was a small boat in a deep sea; and the sea itself was a moaning, private thing, full of contempt and disgust, a thing to which a partner was necessary but not welcome. I could no longer direct; and my boat was overwhelmed by waves, suddenly controlled by her, driven towards the rock, where a cry rose, loud and tortured, and I was among the breakers, ship-wrecked—
>
> (79)

Davies cites this passage and says of it that Golding, "seeking expressive imagery, does call upon the sea, and for a few moments the words break into fire" (110). This section indeed has poetic rhythms, figures, and other such elements. The ocean/sea metaphor is of major emphasis, but even more striking is the negativism of the passage, which does not impress one as essentially exploitative, though one might claim that the exploiter is exploited, for Oliver meant to use Evie but she uses him.

Examination of the quotation as language, as words and phrases, shows a preponderance of expressions that denote and/or connote not pleasure but pain. Obvious negatives include:

hurt	private thing (both participants neuter,
beat	depersonalized, as small boat, thing)
lost	full of contempt and disgust

contractings and stretchings	a thing
of her body (as if on the	not welcome
rack)	could no longer direct
would not consent	overwhelmed
an object, no more	controlled by her
a turning away	driven towards the rock
both eyes shut	a cry
forehead lined	tortured
anguished journey	among the breakers
dark, agonizing and wicked	ship-wrecked.
moaning	

Other less plain negatives include such locutions as "tattoo" (as unintermitted pounding or continuous pricking), "apparently boneless" (a nonpositive seeming), and "undulations" (as unstable risings and fallings, like waves).

The ineluctable conclusion is that this union, superbly complete physically (however negatively stated), does not unite but irreparably separates the partners. As Evie and Oliver walk away in discontent from their joining, they engage in a screaming match, ending:

> "Thought you'd got something for nothing, didn't you?"
> I stared back, my teeth clenched, hating the whole female race. As if she could read what was inside my head, she muttered at me.
> "I hate men."
>
> (80)

And *this* is love.

When Sophy Stanhope goes out deliberately to lose her virginity:

> She looked curiously at the man who was now evidently delighted with life.
> "Is that all?"
> "What d'you mean?"
> "Sex. Fucking."
> "Christ. What did you expect?"
> She said nothing, since it was not necessary.
>
> (*Darkness Visible*, 136)

So also is *this* love.

But such love violates moral and religious prohibitions or sanguine expectations. Golding's view is that "at some point in heterosexual relationships, one person exploits the other; this . . . is sinful" (*Talk*, 112). The connection between sex and the "voice of generations of chapel" (*The Pyramid*,

100) cannot be severed because, like Milton's postlapsarian Adam and Eve, "in lust they burn" (*Paradise Lost*, IX, 1015). The author of the pornographic classic *My Secret Life* (c. 1890) "could only have resorted to a moralistic and quasi-theological vocabulary to describe his behavior; even the current medical terminology . . . was still largely derived from moral and religious conceptions" (*The Other Victorians*, 166). The association with sin/crime of extramarital, premarital, and even marital, sexual performances was general in Victorian times and, in the late twentieth century, with God dead and religion, to some degree, displaced, this pairing is widespread and vigorous, despite the New Morality.

Golding is prone to cause such construing of sexual matter in his writing. There are, coincidentally, some correspondences between Sammy Mountjoy's landscape drawn in his rough workbook and Steven Marcus's description, "The essential imagination of nature in pornotopia, then, is this immense, supine, female form" (*The Other Victorians*, 272). Sammy's drawing is interpreted as prurient by his fundamentalist teacher of religion, who rushes him to the headmaster: "Suddenly he did what Miss Pringle had done—turned the book so that my lovely curved downs were upright, the patch of intricate woodland projecting from them" (*Free Fall*, 207). This unpremeditated figure is male, plainly, not female; the similarities other than the likenesses of the human body to the landscape and the general conception are in certain identical words—"hillocks," "middle distance"—virtually unavoidable in the context. But the seeker after lasciviousness will find lasciviousness.

In her sexual adventure with Bobby Ewan in the opening pages of *The Pyramid*, Evie loses her gold cross. The cross—related to the Tree of Paradise, the Crucifixion, and many other things—is a primary religious symbol to Catholics and Protestants alike. Evie's father—a sexual figure in two senses—cries the loss to Stilbourne: "Lost. In Chandler's Lane, between the chaplofese and Chandler's Close. Hay gold cross hand chain. With the hinitials hee bee. Hand the hinscription 'Hamor vinshit Homniar.' Ther finder will be rewarded" (25). Oliver, given the cross by Henry Williams, returns it to Evie and receives his sexual reward.

The church/sex tie is emphasized by Evie's Romanism, which Oliver goggles at: "I had never met the Roman Catholic Church outside a history book. To come across it living, so to speak, was like finding a diplodocus" (68). Moreover, Evie has come from dusting in the Roman Catholic church and she wears the "celebrated, the notorious cross" (69). Upon this occasion their first coition occurs, Oliver's "reward" for returning her cross.

In *Darkness Visible*, the interconnections among church, cross, and sex are made explicit in the metaphoric crucifixion of Matty and the literal effort to unsex him:

> Matty flung himself down. He lay, his legs stretched down the first line, his arms held wide on either side along the second. The Abo at once leapt to his feet. The cloud in his face was split by a wide flash of white.
> "Fucking big sky-fella him b'long Jesus Christ!"
> He leapt into the air and landed with a foot on either outstretched arm, a foot in the crook of either elbow. He stabbed down on this side and that with his fire-hardened spear into the open palm. He jumped back high, and he landed with both feet in Matty's groin and the sky went black and the Abo disappeared into it.
>
> (64)

Harry Bummer is motivated, at least in part, by his taking Matty for a preacher; the veterinarian who rescues Matty thinks so (65). Also, Harry's pidgin "sky-fella" appears to equal slang "sky pilot," especially since "him b'long Jesus Christ" and Matty has shown his Bible. Passing over such obvious words as "lay," "split," "fucking," "stabbed," and "groin," one notes that Harry's spear is indubitably a phallus and the repeated word "leapt" possibly alludes to the Shakespearean phrase "leaping-house" (brothel).

As sweeping as Golding's Shakespearean reference is, his Biblical and musical references are probably more extensive. Golding's father "played the violin, the 'cello, viola, piano, flute."[14] So, too, does Golding, who thereby has acquired a substantial musical knowledge, of which he makes relevant use.[15] Music functions conspicuously in *The Pyramid*, and Golding mentions, in particular, three compositions for piano: the Chopin Etude in C Minor, Op. 25, No. 12; the Beethoven Sonata No. 23, in F Minor, Op. 57; and the Chopin Polonaise No. 6, in A-flat Major, Op. 53.

Although the C Minor Study seems to Oliver "so exactly to express and contain my own dry-mouthed and hopeless passion for Imogen [Grantley]" (48), whom he so grossly misjudges and etherealizes (Evelyn De Tracy aptly identifies her as "a stupid, insensitive, vain woman" [145]), it comes to "contain not only Imogen, but Evie" (50). Since Oliver has just had a protracted kissing bout with Evie, with his "loins stirring" and "body burning" (49), the relation between music and sex is established. A further connection may be seen in Golding's employment of the ocean metaphor in Oliver's second intercourse with Evie (above, p. 180), for the C Minor is one of the five titled etudes among the twelve of Opus 25 and is called "Ocean."

In the chat with Evie in which he identifies the C Minor etude, he thinks of "the semiquaver passages of the Appassionata" (47). Suitably, the publisher's (or Czerny's) title for the F Minor Sonata, "Appassionata" (passionate), is feminine gender in Italian; so also, for that matter, is "sonata." Oliver thinks as well of "the left hand octaves of the Polonaise in A flat major" (47), an item of significance in his physical clash with Bobby Ewan; this Chopin work often is titled *"L'Héroique,"* an epithet of strong irony as applied to Oliver *in propria persona* or in the fight.

The vocabulary of music is writ large in scenes of physicality, to which it may not seem customary or literally appropriate. For example, there is derisive, it may be sardonic, use of music terminology to puncture the hubris of the character who makes more than warranted of less than overwhelming circumstances bearing down the resistance of a self-proclaimed hero. The model instance comes in Pincher Martin's enema on Rockall:

> He felt himself loom, gigantic on the rock . . . He became a hero for whom the impossible was an achievement. He knelt and crawled remorselessly down the rock . . . now there was background music, snatches of Tchaikovsky, Wagner, Holst. It was not really necessary to crawl but the background music underlined the heroism of a slow, undefeated advance against odds. The empty mussel shells cracked under his bones like potsherds. The music swelled and was torn apart by brass.
>
>   (164)

One may surmise that the potsherds are an artful glance at Job, who, without fault, was grievously mistreated and therefore seen by Pincher as a parallel to his poor, mistreated self.

"He came to the pool on the rock with the one weedy limpet and three prudish anemones" (164). It is not original to remark that the prudish anemones form a rare and noteworthy image, but I suggest additionally a subtle allusion to Mary Lovell. Sixteen pages earlier, the "aspirations" of Mary's voice are said to be "prudish and social" in a passage about Pincher's physical obsession with Mary immediately preceding the rape; and "anemone" (i.e., sea anemone, *Metridium dianthus*) is an apt metaphor for the female genital organs. The bodily proximity of the vagina to the anus and its analogousness to the anemone likewise seem pertinent.

> The strings were working too, and woodwind was added and a note or two of brass. Presently, and soon there would come the suspended chord that would stand the whole orchestra aside for the cadenza. . . . The music

rose, the sea played and the sun. The universe held its breath. . . . the orchestra thundered to a pause.

And the cadenza was coming—did come. . . . Spasm after spasm with massive chords and sparkling arpeggios, the cadenza took of his strength till he lay straining and empty on the rock and the orchestra had gone.

(164-165)

This is the very extremity of comic exaggeration. Hilarity has nothing further to say, once the universe has held its breath over Pincher's enema.[16] But, Golding turns quickly to the underlining contrast; as with Oedipus, arrogance causes Pincher to misunderstand: "Now I shall be sane and no longer such a slave to my body" (165). He is wrong on both counts: remember Euripides' "Those whom God wishes to destroy, he first makes mad" and Pincher's enslavement to the flesh during his life and after his death.

Like an enema, a fistfight is all-but-purely physical. The crucial points in the fisticuffs between Robert Ewan and Oliver are accentuated with music phrases. At the outset, Oliver mentions his "left hand octave-technique" (30); the battle of social unequals goes against him until he hits Robert "with my octave technique, fortissimo, sforzando, in the pit of the stomach" (31). Oliver follows up his advantage—in a manner he later recognizes to be "cheating. I had stuck my knee in his balls" (42)—to knock Robert with a bloody nose into the bracken, from which come faint noises, "variations on the theme of 'Ooo'" (31)

More important to the present concern than the enema or the fight is the seduction of Beatrice Ifor by Sammy Mountjoy. After four years of unsuccessful efforts to bed Beatrice, Sammy finds that she is frightened by the idea of his going mad: "She gave me the lever I wanted." This is followed by a paragraph full of negatives:

Once a human being has lost freedom there is no end to the coils of cruelty. I must I must I must. They said the damned in hell were forced to torture the innocent live people with disease. But I know now that life is perhaps more terrible than that innocent medieval misconception. We are forced here and now to torture each other. We can watch ourselves becoming automata; feel only terror as our alienated arms lift the instruments of their passion towards those we love. Those who lose freedom can watch themselves forced helplessly to do this in daylight until who is torturing who [sic]? The obsession drove me at her.

(115)

Among the negatives are:

lost	We can watch (helplessly)
no end	becoming automata
coils of cruelty	terror
I must (indicative of obsession)	alienated
damned	lift the instruments (like weapons)
hell	passion
forced	lose
torture	helplessly to do
disease	torturing
more terrible	obsession
misconception	drove.

Then, like Oedipus or Pincher, Sammy misunderstands through egotism: "But, of course, once she had got over her fear and we were bound so closely together by lovemaking, there would be no end to the brightness of the sunlight future" (115).

To a degree unconsciously, Sammy acts out his role as declared to Beatrice: "My madness was Wagnerian. It drove me forth on dark nights forsooth striding round the downs. I should have worn a cloak" (115). He recognizes, in part, that he is posing, but at the same time he is taken in by his pose. Hence he provides a self-justification for his falsehood to Beatrice.

Beatrice, with palpable resignation, comes to Sammy's cheap bed-sitter, acquired "as a place to seduce her in" (111). Sammy has little to tempt with in this bare, unattractive, simulated lovenest: "I could not surround Beatrice with luxury, had no gipsy violinist to shudder his way into her ear. That room, with its couch bed, narrow for two unless they were glued together or superimposed . . ." (111). This witty description in negatives emblemizes his futile efforts. Then, Sammy having discovered and utilized madness, Beatrice is lost:

> She only put up a token fight. She was my sanity. I would take any consequences that ensued would I not, who was so breathlessly assuring her that there would be no consequences. And then Beatrice of four years' fever lay back obediently, closed her eyes and placed one clenched fist bravely on her forehead as though she were about to be injected for T.A.B.
>
> (117)

The clever phrasing—ironic and sympathetic to youthful, sentimental conceptions derived from popular melodrama—points up the universal silliness and indicates empathetic feeling for the uncritical agonizing of youth.

Nonetheless, one finds a high percentage of negative wording, implicative of the painful, the undesirable.

All preliminaries done, the yearned-for moment of surrender, copulation, release, satisfaction, peace, has come:

> Why should it be that at this most triumphant or at least enjoyable moment of his career, the sight of the victim displayed humble, acquiescent, and frightened should not only be less stimulating than the least of his sexual inventions but should even be damping and impossible? No, said his body, no not this at all. That was not the thing I meant, thing I wanted. How far was I right to think myself obsessed with sex when that potency which is assumed in all literature was not mine to use at the drop of a knicker? It seemed then that some co-operation was essential. If she were to make of herself a victim I could not be her executioner. If she were to be frightened, then I was ashamed in my very flesh that she should be frightened of me. This did not seem to me to tally with the accepted version of a man who was either wholly incapable or heroically ready, aye ready. There were gradations. But neither I nor Beatrice were prepared to admit them. On the other hand my feelings about her were without doubt obsessive if not pathological. Should they not then make my achievement of her easy: But she, out of my suggested madness and her own religious taboos, was incapable of thinking about this moment, this pre-marital deed, without a sense that was at once one of sin, one of fear, one of love, and consequently one of drama. Unconsciously we were both setting ourselves to music. The gesture with which she opened her knees was, so to speak, operatic, heroic, dramatic and daunting. I could not accompany her. My instrument was flat.

> (117-118)

The tone of this treatment of sexual intercourse (literally, miscarried intercourse) differs from and is a composite of factors from Golding treatments analyzed before. Examples are:

> (the negative) No . . . no not this at all. . . . not the thing
> (the minimizing) humble, acquiescent, damping
> (the embarrassing) displayed, wholly incapable
> (the painful) victim, frightened, ashamed
> (the unbalanced) obsessed, pathological, madness
> (the prohibiting) sin, taboos, pre-marital, daunting
> (the humorous) that potency which is assumed . . . at the drop of a
> knicker.

Besides these categories, there are the quasi-musical, the musical, and the comico-musical:

setting ourselves to music	accompany
operatic	instrument
heroic	flat.
dramatic	

Beyond the music terminology, the manifest double entendre of "My instrument was flat" implies that "instrument" is to be understood as one of the "common eighteenth-century epithets for penis"[17] and "flat" points back to Sammy's lack of sexual potency, remarked early in the quotation.

Altogether inglorious and transitory are the humor and music of this lamentable episode. "But," Sammy tells us rather superfluously, "of course there were other occasions." These uncheerful ceremonies are reiterated dismally: "I never seemed to get near Beatrice, never shared anything with her. She remained the victim on the rack. . . . She was beginning to look up, to belong, to depend, to cling, to be an inferior in fact, however the marriage service may gloss it. Instinctively she was becoming what she believed to be a wedded wife. Her contribution, after the heroic sacrifice, was negative" (118-119). A waste and unutterably sad.

Sammy's own aphorism "love selflessly and you cannot come to harm" (33) does not operate in this case. A few pages earlier, Sammy puts forth his youthful view of sex: "A young man certain of nothing but salt sex; certain that if there was a positive value in living it was this undeniable pleasure. Be frightened of the pleasure, condemn it, exalt it. . . . the tickling pleasure, the little death shared or self-inflicted was neither irrelevant nor sinful but the altar of whatever shoddy temple was left to us. But there remained . . . the knowledge that if this was everything it was a poor return for birth, for the shames and frustrations of growing up" (108).

One naturally does not attribute to an author a view held by his fictional character, but this view is hardly one that Golding would find uncongenial. Sammy Mountjoy is a character whose life reverses Golding's: "All the terms of my life were turned upside down [in *Free Fall*]"; to my assertion that Golding took his "respectable schoolmaster's home kind of background and postulated [in *Free Fall*] that the son was a slum child," he responded, "Yes, yes" (*Talk*, 79, 80). In any case, Sammy's attitude toward sex—including the offstage and unconvincing alliance with Taffy—can be deduced from what Golding has written, just as Calvinism can.

Turning now from heterosexuality to homosexuality, one finds that the homosexual acts in Golding's works have the veil of charity drawn over them. They occur offstage ordinarily and are reported; instances are Pincher Martin and "that crude and unsatisfactory experiment" (90) with "that boy with his snivelling, blubbered face" (91) and Mr. Pedigree's transactions with his boy in *Darkness Visible*. But in *Clonk Clonk* Golding's gentlest and most detached, not to say sympathetic, description of homosexual love comes onstage in his

narrative, not dramatic, presentation of the "unselfconscious" love of the
Leopard Men:

> They talked all at once but paid little heed to what anyone else said. . . .
> it was not useful speech. It was no more than an expression of an emotion-
> al state, so that in that sense, each Leopard Man was talking or singing to
> himself. Mime of the body, song of the throat, it was a communication at
> once total and imprecise as the minds that lay behind it. It conveyed . . .
> pleasure in the thought of sleep and love—love as unselfconscious as the
> sleep. One laid down his three-stringed bow, one his hand drum. They
> put off weapons so that there was a scattered jumble before the splayed
> roots. They snuggled, old and young together into the natural rest places
> between the roots so that the trunk seemed to grow a frill of brown skin
> and sliding muscles. The dappled shade shifted over them. The singing
> became a crooning, murmuring sound as they hugged and cuddled and
> made love. There was much stroking and intimate sharing till heat and
> satisfaction sunk them towards sleep. [18]

The reader ought to observe that this passage contains no negations, no
evasions (comic or otherwise), as do virtually all Golding's sex scenes.

Golding once defined sexual sin as "exploitation of one person by another"
and insisted there is no sin in the absence of exploitation. He further said that
the heterosexuality or homosexuality of the relationship had nothing to do
with the case (*Talk*, 111, 112). But, when callousness or exploitation enter
the sexual conjunction, sexual culpability, vice, Biblical "transgression of the
law," enter.

The ultimate instance is Golding's inversion of Melville's Billy Budd and
John Claggart in the persons of Billy Rogers and Robert James Colley in *Rites
of Passage*. [19] When Lieutenant Summers says, "Mr Colley is willing himself to
death," Edmund Talbot's skeptical response is "Come!" (153). A hundred
pages later, smug, imperceptive Edmund finally realizes what brought Mr.
Colley to will himself to death. Captain Anderson's assertion is plain: "It is
likely enough that the man, helplessly drunk, suffered a criminal assult by
one, or God knows how many men, and the absolute humiliation of it killed
him!" (251), and he uses the word "buggery" to Foretopman Rogers (254).
But it takes Edmund's reading of Colley's papers, which he had removed
surreptitiously from Colley's cabin (157), to break light upon Edmund, who
confesses to his "Honored godfather," "I do not know how to write this"
(276), then rehearses for the reader's benefit the pertinent facts. The critical,
inescapable "physical truth" is:

> Then Colley in his letter—*what a man does defiles him, not what is done by*

others—Colley in his letter, infatuated with the "king of my island" and longing to kneel before him—Colley in the cable locker, drunk for the first time in his life and not understanding his condition and in a state of mad exuberance—Rogers owning in the heads that he had knowed most things in his life but had never thought *to get a chew off a parson!* Oh, doubtless the man consented, jeeringly, and encouraged the ridiculous, schoolboy trick—even so, not Rogers but Colley committed the *fellatio* that the poor fool was to die of when he remembered it.

(276-277)

The sexual intimacy takes place offstage, of course. What the reader sees of the affair is the public climax of Colley's drunkenness: "A young stalwart had him in charge. This fellow was supporting Mr Colley, whose head lay back on the man's breast." Colley is oblivious, blacked out; he extends his arms "as if to embrace us all" and exclaims, "Joy! Joy! Joy!" Then, with his face thoughtful, "He turned to his right, walked slowly and carefully to the bulwark and pissed against it" (117). Colley next delivers a benediction. "Then there was a commotion I can tell you! If the man's uncommonly public micturation had shocked the ladies, to be blessed by a drunk man in a canvas shirt caused screams, hasty retreats, and, I am told, one *evanouissement!*" (118). This distressing burlesque ends as Colley is led from the deck. Useful as the crudities of low comedy are to reduce the shock of the innocent's inconceivable behavior, the shock remains and is intensified in retrospect when the reader comes to understand together with Edmund Talbot.

Despite all the evasiveness and all Golding's shifting back and forth between reticence in the presentation of sexual behavior and a sort of uneasy four-letter-word insistence upon it, there is no question but that sex, seen one way or another, is persistently central to Golding's fiction. This emphasis seems a little unlikely, given the diminished roles allotted to the females, who usually have their primary functions as foils or revealers to the protagonists, nearly always male. The genuine exceptions are Palm in *Clonk Clonk* and Sophy in *Darkness Visible*.

Precisely what Golding meant when he referred to sex as a "relative triviality,"[20] one of course does not know; nevertheless, the degree of preoccupation with this subject in his writing suggests that the relativity might be trivial but not sex itself nor the practice thereof.[21] From a Christian viewpoint (affected by Genesis 18-19 and Revelation 17-19), sexual activity may be "*wrong, wrong, wrong!*" as Oliver's father "burst out" in "the voice of generations of chapel" (*The Pyramid*, 100). But, however reluctantly, Golding does not hold aloof from the sexual trauma, and however uneasily he confronts it, exploitative sex is very much Golding's subject.[22]

NOTES

1. Jack I. Biles, *Talk: Conversations with William Golding* (New York: Harcourt, 1970), 86.

2. William Golding, *Lord of the Flies* (New York: Coward-McCann, 1962), 161–162.

3. See E. L. Epstein, "Notes on *Lord of the Flies*," in William Golding, *Lord of the Flies* (New York: Capricorn Books, 1959). Cf. Claire Rosenfield, "'Men of a Smaller Growth': A Psychological Analysis of William Golding's *Lord of the Flies*," *Literature and Psychology*, 11 (Autumn 1961), 93–101.

4. William Golding, *Pincher Martin* (London: Faber, 1956) 95–96.

5. William Golding, *The Pyramid* (London: Faber, 1967), passim.

6. William Golding, *Rites of Passage* (New York: Farrar, 1980), 85–86.

7. Sir Leslie Stephen, *History of English Thought in the Eighteenth Century*, 2 vols. (New York: Harcourt, 1962), II, 373. Stephen attributes to Robert Southey a similar view: "not more laudable in its purpose than vicious in its style, and therefore one of the most popular ever written" (II, 372).

8. The Victorian physician William Acton, author of *The Functions and Diseases of the Reproductive Organs* (1857), bears down upon the conception that sex is "a universal and virtually incurable scourge. It cannot ultimately be controlled, and serves as a kind of metaphor for death, as cancer does today." See Steven Marcus, *The Other Victorians: A Study of Sexuality and Pornography in Mid-Nineteenth-Century England*, 2nd ed. (New York: New American Library, 1977), 28.

9. Rolfe Humphries, trans., *The Aeneid of Virgil* (New York: Scribner's, 1951), 173.

10. The most important exceptions are found in the comforting intercourse of the gentle People of *The Inheritors* (London: Faber, 1955).

11. Another instance, at the extreme from Pincher's virulence and violence (and without the sexual aspect), is little Henry's fascination with dominance over the tiny, transparent scavengers on the beach: "He became absorbed beyond mere happiness as he felt himself exercising control over living things. He talked to them, urging them, ordering them. Driven back by the tide, his footprints became bays in which they were trapped and gave him the illusion of mastery" (*Lord of the Flies*, 69).

12. Cecil Davies, "'The Burning Bird': Golding's *Poems* and the Novels," *Studies in the Literary Imagination*, 13: 1 (Spring 1980), 101; reprinted in this volume. Cf. "The Novels Foreshadowed: Some Recurring Themes in Early Poems by William Golding," *English*, 17 (Autumn 1968), 86–89.

13. There are strong implications here of Evie's incest with her father, indications subsequently confirmed when Evie accuses Oliver of telling about "Me 'n' Dad" (110). Cf. Sophy Stanhope's lust for her father—an incestuous desire apparently never consummated: "her splendid, idiotic body took charge, and before him, her unbra'd breasts rose up, their vulnerable, tender, uncontrollable, enslaving points hardened, stood out and lifted the fabric of her shirt in a sign as clear as if it had been shouted" (William Golding, *Darkness Visible* [London: Faber, 1979], 186)

14. William Golding, "The Ladder and the Tree," *The Listener*, 24 March 1960, rpt. in William Golding, *The Hot Gates and Other Occasional Pieces* (London: Faber, 1965), 168. Occurring throughout his writing, Biblical references are especially prominent in *Darkness Visible*.

15. Scholarly attention to Golding's use of music has been quite limited. For a lengthy study of this subject, see Bernard Crook, "The Use of Music Vocabulary in William Golding's Novels," M.A. thesis, Georgia State University, 1971. For a few brief comments, see Avril Henry, "William Golding: *The Pyramid*," *Southern Review: An Australian Journal of Literary Studies*, 3 (1968), 5–31.

16. In the quotation from *Lord of the Flies* (1954) (above, pp. nos) the intercourse (incest?) is blurred by figurative language; but in *Darkness Visible* (1979) the act is called by its vernacular name (above pp, nos). Golding's alternating between extremes in his choice of diction can be exemplified clearly by a simple contrast. In *Lord of the Flies*, Simon struggles "to express mankind's essential illness":

> "What's the dirtiest thing there is?"
> As an answer Jack dropped in to the uncomprehending silence that followed it the one crude expressive syllable.
>
> (103)

The expressive syllable goes unexpressed, but Sophy of *Darkness Visible* expresses it; and the description of her washing after loss of virginity is unexpectedly graphic:

> The thought . . . started her even more elaborately probing and washing, pain or not; and she came on the other shape, lying opposite the womb but at the back, a shape lying behind the smooth wall but easily to be felt through it, the rounded shape of her own turd working down the coiled gut. . . .
>
> (138)

17. Robert Kiely, *The Romantic Novel in England* (Cambridge, Mass.: Harvard Univ. Press, 1972), 88. Cf. Hugh Rawson, *A Dictionary of Euphemisms & Other Doubletalk* (New York: Crown 1981), 147.

18. *The Scorpion God: Three Short Novels* (London: Faber, 1971), 77–78.

19. It ought to be observed that James Colley has the same initials as John Claggart, but Golding's indirect communication is subtlest in his changing Budd to Rogers: "Roger" is one of the personal names given to the penis and, by extension, to the sexual. Cf. D. H. Lawrence's title for the second version of *Lady Chatterley's Lover* (1928), that is, *John Thomas and Lady Jane* (written 1927; Italian publication 1954; English publication 1972), "John Thomas" being another of the several personal names so used; similarly, "Lady Jane" denotes the female genitals.

20. William Golding, "Fable," *The Hot Gates*, 89. The essay concerns *Lord of the Flies*, and the sentence reads, "The boys were below the age of overt sex, for I did not want to complicate the issue with that relative triviality." Cf. Sophy's numerous uses of "trivial" (e.g., *Darkness Visible*, 137–139, 186).

21. Golding's most recent book—*The Paper Men* (London: Faber, 1984)—is amply sprinkled with four-letter words and other indecencies, having perhaps a higher percentage of such than his other book. (Incidentally, *The Paper Men* is, at least in one respect, regrettable: inevitably it will be understood in the future as substantially more autobiographical than it in fact is, and it will give posterity a conception of Golding as a nasty man, splenetic and malevolent, which he is not. Despite some correspondences, Wilfred Barclay is not William Golding.)

22. Nothing in this essay is intended to associate Golding's own attitudes concerning sex—whatever they are or have been, present or past—with those attitudes to be deduced from his fiction. The vocabulary accepted in public expressions regarding sexual matters

has become far freer since World War II than before, as have sexual behavior and mores; hence, that the relevant language in fiction has turned more and more to the physical idioms of the vernacular has been a matter of course. The use of such wording is likewise increasingly evident in Golding's writing. But to touch upon certain changes in Golding's personal views, volunteered in private conversation, seems fair, permissible, and germane. Shortly after publication of *Darkness Visible*, Golding acknowledged that young people had taught him something on this subject. They are right, he said warmly and approvingly, to bed and live together for a time to learn if they are suited to one another and want to continue on a long-term basis. If and when they find they are, in fact, compatible and content, they may then desire to "settle down and raise a family" and, as a consequence of this experimentation, may live with a greater expectation and possibility of being "happy ever after." That "freedom which stemmed from the pill" (*Darkness Visible*, 142) provides the opportunity for experimentation and conclusion; even more important, it prevents the infant victim's being unwanted or having helplessly to face an inevitable rupture of its family.

Golding and the Nobel Prize

RICHARD BRADFORD

The award of the 1983 Nobel Prize for Literature was attended by a degree of controversy exceptional even by the standards of that institution. When the Nobel Committee's decision was finally announced, the Swedish Academician and novelist Artur Lundkvist made an unprecedented attack on Golding's literary status and on the allegedly biased selection procedure of the Academy. He went so far as to call Golding "a little English phenomenon of no special interest," and his personal criterion for laureateship seems to have been based upon a notion of literary imperialism whereby an author's standing depends upon his having "influenced" as many diverse literary "schools" as possible. Lundkvist's candidate, Claude Simon, according to his champion, has had a substantial effect upon the development of the Latin American novel.

These histrionics in Stockholm would seem to have overshadowed all other discussion, since there appears to be no other reason for the curiously muted response of the British literary establishment to the first Englishman to win the prize since Sir Winston Churchill. Phillip Howard, the *Times* literary editor, simply listed Golding's publications and noted that he was probably the British novelist "most likely to survive" (*Times*, 7 October 1983). The other "serious" British newspapers, *The Guardian, The Sunday Times*, and *The Observer*, were similarly unforthcoming, and the literary weekly, *The Times Literary Supplement*, and the fortnightly *London Review of Books* ignored the event entirely. The most interesting questions were asked by the Swedish press: *Dagens Nyheter* (7 October 1983) raised the subject of Golding's having

195

been preferred to his more prolific and, it must be argued, more widely read countryman Graham Greene, noting that for some years there had been speculation in the United States, and most recently in *The New York Times* about whether it was now too late for Greene to be seriously in contention for the award. *Helsingborgs Dagblad* questioned Phillip Howard on this matter and received the answer that Greene, Golding, and Anthony Burgess were indeed the three greatest living British novelists. He said that it was surprising that Greene had not received the prize before, but that, he added, was nothing to do with its award to Golding. "Golding is more didactic and more precise than the others. He is easier to read than Greene and Burgess because the moral corruption in man's heart is more black and white in Golding" (*Helsingborgs Dagblad*, 7 October 1983).

What I believe Howard meant, in reference to Greene at least, is that, in attempting to abstract a moral "attitude" from his novels, the reader is often thwarted by the feeling of total despair which descends upon his protagonists as they deal with a squalid and hellish world; and any form of religious reference usually appears as a ritual, an aggravation of that despair which seems merely to heighten their certainty of damnation. Of course, novels are not primarily in the business of moral education, but what one might term Greene's idiosyncracies—what was recently called his "making his form of Englishness a universality for artistic purposes,"[1] and his apparent obsession with danger and squalor for their own sake—do not really harmonize well with Alfred Nobel's description, in his will, of "the person who shall have produced in the field of literature the most outstanding work of an idealistic tendency."[2] Imputing an "idealistic tendency" to Greene, beyond a sceptical and probably heretical Catholicism, would be a difficult operation. And a sense of ethical or philosophical progression, beyond the mellowing and political phlegmatism brought about by age, is not evident in his work. His two recent and recognizably canonical novels *The Honorary Consul* (1973) and *The Human Factor* (1978) look suspiciously like a reshuffling of the familiar counters marked "international politics," "treachery," "religious speculation" and "Englishness."

This article is by no means an attempt to denigrate Greene's art. Indeed *The Human Factor* contains some interesting meditations, mainly those of the South American novelist Saavedra, on the problem of reconciling political relevance and timeless artistry in the novel; but such concerns for Greene manage to look oddly peripheral and whimsical when placed beside Golding's agonized investigations of the capacity of words to comprehend the human condition. This article is intended to examine a particular aspect of Golding's work as it was seen by his sponsors and the Nobel adjudicators in 1983 and which is normally conferred only by death—a sense of both *development* and *completion*.

In their original study of Golding, Mark Kinkead-Weekes and Ian Gregor conclude that they "might incline to regard Golding's achievement from *Lord of the Flies* to *The Spire* as a continual progress, in that in his last novel he seems to have found a satisfying shape for myth." But of course *The Spire*, as they knew, was only Golding's "last" novel in the sense that it formed an interesting and thematically neat terminus for their intertextual speculations, and they add that the sense of resolution, both moral and technical, found in *The Spire* leaves "the artist free for further exploration."[3] All criticism of Golding must share a version of Eliot's belief that "after the supervention of novelty, the *whole* existing order must be, if ever so lightly, altered; and so the relations, proportions, values of each work of art toward the whole are readjusted. . . ."[4] The "whole" presented to the world and to the Swedish Academy in 1983 included *Darkness Visible* (1979) and *Rites of Passage* (1980); and in the nature of the "readjustments" created by these two novels to a corpus of work discontinued thirteen years earlier must lie some hope of reconciling the reverberations and complexities of Golding's *oeuvre* with the rather terse Nobel citation which has him "illuminating the human condition through the perspicuity of his realistic narrative and his use of universal myth."

The Pyramid dismayed many of the critics inured to the conventions and expectations of what might be termed the "Goldingesque"—Denis Donoghue in *The New York Times Book Review* was sufficiently affronted to call the work "an embarrassment." The monolithic symbolism which dominated the earlier works—the resonant microcosm of *Lord of the Flies*, *Pincher Martin's* pinnacle of isolation, Sammy Mountjoy's mental dramatization of the Fall, and *The Spire's* obsessive examination of a sacred and profane aspiration—are not merely *themes* but structuring principles which sustain often refractory and self-referring narratives. *The Pyramid* contains no such architechtonic complexity; it is instead something of a *Bildungsroman* in which the allusive coherences of "myth" and "fable" are replaced by a set of less universal referents—those provided by the structures and tensions of English society over the previous forty years.

The question raised by *The Pyramid* was whether Golding had exchanged his faith in the power of myth to comprehend the apparent chaos of con-

temporary life for the techniques of nineteenth-century classic realism and
those of the modern sociologist. In Golding's 1975 *Guardian* review of Paul
Fussell's *The Great War and Modern Memory* he discusses what would appear to
be this very dilemma:

> The Second World War came near to demolishing all the assumptions of
> the first one and uncovered entirely different areas of indescribability
> . . . . The experience of Hamburg, Belsen, Hiroshima, and Dachau
> cannot be imagined. We have gone to war and beggared description all
> over again. Those experiences are like black holes in space. Nothing can
> get out to let us know what it was like inside. It was like what it was like
> and on the other hand it was like nothing whatsoever. We stand before a
> gap in history. We have invented a limit to literature.[5]

But four years later, at the beginning of *Darkness Visible* Matty does emerge
from the black hole to tell us what it was like inside. The whole vivid scene
seems intended to evoke another eerie encounter in the blitz like the passage
from *Little Gidding* where the "face still forming" presents itself and delivers
its prophecy:

> From wrong to wrong the exasperated spirit
> Proceeds, unless restored by that refining fire
> Where you must move in measure, like a dancer.[6]

Golding offers no strategies of consolation like those Yeatsian hints from the
"familiar compound ghost." Eliot's "half recalled apparition" provides a form
of solace, confers some meaning on the "hell" of the blitz; but Golding's witness, the "bookseller" (Goodchild himself?), provides a different keynote to
the proceeding vision of the chaotic and intractable postwar world. "Was it
the Apocalypse? Nothing could be more apocalyptic than a world so fero-
ciously consumed. But he could not quite remember."[7] The various forms of
evil which thread their enigmatic way through Matty's biography—Pedigree's
pederasty, his own "crucifixion" by the aborigine, Sophy's sadism, Toni's
lurking, inexorable terrorism—constantly resist any form of categorization
that one comes to expect from Golding's fabulous and mythopoeic strategies.
Jocelin on his deathbed in *The Spire* is at least allowed some partial consolation
in his *understanding* that in seeming "*like the appletree*," *The Spire* had involved a
miraculous transformation of the natural *through* the aspirations of fallen man.
The burden of incomprehension for Matty, his fellow denizens of a fallen
world, and indeed for the reader, is never, even partially, removed. Matty's
question in Part I—"What am I? What am I for?"—is never answered, and
the conflagrations which attend his "birth," his life, and his death might be
Old Testament or they might not.

When Sophy and her father confront the appalling facts of their existence, we are tempted to regard the exchange as a clue to the "meaning" of the novel, a comfortable reassertion of the old misanthropic Golding exposing the inescapable depravity and cruelty of human beings:

> He stopped; then went on in his normal, cold voice.
> "I don't want to seem unwelcoming. But—"
> "But you're busy with your toys."
> "Precisely."
> "We're not very wholesome are we?"
> "That's a good word."
> "You, Mummy, Toni, me—we're not the way people used to be. It's part of the whole running down."
> "Entropy."
>
> (185)

But Golding in his Nobel Lecture seems to deny the reader any confidence in the attempts of these people to understand themselves or their predicament. Matty's vague intuition of his mission to purify, Sophy's nihilism, Bell's and Goodchild's amateur mysticism, are all simply points of view, none of which is allowed any sort of thematic priority within the novel:

> When I consider a universe which the scientist constructs by a set of rules which stipulate that his constructs must be repeatable and identical, then I am a pessimist and bow down before the great god Entropy. I am optimistic when I consider the spiritual dimension which the scientist's discipline forces him to ignore . . . . We know, or at least it is scientifically respectable to postulate, that at the center of a black hole the laws of nature no longer apply. Since most scientists are just a bit religious and most religious are seldom wholly unscientific, we find humanity in a comical position. His scientific intellect believes in the possibility of miracles inside a black hole, while his religious intellect believes in them outside. Both, you could say not wholly in jest, now believe in miracles: *credimus quia absurdum est*. Glory be to God in the highest. You will get no reductive pessimism from me.[8]

And *Darkness Visible* does at crucial points veer into comedy at the expense of all sorts of reductivism. One suspects that Bell's and Goodchild's search for evidence of a timeless continuum through Matty is merely the somewhat meretricious attempt of two elderly sentimentalists to escape the world of "Harold Krishna, Chung and Dethany Clothing, Bartolozzi Dry Cleaning" and the "Mama Mia Chinese Takeaway" (all comically conflated paradigms of a polyglot commercialism).

Edwin spoke over his shoulder.

"Different when I came, wasn't it, after the war? London wasn't crawling all over us. The Green was still a village green—"

(202–203)

The most remarkable "comic" deconstruction of reductivism creates the
book's suspiciously over-dramatic *dénouement*, with Matty consumed by the
"refining" fire of the terrorist attack. His return to the flames from which he
emerged is brought about by his failure to meet an appointment with just
about the only people in the book willing to accept him as something more
portentous than a deformed simpleton. He is prevented from reaching town
by a puncture in his bicycle tire (240). Is this contingency, fate, or a joke on
the unreliability of "inspiration"?

Rites of Passage provides an answer to those who would question the legitimacy of a world view based, apparently, on whimsically systematic scep-
ticism. It is clear that the book, like its predecessor, grew out of the
thoughtful reassessments which took place in the seventies and which emerge
periodically in the reprinted essays and journalism of *A Moving Target*. And it
is perhaps significant that when asked by British journalists why he thought
he had received the Prize he should, and it is not clear with what degree of
flippancy, cite this collection of nonfiction.[9] One of the most interesting
pieces in the collection, "Intimate Relations,"[10] concerns the psychological
and literary implication of the keeping of journals or diaries. Golding begins
with a psychological curiosity, the journal of Jimmy Mason. Mason was a
probably psychotic, nineteenth-century peasant boy who kept a weird record
of his Essex village life as a sort of confirmation of his own existence, as if by
petrifying the flux of his life he might preserve some balance between the
possibility of his own insanity and the genuine fear that someone was attempting to kill him (104–107). The correspondences between Mason's record of
his existential torment and Matty's journal in *Darkness Visible* are quite
obvious, but the real significance of Golding's essay lies in the link it provides
between the deferments and blind alleys of that novel and *Rites of Passage*.

Rites of Passage is the journal of one Edmund Talbot, a well-connected Regency gentleman who reports his passage to Australia to his powerful and urbane patron. And there is a journal within a journal, that of a young clergy-
man, J. C. Colley, who dies "of shame" when, after his ritual humiliation at
the hands of the crew and the immigrants, he is forced to confront the possibility of his own homosexuality. The novel is something of a psychological
adventure story as Talbot investigates the arcane procedures of shipboard life,

the characters of his fellow passengers and the complexity of circumstances leading to Colley's death. But the real burden of significance rests upon Talbot's developing awareness of his own inability to discharge his duty in faithfully recording the events of the voyage. The work is, in the end, a meditation on the nature of writing and the relativity of "truth." In this process Golding seems to be examining his own endeavors in this field, an act which could hardly be more appropriate for a writer whose one aim has been to *tell* us something about our own nature. Self-canonizing allusions abound. Talbot's first impression of life on the rather antique vessel is the stench, which his servant, Wheeler, reveals as issuing from the ballast.

> "It's sand and gravel you see. The new ship has iron ballast but she's older than that. If she was betwixt and between in age, as you might say, they'd have dug it out. But not her. She's too old you see. They wouldn't want to go stirring about down there, sir."
> "It must be a graveyard then!"
> Wheeler thought for a moment.
> "As to that, I can't say, sir, not having been in her previous. Now you sit here for a bit and I'll bring a brandy."[11]
>
> (5)

The similarities between this episode and the description in *The Spire* of that "form of life . . . which ought not to be seen or touched," that nexus of evil, the "pit dug at the crossways like a grave made ready for some notable," cannot be accidental. But in *Rites of Passage* Golding is playing a different game. His, or rather Talbot's, intuitions of some lurking preternatural sickness peculiar to the ship and infecting its passengers and crew are a comically accurate dramatization of the certitudes and complacencies of "mythologizing" the world. Pincher Martin's deluded attempts to impose a pattern on the rock, his creation in stone, of a human form as token of his existence there is paralleled by Talbot's literary strategy to convey his own sense of pervasive evil on the ship:

> As for the Navy—well, it is literally in its element. Its members stand here and there encased in tarpaulin, black with faces pale only by contrast. At a little distance they resemble nothing so much as rocks with the tide washing over them.
>
> (17)

But the chief resonance derives from the ritual murder in *Lord of the Flies* which is recalled in the dipping of the Reverend Colley in a urine-filled tarpaulin, his enforced drunkenness and his resulting act of fellatio with the devilishly handsome sailor, Billy Rogers. Colley commits a form of suicide and much of Talbot's later narrative is concerned with a self-indulgent assessment of his own guilt (he had shunned Colley's company, and had been having a clandestine sexual liaison at the time of the sacrilegious baptism), and the amount of blame he feels that he can apportion to his fellow passengers and the crew. In the process the whole of the voyage becomes demystified. Captain Anderson's dark antipathy to all things clerical, which seems a symptom of a wider malevolence abroad in the ship, is revealed as simply the result of his being the illegitimate offspring of a nobleman conveniently farmed out as the stepson of a country parson. The enigma of why none of the crew is willing to speak of the purser, a shadowy figure ensconced with his ledgers in the depths of the ancient vessel, dissolves when Talbot learns that they all owe him money. "Colley's Letter," the journal within a journal, yields up nothing but a record of doomed naiveté.

Talbot's "conclusion" for his patron is written with a certain tinge of disappointment. There was no real evil pact between the crew members and the captain, no atavistic corruption communicated by the fabric of the vessel itself; just ignorance, stupidity, and a concatenation of petty miseries. Talbot ends with the glib and pompous elevation of Colley's ordeal to the status of a moral precept. "In the not too ample volume of man's knowledge of Man, let this sentence be inserted. Men can die of shame" (278).

The point of all this lies not with our recognition of another perspective on man's moral turpitude, nor even in our realization that Talbot's narrative is a series of inconclusive clarifications and distortions, but rather in the fact that he writes at all. His style is immensely self-conscious, he is continually aware of himself in the process of recording, or rather mediating, experience. He continually forgets what the date is and where he stands at any particular point in relation to the rest of the narrative, so it is not surprising to find Sterne acknowledged as a literary progenitor (72). I do not think it is too eccentric to claim that *Rites of Passage* is Golding's novel *about* writing. "Intimate Relations" traces much of the reading Golding must have done to develop such an impressive grasp of the style of an eighteenth- or early nineteenth-century "public" diarist (Admiral Hervey's Journal seems likely to have been the basis for Captain Anderson's family history), but it is the *nature* of writing in this peculiarly personal form which interests him most. "But the diary reveals not that to err is human but that to be mixed and mixed up, to be inconsistent, irrational, clever, and sensible is in general what we are" (123). This seems a pretty adequate assessment of Edmund Talbot, but it hardly seems necessary to write a novel to tell us that this is what we are like, and indeed this was not Golding's intention. At the beginning of "Intimate Relations" he proposes a connection between what we regard as the accidental memorials of prehistoric man and the modern habit of keeping a journal.

> There is a cave in the Auvergne where if you peer into a pool you can see a single footprint and by it the mark of a stick in what was once soft mud. That capacity we all have called kinaesthesia, a sympathetic identification with someone else's body movement, interprets signs instantly. We feel how the person lurched, saved himself or herself from falling deeper into the pool by stabbing down and leaning on the stick. . . . They were leaving a sign; and the obscurity lies in this, that such a sign has latent in it some of what we have called sign, symbol, emblem, metaphor, simile. Some of that same obscurity surrounds the question of why we modern people of every age, rank, calling, sex, belief have left records of one sort or another. We have kept journals.
>
> (104)

Edmund Talbot is indeed saving himself "from falling deeper" in the sense that his writing allows him some stability, however complacent or spurious, within a bewildering jumble of moral categories and circumstances.

Thus it is possible to suggest that with the publication of his last novel prior to the award of the Nobel Prize (*The Paper Men* emerged five months afterwards) Golding had appeared to have conferred a satisfying sense of intellectual rigor upon his work. The two new novels confronted those very charges of "exaggeration" and "predictability" which had been a rallying point for hostile critics ever since the aggressive assessments of James Gindin and Martin Green.[12] The following extract is from a lecture intitled "Belief and Creativity" delivered in 1980 and reprinted in *The Times* as a sort of unofficial acceptance speech the day after Golding received the Prize.

> Though in general terms I would still assent to the philosophical or theological implications about the nature of man and his universe presented in the book [*Lord of the Flies*], today, a generation later, I would qualify them as subtler and less definable than I once thought. God works in a mysterious way, says the hymn; and so, it seems, does the devil—or since that word is unfashionable I had better be democratic and call him the leader of the opposition. Sometimes the two seem to work hand in hand. Sometimes neither is on call even if you call them louder. They are asleep or away hunting perhaps—perhaps hunting each other. Not to refine upon it, my mind is all at sea.[13]
>
> (198)

It is not that Golding has lost faith in the capacity of man to comprehend his own condition; rather he has adjusted his concept of fiction as a vehicle for conveying such verities. His later skepticism is not Greene's world-weary version, but a transference of allegiance from his reliance on the novel as the embodiment of a truth to a belief in the status of fiction itself as a token denial of all forms of reductive determinism:

> Put simply, the novel stands between us and the hardening concept of statistical man. There is no other medium in which we can live for so long and so intimately with another character. That is the service a novel renders. It performs no less an act than the rescue and the preservation of the individuality of a single being, be it man, woman, or child.
>
> (Nobel Lecture, 210).

If the Nobel Prize has any "meaning" beyond the conferring of a usually brief celebrity and the increase in book sales, it must be as a directive to retrospective reassessment. I have, in this article, attempted to indicate a number of crucial changes in the direction of Golding's thought and art in the seventies which converge upon his apparent wish to approach his writing in a way which urges literary, or rather writerly, and ethical values toward a single technique; and it seems clear from the consiliences between the Nobel Lecture, the nonfiction, and the two later novels that he himself was aware of such a development. It is impossible to say whether this fresh stance taken up in a later period actually influenced the award or whether, as the citation suggests, it was made for his earlier, as Howard put it, more "didactic" work. What it *has* done is to highlight the undoubtedly self-conscious tension between the recent "skeptical" fiction and the period which concluded so perplexingly with *The Pyramid*.

NOTES

1. John le Carré in *The Listener*, 4 October 1979, 443.
2. For a full English translation of the will see Nils K. Stahle, *Alfred Nobel and the Nobel Prizes* (Stockholm: The Swedish Institute, 1978), 12.
3. *William Golding: A Critical Study* (London: Faber, 1967), 256–257.
4. "Tradition and the Individual Talent," *Selected Prose of T. S. Eliot*, ed. Frank Kermode (London: Faber, 1975), 38.

5. Reprinted in *A Moving Target* (London: Faber, 1984), 102.

6. *The Complete Poems and Plays of T. S. Eliot* (London: Faber, 1969), 195.

7. *Darkness Visible* (London: Faber, 1979), 15.

8. Reprinted in *A Moving Target*, 204–205.

9. See *The Times*, 8 October 1983.

10. *A Moving Target*, 104–125.

11. All references are from the second edition (New York: Farrar, 1982).

12. James Gindin, "Gimmick and Metaphor in the Novels of William Golding," *Modern Fiction Studies*, 6 (Summer 1960), 145–152; Martin Green, "Distaste for the Contemporary," *Nation*, 21 May 1960, 451–454.

13. Reprinted in *A Moving Target*, 185–202.

Sybille Bedford: Most Reticent, Most Modest, Best[1]

ROBERT O. EVANS

> Faith is not believing something which our
> intelligence denies. It is the choice of the
> nobler hypothesis. Faith is the resolve to
> place the highest meaning on the facts
> which we observe.[2]

During that particularly hot summer of 1936, in Sanary at the unfashionable end of the French Mediterranean coast, Aldous Huxley finished *Eyeless in Gaza,* the book Sybille Bedford has said served as a sort of blueprint for the nobler hypothesis most of Huxley's work expresses.

Then, for Huxley there came a brief respite, a period of boredom or flatness—Bedford calls it "accidie"—and, perhaps, for Maria Huxley a short relief from the many obligations that seemed to wear her down, spend her energies, and threaten her health. For not only did she keep house for the family, doing most of her own work, but she also typed Huxley's manuscripts, and that summer she was struggling to learn shorthand. She even "found the time to type a chunk of a long novel" for Sybille Bedford,[3] who at twenty-five was spending one of her prolonged visits with the Huxleys.

One wonders now what that long novel was? Might it have been an early piece of *A Legacy?* Sybille Bedford, the most reticent of writers when it comes to herself (and one of the most modest), has not said. Nor does she anywhere suggest that she learned the craft of fiction from the eminent novelist with whom and with whose family she had such a close relationship over many years. If she did learn anything from Huxley, I think it must have been that the goal of the novelist should, in the long run, be to encompass that nobler hypothesis mentioned in the strange prayer printed by Gerald Heard, for in style and content her work is as different from Huxley's as that of two writers living in proximity in the same century could be. And perhaps the conclusion that she shared Huxley's devotion to a higher purpose as the end of art is more startling than it at first seems, for when *A Legacy* finally was published in 1956 reviewers certainly did not hail Sybille Bedford as a writer given, in Matthew Arnold's sense, to high seriousness. *Time* praised her for her tart and feline wit; Evelyn Waugh liked her "cool, witty, elegant" sometimes "uproariously funny" scenes; and Sybille Bedford herself seems to think of her work as domestic comedy. Despite an English Penguin edition (never available in the United States), the novel was soon more or less forgotten, though there has been, twenty years later, another American paperback reprint.[4]

A Legacy was followed by two other works of fiction, *A Favorite of the Gods* (1963) and *A Compass Error* (1969). These two have recently been reprinted in England and were reviewed at some length by Francis King in *The Spectator* (18 February 1984).[5] One might argue that a writer must have considerable merit to command first place in a review fifteen years after publication on the strength of a reprint. Excepting perhaps the chunk of long novel Maria Huxley typed in 1936, this appears to be her whole production as a novelist, though she has published several notable nonfiction books. *The Sudden View* (1953) is an extraordinary travel book mostly about a journey to Mexico, the best Mexico book since Graham Greene's. (It was published in the United States under the title *A Visit to Don Otavio.*)[6] It concerns a lengthy trip she made in the company of Esther Murphy Arthur of New York (the daughter-in-law of the American president, Chester A. Arthur), identified in the book only by the initial "E." *The Trial of Dr. Adams* (1959) is a piece of legal journalism dealing with the trial of Dr. John Bodkin Adams at the Old Bailey in 1957. Dr. Adams was charged with the the murder of an 82-year-old woman patient for the purpose of gaining a small legacy. His trial was the sensation of the day, especially when Dr. Adams was acquitted and then immediately arrested again for a similar crime before he even had time to leave the court-room.

Another nonfiction book, *The Faces of Justice: A Traveller's Report* (1961),[7] compares the legal processes in England, Austria, Switzerland, Germany, and

France, and is so enthralling and informative that it has sometimes been used as a textbook in courses in comparative law in the United States and Germany. And in 1973–1974 she published an extensive biography of her friend, Aldous Huxley, a work that has met with mixed reception from academic critics who have not always shared her preferences among Huxley's novels.

Three novels is not very much for a writer for whom I am about to claim serious stature. Still, it is quality and not quantity that really matters. Even more prolific writers have been remembered for less. Who now reads anything by Gustave Flaubert except *Madame Bovary?* With Sybille Bedford the problem of weighing her merits is doubly complicated, for the two later novels (*A Favorite of the Gods* and *A Compass Error*) are actually novel and sequel; that is, parts of the same story. One is a continuation of the other, though either will stand scrutiny as an individual work. Three books then and only two stories, but what stories they are!

A Legacy is told in the first person through childhood memories by Francesca, the daughter of a German baron, Julius von Felden, and his second wife, an English woman, Caroline Trafford. (There is a strong hint in the book that Francesca may not actually have been von Felden's child). The narrator, whose name we learn only after some two hundred pages, begins the story with her birth in the suburb of Charlottenburg in Berlin (now near the center of West Berlin) and leaves the reader when she reaches the age of nine, when her mother separates from von Felden and returns to England. In between she explores her memories of two families that may be taken as proto-types of importance in the years of formation of nationalist Germany.

These are the von Feldens, minor Bavarian aristocracy, Augustans as she calls them, more given to tinkering with machines in the potting shed than to great scientific discoveries, educated if not exactly brilliant, allied closely to the southern Catholic aristocracy in an emerging nation for which the church once had high hopes and ambitions. The second family are the Berlin Merzes of Voss Strasse, wealthy, Jewish, introverted, comfortable upper-class bourgeoisie, with whom Julius von Felden became connected through his first marriage to the daughter Melanie, who died before Caroline Trafford entered Julius's life. During the short term of his first marriage Julius, who had wasted his patrimony, lived on an allowance from the older Merzes. A brief excursion into the foreign service had been unsuccessful, though Julius was well enough liked in the embassies abroad for his indisputable charm. When Melanie died and Julius married again, it never occurred to the Merzes to stop the allowance; in fact, they actually raised it. They were then bringing up Melanie's child, Henrietta, and perhaps they felt they needed to placate the father to keep the grandchild, though neither narrator nor author ever says so. Much of what Sybille Bedford accomplishes in the way of story line she does by hints which propel the reader gently toward the conclusions she wishes. So Julius spent part of each year in the Merz household at Voss Strasse, even after his second marriage and the birth of Francesca. Caroline's child was not, however, born in that forbidding house. Such a thing would have been unthinkable. For birthing purposes Caroline and Julius took a flat, but to Voss Strasse they moved when Francesca was three weeks old.

Such a summary provides only the sketchiest of introductions to Sybille Bedford's extremely complex plot, which deals partly with the confluence of these two very different families during the rise of German nationalism—one might say the making of the modern Germany which three times plunged Europe and the world into war. The one, the von Feldens, a southern family, was perhaps culturally more French than German. French was the language they spoke at home, though with the local priest, who knew no French, they spoke Latin at table. The other family, the Merzes, were Jewish, rich by the standards of their day, mercantile, Berliners.

Through the marriage of Julius's older brother, Gustavus, to Clara Bernin, the von Feldens attached themselves to the Catholic aristocracy at a time when the church could place Bernin and later Gustavus in positions of great power. Bernin and Gustavus become Bismarck's successors. The von Feldens are also connected, though by an accident contrived by the author rather than through blood or marriage, with the Prussian aristocracy, that militaristic element that stocked Germany's rising officer class. Julius's younger brother, Johannes, is shipped off by his family to a Prussian military school (a new school, very Prussian, though actually set in southern Germany), where he suffers terribly, escapes, is returned, and eventually goes mad. Ironically, in the Watergate type of cover-up that follows, Johannes is commissioned and regularly promoted, until many years later an incident occurs which brings his case to the attention of the press (another element beginning to exercise power in rising Germany). The von Felden affair becomes a national scandal, a *cause célèbre*, on which the plot of the novel eventually turns.

The plot of *A Legacy* is much more complex than this—to reveal it entirely might spoil the suspense for readers who have yet to discover Sybille Bedford's attractions. The point to be made here is that we are dealing with a very large tapestry, one with many strands and themes which the author skillfully weaves together to bring about the eventual dénouement. But the events, controlled as they are for the reader by the memories of a child, are not in themselves greatly important. The scandal has its interests, and the people who contribute to it are interesting also as characters. They are cultivated and fascinating people, sometimes even a little zany—like Julius, when he arrives in Berlin in the company of two monkeys only to find the German hotels will not accept animals as registered guests. Sometimes they are shocking—the hazing Johannes suffers in the Prussian military school. Sometimes sad—Edward Merz's gambling away his fortune. Sometimes cruel—Edward's wife, Sarah, refusing to pay his debts. (She is a rich Frankfurt aniline heiress who understands the value of the Deutschmark.) Sometimes charming—Julius and Sarah are both collectors of impeccable taste; a picture presented to Caroline by Sarah—painted by Claude Monet—plays an important part in the unfolding of the plot. (We are dealing with the period when Impressionists were barred from the main exhibits, but Sarah has the foresight to recognize their coming value.) Sometimes poignant—as when Melanie has herself baptized in order to marry Julius, only to discover that she had the ceremony performed by a Lutheran minister instead of a priest. Such incidents are all part of the panorama that Evelyn Waugh, naturally, appreciated when he read the novel. But the incidents, many of them hilarious, are not there simply to delight the reader. They contribute in a major way to the development of plot and character—as a pet pony named Fanny, who likes to take the notes out of one's case and count the sum, finally takes out a real note which reveals information long hidden that brings about the termination of the marriage of Julius and Caroline.

Out of context the recitation of such incidents sounds precious, but in a large novel they are all brought about quite naturally. Unfortunately, they seem to have clouded the eyes of Sybille Bedford's reviewers and distracted them from her more important themes, for what she has prepared for us is a social history of the emerging Germany that was to become, when nationalism reached its apex, the *Reich* that was to have lasted a thousand years. She is, in my opinion, a better historian or sociologist than any of the professionals who have tried to explain Hitler's Germany. All of the elements she examines were there from Bismarck's time, none of them in itself perhaps dangerous—but mixed together, explosive. Sybille Bedford never claims to deal with all of the components of national socialism, nor for that matter with any one of them, in a direct, critical fashion, but she paints her canvas carefully with the novelist's all-seeing eye and with real erudition.

A major theme, then, of *A Legacy* explains how the Germany that gave us

Beethoven and Wagner, much of modern medicine and science, and a highly
developed civilization, could become under Hitler the archenemy of the very
values the country helped to create. In the interactions and the power
plays—brought about because of conflicting ethical systems among various
segments of the population—Nazi Germany arose, a nation that could ex-
terminate six million Jews, a nation those of us who belong to Sybille Bedford's generation remember as a threat to the entire structure of western
civilization. No one, nor no one party, was singly at fault, but what happened
was the result of the way people behaved. Many compromised their principles
when they should have stood firm, whatever the immediate reasons, and
gradually the door opened upon barbarism. Had Germans behaved differently, the Nazis might never have come to power. That, in sum, is the author's
nobler hypothesis!

There is, of course, no doubt where Sybille Bedford's sympathies lie. She is
an English woman making no excuses for the Germans. Still, on the whole she
treats them fairly, except perhaps in her descriptions of the Prussian military
mentality. There she offends our sensibilities, though she carefully points out
that Prussia was not all of Germany nor even the most important part. (One
need only recall writers like Eduard Graf von Keyserling to realize that not all
of Baltic Germany was militaristic at heart.) The Prussians are the worst element in her novel, but it was not their political victories alone that paved the
way for national socialism. All Germans were responsible (if indeed any of
them were and history is not just a tragic accident). Sybille Bedford shows us
how through, among other things, numerous planned asides. "Nobody here is
allowed on the grass"[8]—a remark about Berlin. *"I've never seen such
manners"*—Caroline attempting to escape from a bad district in the city by
cab, only to have a man try to snatch the vehicle away from her (213). "Who
said Prussia was a police state?" (266)—an ironic remark from Sarah. "Caroline is an English gentleman" (263). "The Kaiser and Kaiserin announced a
Court Ball, and there was after all a brand new battleship" (278).

The writer claims no special insight. Instead, she applies her intellect to
intelligible phenomena and permits the reader to draw the inevitable conclusions. She is writing about people first of all and then about a nation, one
which was to bring the democracies to their severest trials. Sometimes she
explains: "Bismarck's successful wars . . . brought at once a tide of big
money, big enterprise, big building, big ideas which blurred demarcations
between castes, swelled military and domestic discipline into Wagnerian displays and atrophied the older traditions of economy, frugality, and probity.

Tradespeople were coining money, the middle classes were getting rich and the rich became opulent. The pay of the bureaucracy remained lean, but its members were puffed with self importance" (14). She follows with a more extensive discussion of German politics. The liberals in the rising nation worked hard for a union, hoping to curb the power of the princes. They got the Kaiser and World War I and later Hitler and World War II. Prussian nationalists hoped for hegemony over Austria. Some lived to see the Austrian empire destroyed and later the *Anschluss*. Free traders wanted to get rid of archaic monetary conditions. Democrats wished to extend the franchise. Labor leaders wished to unite the working class. Socialists hoped for the expansion of trade unions. And the army—one supposes that at first they wished merely to expand and become more powerful in the state. All of these worthy ambitions working upon one another brought about unforeseen results: high tariffs, the Imperial Constitution of Versailles, anti-socialist legislation, Alsace-Lorraine (and the lasting enmity of France), Bismarck, later Hitler. All the stuff of history, the course of human events. Sybille Bedford, of course, is not the first novelist to trade in this kind of coin. *War and Peace* is much the same kind of book. In both the nobler hypothesis arises from an explanation of great events which somehow boggle our imaginations and challenge our intellects.

This aspect of *A Legacy* raises the novel to a serious level far beyond drawing-room comedy. It is in the political explanations, which hinge on the variety of people that merged to comprise a unified Germany, that the deeper themes lie. To say that is not to deny the charm of the characters or the delight we take in hilarious incidents. The book is full of such things. Julius von Felden is an absolutely charming person, even if he turns out to be superficial and sometimes less than honest. (He presents the Merzes with two beautiful china dogs—supposedly antiques, but they are really fakes.) Grandpa and Grandma Merz provide wonderful (if minor) portraits—the old gentleman with his passion for a well-turned ankle sometimes supplied by paid female companions—Grandma with her interminable game of Grabuge played with 144 decks of cards, all spades.

On the whole, I think the women come off best. Caroline is not only an English "gentleman"; she is a woman of principles, though certainly not Victorian in conduct. Sarah Merz, despite her cold-hearted refusal to pay her husband's debts, is also a woman of principles and a person of extraordinary intelligence. Clara von Felden, the Catholic sister-in-law, is something of a religious fanatic, but she, too, has high principles. These are memorable portraits any great novelist would be proud to own.

There are other devices in *A Legacy* that help carry the themes and make the book highly readable. Among these, the gnomic wisdom offered by the narrator (true, she was only a child when the story took place, but she was grown up when she wrote it). She begins a chapter with a commonplace allusion to Shakespeare:

> Tomorrow, and tomorrow, and tomorrow. . . . Life, in the neat sad dry little French phrase that bundles it all into its place, life is never as bad or as good as one thinks. *La vie, voyez-vous ça n'est jamais si bon ni si mauvais qu'on croit.*
>
> (158)

Or again:

> We are said to reinvent our memories; we often rearrange them.
>
> (171)
>
> Girls of course are never sure of their welcome at all, or that was what one heard.
>
> (172)
>
> All vast dreams are shocking. To small people.
>
> (210)

And Caroline to Julius:

> We had better get married all the same, don't you agree?

Julius, charming sophisticate, in response:

> Whatever you prefer. Unmarried lasts longer.
>
> (216)

There are also many allusions, figures of speech, verbal devices in this book. Sybille Bedford has all the stylistic finesse we have come to expect from the best English writers of our time, and ours has been a century of great stylistic experimentation: think of Virginia Woolf and the stream of consciousness, or James Joyce and paranomasia, or—more recently—Anthony Burgess's *Napoleon Symphony,* where he often omits the predicate forcing the reader to finish his sentences.

Sybille Beford is also given to the utmost economy. She can say more in a few words than many writers in a whole chapter. Economy of diction, to be sure, is no new thing (Jane Austen), but Sybille Bedford sometimes accomplishes that in startling new ways. She introduces speakers who are not part of the novel at all, as if we could overhear tidbits of conversation about events in the book. For instance, when Sarah refused to pay the gambling debts:

> "Young Mrs. Merz took a great deal on herself."
> "Any assets?"
> "Only personal. Merz's got a motor."
> "Not much prospect of a discharge!"
> "Not a chance."
> "Much the best thing for him."
> "It'll look fishy though. If they go on living in that huge house of theirs—"
> "*It will look damn fishy.*"
> "Who acted for Mrs. Merz?"
> "Benjamin & Bleibtreu. Her people's people."
>
> (16)

Unidentified Berliners, clubmen perhaps, gossiping about the bankruptcy, a simple effective device. But "Bleibtreu"? (Stay true.) One of these Shakespearean word games: a rose by any other name. . . .

Sometimes Sybille Bedford becomes rather more complicated, as:

> From behind shuttered windows, Melanie was watching.
> "Oh, Jules, what's that? Where does it come from?"
> "Won't they drop it?"
> "Can we have it out at once? Where are you going to put it?"
>
> (134)

These three remarks pertaining to the same event were actually made at different moments as Julius brought an article into the house, but the writer has compressed them into a single passage, to save time and space and perhaps secure emphasis.

Another device of a different sort, perhaps borrowed from Conrad, seems to demand our attention. That is the use of a lie as a sort of summary of unethical conduct. In *Heart of Darkness* Marlow tells two deliberate lies. The first, for business reasons, is to enable him to get rivets to repair the boat. The end justifies the means. By Conrad's standards it is a bad lie. The second is the lie Marlow tells at the end of the tale to Kurtz's European fiancée, intending to give her some small comfort. Kurtz died, he tells her, with her name on his lips. We know nothing could be further from the truth. But this time it was a good lie. The existential problem (Kierkegaard wrestles with the same point; see his discussion of Abraham's willingness to sacrifice his own child) has to do with the intention behind the action. At the end of *A Legacy* Gustavus commits suicide, thus in the eyes of his wife Clara endangering his immortal soul. If, however, he did not die immediately, if he lingered even for a few moments, there is always the hope that he repented and thus saved his soul. Caroline, who discovered the body, is asked to give Clara that hope. "I do not think I can," she says. . . . *"There have been too many lies. . . .* Now it must have a stop. . . . I'd do anything to be of help to her. Only, do not ask *me* to set up the next lie" (300). The tone is quite different, but the subject might have been extracted from Graham Greene's *The Heart of the Matter.*

Like Greene, Sybille Bedford is concerned with ethics, with human conduct, with the nobler hypothesis. *A Legacy* is a very full book on both national and personal levels. Though it suggests rather than prescribes solutions, it deals with ethical actions, some of which are of great importance to her readers, particularly those whose history goes back to World War II. In this double sense, then, this is a very deep book indeed, one that has been too little read and too little appreciated.

A Favourite of the Gods and *A Compass Error* also treat ethical matters, but without the historical skeleton of *A Legacy.* They are more personal books; indeed they are so charming (and so fluffy) that it is again easy to mistake the deeper meaning—or to miss the point.

A Favourite of the Gods deals primarily with Constanza and once again is told mostly in the first person, through the voice of a young girl, her daughter Flavia. The story begins with Constanza and her daughter on a train from Italy bound for Nice, where Constanza plans to catch the Calais Express. She is going north to be married for the second time. Suddenly Constanza notices that the ruby ring which belonged to her Italian father and was perhaps her most prized inheritance from him (*valeur sentimentale*) is missing. The Calais Express, too, is missed. They continue toward Toulon. Finally they disembark at an unfashionable seaside town (like Sanary?) in an unfashionable season; take rooms in a hotel (later they will rent a villa); send telegrams to the abandoned fiancé, Lewis (who never appears); and "'It doesn't look,' Constanza said, 'does it, as if we were getting off tomorrow or the next day?'"[9] In fact, they stay for eleven years. (I can think of only one comparable incident in contemporary English fiction, in Nancy Mitford's *The Blessing,* when the heroine, left stranded without money in a Paris railway station, is assisted by a gallant Frenchman, who drops her mink coat in a trash can, promising to buy her a more suitable sable.)

The story proper is Constanza's, as the division titles indicate: "A Rational Education," "The Story of a Marriage," etc. It begins, however, with Constanza's American mother, who married an Italian nobleman, eventually left him (to his astonishment) because of his infidelity, took her daughter to Eng-

land, and in time married her off to an ambitious young man. Flavia is the
result of that marriage. At one point Flavia tells her mother that she thinks
Constanza is marrying Lewis for her sake. This remark prepares for a typical
Sybille Bedford anachronism; referring to her first marriage, Constanza says:
"I married for love to please my mother—it does sound queer" (18-19). It was
queer! The first husband, Simon, divorced Constanza to marry another
woman better able to further his ambition. Many years later Constanza makes
another marriage contract she won't keep, but after eleven years in the south
of France she does meet a Frenchman, separated from his wife, a man with
whom she believes she can live happily. Her emotional trials are many, but at
the end of the novel all seems to come out well. Constanza was, after all, a
favorite of the gods. But before we learn that, we watch her as a young girl in
Italy, as a debutante in England, and also follow her mother's strange life with
her Italian husband and later as the virtually untouchable principessa. This is
a social drama, mostly comedy with a rather light touch (shaded a bit by
Henry James's *The Portrait of a Lady*, perhaps), but there are serious themes,
too.

"Mr. James," Flavia asks, "what is wrong with human affairs?" Her wise,
kindly old mentor can only suggest that she "Wait for Evolution" (136).

Or Constanza on marriage for love: "One doesn't marry like that, just like
that. For a bit of love" (154).

Or Mena, the trusted maid, on the role of women: "Some women get to
hate their men" (165).

Or Simon to Constanza, on war: "May I only remember it in my night-
mares. People going through with it is the final proof that we are all insane"
(177). There is, in fact, quite a lot about war in the book, especially when the
author deals with the people who experienced World War I. Most of it reflects
the general attitude, the disgust with the horror of stalemated trench warfare,
of most writers of the time.

Or, again, Anna, the principessa, upon being told there was revolution in
Germany following World War I: "Whatever that means, they won't stand
for another war." And Constanza, responds, "Nobody will that" (202). How
wrong we all were.

And much later, about Michel Devaux, the man Constanza finally picked:
"Now he's alone and writes books. . . . He tells us that the first step towards
sane government is the renunciation of war as an instrument of policy. . . .
Que voulez-vous, mesdames, c'est un homme à principes" (267).

These are but samples, and war and marriage but a few of the serious themes touched on by the writer. Early, in *A Favourite of the Gods* she had her say, through Constanza, about religion—or at least about the church. A young man named William, an Anglo-Catholic, has come to visit in Rome. "How do you feel about Infallibility . . . ?" he asks Constanza. "That's easy, like the Immaculate Conception and all that. God is omnipotent, isn't he?" "But why should God *want* to make the Pope infallible?" "Because we are the One True Church." "Do you *really* believe that?" And Constanza, "I'm not at all certain. . . . It does seem odd that *everybody* else should be wrong, the Protestants and the Greeks and the people who think there isn't any God at all; the Buddhists, too" (47–48).

But Sybille Bedford does not examine religion or the church very closely. She lacks the interest in theology of a Graham Greene or an Evelyn Waugh. She dispenses with religion quickly and rather flippantly, but she does not avoid the subject. It is, after all, part of being human. Her themes, even when concealed in the most lighthearted of stories, are the same serious themes major writers of the century examine. One cannot quite afford to dismiss *A Favourite of the Gods* as social comedy. As the reviewer of *The Spectator* reminds us, Constanza dies in a ditch in France "riddled by German machine gun bullets."

It would be even harder to dismiss *A Compass Error* for levity. It is much less lighthearted, and Flavia, whose story it is, is far less lucky than her mother. The story begins with Flavia left alone in the villa on the French seacoast. Anna is dead. Constanza has fled with her lover, Michel, keeping her whereabouts secret (except from Flavia) because discovery would ruin Michel's divorce case. Like Constanza, Flavia now has her first sexual experience, only in this novel it is a lesbian affair with an older woman.

Flavia is supposed to be spending her summer reading for her university entrance exams. A rather intellectual, lonely girl, she picks up with an artist's family and begins her first love affair with the wife. The portraits Sybille Bedford draws here are wonderfully interesting, and one wonders how much they may be indebted to Sanary and her own holidays with the Huxleys. But where sexual experience for Constanza eventually led to a pleasant fulfillment with Michel, there is no such happiness in Flavia's future. She forms a new liaison with another attractive, older woman, and because of it she reveals her mother's (and Michel's) retreat. This is enough to spoil their escape, and Flavia blames herself even though she gave nothing away directly. She simply made it possible for her *femme de monde*, Andrée, to discover what she had seduced the young girl to find out. Thus, Constanza and Michel are never married. Flavia never goes to the university. The end results, we are told in the epilogue, are tragic, though Flavia "has often come near to absolving herself." Come near to absolving—after World War II, after Michel spent his war in retreat in some corner of unoccupied France and Andrée is decorated by both the British and the French, after Flavia—did nothing!

If we put the two books together and make them one long novel dealing with major themes of the times, they are a considerable accomplishment. What Sybille Bedford is concerned with primarily is ethical action, what principles amount to, what right principles are, and how we should survive our own sentimental education and recognize such things. This is important stuff for a novelist, and Sybille Bedford is a novelist of absolute integrity bent on telling her readers the truth. That she clothes it in delightful European scenes, in comic incidents and in allusions to her extensive reading in several languages should only make the novel better, not conceal its true value, but the reviews have hardly done better with A Favourite of the Gods and A Compass Error than they did with A Legacy.

Many of the techniques she uses in A Legacy, particulary those aimed at economy in writing, appear again in the later books (and in her nonfiction, as well). There are a few new devices, of course, and the texture is perhaps even richer in the later books. In A Favourite of the Gods, for example, we hear of Mr. Asquith, Keir Hardie, Winston Churchill, and Lloyd George only a few lines away from Cezanne and Picasso, Stravinsky and Debussy, almost on the same page with G. B. S., H. G. Wells, and D. H. Lawrence, E. M. Forster, Marcel Proust, T. S. Eliot, the Sitwells, Ezra Pound, and Gerard Manley Hopkins—even d'Annunzio. The texture is loaded with contemporary European references, a strong plus value for the reader.

Who is to say how time will eventually deal with Sybille Bedford? At any rate there has been a reprint of A Favourite of the Gods and A Compass Error since I wrote that line for the slightly different version of this piece published in Studies in the Literary Imagination. But Sybille Bedford remains very different from most contemporary English novelists. Her canvas is so much larger. Her ethical considerations are more reminiscent of Conrad (or Tolstoi) than Iris Murdoch or Muriel Spark or Doris Lessing. If Olivia Manning paints as broadly in The Balkan Trilogy and The Levant Trilogy, she seems much less concerned with the nobler hypothesis than Sybille Bedford. She deals with life in a larger sense than Olivia Manning does with Harriet Pringle or Muriel Spark with Miss Jean Brodie. She can be just as ironical, just as funny, and just as delightful to read, but she is a lot harder to ignore. If I sound complimentary, it is deliberate. "Too complimentary," she wrote to me, "because what you say about my having got some inches nearer to explaining all those German wars rather scares me. If I have explained anything, it was by help of instinct, not tangible knowledge."[10] Perhaps! But it is fatal to believe an author about his/ her own work. The final test lies on the printed page, and there it is hard to fault Sybille Bedford, except perhaps for having spent so much of her extraordinary energy and insight on nonfiction, though those works too deserve praise.

NOTES

1. Sybille Bedford was born 16 March 1911, daughter of Maximillian von Schoenebeck and Elizabeth Bernard. She married Walter Bedford in 1935. That is absolutely all the personal information she has supplied to the usual biographical sources.

2. Aldous Huxley in Gerald Heard, ed., *Prayers and Meditations: A Monthly Cycle Arranged for Daily Use* (New York: Harper, 1949).

3. Sybille Bedford, *Aldous Huxley: A Biography*, 2 vols. (London: Chatto and Windus; Collins, 1973–1974), I, 336.

4. I am pleased to report a new American paperback edition of *A Legacy* by the Ecco Press in 1976.

5. King's review is titled "Women, War and Crime," 21.

6. A new edition from Collins with the American title was dated 1960.

7. A Touchstone paperback edition (Simon and Schuster) is available in the U.S. Two chapters appeared earlier in somewhat different form: "England: An Ordinary Trial" in *Vogue* and "Paris: Summary Justice" in *Esquire*.

8. *A Legacy* (New York: Simon and Schuster, 1957), 113. Subsequent references to this edition appear parenthetically.

9. *A Favourite of the Gods* (New York: Simon and Schuster, 1963), 20. Subsequent references to this edition appear parenthetically.

10. Letter to the writer, 8 July 1977.

"No Idle Rentier": Angus Wilson and the Nourished Literary Imagination

MARGARET DRABBLE

A ngus Wilson is without question one of the most important British novelists writing today, and some would say the greatest. He has behind him a solid body of work: three collections of short stories, seven major novels, and a wide variety of critical and biographical studies. When one attempts to describe the quality of his achievement, one is almost daunted by its range, richness, and diversity. He is a brilliant comic writer, with the keenest eye for social pretension and manipulation; he also writes of loneliness, doubt, breakdown, and inner confusion. He dissects English society with a knowing familiarity, yet is widely travelled, and equally at home in foreign settings and with international themes. He loves extravagant set pieces—plays, crowd scenes, parties, public meetings—yet can also describe the bewilderment of an elderly lady confronted for the first time by an automatic washing machine. He is fond of the macabre, the exotic, the bizarre and the camp, yet writes with deep sympathy of a Quaker's search for truth through self-abnegation. The moment one has decided that he is writing a comedy of manners with an edge of *haute-bourgeoisie* snobbery, he turns the whole book upside down and exposes the snobbery of the snobs. He castigates dullness, yet writes with respect and insight of the civil servants and administrators of this world, battling on in face of the world's conviction that they are dull. A master of parody and pastiche, he has his own unmistakable center. A "traditional" novelist, in the sense that he employs elaborate plots, displays a great feeling for sociologically significant material decor, and fills his works with Dickensian "characters," he also uses a dazzling variety of shifts, tricks and fictive devices, a splendid (but rarely intrusive) display of literary allusions and echoes, and a highly sophisticated and complex narrative technique. Sophisticated in all ways, and immensely discriminating, his writing also embraces coarseness and relishes vulgarity in its many manifestations. Farcical, serious, malicious, compassionate—in short, a novelist for all seasons.

This multiplicity is not only evidence of his great talents: it is also at the core of his work. He is a writer who is never satisfied with the simple, or with the already achieved. He moves on, rejecting label after label, restlessly enquiring, balancing, and reassessing, extending his range with each new work. The success of his first collections of stories, *The Wrong Set* and *Such Darling Dodos* (1949 and 1950), brought him fame as a social satirist, earning him such epithets as "merciless" and "savage," but like his own character Margaret in *No Laughing Matter* he soon found this kind of recognition restricting and moved into larger fields, writing, with equal and increasing success, of wider themes, drawing together the random subjects of his stories into a more comprehensive portrait of British life. He has never abandoned his skill for spotting the eccentric, for exposing oddities and inconsistencies of speech, dress, and attitude—in his latest novel occurs the wonderful and characteristic sentence, "I thought an entree was what people like Mama call what people call starters"[1]—but these flashes have become part of the pattern of the whole, rather than the fabric itself, and in his later works he rarely allows himself the undisguised dislike manifested in such portraits as that of Gwen in "Rex Imperator":

> Gwen Rutherford did not reply, she was too busy settling herself on the sofa. It was a process acquired through years of competition for the best chairs in private hotel lounges and it took time. First a place had to be found for Boy, her white West Highland terrier, then there was her own ample body to be spread, next she had to put out on the seat beside her a jade cigarette holder, a shagreen cigarette case, her knitting and her Boots' library book; she would also have liked the newspaper, but Mr Nicholson had taken that. She sat bolt upright with her large bust and her short thick arms held defiantly forward. Her fat face with its bulging eyes was blotched from an over-hasty make-up, the lines of her plump cheeks ran in deep sulk at each side of her small pouting mouth. She looked like

the British bulldog at bay rather than a once beautiful woman soured by seven years of legal separation. Long after most women had grown their hair again, Gwen had retained her peroxide shingle and the rolls of blue stubbled fat at the back of her neck added to the bulldog illusion.[2]

Not a pleasant caricature; his early experiences of private hotels stocked Angus Wilson's imagination with some frightening visions.

His first two novels, *Hemlock and After* (1952) and *Anglo-Saxon Attitudes* (1956), both contain figures who are cruelly satirized: the pretentious, manipulative, cultured, snobbish, sensitive, destructive Mrs. Craddock, with her fancy geese and her tame son; the self-deluding Scandinavian wife, Inge Middleton, with her ludicrous Christmas celebrations and her ignorance of her own children; Ron, Vin, Larrie, and Yves, an unpleasant quartet of ineffective con-men; the historical novelist Clarissa Crane, who is summed up so devastatingly by an elderly professor as a "time-waster"; the crazy and wonderful Rose Lorimer, an academic in fur coat and straw hat with roses nourishing strange fantasies about pagan Christianity; the mean, paranoid, wife-bullying Professor Clun (in fact a gallery of academic portraits that surpasses Mary McCarthy's in *The Groves of Academe*); yet they also contain much more. Both novels have male protagonists, successful novelist Bernard Sands and successful historian Gerald Middleton, both aging, guilty, intro-spective, pursued by a sense of failure, and anxious to put right the mistakes of a lifetime, and neither seen through the eyes of satire. The novels contain preoccupations with justice, evil, responsibility, the possibility of self-knowledge. They raise the complex questions that dominate Wilson's later works: the relationship between manners and morals, between the claims of the world and the claims of the self, between activity and retirement, between town and country, the civilized and the wild, between multiplicity and in-tegrity, between (as a later character defines it) fun and duty. The comic effects are superb—on a large scale there is the collapse of Sands's idealistic project for establishing a Writers' House, Vardon Hall, which ends in a scene of operatic disaster; on a smaller scale there is Middleton's attempt to vary his usual Christmas gift of a cyclamen to his one-time housekeeper Mrs. Salad. Mistakenly he presents her with a poinsettia, which she greets with disgust:

> "Oh, it's a lovely foreign thing. Bright as blood," Mrs Salad said in her old, croaking tremolo, and she peered at it through the haze of mascara's moisture that always clung to her eyelashes and stuck in little beads on her black eye-veil. "I dare say it'll draw the flies. But lovely for them that likes bright colors. Just like the stuff the girls put on their finger-nails

now. Like a lot of old birds giving the glad in the Circus, or the York Road, Waterloo, more likely. Trollopy lot."

And Mrs Salad's black-dyed curls and fur toque with eye-veil shook in disgust. . . .

The camp, the malicious, and the macabre still flourish, but the novels are not primarily comedies.

The Middle Age of Mrs. Eliot (1958) is neither comedy nor satire, though, again, it contains elements of both. Its structure is more traditional than that of its two predecessors, and unlike them, it is a journey into the future rather than a reassessment of the past. Its protagonist is a woman, a choice which gives the author a well-judged distance from his creation (Sands and Middleton sound occasionally like apologists, even when most harsh on themselves). Like Mrs. Craddock, Meg Eliot is a cultured woman, but culture here is not subjected to mockery but to investigation. Her favorite novels include *Emma, The Mill on the Floss, The Small House at Allington*, and *Daisy Miller*, a telling collection, and one of the novel's lovely subtleties is the varied way in which it demonstrates that the reading of novels (and the writing of them?) can be either an escape into the past or an attempt to make sense of the present. The plot, as Mrs. Eliot's reading matter might suggest, has a classic structure. At the opening of the book Meg Eliot is, like Emma, handsome, clever, and rich, seeming to unite the best blessings of existence. She is, though childless, very happily married, has a wide circle of friends, and busies herself with voluntary social work and a pleasant if expensive hobby—she collects porcelain. Like Emma, she prides herself on her ability to manipulate others for their own good, and on her kindness to the less fortunate—notably to three women friends who have fallen on harder times, whom she thinks of as her "lame ducks." We see her in action, gracious, witty, seemingly self-aware, tying up her various obligations before departing with her husband, Bill, for a visit to the Far East. On the journey, disaster strikes. Bill is killed by an assassin's bullet in a foreign airport, and Meg Eliot returns to find that not only is she suddenly poor—her husband died in debt, unexpectedly to her but not to the reader—but that all her occupations have gone. Her change in status, and the growing awareness of that change, are charted with the keenest insight; she finds herself the victim of those she once patronized, a woman without place, fortune, protection, or skill, a lame duck indeed. Her attempts to reenter society, her false starts, her failures, her breakdown and slow recovery take us into many corners of English life—the world of decayed gentlefolk, the hard struggles of single professional women, the fringes of

Bohemia, the grind of a shorthand-typing course, the respite of her brother's nursery garden in Sussex. The novel records the progress of a human being toward self-knowledge and toward knowledge of the world she lives in, a world of which, as she admits, she had been dangerously ignorant.

I must confess that this seems to me an almost perfect plot, and perfect for Wilson's purposes. Through it, he explores the hypocrisies of society, displaying as he does so a profound sympathy with the lonely and the powerless, and a deep respect for the fighting spirit with which Meg Eliot faces the reality that has been thrust upon her. Like a true heroine, and a worthy successor to her fictional counterparts, she rejects the easy answers—marriage, a life of borrowing and sponging, a quiet life in the country with her brother, the comforts of religious mysticism—and battles on, determined to earn her own living, determining never to be taken by surprise again. At the end of the novel she is happily engaged as secretary to a Labour M. P., but thinking of moving on. Restlessness, or curiosity? A little of both, but certanly she recongizes that for her change and engagement with life are both essential.

The whole book is so solidly constructed and carefully accomplished that one might well wonder where the ever-restless Wilson himself might move next. He was in his mid-forties when it was published, an age when most novelists have found their voice and form, an age for consolidation. Here was a straight success, a moving story of triumph over tragedy, a story with a very wide appeal, restrained, balanced, apparently middlebrow, an apology to the middle-class reader for past satire at the expense of middle-class readers, a settling of accounts with womankind in general (for women had not shown too well in previous Wilson novels). A marriage of Virginia Woolf and Arnold Bennett, as Wilson claims the novel was described. Why not simply repeat the same formula?

But like his heroine, Wilson is not fond of repetition. His next novel, *The Old Men at the Zoo* (1961), is quite different—a not too fantastic fantasy, set in what was then the near future. *The Old Men* is about politics, about freedom and restraint, about responsibility and democracy. Its narrator, Simon Carter, is Secretary of the Zoological Gardens, and the Zoo's staff serve as a microcosm for government. (Wilson worked at the British Museum between 1937 and 1955, a member of the library staff, and in this novel he displays a useful familiarity with administrative problems and the administrative temperament that most novelists conspicuously lack.) Vanished are the polite archaic shades of Austen and Trollope: we are in a world of violent color, of savage events, of bestiality (literally), and of war. Dickens? Zola? H. G. Wells? Men are seen and described in terms of the beasts they keep. They are corrupted by power, lost in the attempt to preserve a civilized balance between the ordered and the free, between the state and nature. "Limited liberty" is the slogan with which Carter and his colleagues attempt to establish a wild zoological park, a glorified Whipsnade, a project as idealistic and as doomed as Sands's attempt to provide a home for writers—for it is undermined not only by its own staff and their intrigues, but by the outbreak of European war. The plot sounds and is bizarre, but, as one might trust from Wilson, its symbolism is not disembodied (the descriptions of animal behavior show how deeply he studied and felt for his subject), nor does it refuse the incidental delights of the other works, including a portrait of the Director's naive wife, Mrs. Leacock, whose favorite adjective is the schoolgirl "mouldy," and who hopes to pacify an outraged and contemptuous aristocratic neighbor with a little gift: "So I just popped a pot of bramble jelly I've made into a bag with a little note saying that it was a poor thing, but my own. You see with someone so rich there's nothing you can do for them. But I daresay they never think to give her anything homemade. . . ."

(Wilson is always hard on this peculiarly English brand of childishness: Mrs. Leacock insists on referring to her husband as "Daddy" even when no children are present, and despite the fact that her daughter, a nymphomaniac, is in her thirties; the daughter in turn complains that her father "still calls his prick his weewee." A similar regressive clinging to family talk can be found in many other works—for instance, in the short story "Crazy Crowd" and in the character Susan in *No Laughing Matter,* who refers to her unfortunate youngest son as P. S., for Post Script. Wilson has little patience with this kind of whimsy.)

The Old Men at the Zoo is a somber novel, showing a Europe which returns to the violence of the 1930s, where nationalism and neo-Fascism flourish. But even from this dark scene, there is no escape through withdrawal, no retreat into the quiet garden. Carter is a keen naturalist who likes to reread *Tarka the Otter* and whose greatest joy is to watch badgers at play; yet through the fortunes of war he finds himself forced to kill the things he loves in order to eat them; his murderous task is aided, ironically, by a brutal village boy so far removed from natural life that he has never seen even a rabbit, and who can do little but lament the absence of "proper tinned stuff from Norwich." (For Wilson's own analysis of this scene, see his autobiographical study, *The Wild Garden*).[3]

His next novel, *Late Call* (1964), is very far removed from fantasty; indeed, its subject matter is positively banal. It relates the story of a fat elderly woman, Sylvia Calvert, who retires as manageress of a hotel and goes to live with her son, Harold, headmaster of a comprehensive school in a New Town in the Midlands. The whole plot revolves round little domestic intrigues and disputes: her gambling husband, Arthur, is always borrowing money; her granddaughter, Judy, is in with the county set; Harold mourns his dead wife; grandson Ray doesn't seem to be interested in girls. Will Harold get together with big-bottomed Sally Bulmer? Will Arthur's coarseness offend Judy's friend Caroline Ogilvie? Will Sylvia ever learn to use the Roastomatic? Will Ray and his friend Mr. Corney come up against the law? The whole thing is like a parody of the soap operas to which Sylvia herself is addicted. (Angus Wilson's pastiche soap opera about prison life, "Wardress Webb," was shortly followed in real life, if so it may be called, by a remarkably similar TV series called "Within These Walls," starring Googie Withers; thus does art imitate art. Similarly, I switched on a television program about the Edinburgh Festival the other night to find myself watching a performance of actors portraying the tribal life of baboons that could only have been a continuation of the work of Ned's troupe in *As If by Magic,* whose previous dramas had included a drama called "Batteries," with chickens, and one called "Territoriality," with elands and gazelles. Angus Wilson should beware of what he imagines next, for we are surely going to be watching it in three years' time.)

In middle-class and lower middle-class soap opera land, Angus Wilson boldly relinquishes all his familiar touchstones, for it is a world where echoes of Woolf and George Eliot and jokes about the reputations of Etty and Wilkie mean nothing—a world where almost all the cultural framework is drawn from Syliva's own reading and viewing, apart from a fine account (through Sylvia's reactions) of a local amateur performance of *Look Back in Anger,* which horrifies her, when she wakes to pay attention, by Jimmy Porter's violent ranting about Alison's mother, "who ought to be dead." This is the focus of Sylvia's struggle—her sense of her own redundancy. Her struggle is not un-like Meg Eliot's, but she has none of her weapons, being ill-educated, old, and socially inferior to her relatives: her clever son is a characteristic product of the new postwar world, upwardly mobile, ambitious, deeply involved in community politics, proudly provincial, painstakingly progressive even to the extent of smiling with happy approval when ton-up boys with rowdy motorbikes shatter the peace of his neighborhood. Yet Sylvia's spiritual journey towards a new sense of purpose is treated with entire seriousness, and she emerges with great dignity, despite (or because of) the fact that she embodies many of the qualities that the earlier Wilson had found ridiculous: she is ignorant, has poor taste, and is fat. Obesity, in some of Wilson's satire, seems almost to be a crime in itself; Mrs. Curry, the procuress in *Hemlock and After*, is grotesquely fat and almost a personification of evil, as though appearance and morals held some direct correspondence. But Sylvia's size is a theme of sympathy rather than laughter. She waddles and puffs, even at the most dramatic moments of the action, and there is a shocking scene in which, on the way out for an evening's entertainment with her family, she slips and falls: "The pain and the shock were not enough to drive from her a dreadful picture of herself—a fat useless old woman dolled up to no purpose, a sprawling ugly furry mess on the pathway. She could sense that the cheap imitation hat had fallen rakishly to one side, and that the white hair straggling down her face was spattered with blood from her hand. . . . She felt herself to be a huge sack of coals as they lifted her from the ground and supported her back into the house."[4] In such scenes, Wilson's effort of imagination is triumphantly vindicated; he has entered into the mind and heart of a woman from a background utterly remote from his own, and in showing us the world through her eyes, he enlarges our sympathies as much as he has enlarged his own.

Predictably, *Late Call* was hailed as evidence of a new, mature compassion, and a sign that the novel of social realism was not yet dead. Equally predictably, Angus Wilson was not content to rest here. His next work, *No Laughing Matter,* which he described as his best, is yet again a new departure, and by far his most ambitious. When I first read it, despite my immense admiration, I must admit that I felt a slight regret that he appeared to have abandoned the traditional novel of which he had been a partisan, and with which I associated myself. He had seemed to stand as living proof that there was still life in the old forms, and that they could be adapted to the complexity of the post-Woolf, post-Joyce era; was he now to desert us for the avant-garde, for the barren wastes of intellectual play which literary critics so enjoy, abandoning through a desire for novelty the territory he had so decisively conquered? In fact my initial reaction to *No Laughing Matter* bears some relation to his own initial reactions to Woolf, which he described in *Studies in the Literary Imagination*[5]—a feeling that this was too rarified and literary for my taste, that it belonged to the realm of art rather than life—and like him, I have lived to change my mind. It is, as he says, his finest work, but it is of such richness that it requires many readings. (Having said that, I must record that when my husband went off with our new copy to work one Saturday morning when I was in the middle of my first reading, I took a taxi into town and bought another, poor though we were in those days, so anxious was I to continue it—so, even the first impact must have been considerable.)

On one level, *No Laughing Matter* is the story of a family and its fortunes, and a social history of Britain spanning more than fifty years of twentieth-century life: a thoroughly conventional project, and one that Thackeray, Trollope, Bennett, and Galsworthy would all have applauded. (Indeed, in one of the novel's multiple ironies, one of the characters ends up watching *The Forsyte Saga* on television.) The six children of William and Clara Matthews (failed writer and faithless wife) occupy the center of the stage, with supporting cast of grandmother, aunt, cook, husbands, wives, lovers, colleagues, grandchildren—but already we are confronted by the complexity of the novel's subject, and the corresponding complexity of Wilson's narration. For, from the first page, we are in a shifting world of theatrical effects, distorting mirrors, kaleidoscopic refractions, burlesques, imitations, shadows of shadows. The Matthews family is much given to posturing and self-dramatization, and we see them, their actions and their views of one another through innumerable filters. Wilson's work had always emphasized the human need to play roles, to adopt manners and strike attitudes, but here that need becomes the texture of the book itself. The six children, in the early sections, find release and reconcile themselves to their painful and often squalid family life in a variety of ways; they daydream in solitude, composing their own future; they rearrange reality; they pursue solitary fantasies; and they also invent a corporate fantasy, The Game, in which each child takes on the role of one of the oppressive adults on whom they are dependent, and whose characters and destinies forge their own. The Game, which runs throughout the novel, centers on the favored handsome son Rupert's impersonation of his weak and despised father, Billy Pop, the Billy Goat, the White Slub; and the impersonation by Marcus, the unwanted dark outcast changeling baby, of his mother, the Countess, the Black Bitch, the Tigress. (Rupert becomes a successful actor, whose professional progress is also a charting of the history of British theater; Marcus becomes a homosexual with a flair for exotic decor and design, famous, as a minor character unkindly puts it, for his "green balls.") The Game is counterpointed by a succession of scenes from plays in the manner of dramatists as varied as Coward, Chekhov, Shaw and, finally, Samuel Beckett, each shedding a different light on the characters and on the cultural milieu which they inhabit. And within this framework are dozens more variations, most notably, perhaps, those of Margaret, who becomes a successful novelist (though she fears she is labelled as a "writer's writer," overconcerned with technique); her career is launched, as was Wilson's own with short stories in which she takes revenge on her family for the embarrassments of her youth. One of them, produced at length, recounts in fictional terms the "real" wedding of Margaret's twin sister, Sukey, and is prefaced by a quotation from a review which reads "The ironies of Miss Matthews' stories expose our most cherished evasions." Irony indeed, and Margaret discovers that although writing can cure, it can also kill. Even Sukey, the dull, sensible, domestic member of the family, turns to fiction to solve life's problems, and writes little tales of domestic life for the BBC, carefully eliminating the uncomfortable and complex, with titles such as "How to Climb Snowdon without a Tin Opener," "When Santa Left Too Many Cricket Bats," and "Why Can't We Take the Rhino Home." Quentin, the eldest, a disillusioned socialist, converts his personal and political despair into highly popular television cynicism and punditry. Gladys, an efficient business woman involved in a ruinous affair with an inefficient business man, comforts herself by seeing herself as Podge, the fat and lovable Cockney. (Gladys, in fact, is a redeemed version of Gwen Rutherford, even to the point of imitating for her siblings a bulldog with such startling verisimilitude that they are all, despite their manifold anxieties, reduced to the laughter of childhood.)

Yet, despite the constant shifting of style and focus, the fictions within fictions, the multiplicity of echoes (in the first pages alone we are referred to cinema newsreels, films of the Wild West, Wordsworth, Bret Harte, Whitman, music hall, and Marie Lloyd), there is nothing remotely confusing or artificial in the presentation of character and action. There is none of the arbitrary uncertainty and maddening fluid impermanence that haunts so many twentieth-century expositions of the multiplicity of personality. The major events of European history—the Great War, the rise of Fascism in Germany and London's East End, the Spanish Civil War, the growth of totalitarian tyranny in the Soviet Union, the Second World War, Aden, Suez—are woven into the family history with consummate artistry, yet with none of their weight diminished. The six protagonists and their supporting cast are not abstractions; they exist on every level of the self. They have faces, clothes, voices; they eat, they quarrel, they misunderstand themselves and one another, they grow old. In this novel, more than in any other I know, we see people—real, recognizable people, in the most old-fashioned sense—in the act of becoming what they must ineluctably be, despite the shadow selves that they might have been, the impersonations that they carry with them. We seem to see into the heart of the family nexus, into the mystery of developing personality. It is a truly remarkable achievement, and seems to me to be, much more than *The Middle Age of Mrs Eliot*, a true fusion of the many traditions of British fiction. An inexhaustible book, and on so generous a scale that it can be reread over a lifetime.

Of Wilson's last published novel, *As If by Magic* (1973),[6] I shall say little, largely because I know that I have not come to terms with it. Its theme is enormous—no less than the duties of affluence towards the Third World, and the possibility of individual engagement and responsibility within a capitalist society—and its form is extraordinary. Dickensian farce rubs shoulders with scenes from de Sade, dissertations on D. H. Lawrence and Tolkien mingle with Henry James and Shaw. On the last page the heroine, sick of her inescapable habit of seeing life through the spectacles of old books, cries "Damn English Literature! Damn the past and the future! I have enough to do making something of the present. But neither the past nor the future were escapable"—a cry of despair, of challenge, of acceptance of challenge. If anyone can make sense of the present, it is Angus Wilson. John Updike remarked recently that writing fiction in the seventies, this global decade, becomes increasingly difficut, a view which many novelists would endorse, and *As If by Magic* is an attempt at a global novel, ranging from London to Morocco, from Japan to Ceylon and Goa; its hero on his travels seems to hear "a high, distant overtone of perpetual woe. Could it be the natural noise of the world, as he began to fancy?" And if so, what fiction can cope with such knowledge?

But let me end on a more positive and more personal note. My respect for Angus Wilson's work will by now be evident; I hope I have also managed to indicate what a joy it is to read. His wit has been acclaimed by all his critics, but I would like to pay tribute to his immense store of sheer information, if that is not too dull a word for it. His books are packed with out-of-the-way facts about gardening, archaeology, agronomy, educational theory, political history, esoteric religions, interior decor, Stonehenge, women's fashions, and cookery. Mary McCarthy has said that the novelist has "a deep empiric love of fact," and that facts are part of the proper texture of novels. I agree. My son, having just finished *Anglo-Saxon Attitudes* for the first time (and watching him read it was almost as enjoyable as my own first discovery) said with a sigh of admiration as he finished it, "But how does he *know* so much?" "I suppose he finds it out," I replied vaguely—but how much he has found out, and to what use he has put it! What I have learned from him has become part of my own store of knowledge. I rarely see a rhododendron or a calceolaria without recalling his strictures upon these flowers in *The Middle Age of Mrs Eliot;* I never rinse the rice without recalling that Harold's dead wife, Beth, used to rinse it three times. (In fact before I read *Late Call* I don't think I realized one had to rinse the stuff at all.) I am sorry to say that I used not to know that it was more chic to read novels than biographies, nor had I even thought to enquire who designed the Raven's Cage in London Zoo. (Decimus Burton, of course.) In *As If by Magic* one character asks another how she knows that a certain kind of duck is called a mandarin, and she replies, "Oh, I've always known. Idle rentier women are magpies. They collect any random fact in sight. . . . I've got nothing but idle vision, but at least I must name what I see." Angus Wilson is no *idle rentier* (though he has created some memorable ones), but he too likes to name what he sees and his readers are all in debt to his insatiable curiosity, to his conviction that the literary imagination nourishes itself in the real world of events, as well as in the world of fiction.

NOTES

1. *As If by Magic* (London: Secker & Warburg, 1973), 202.
2. *Such Darling Dodos and Other Stories* (1950: rpt London: Secker & Warburg, 1959), 12-13.
3. (London: Secker & Warburg, 1963), 87-90.
4. *Late Call* (London: Secker & Warburg, 1964), 103.
5. See "The Always-Changing Impact of Virginia Woolf," *Studies in the Literary Imagination,* 11: 2 (Fall 1978), 1-9. Reprinted in this volume.
6. Wilson's new novel, *Setting the World on Fire*, was published in the spring of 1980. [Ed.]

Olivia Manning's *Fortunes of War:* Breakdown in the Balkans, Love and Death in the Levant

ROBERT K. MORRIS

> Two more years were to pass before the
> war ended. Then, at last peace, precarious
> peace, came down upon the world and the
> survivors could go home. Like the stray
> figures left on the stage at the end of a
> great tragedy, they now had to tidy up the
> ruins of war and in their hearts bury the
> noble dead.
> —*THE SUM OF THINGS*

The short, valedictory "coda" to Olivia Manning's six-volume novel sequence, *Fortunes of War,* writes finis to one of the most remarkable books published in the past twenty-five years, while leaving inconclusive the fates of its equally remarkable hero and heroine, Guy and Harriet Pringle, whose four-year odyssey in the Balkans and the Levant the series has charted.

This is, of course, as it should be. From the first pages of the first volume—when, "in the confusion of a newly created war," a young, wondering Guy and Harriet roll toward Bucharest, their night train skirting a dark pine forest, "the light from the carriages [rippling] over the bordering trees"—to the last pages of the last—when, in 1943, "his youth behind," twenty-one-year-old Lt. Simon Boulderstone stands at the rail of a destroyer, watching "the glimmer of the blacked-out shore, the last of Egypt"— *Fortunes of War* has been unwavering in its depiction of the human condition as open-ended. In Miss Manning's fiction, life is a continuing quest and question: a kaleidoscope of paradoxes and ironies that shape and shift character and in turn are shaped and shifted by them. Under normal circumstances such patterns take on unexpected permutations. How much more unexpected personal change is when carried out against the ever-changing and most impersonal of backdrops—war.

For the world at war is Miss Manning's world. And, as true to life as to her novelistic vision, the "stray figures" who happen into it—to grapple, ordinary as they are, with the extraordinary; to love, marry, mature, succeed or fail, live or die—are merely left to anonymous time and history after the great tragic backdrop has been removed. Yet, like the controlling image of the Levant trilogy—the pyramids—all of *Fortunes of War* is a monument to days that once shook the world and now slip, year by year, further from our memory. What makes Miss Manning's record so viable—nay, phenomenal—is the labor and art which have gone into perfecting the smallest details of its construction. Though each of the novels is self-contained, taken together their effect is solid, overwhelming, enduring. This, in part, is due to the heft of Miss Manning's well-wrought words—over half a million of them. But there is more. Scene by scene, character by character, theme upon theme, the six parts of *Fortunes of War* are pieced together to become a pyramid of its own—the foundation laid in *The Great Fortune* and rising to the apex in *The Sum of Things*.

Twenty years of actual time and four of fictional time separate these first and last volumes, and throughout it all Miss Manning sticks by the original paradox that furnishes the groundwork for the series: the idea that Guy and Harriet can build their lives (together and independently) in a world that is progressively breaking down.[1] The breakdown begins in Bucharest shortly after the invasion of Poland. Part comic-opera Ruritania in its feudality, its gilt and gaudiness; part political nightmare in its ferment of royalist, liberal, and fascist factions; neutered by its fence-sitting neutrality, Bucharest acts as a touchstone for the tremors of history that initially leave the Pringles shaken if uninvolved, but eventually put them at "the center of things,"[2] and then—with the fall of France and England's entry into the war—at the epicenter.

Guy and Harriet share in common their youth, energy, optimism, and English passports, but there the surface likenesses end. The world in

1939–1940 was a disastrous complexity, the anarchic shenanigans in Rumania—trapped between the Nazi eagle and Russian bear—but one face of the real chaos soon to ensue. To fathom anything but the moment-by-moment events themselves was, as Miss Manning suggests, difficult, if not impossible. Yet if one could not actually *understand* the confusion, one could *react* to it. Which, precisely, in opposing but complementary ways, is what Guy and Harriet do. Guy, a lecturer in English literature at the University of Bucharest, is free, enthusiastic, generous, frank, idealistic. Harriet, his bride, is constrained, a trifle reactionary, sensitive, logical, circumspect, and realistic. Such pointed differences are modified and amplified over the course of the sequence; here, in the earliest volumes, Miss Manning uses them to show Guy's and Harriet's alternative responses to uncertainty and to show how each goes about seeking permanence as ballast in a sea of change.

The major quest in the Balkan trilogy is Harriet's. Uncertainty begins as an emotional response to the physical condition before it is taken as the condition itself. Arriving in Bucharest from relatively fixed circumstances of life in England, she finds herself ill suited to enter either into Guy's professional or social life. Though the wife of a man accepted by the Rumanians because he is an Englishman and therefore an "ally," and valued by the "organization" and his students, Harriet remains for much of the first trilogy an outsider in the country and in Guy's circles. At times, in fact, she is thoughtlessly, though never maliciously, excluded by him. Guy's sweetness and goodness seem to extend to everyone but Harriet, whom he dearly loves but shamefully takes for granted—a blind spot that is to affect both their visions.

Harriet, a staunch realist but scarcely a tower of strength, moves between depression and confusion in searching for some niche in the disintegrating society of Bucharest during the "phony war." She represses any intimacy with Guy's friends (male or female) or with his favored students. Her only refuge is a growing friendship with one of Guy's more sober, pessimistic colleagues, Clarence Lawson, and with Bella Niculescu, an Englishwoman married to a Rumanian. Yet withdrawal and retreat seem to be her problems. Harriet at first responds to life, rather than living it, mainly because she is so riddled with uncertainty that even here she is uncertain which game to play. She is drawn toward Guy's hyperactive life of action that lacks serious accomplishment, of intellectual stimulation without serious thought. Wanting to be her own woman, however, she is also led into feeling that living for the unexpected, crowding life with a great deal of busy, fussy things cannot enrich or fulfill for very long. Like Rumania, she is sitting between two stools.

Both of which are about to collapse. Even as Guy directs his amateur production of *Troilus and Cressida,* Dunkirk is being evacuated, the Scandinavian countries are being invaded, France is about to capitulate. Harriet—uncast in the play—is less moved by the plight of the world or the imminent "fall of Troy [i.e., Bucharest]"[3] than by Guy's madcap scheme to carry on his escapist pursuit while the world crashes about them. Or is it, really, that she wishes she could do something with life, rather than continually thinking about it?

> Harriet stared up at Guy, her heart melting painfully in her breast, and asked herself what it was for—this expense of energy and creative spirit. To produce an amateur play that would fill the theatre for one afternoon and one evening and be such an ephemeral thing. If she had her way, she would seize on Guy and canalise his zeal to make a mark on eternity. But he was a man born to expend himself like a whirlwind. . . .[4]

Miss Manning's metaphors are hardly fortuitous. Whatever shortcomings Guy has—and most of them are in his relationship with Harriet—he is filled with vitality and energy; a life-affirmer who won't even acknowledge that the disintegration and decadence about him could possibly alter his priorities. Harriet, on the other hand, interprets the worsening world situation as narrowing her and Guy's alternatives. Their course lies between desperation and desperation.

It is easy to understand why anyone could think that way. As *The Spoilt City* opens, it is 1940. Rumania has been steadily ceding territory on the demands of Russia; she is shortly to lose Bessarabia and Transylvania. Pro-Nazi sentiment restores the Iron Guard to power and elevates the dead, once-reviled Codreanu to something of a deity. The drill and tramp of the Guardists' boots drown out the irresponsible laughter of the cafés; the music of the nightclubs yields to "Capitanul," the theme song of the Guards, who come to strike, at first, irritation, then incredulity, and at last, for some, terror. Anti-Semitism and Jew-baiting drive families like the wealthy Druckers into hiding or to flight; once-friendly Rumanians estrange themselves from the Pringles; their colleagues bolt for Greece; even the pathetico-comical Prince Yakimov, Harriet's personal plague and "the social pander of all ages," flees Bucharest when his opportunism fails to gain him security.

Only Guy and Harriet resist to the last this expediency as a way of existence—clinging more fiercely to each other despite the rift in their ideals and the breaking down of expectations, yet never once really seeing eye to eye. As much as she "never lets reality out of sight," Guy "keeps it at bay"; as much as she grows more interested in people for themselves, she sees that his interest in great problems is a "lack of fundamental interest in the individual"; and as much as he believes in "Western culture and democratic ideals," she can understand that idealism is a living thing—not an historic or isolated phenomenon—equally concerned with the reality of the moment as abstracted into creeds or philosophies. Realizing that life is more and more a contradiction of ideals, no matter how realistic they seem, Harriet begins to abandon her old, shopworn beliefs. As the world order breaks down, the personal ordering of her life is fashioned anew. Living under impermanence hews out new attitudes and sensibilities, makes her aware of choices and responsibilities that under routine living are generally absorbed by habit: a condition of life, by the way, that neither Guy nor Harriet is to experience over the remainder of the sequence.

For one moment, however, there is an interlude that masquerades as permanence. Together (at the opening of *Friends and Heroes*) in the "indolent sunshine" of Athens, "where the fate of Rumania was a minor fracas, too far away to mean anything," Guy and Harriet feel a sense of security and integration. Both are fleeting. *Friends and Heroes* does for Greece what *The Great Fortune* and *The Spoilt City* do for Bucharest: follows her fortune to misfortune. Greece's early victories over Italy momentarily delude her into believing she can repel the forces of Hitler and Mussolini. But euphoria degenerates into futility when the Greeks fail to reincarnate another Thermopylae in the face of an Italian offensive, and the novel ends with northern Greece falling to the Nazis as Guy and Harriet embark from Athens, just one jump ahead of their armies.

But a good deal before this, Harriet has come to acknowledge that breakup and breakdown are the norms, that permanence no longer exists in the world as she knows it. One consequence of this is her aborting any attempt at a love affair with the dashing, Byronic Charles Warden. Adultery would of course only raise uncertainty to a higher exponent. But, more telling, can a realist like Harriet commit herself to "a romantic figure, marked down for death?" Harriet is a survivor, "required to live"; Warden of the heroic stamp, doomed.

And so she casts her lot with friend, instead of hero; or, one might say, her almost-liaison with Warden helps bring Guy down from the pedestal she has set him on and dispel the nimbus of saint, the aura of hero with which she has surrounded him. Harriet sees Guy in the clear, cold light; he is human and fallible, a well-meaning but selfish idealist—selfish because it is really himself that he has pleased all along in his grand, energy-consuming, ephemeral projects. Yet Harriet does not make her tacit pact with Guy out of wounded pride or feelings of neglect and self-pity, any more than she "jilts" Warden because she sees him as another order of being who would complicate her already troubled and confused values. It is rather that Harriet must have some fixed point of reference in a world gone mad, some hold on certainty in a time when everything is uncertain. And that is Guy, who, "whatever his faults, [possesses] the virtue of permanence."

In some ways this is second best. But for Miss Manning's heroine in 1941, there was no first best. What Harriet is left with at the end of the Balkan trilogy is a great deal of growth in a very short period of time. It will take Guy another three volumes to reach even the halfway point where Harriet is at the conclusion of *Friends and Heroes*. The repeated breakdown of things for the Pringles—the breakdown of the Balkans, of old values, of dependency on others, of illusion (particularly in Harriet's case)—is actually the dismantling of all mechanisms that logically control life. Once one grasps this illogic of entropy, it is almost possible to understand life—or what, under such circumstances, passes for it.

There is much less ambiguity in Miss Manning's mind about death, which enters the Pringles' circle in *Friends and Heroes* and is to remain her preoccupation for all of the Levant trilogy. It is Prince Yakimov who dies. Bundled in his immortal overcoat ("given to [his] Dad by the Czar"), dragging on his eternal cigarette, Yaki is shot by a security guard during a blackout in Athens. Yaki's death is both pathetic and comic, and, in being senseless, prototypical of all the other senseless or stupid or cruel or violent or tragic deaths Miss Manning later records. For, senseless as it is, it makes perfect sense, given Miss Manning's inescapable premise that most of the world has gone mad. How could it be otherwise? In a world where "killing, destruction, and turbulent hatred" pass "for normal life"; in a world where war produces "anxiety instead of expectation, exhaustion instead of profit"; in a world that through progressive life-denying measures grows increasingly thanatopic; in a world in short, where one can hardly think of life as real, but of death as all too real, perhaps the great mystery provides all the clarity one can expect: about itself *and* life.

Seeing death "steadily" and seeing it "whole" (*pace* Matthew Arnold!) is what, I think, the Levant trilogy is mainly about. Miss Manning does for "it" what she does in the Balkan trilogy for "breakdown": views it roundly, and without possibly exhausting its meaning, shows its effect on the ones who survived some of the gloomiest and bloodiest days of the Second World War.

In a large way, Miss Manning's entire sequence syllogizes before it elegizes. Breakdown/impermanence/uncertainty lead to the central disruption of life at any time of history: war; war, in turn, gallops on wildly with its grimmer brother, death; and death, in its turn. . . . In some of Miss Manning's finest writing we see its permutations and consequences born from the almost mini-apocalypse being visited on "the cradle of civilization." The Levant trilogy is one of the most vivid pictures of what was happening to a handful of lives, stitched by threads running from Alexandria to Cairo, Memphis, Luxor, Damascus, Jerusalem, into the vast tapestry of the desert, as the "rough beast, its hour come round at last, / Slouches towards Bethlehem to be born."

Historically, of course, it hadn't and it wasn't, though in 1941, as the Levant trilogy opens, it isn't certain that the Nazis won't overrun the mid-East, no slouches Rommel or they. Tobruk has fallen. Alexandria seems fated to fall. Onto the Cairo scene comes Second Lieutenant Simon Boulder-stone—young, green, drafted—one of the rocks of central consciousness on which Miss Manning is to build the last two faces and apex of her pyramid. Simon is not merely a new character in the sequence; his is a fresh point of view that complements Harriet's. Harriet is a year older than Simon, wiser than he, but not wise, though she counts herself as a different generation, having lost her freshness and innocence in the Balkans. Yet both she and Simon are strangers in an even stranger land, lonely, insecure in their attachments, vague of purpose, fearful and cutoff. Harriet has been bounced from Rumania to Greece to Egypt, where War and Death, along with their other apocalyptic brethren, Hunger and Plague, thrive, but where Guy doesn't, thanks to the bad agency of his old supervisor, Gracey. Simon has been whisked from basic training on Rugby fields and thrust into a war where "bullets can kill a man." Miss Manning's purpose is to study that war—at the front and on the home front (if inhospitable Cairo can be called such by its English population)—and she chooses to come at her themes from two different directions and on two different levels.

Not, however, at first. She rather artfully brings Simon and Harriet together at the opening of *The Danger Tree* before their independent narra-torial consciousnesses go their separate ways. It is, as a matter of fact, over death—a death—that they meet. Simon, looking up Edwina Little, who is supposedly the girl friend of his brother, Hugo, in the lines, is taken by some of her friends and Harriet's to pyramid ruins outside of Cairo, and thence round to the home of Lord Hooper, a British official. The reader is galvanized from the boring and stuffy banalities by the shriek of brakes, slamming doors, the entrance of Lady Angela Hooper and two safragis carrying "the inert body of a boy," Angela's son, "killed by a hand grenade he picked up."

> One eye was missing. There was a hole in the left cheek that extended into the torn wound which had been his mouth. Blood had poured down his chin and was caked on the collar of his open-necked shirt. The other eye, which was open, was lackluster and blind like the eye of a dead rabbit.[5]

Angela won't believe he's dead. Lord Hooper tries to feed him gruel through a hole in his cheek, then carries him, followed by Angela, still in shock, to his room to "sleep."

The scene is crucial—my only reason for having dwelt on it so long—for its tendrilling out to touch on many other related things in the book. The death of Angela's son is significant in her leaving her husband and taking up with Bill Castlebar, doomed also to a freakish death of sorts. Horrible and tragic one moment, the death of the young boy loses its immediacy, Harriet reflects, when juxtaposed beside the deaths of all young "dying in the desert before they had had a chance to live." And yet, she concludes, "the boy's death was a death apart." The paradox is amplified when Harriet and Simon, trying to forget the incident, climb the pyramids outside of Mena. Harriet tells him how she happened to be with Hugo on his twenty-first birthday, recalling silently how she intuitively knew he was fated to die. He of course is. Simon's quest in *The Danger Tree* is the quest for his brother, and Hugo's death is the end of the quest: a death that is another "death apart." The singularity of both deaths that enclose *The Danger Tree* in tragic parentheses somehow suggests their universality. Death is both singular *and* universal: like the pyramids themselves—keeping their ghostly wardership over the dead, the dying, and those who will die—"a greater darkness in an area of darkness."

It is an area that Simon will get to know too well before the sequence concludes some five hundred pages later. His is perhaps the major progress over the landscape of death and through the City of the Dead: a tortured, tortuous trek through the darkness that offers scant illumination. Over that territory Simon wanders, in fact as well as in spirit: a pilgrim without a guide. Inured today as youth is to violence—the media's factual or fictional exploitation of crime, war, revolution, terrorism, etc., had made them so—young men like Simon grew up in the thirties knowing little of it. Old age, illness, accident. This was normal death; normally the normal conclusion to a normal life: the end of being, not the wellspring of it! Until the war. Young men who had never looked on death nor (many of them) even seen a dead person were suddenly drafted to be its grim agent and to kill. Many wouldn't or couldn't.

Many didn't. Many—most—who didn't want to, did or had to. Simon is one
of the latter, a sort of *soldat moyen sensuel* whose rawness, youth, innocence, and
sensitivity are leveled or twisted or warped through his encounters with
death.

The changes are long and complex. Miss Manning makes a good start,
however, in Simon's first battle and the events leading up to it.[6] On patrol in
the desert, he is initially "awed" by the sight of dead Germans, then
"surprised" that one of them looks like his batman, Arnold. Under fire and
firing, Simon is "amazed" that his attempt to kill has been successful. As Miss
Manning continues:

> The satisfaction intoxicated him. In his excitement, he lost all sense of
> danger. . . . In an ecstasy of joy, he rushed into a fusillade of machine-
> gun bullets, thinking he had discovered the thing he wanted all his life.
>
> (156)

His "euphoria" is short-lived. Minutes later Arnold is dead, Simon in "fury" is
engaged in hand-to-hand combat with a young, blond German soldier not
unlike the dead one he was awed by. But, as he blows off the German's face he
feels neither awe nor surprose nor amazement—only "hatred."

To weather these rapid-fire alterations of emotion, anyone's psyche must
retreat or set up defenses. Simon's does both. Lonely and friendless on his
arrival in Egypt, he now becomes aloof, almost a loner, "his instinct . . . to
avoid any relationship that could again inflict on him the desolation of loss."
Baggage not crucial to survival—that is, thoughts of home, family, wom-
en—is jettisoned. And once unencumbered, Simon can settle into normaliz-
ing what is unnatural.

> In spite of the heat of the day, the cold of night, the flies, the mosquitoes,
> the sand-flies, the stench of death that came on the wind, the sand blow-
> ing into the body's interstices and gritting in everything one ate, the
> human animal not only survived but flourished. Simon felt well and
> vigorous and he thought of women, if he thought of them at all, with a
> benign indifference. He belonged now to a world of men: a contained,
> self-sufficient world where life was organized from dawn till sunset. It
> had so complete a hold on him, he could see only one flaw in it: his friends
> died young.
>
> (197)

This is one of the best understated bits of irony in the entire *Fortunes of War*,

summarizing and anticipating Miss Manning's near classic respect for hamartia. The tragic flaw can be found in something as innocuous as the poisoned
stem of the mango—the fruit of the "danger tree"—as well as in things more
capacious—things like time, place, and character. One flaw is all that is needed to mar perfection—or, more accurately, the appearance of perfection.[7]
And the sooner one realizes these flaws exist—Miss Manning does not believe
that "human kind cannot bear very much reality," as I hope to make clearer in
my discussion of Guy, below—the better one's chances for squaring up to life
and death.

Simon's blend of cynicism and tenderness in the passage quoted is perhaps
inadequate preparation for his discovery that Hugo bled to death after having
both legs shot off; but now death becomes a reality for him and the impulse to
his fatalism—which, in war, may well be the same thing. "He felt death as
though he and Hugo had been one flesh and he was possessed by the certainty
that if he returned here, he, too, would be killed" (204). The feeling brings on
a true catharsis, purges him of grief and anguish, and goes on, we see in the
second volume, to promote a saving, if not completely salutary, stoicism.
Simon, on leave to Cairo at the opening of *The Battle Lost and Won,* once again
views the pyramids, this time without wonder, "for now there was no wonder
left in the world." Some poison has indeed leached into Simon's sweetness,
but not mortally. If he has lost wonder, he hasn't lost hope: as Miss Manning
makes clear by replacing "the danger tree" with a solitary palm:

> . . . hemmed in by buildings like a bird in too small a cage, he ached
> with pity for it though the tree itself conveyed no sense of deprivation. A
> human being in similar case would have been bemoaning his misfortune
> but the tree, swaying in the hot wind, spread itself as though rejoicing in
> such air and light as came to it.
>
> (210)

Simon is of course the tree; lonely, detached, stoic. As for "rejoicing," there is
little cause for it in *The Battle Lost and Won.* It gains wider scope in *The Sum of
Things,* ostensibly a book of peace, where Harriet and Simon both reach out
for "air and light" from their congruent, claustrophobic worlds. But if, here,
Simon loses one battle with himself, he wins another: he survives.

The odds are heavily against it, though Miss Manning's title does suggest
from the first the neat correlation between Simon's emotional struggle within
and the desert war without. The two come together in Miss Manning's finest
and most brilliant picture of the front: Montgomery's counterattack against

Rommel and the first battle of El Alamein. (269ff.) Simon, now a liaison officer, is ordered to take a signal to the vanguard of Monty's forces—wherever that might be! Under a ghostly full moon, by jeep with his driver, Crosbie, then on foot alone, Simon picks his way over mine fields, through mortar barrages, raging fires, and driving smoke, and accomplishes his mission. A rain of death lashes him everywhere he goes. He realizes that if Hugo had not died when he did, "he would, as likely as not, have died in the present battle." Death seems inevitable; the *only* thing that seems inevitable. Simon is himself almost killed. But he is ordered by the corps commander to dig in; he does, passes out fatigued as the battle reaches its height. From the Armageddon of the night before, he wakes to the Day of Judgment:

> He woke at daybreak to find himself alone in the trench. . . . He had the field to himself—but not quite to himself. Burnt out tanks stood about him like disabled crows and the smell of burning was heavy in the air. There were dead men and men not yet dead, and the Brens were returning to pick them up.
>
> As the sun topped the horizon, the first, subtle light of day swept like a wave over the desert and about him, and passed on, lighting up desert and more desert, miles of desert that had once been no-man's-land. . . . it was in no-man's-land that Hugo had died. He had bled to death like the dead left behind by the battle and perhaps he had lain here, on this barren ground that was now the field of victory.
>
> Walking back among tanks as useless as the sand they stood on, stepping over the bodies of lost young men, Simon asked, "Is this what Hugo died for? And am I to die for this?" There was no one to answer him and as he realized how hungry he was, he forgot his own questions and started to run.
>
> (280–281)

Again, I must apologize for so long a quotation, but Miss Manning's talent for wedding scene, emotion, idea, and character can't be gained through paraphrase. Simon's overwhelming question formulated in the overwhelming desert is *the* overwhelming question of young men at war, who, whether fighting on the side of right or wrong (?), winning battles or losing them, still seem to die. The great principles behind wars are seldom evident on the battlefield; waste and carnage, on the other hand, are. To a soldier, death is both impetus and result, omnipresent, the alpha and omega.

Simon's question—"Am I to die for this?"—leaves ambiguous the values one dies for, while implying that one *will* die; it merely seems to be the corollaries—"When? Where? How?"—that need ironing out. Simon and Crosbie come through the attack on El Alamein without a scratch; and then weeks later, diverting their jeep from the road to seek some attractive shade under a tall palm—like "the single palm he had seen and pitied in Cairo. This similar palm, swaying in the wind . . . like something known and loved"—they are blown up by a booby trap. Crosbie is killed; Simon, legs paralyzed, rescued by an ambulance before he meets Hugo's fate of bleeding to death. Fate! Fortunes of war! Ultimately they are one and the same. The battle, lost *or* won, always rages, of course—fate on one side, character on the other—but never as intensely as during the war when the one, if not actually annihilating the other, must in some way change it. Even those who don't live (like Simon) on intimate terms with death, find it a familiar that shapes them.

Simon's attitude toward death, his relationship with it, is the one extreme; Guy's is the other—at least for the first half of the Levant trilogy, when we are back with the old Guy we knew too well in the Balkans: simple; good; charismatic; the self-sacrificing friend (and shoddy husband); the hardworking teacher, more dedicated to his students than to his wife; the life of the party (to all but Harriet); the patriot, ridden with guilt feelings for not being able to fight in the Spanish Civil War or the present one because of his myopia (literal and figurative). For the first half, I say, myopic, idealistic, solipsistic Guy sweeps death under the carpet. "You know how I hate things like that," he replies to Harriet's entreaties to have him visit the Khalifa tombs with her. "Useless bric-a-brac, death objects, *memento mori!* What point in making oneself miserable?" (248) Death, for Simon, is the sole reality; for Guy it is the purest example of his "refusal to recognize reality": a disarming idiosyncrasy until it becomes, as Harriet sees, a dangerous flaw:

> To someone moving so rapidly through life, reality and unreality merged and were one and the same thing. There were times when she felt he drained her life as well as his own, but he had physical strength. He could renew himself and she could not.
>
> (374)

Like all Miss Manning's characters, Harriet is susceptible to self-irony. Correcting Guy's flaw, renewing (i.e., re-creating rather than merely refreshing) him is what *The Sum of Things* —the final volume of *Fortunes of War* —is about. But it is also about Harriet's renewal and Simon's; and both in Miss Manning's masterfully engineered summation, are connected with Guy's. Harriet, escaping the "killing element" of Guy, oblivious of reports of her death, moves reluctantly over the Levant from Damascus to Jerusalem, yet gains a new sense of her worth and a new independence of mind and spirit. Simon, brought back from the dead, but a bitter, hopeless, despairing paraplegic, is saved from suicide and regenerated through Guy's ministrations. And Guy himself—the third pilgrim journeying through this dark night of the soul—unable to turn his face on dying and death, moves by little revelations to recognize his hamartia.

The catalyst for his change is the news that Harriet has gone down with the torpedoed passenger ship bound for England. No one doubts that Guy has loved Harriet all along, but by the same token he has been insensitive to her needs, seeing "marriage as a frame to hold an indiscriminate medley of relationships." Rumors of her death shatter the frame. In his own way he is as uprooted and lost as Harriet, each at different ends of the Levant; his need to be needed takes him to Simon, when Edwina Little begs him to become her surrogate. It is on his first visit to Simon that Guy breaks down while talking about Harriet, and this expression of his feelings—wrenched from him for the first time over six volumes—is synchronized with the return of feeling to Simon's legs: "a trickle of life." The trickle leads into Guy's own sensibilities. Hating "death and everything to do with death," Guy nevertheless is forced to concede its symbiosis with life:

> Guy felt betrayed by life. His good nature, his readiness to respond to others and his appreciation of them had gained him friends and made life easy for him. Now, suddenly and cruelly, he had become the victim of reality. He had not deserved it but there it was: his wife, who might have lived another fifty or sixty years, had gone down with the evacuation ship and he would not see her again.
>
> (414)

Guy's devotion to Simon is, I think, a new "marriage" of sorts, not without the ambiguities or shortcomings of the old. Guy's awareness of reality doesn't entirely purge him of his egocentrism. He is still, undoubtedly, selfish. Consumed by the compulsion to get Simon well, Guy lectures, directs, organizes him, trying to bring him into his (Guy's) orbit. Charity, remorse, pity, even self-pity are the impulses to Guy's humanitarianism, but this selfishness keeps the machine running. It is a paradox that readers of Miss Manning must learn to live with. And, anyway, worse ends have come of better means. The paradox becomes somewhat explicable when we finally realize that Guy's need to *save* someone is inseparable from his need to *have* someone. With Miss Manning's shift in narratorial point of view (some of the central chapters in

The Sum of Things filter through Guy's consciousness) we see that everyone else's fear in *Fortunes of War* —loneliness—is also Guy's. Harriet, in short, has not been entirely right about him, as he has not about her. Guy can handle—or mishandle—only one permanent and abiding relationship at one time. But he must maintain *that* kind of connection. Harriet's "death" brings Guy to the nadir of his night journey; his rehabilitation of Simon brings him into the light. But Simon, likewise returned to health, changes ("He had been a sick, despondent boy; now he was a young man conscious of his strength and his individuality in the world"), grows away from Guy and leaves him. With Simon gone, with the further realization that the only thing he has left in life is teaching, and that the work is fraudulent ("he had been peddling the idea of empire to a country that wanted one thing; to be rid of the British for good and all"), Guy slips back into his dark night once more, a lost soul weighed down by his two losses. After this, what consolation?

The consolation is Harriet, who "returns from the dead" mere pages from the end of Miss Manning's sequence to redeem Guy from guilt and apathy, and to reconcile the changes each has undergone in their separation. Harriet does not quite step down from her pedestal to amaze everyone, for Guy has never placed her on one; in Miss Manning's interesting twist to her "winter's tale," Harriet steps up: no shadow of Guy, no reflection, no statue, but very much her own woman:

> She was free to think her own thoughts. She could develop her own mind. Could she, after all, have borne with some possessive, interfering, jealous fellow who would have wanted her to account for every breath she breathed?
> Not for long.
>
> (566)

In the real world—and Miss Manning in her writing is as close to that world as one generally comes—time does not work the same sort of amnesty as it often does in fiction. Nor do many of us have the opportunity of "dying" to be born again. What is so starkly real about *Fortunes of War* is that of the characters in it, only Guy and Harriet have a story that comes close to a "happy ending," and, given the novel's ambiguous optimism, not all that happy either. They are, in a limited way, renewed. They can feel again—or, in Guy's case, *really* feel for the first time. Yet Guy and Harriet, I repeat, are exceptions. *Fortunes of War* is very much a novel of the failure of feelings: a failure brought about by the betrayal or deadening of them. And the greatest failure is that of love.

It fails in Miss Manning for the same reasons it does so in the work of most modern writers: it fosters false illusion, creates dependencies, casts one into uncertainty and confusion, aborts and perverts personality, even destroys. Love, Miss Manning suggests, is a heavy investment that brings in few returns. There is a bit of joy, a little happiness, moments of excitement, perhaps an instant or two of supreme passion; but mostly there is grief, anxiety, pain, frustration, anger, and disappointment. War, once again, speeds up all processes, throws them into sharper relief: the abstract nouns of feeling and emotion subject to the same fortunes as Miss Manning's characters.

Start again with Simon. His hasty wartime marriage to Anne—a week before he ships out for Egypt—is based on obligation rather than love. He leaves behind a girl he hardly knows as wife or lover, finding immediate substitutes for affection in friends on board ship, and then having to leave them behind at Suez. Simon has no one. The only person who really means anything to him is his older brother, Hugo. An offstage character in the Levant trilogy, Hugo looms large in Simon's education. His death leads Simon to the realities of death; his "girl," Edwina Little, "the most gorgeous popsie in Cairo," frees Simon from the romantic illusions that come to crush the hopes of Edwina herself.

Hers is perhaps the saddest story in the trilogy. Edwina—the playboy bunny of the embassy and officer set in Cairo—is lovely, desirable, popular, promiscuous on the one hand, flighty, flirty, superficial, indecisive on the other (though with the "one hand" being what it is, her men don't generally bother about "the other"). Because Simon thinks she's "Hugo's girl" (Hugo, in reality, was, like most of Edwina's men, only a couple of nights' stand), and because he's very young and inexperienced with women, Simon can't see through the facade; then, with Hugo dead, and Simon dewy-eyed about, smitten by, yearning for Edwina, he doesn't want to. Miss Manning's irony seems both obvious and bitter. Hugo's "gorgeous popsie"—ideal woman-love object—is meretricious and phony, as much of an illusion as any empty abstraction ("duty," "honor," "freedom") spawned by war.

And yet what we at first take for one sort of mental and spiritual flaw at odds with Edwina's bodily perfection, is quite another: scars, in fact, that have felt many wounds. Why is she promiscuous? Why does she allow herself to be exploited by men? Why does she grub and connive and prostitute herself, demean and humble herself to snare a husband? It is not a defect in character merely. Behind Edwina is a philosophy of love and feeling born of pathos and nurtured by suffering and death. War dictates to her the way she should love. As she tells Harriet, no stranger herself to impermanence and uncertainty:

> "These poor boys! You meet them . . . you . . . " She paused, catching her breath.
> "You give them your heart?"
> "Yes. And then they go back and get killed." Edwina, putting her forefingers under her lashes to lift the wetness away, said, "Oh, dear!" and sniffing, gave Harriet a rueful smile that was a comment both on the futility of grief and her own incorrigible frivolity: "What's to be done about it? Cry one's self sick? What good would that do?"
>
> (213–214)

One pities her in this and then censures her later for her neglect of Simon in the paraplegic ward (though it *is* her neglect that brings Guy onto the scene). Simon is quick not to understand her rejection of him, and, when on the mend, equally aware why she had to reject him. Why should the life style of any energetic and beautiful woman turn into a death style? Why should she sacrifice herself to a cripple, just because he happens to be the brother of someone she went to bed with a few times? Simon is freed finally from the magnetism of her sensuality; and Edwina, too, is freed from flogging it, settling for a second-rater as a husband (after losing a lord and failing to "comfort" Guy in the months after Harriet's "death"), but becoming worn and blasted by the pace of the life she leads.

Edwina's questions are no less than those of Lady Angela Hooper, who escapes from one lovedeath only to experience, after a wild and erratic interlude of flight and lovemaking, another. Where Edwina's fixaton is on many men, Angela's is on one, Bill Castlebar, the poet; where Edwina's love story is sad, Angela's is tragic. The death of her son causes her to seek love and living elsewhere, and when she finds Castlebar—seedy, dissipated, alcoholic, but not untalented—she takes up with him as a mother, as well as a mistress. Angela is not blind to her defects or Castlebar's. So long as she can keep him wet and relatively healthy (a kind of fluid dildo!), he'll continue to make love to her and she'll continue to suppress the pain in her past life and the absurdity of her present one. Booze is Castlebar's anodyne and sex is Angela's: the boredom of overabsorption from/in either warded off by their many and continual transplants around the Levant. Liberated from her stuffy, conventional life by her son's death, rich, generous, vastly unreliable, Angela has, to the envy of Harriet, learned to live with uncertainty so long as she has the relative permanence of Castlebar who eventually graduates from stud-son substitute to friend and lover. Castlebar is almost an anomaly. Weak, cowardly, emasculated by his wife, Mona, who is loud, pushy, and insensitive, and has little to commend her but a passé soprano and "splendid breasts," he seems to have enough will and dedication to be a good poet; he certainly has enough staying power and intelligence and charm to remain Angela's obsession, and to turn her from mother-mistress to mistress-lover. Their idyllic interlude in Jerusalem—where they restore each other to mental and physical health, and rescue Harriet to boot—apparently foreshadows love conquering all.

It doesn't. It is withered once again by death, catching Angela up in its tragic, recurring cycle. The *déjà vu* is Harriet's, as she, Angela, and Castlebar (quietly nursing an undisclosed malady that has lingered on undiagnosed) head out to see the pyramids at Mena and Harriet feels "an odd apprehension. She and others had been shown this village on the day Angela's child had died." A few weeks later Castlebar dies, not actually a victim of war, but of typhoid, accelerated by alcoholism. In various shapes, death hangs heavy and dark and certain over Egypt, lightened only briefly by something as fragile and uncertain as love.

Those who can experience even these fleeting moments, implies Miss Manning, have something; those who can't, don't. Love, however risky and impermanent, quickens feelings that are so easily deadened in a world where the facts and artifacts of death are everywhere. Aidan Pratt—who has "lost the sense that anything's worth keeping . . . the sense that anything left had value"—is one of those who can't. His singular story is perhaps the darkest in all of *Fortunes of War;* his gloom, self-absorption, pessimism, defeat, the heaviest to bear. On three sides Pratt's life has been deformed; and all three of them can be chalked up to the times:

First there is his abortive acting career:

> My career had just started when war broke out. When it's over—if it ever is over—I'll be verging on middle-age. Just another not-so-young actor looking for work. In fact, a displaced person.
>
> (166)

Then there is his two weeks of hell in a lifeboat:

> It was early in the war and I had declared myself a conscientious objector . . . . I was directed on to a ship going to Canada. . . . There was a crowd of kids on board, being evacuated. . . .

The ship is torpedoed. Thirty-five people, including nineteen children, are crammed into Pratt's lifeboat. There are no oars. Food runs out in four days. After a week, people begin dying of thirst and exposure, until only five are left:

> We'd rigged up a shelter for the smallest children and when there were no children left, we took it in turns to sleep there. The last time I crawled in, I said to myself, "Thank God, I needn't wake up again!"

But he does. A reconnaissance plane spots them and a ship picks them up:

> "And they were all alive [Harriet asks]: Kirkbride, the old man and the lascars?"
>
> "Yes, I was the only one who died. And I should have stayed dead like the poor little brats we threw overboard. Some of them too light to sink. It was ghastly, seeing them floating after us. I should have died."
>
> (318–320)

Finally, there is his love for Guy

> Crossing the Midan to the restaurant door, Guy could see through the glass into the brightly-lit interior where Aidan was sitting on a sofa. He was, as promised, waiting for his guest, looking for him but looking in the wrong direction, his dark, somber eyes betraying a longing that brought Guy to a stop.
>
> Guy, reaching the pavement, paused in the darkness of the street, reluctant to enter, knowing that he was the longed for object.
>
> (514)

This is the most explicit reference in the trilogy to Aidan's homosexuality. Generally Miss Manning has got at it with shading and innuendo: just enough to suggest that it joins the other "abnormal" relationships, though Aidan's deviation is a bit more acute in that (1) it is forever inopportune in the contexts of Cairo's egregious heterosexuality and English morality,[8] and (2) it is frustrated by the love object itself. Guy has been repeatedly cool to Aidan throughout, but here, during their last meeting in the Cairo café, he is as square and gelid as an ice cube. Why Guy is so bitchy and beastly is, I think, part of Miss Manning's design to anticipate Aidan's tragedy. When Aidan, leaning from the train window, reaches out to touch Guy, and Guy withdraws—probably his most *consciously* unfeeling act in all of *Fortunes of War* —I would put that as the moment that Aidan decides to shoot himself. "A clean break, a tidy break," thinks Guy, walking home from the railroad station, relieved that Aidan needn't occupy himself any further in "the pursuit of hopeless illusions." The pot calls the kettle black, and irony and truth simmer together in both. Guy has, of course, no idea how desperate Aidan is nor how much he needs him. Certainly by the end of the interview, Aidan hasn't too many shreds of illusion to tuck away. Boxed in on three sides by a war that has ruined his career as an actor, brought about his living death, cut him off from love, he has found life only futile. The fourth side—suicide— completes the square.

"The war had trapped him," Guy explains (without really explaining) to his friend, Dobson, "and he probably took this way out." To which Dobson replies: "The war's trapped a good many of us, but death's a pretty desperate escape route." One admires Dobson's blunt existentialism, and I've no doubt Miss Manning partially approves of it as well—but there is no denying that *Fortunes of War* shows that loving and living are perhaps as desperate. The sequence does, after all, end with the dreary, almost farcical wedding of Edwina with Tony Brody (a Colonel Blimp *ab ovo!*); the death of Castlebar and (thanks to Mona) a travesty of a funeral; Angela's despair; Pratt's suicide.

And yet as with all open-ended novels that have taken on the monstrous problems of loving and living, the dénouement to *Fortunes of War* purges a good deal of the pessimism and produces a kind of final, unfinal optimism. The sadder, more somber lives fall away (figuratively) from Miss Manning's apex, and when the final block is set in place, Harriet and Guy and Simon are on top. "When we climbed the pyramid," Harriet says in her farewell to Simon, "the war was at its worst. Now it's turned around."

As have their lives. Simon has grown into manhood and maturity, in full control of his mind as of his body. No longer obligated to Anne (who has written to him a "Dear Simon" letter), no longer obsessed by Edwina, no longer chained to the ghost of Hugo, Simon is free, and "his sudden freedom produced an emptiness like an empty gift box that in time would be filled with gifts." Freedom still brings anxiety; that is the price we pay for it. But what will fill Simon's gift box, we assume, will be due to choice and character, more than fate or fortune: the same thing, in fact, that will fulfill Guy and Harriet's gift of themselves to each other.

True to her thesis throughout *Fortunes of War*, Miss Manning has taken them through many experiences and changes to find some sense of permanence in a marriage acceptable to both. What the Balkans and Egypt and the war have taught them about that, and about a dozen other things, is considerable: yet it can only be measured by the distance they have come and the height they have climbed. How much further they had to go—if they were to go further—we shall, alas, never know. Olivia Manning died of illness not

long after completing the final volume in the series: refusing to surrender in
her own lost battle before seeing to it that her greatest hero and heroine were
on the way to winning theirs.

NOTES

1. I have explored this theme in a somewhat lengthy analysis of the Balkan trilogy: see *"The
   Balkan Trilogy:* The Quest of Permanence" in my *Continuance and Change: The Contemporary
   British Novel Sequence* (Carbondale: Southern Illinois Univ. Press, 1972), 29–49.

2. "The Center of Things" is the title of Part Two of *The Great Fortune.*

3. "The Fall of Troy" is the title of Part Four of *The Great Fortune.*

4. *The Great Fortune,* 287.

5. *The Levant Trilogy* (New York: Penguin Books, 1982), 35.

6. This sequence can be found starting on p. 148 in *The Levant Trilogy* (New York: Penguin,
   1982).

7. A few citations in support of this theme are: *Ibid.,* 15, 43, 77, 81–82, 88, 114, 123, 374.

8. As recently as the late fifties, anyone convicted of homosexuality in Great Britain was
   subject to a stiff prison sentence. Needless to say, few came openly out of the closet and
   indeed the closets were very full. "The love that dare not speak its name" was silent as the
   tomb. At another time and another place Aidan might have simply said "I love you," and
   suffered a rebuff. In 1942 it was unlikely he'd say anything explicit, given his character
   and Guy's.

The *Nouveau Roman*, Russian Dystopias, and Anthony Burgess

ROBERT O. EVANS

T wo of Anthony Burgess's early novels, *A Clockwork Orange* and *The Wanting Seed*, present an inverted vision of society at some date in the not-too-distant future. Thus both are dystopias or anti-utopian novels in the broadest sense. Burgess himself prefers the term *cacotopia*; "it sounds worse than dystopia," he says in a much later work, *1985*.[1] Both the early novels appeared in the same year, 1962, suggesting that Burgess became interested in an anti-utopian approach to literary structure somewhat before that time, had his fling, and went on to other, possibly better, subjects. Then, several years later, in 1978, he returned to the earlier interest with *1985*, which is both a fictionized essay on the subject of cacotopias, the language *Newspeak*, and Orwell's *1984*, and a novella in the same spirit. The essay part of *1985* tells us a good deal about Burgess's preferences in the genre, making clear a good many things about the earlier novels that had been matters of speculation among the critics. For instance, *1985* is firmly rooted in Orwell and pretty much ignores Aldous Huxley's *Brave New World*, that other famous English dystopia from the era. Orwell dealt primarily with a society constructed in denial of freedom and personal liberty, subjects close to Burgess's heart; Huxley was more concerned with the loss of pleasure.

Of the two earlier books, *The Wanting Seed* has gone virtually unnoticed, while *A Clockwork Orange* quickly became a *succés de scandale*. For a time it seemed as if it might even supplant the vogue (especially among American high school and college readers) for William Golding's *Lord of the Flies*, the in book of that era, which itself had supplanted Salinger's *The Catcher in the Rye*. *A Clockwork Orange* never quite attained those heights, though it did a good deal for the author's reputation and perhaps his financial independence as well. A decade later it enjoyed something of a revival with the production of Stanley Kubrick's fascinating film version.

Both earlier books and *1985* deal with what might be called relevant social matters, reflecting concerns of their generation. *The Wanting Seed* might be considered an essay on the population explosion—almost a Malthusian document—while *A Clockwork Orange* deals primarily with teenage violence and amorality. *1985* presents a larger canvas, freedom in the modern world (to borrow a phrase from Maritain). A still later work, *The End of the World News*, only a third of which is properly a dystopia, deals with the end of the world, or, more precisely, how people might behave in the face of a planetary cataclysm. There we find Burgess expanding his range of interest immensely, not simply using anti-utopian machinery to discuss still another aspect of twentieth-century society. Both earlier novels are heavily larded with violence, so much so that,were they not set in the future, and identifiable with a number of other works with similar concerns, such as Eugene Zamyatin's *We* or Orwell's *1984*, one might suspect Burgess of borrowing a page from the French *nouveau roman* and hanging his two 1962 books on fictive structures dependent on violence for their very shapes. To quote Neville Chamberlain, and disagree with him, we have not found much "peace in our time."

Who can say why the public in the early sixties took avidly to *A Clockwork Orange* and ignored *The Wanting Seed?* Both are shockers, but perhaps the public likes to be shocked by some things while others remain taboo. Whatever the reasons, it is hard to understand why the critics in those days followed the tastes of the public instead of their own insights. *A Clockwork Orange* received a reasonable amount of attention; *The Wanting Seed* is still wanting, though, I am tempted to argue, there is not really very much difference in literary quality between the two. But perhaps before we attempt any judgment of Burgess's social commentaries, we should ask ourselves just what kind of novels we really have here. The real question, it seems to me, comes down to alternatives: are we dealing with a new twist in a fairly recognizable anti-utopian convention, brought about by the changing sensibility that followed World War II, or have we, alternatively, novels that borrow machinery from the earlier convention where it is convenient to do so but are really more closely related to the revolution in the novel that we associate, in France at least, with the term *nouveau roman*? In short, had these works been written by Alain Robbe-Grillet, or Michel Butor, or Nathalie Sarraute, had some of the elements of the inverted utopia been de-emphasized, would we consider Burgess's earlier books something else again, something more worthy of serious critical attention?

Such questions suggest the whole complex subject of genre. For purposes of such a discussion, I suggest certain criteria. First, not all literary works belong to a genre (consider, for example, Franz Kafka's *The Castle*—with what genre should it properly be associated?). There is some question among critics whether examples of the *nouveau roman* belong under the rubric *roman* at all. It is possible that Robbe-Grillet was simply bogged down in terminology when he entitled his essay *Pour un nouveau roman* in 1963. He might have done better to stick with Jean-Paul Sartre's phrase *anti-roman*, coined in the preface to Mme Sarraute's first novel, *Portrait d'un inconnu* in 1948. The question about the French works is whether they are novels at all in any understandable genre-sense. That question may also be germane for *1985* and *The End of the World News*. It is not quite so clear whether we can ask it of Burgess's earlier works, for they resemble what we expect the novel to be much more than, say, Robbe-Grillet's *La jalousie*. Still, there is an ethereal, anti-novel quality about Burgess, even in the early works, which has gone unnoticed but which Kubrick seems to have understood (or perhaps sensed) when he turned *A Clockwork Orange* into a film. While we may not immediately notice any resemblance between *A Clockwork Orange* and *Last Year at Marienbad*, they are surely more closely related to each other than either is to, say, *The New Centurions* or a Clint Eastwood saga.

Next (on my list of criteria), fictive structures may be generic—that is, they may be conventional and fit into definite genres—or they may be otherwise. They may be mimetic or metaphoric—and there is a good deal of ground in between. In any case, the fictive structure should be calculated to be a means for the expression of truth as the writer sees it. Accordingly, as Vivian Mercier puts it, "The history of the novel . . . may be summed up in a single phrase: the quest for realism."[2] Ah, but as Bacon puts it, "What is truth?" Have we in Burgess perhaps a struggle towards a new fictive structure calculated to express a particular sort of truth pertinent, perhaps even necessary, to our times, a structure less easily identifiable than that in the French *roman*, because it still adheres more closely to conventions than a book by Robbe-Grillet, or because there is no English manifesto comparable to *Pour un nouveau roman*, or, as has been said of our Romantic poets, because the English unlike the French do not form schools? And if what we find is such a structure, then what exactly is the truth Burgess is expounding?

Two decades ago it was virtually impossible to answer such questions about Burgess or even to clarify his position in contemporary literary history. But since the essay portion of *1985*, together with the long list of Burgess's titles since 1962, the task has become somewhat easier. Still, it may be salutary to begin with a brief examination of the anti-utopian convention (or even the utopian novel itself, if we can decide what is utopian and what is not). The name, of course, comes to us from Sir Thomas More, a saint whose early literary reputation rests on his skill as a polemicist. (The man who was later canonized described the Protestant Reformation as "lousy Luther's abominable bitchery.")

More's *Utopia* is itself a much debated book. Is it perhaps a continuation of a convention begun by Plato in *The Republic* or a somewhat pale inversion of that work? Is it a political document to be taken seriously, or was it, as Erasmus thought, a heavy-handed piece of humor to be compared with his own *The Praise of Folly*? Or, a twentieth-century reader might ask, does it exist somewhere between the two? However we may answer such questions, we must at once admit that any resemblance between Burgess's early books and More is quite coincidental. Burgess writes from a very different political climate, for a far vaster audience than More ever dreamed of, and from a society with immensely altered sensibilities. His direct debts are instead, I should argue, to the twentieth-century anti-utopians, particularly Zamyatin and Orwell, though that is not to claim that he is simply providing an updated version of his predecessors' work. Still, in one respect there may be a less tenuous connection between Burgess and More, for the moral position both espouse is rooted in Roman Catholicism. A host of contemporary English writers may be numbered among the Catholics: Evelyn Waugh, Graham Greene, Muriel Spark, John Braine, to mention a few, and most of them employ religious themes now and again, though they are novelists who happen to be Catholics using material they know best rather than Catholic novelists, to make Malraux's distinction—that is, novelists writing to expand the faith. Should there be any lingering doubts about Burgess's convictions, one need only read his *Man of Nazareth* (1979), as straightforward a life of Jesus as one can find—as different from, say, Kazantzakis on the same subject as night from day.

It is worth noting, I believe, that the anti-utopian novel had little appeal for writers in the nineteenth century. It gained attention in the first quarter of our century, particularly after the Russian Revolution and especially after the Bolshevik *coup d'état*. After the fall of Kerensky, Lenin opted for a tightly controlled proletarian society, and after Lenin, Stalin really gave the remaining dissidents who were not in prison or exile plenty of ammunition. But of course revulsion against the Bolshevik takeover did not come about all at once; it took some time for even the Russians to discover what it was they had created. For instance, Sergey Esenin's poem "Inonia" is a populist-agrarian paean in praise of what he thought communism would bring about. Still read in Russia today, it describes a utopian, anti-capitalist republic of peasant farmers. There is not so much as the mention of a single city in it. Esenin of course read his politicians quite wrongly. He seemed in 1917 to believe the Revolution provided the basis for a primitive, democratic community. "Inonia" is a little reminiscent of the theological call to return to the purity of the apostolic church; and indeed when Jesus, in the poem, returns to earth to help the peasants in their struggle, he is shot by a policeman and buried in a common grave with other victims of tyranny. If Esenin had not committed suicide in 1925, he would surely have done so later, in despair, when he saw Stalin systematically starve the peasant class into abject submission.

Later, in 1920, Vladimir Mayakovsky, the roughneck of Revolutionary poetry, published a crude, romantic verse utopia called *The 150 Millions*. In this remarkable poem Woodrow Wilson, the evil incarnation of capitalism, reigns in his palace in Chicago, a city built on a giant screw, while Ivan, the pure communist, wins over the American people to the new politics. It is hard to take such prophecy seriously today, and even Mayakovsky himself eventually grew tired of playing Walt Whitman to the Russians. In his play *The Bedbug* he lashed out at the establishment. Meyerhold produced *The Bedbug*, but it was almost immediately banned for being subversive (though some thirty years later there was a revival under Khrushchev).

Neither Esenin's silly vision nor Mayakovsky's slapstick seems very closely related to the fiction of Anthony Burgess, though Burgess may indeed know these works. (He knows the language.) But they do contribute to the literary climate that produced Zamyatin's *We*, a book Orwell reviewed in the *Tribune* on 4 January 1946, after he was finally able to lay hands on a copy. Since much of Burgess's work, especially *1985*, is deeply rooted in Orwell, and since Orwell was much interested in Zamyatin, one may descry a clear line of inheritance. The earlier Russians, breaking with the past under the encouragement of the Revolution, paved the way for what was to follow, eventually producing in Russia the doctrine of socialist realism with its many exemplars. The early writers are important, it seems to me, for creating a climate that encouraged a new literature, the cry taken up by the Serapion Brethren.[3] This school, under the partronage of Gorky and Zamyatin, met during the winter of 1921 in the House of Art in Leningrad to discuss and (hopefully) chart the future of Russian literature, and no doubt to read to each other what the followers were writing. Paper was in short supply, and many remained for a long time unpublished. The Brethren consisted mostly of prose writers (and mostly of men—there was only one woman, the poet Polonskaya). Most of their names are unfamiliar to westerners, nor do they any longer matter (except a few like Zamyatin and Zoschenko, who have been printed outside of Russia). What does matter is that the school, composed mostly of writers who had been sympathetic toward the Revolution, soon became disabused with the policies of a regime that was stifling the production of genuine literature. In their manifesto, they say:

> We have called ourselves the Serapion Brethren because we object to coercion and boredom, and because we object to everybody writing in the same way . . . present-day Russian literature is amazingly prim, smug, and monotonous. We are allowed to write stories . . . provided they are social in content and inevitably on contemporary themes. We demand . . . that a work of art be organic and authentic. . . .[4]

In *We* the state is run absolutely by a figure known as the Benefactor (Orwell's Big Brother). He is voted into power but once there has no opponents, like Stalin. Thus comes about the Single State. Its philosophy, as Burgess says in *1985*, is simple: "It is not possible to be both happy and free. . . . It is the duty of all good states to bring back Eden and scotch the snake of freedom."[5] Zamyatin and Orwell after him are especially concerned with freedom, as indeed is Burgess (which explains his preference for Orwell over Huxley, whose major concern might be what we call today the pleasure principle). Burgess translates these matters rather loosely into what he calls Pelagian and Augustinian terms, the former spelling determinism, the latter freedom. The philosophical system is loosely Catholic, and there is no doubt on which side Burgess comes down. In an argument between faith and good works he would opt for good works.

It would be going too far to claim that the manifesto of the Serapion Brethren by itself created the literary climate critical of the political regime that characterizes the early days of Soviet Russia; but surely it reflects accurately the feelings of an important group of young, talented writers about events managed by the communists. From such feelings dystopias critical of Bolshevik politics arose. Zamyatin himself is the best example, though his personal disillusionment with the regime predates the founding of the Serapion Brethren. An ironic writer and a merciless satirist, he had from the beginning criticized what he found faulty in society. After the Revolution he found the Bolshevik bureaucrats disgusting and made fun of them at so many turns that Soviet critics soon made him their favorite whipping boy. We need not wait for *We* to take his measure in relation to the authorities. His *Impious Tales* and *Tales for Adult Children*, collections of earlier stories, reveal what he thought about official plans for a new literature. Soviet commissars he found to be poor substitutes for Tsarist officials (whom he also detested). In one tale, for example, a decree is posted: "Cholera is officially proscribed" and again "Famine is strictly forbidden."

But Zamyatin was not opposed to revolution. Rather he interpreted its aims differently from the politicians who controlled Russia after the Bolshevik coup. Even Lenin, when he approached the topic of literature through his spokesmen, became dogmatic. Literature must, the Party insisted, in some way serve the cause whether it served truth or not. According to Zamyatin all dogma was reprehensible; dogma was the stuff true revolution aimed to destroy. Hence the former socialist attacked the regime every chance he had, and we know the price he finally paid. He had become, he said in his famous letter to Stalin, "the Devil of Soviet literature, and since to spit on the Devil is considered a good deed, all the critics did nothing but spit on me as viciously as they could."[6] He was condemned to what for a writer, he says, amounted to capital punishment—silence. But Zamyatin was luckier than most; instead of being liquidated, he was permitted to leave Russia in 1932 and found asylum in Paris, where some five years later he died. His works are still banned in the Soviet Union.

A discussion of Zamyatin as a giant among protesters against the Soviet regime, a political condition that encouraged the writing of inverted utopias, is pertinent, I should argue, to consideration of Burgess's numerous excursions into the convention. We should not forget that *We* preceded Orwell's *1984* (which really deals with 1948) nor that in Burgess we are dealing with an English writer fully cognizant of the shape of Russian literature. For instance, in a different work, *Honey for the Bears*, Burgess has the character Paul turn "to the poems of Sergey Esenin, the young man who had been married to

Isadora Duncan for a year and, after taking to drink and a kind of madness, had written a farewell poem in his own blood and then hanged himself."[7]

Zamyatin has affected almost every Russian writer since the Revolution who became critical of the regime and had to be careful how he expressed himself. Consider the cases of Andrey Siniavsky and Yuli Daniel, who had to publish abroad (as did Pasternak and Solzhenitzyn) under the pseudonyms Abram Tertz and Nikolay Arzhak. These two were arrested in Moscow in 1965 for subversion, tried in 1966, and sentenced to long terms in a concentration camp—to the revulsion of the literate western world.

The influence of the anti-utopian convention is especially clear in Yuli Daniel's *This Is Moscow Speaking*, a novella dealing with Russia in some period in the not-too-distant future—after the declaration on the wireless of Public Murder Day. *A Clockwork Orange* and *The Wanting Seed* of course precede *This Is Moscow Speaking* by many years. Though *1985* follows Daniel's book, there appears to be no direct borrowing of theme or incident. The point is that Zamyatin's passionate appeal for truth, freedom, and reason—though specifically occasioned by political developments in Russia after the Revolution—continues to be spoken by a host of writers who know his work and appreciate his ideals and are familiar with the anti-utopian convention he adopted, though the necessity for such a clarion outcry in western nations is surely less than in the Soviet Union. In sum, then, the dystopian convention received new impetus from the Russian Revolution and continues to receive impetus from closed communist society. The argument is epitomized and perhaps dangerously oversimplified by Ayn Rand in her naive little novel called *Anthem*. Better look at Koestler's *Darkness at Noon* or Solzhenitzyn's *The Gulag Archipelago*. Still, Ayn Rand's polemic against collectivism sometimes states the case well and reveals the debt to her famous predecessor. "What disaster took their reason away from men?" she writes. "What whip lashed them to their knees in shame and submission? The worship of the *We*." (Her interpretation of the pronoun is the same as Zamyatin's.) This, then, is the convention to which *A Clockwork Orange* and *The Wanting Seed* belong; *1985* and *The End of the World News* are linear descendants with a somewhat different focus. They are all criticisms of society, particularly the violent, inhumane, antirational society produced by the communist regimes, even though Burgess's focus in these works is certainly not directed at the Soviet Union.

It may be claimed, consequently, that since the Russian Revolution a new dystopian convention, or at least a new turn, has arisen. There is, however, one aspect of the convention that nearly all dystopian novels except Burgess's share: they are intended to give their readers a warning, usually about some particular state of politics. In *Anthem* we find a diatribe on the horrors of collectivism; in *We* Zamyatin cuts deeper. He examines what happens to a society when it becomes entirely closed. *We* is, after all, set in a mythical place with no contact whatsoever with an outer world—indeed there is no other world except the city. Since Zamyatin was an idealist with some faith in or respect for human nature, there remain a few traces of reason and decency and an almost innate drive for freedom. Thus the few characters that illustrate these aspects of humanity are examined psychologically, but the story, essentially, remains a warning of what will happen if we do not guard the development of our social and political institutions. Much the same thing can be said of *1984*, or Arthur Koestler's *Darkness at Noon*, Alexander Solzhenitzyn's *The First Circle*, or for that matter Edmund Wilson's play *A Little Blue Light* (which has thankfully disappeared from view).

But of what does *A Clockwork Orange* warn us? Social conditions over which we have no control? It is rather—I have argued the point elsewhere[8]—an expression of disgust and revulsion about what has happened to society in our lifetimes. It does not warn us to be careful not to follow a certain political course, as do most of the other books in the convention. It is, to be sure, a subtle work, often pointing a finger at what Burgess considers to be the cause of our situation. The climate of violence, of which Alex is the teenaged exemplar, exists in a Britain in the near future, and the possibility exists that it is man's fallen nature, in conjunction with his institutions, that has brought about this dreadful situation. The book does not deal with the consequences of political action. It is not an attack on a Soviet-like system, though one can hardly doubt that the author had little use for a Russia that could send Siniavsky and Daniel to a concentration camp, and Sakharov to exile and psychological rehabilitation, for speaking the truth as they saw it. Neither is it an attack on the permissive society of the United States, though Burgess implies that at least part of the fault in the England he depicts can be blamed on the two giant superpowers. The violence of the young gangsters is generally considered to be an American trait; the language they speak has close relations to Russian, as I have also said.[9] Burgess tells what he thinks about the superpowers: "As for America, that's just the same as Russia. You're no different. America and Russia would make a very nice marriage."[10]

The Wanting Seed deals in different themes. The subject of this book is man's natural desire to live and perpetuate himself, more particularly the results in some not-too-distant future of the population explosion. We are given a glimpse of a society in which motherhood is not honored, in which love as an encouragement to reproduce is evil, where homosexuality is approved, and where stupid, meaningless war is not a Malthusian catastrophe but an accepted means of keeping the population in balance with the food supply. (One may be reminded of some of the remarks made by pacifists about the American adventure in Vietnam, though Burgess wrote before that time.)

The book grows more disgusting, or more disgusted with human nature, with every chapter, finally turning to cannibalism as a solution for hunger. It is not the events on which the fable is hung that especially concern the reader, but rather the fact that this portrait, too, while outwardly dystopian, is not calculated as a warning—any more than A *Clockwork Orange* is. It is more an expression of vast loathing over what the author, a realist of no mean talent, makes us believe may almost be inevitable. It shakes us as Malthus, in quite a different way, shook the roots of his society. But it does not attribute the troubles of the world to political actions nor to institutions about which we might still do something. No, the worst has already happened. Man has outproduced the food supply. Even the most stringent controls can do nothing to alleviate the situation. From there Burgess predicts a sort of cyclical social progression (which I hardly believe we should take seriously), as hopeless in one phase as it is in another.

Neither A *Clockwork Orange* nor The *Wanting Seed* really fits the dystopian convention Burgess inherited. He borrows some of its devices, but at heart his statements are different. In these novels it is the statement about mankind, not the fictive structure in which it is embedded, that matters. If we search a little deeper, we may conclude that Burgess in these books is really closer to Jonathan Swift than Orwell or Zamyatin. We may discover, if we push matters a bit, that he is really closer to Milton's *Paradise Lost* than any of his predecessors in the dystopian convention. What Zamyatin is saying is that if we persist on the Soviet political course we may destroy something in our society and in ourselves which is precious (though a racial memory may remain). Burgess is saying that because of what we are (translate because of man's fallen nature) something dreadful is bound (or at least likely) to happen and happen quite soon—we can already see the beginnings (especially in A *Clockwork Orange*). In *1985*, in the essay portion, Burgess makes a rough division of mankind into Pelagians and Augustinians. "Bakunin believed that men were already good; Pavlov believed that men could be made good. . . . This was the ultimate Pelagianism."[11] But he reserves his strongest disapproval for B. F. Skinner, appalled by Skinner's title *Beyond Freedom and Dignity*. In such works Burgess found the dissolution of virtually all worthwhile social values: "It was the sense of this division between *well* us and *sick* them [emphasis added] that led me to write . . . *A Clockwork Orange*."[12] The tale that follows the essay portion of *1985* is by way of illustration. He does not say there is anything we can do about this situation, though I hasten to add I am not accusing him of cynicism. (There is, I suppose, a sense in which every writer—I almost said every decent writer—who draws such portraits hopes that his readers will understand them as object lessons.) All Burgess says about his hopes and intentions is that the business of the novelist is to earn a living (see *The Novel Now*), beat the tide of life; that is, get the next story out while one is still in good health and has avoided the statistical accident. Not that he is entirely pragmatic; he does admit that "critics say there are certain persistent themes in my novels—the need to laugh in the face of a desperate future; questions of loyalty; the relationships between countries and between races."[13]

In *The End of the World News* (1983) Burgess focuses his themes a little more strictly. This is a very unusual book, one which relates three disparate stories, a musical comedy about Leon Trotsky's visit to New York, a life of Sigmund Freud, and a science-fiction tale about the end of the world, or rather the end of our planet Earth. It is in the latter that he borrows from the dystopian convention, and then not heavily. The world does not come to an end because of what man has done politically or socially within his institutions. It does not end because he has unwisely produced a population in excess of the food supply, as in an earlier novel; but rather Earth disappears because of a cosmic accident. A planetlike structure called Lynx (appropriately) breaks into the solar system and finally into our orbit, and collides with Earth, destroying it. All this is foreseen by the astronomers and takes a certain length of time. What Burgess examines is the actions of men and women as they prepare for the inevitable, their idle hopes, and the very limited attempts to preserve the race in some sort of spaceship. For that he needs the machinery of science fiction, but his main interest seems to be partly psychological and partly theological. No one has a right to live. God made no promises of eternal life in the sense of mankind perpetuating himself through the generations forever. The solar system had a beginning, and it must have an end. What Burgess does is push that end into the not-too-distant future once more. Theologically his positions are traditional. The fictions in which he presents them are what we find unusual. We should not forget that Burgess is, after all, a Catholic.

Should we then dismiss his books as latter-day examples of the dystopian convention cut rather finer than the predecessors? Not quite, I think, for though he rather obviously uses the convention, he is not playing Cassandra for his audience. Burgess is certainly not a conventional artist, and he has perhaps been much misunderstood. Some critics and many readers take him for an *avant-garde* liberal, but if we dig deeply into what he has to say, that is exactly what he is not. He has little sympathy for theories of progress or the perfectibility of mankind. He is much more traditional in a Christian sense, closer probably to William Golding than to George Orwell despite his pervasive interest in the latter. He strives to express the truth, as he sees it, in the most original way he can. He is an experimenter, in the sense that Shakespeare was, a writer never content with something he had produced no matter how nearly perfect it may seem to the reader. He is in constant struggle to find a form (and a language) for the truth he expresses.

In that respect he reminds us again of Zamyatin. One of the charges levied against Zamyatin and the Serapion Brethren was that they were too much concerned with form—they were, in an age which denigrated not only form but even good writing, formalists (though strictly speaking we reserve that term for the school of criticism that grew up in Russia beginning before the Revolution). This is not the place to discuss Zamyatin's "functional expressionism" that he preached to his followers nor the "mother image" on which his works often hang. But there is a resemblance between what he tried to do with his writing and what Burgess seems to wish to accomplish. Both strive, as genuine artists, for a means of expression equal to the subjects which to them are serious, important, and quite unpleasant in terms of the societies in which each lives. I once wrote that Zamyatin is by far the better writer, that his books have a polish and subtlety of technique beyond Burgess's power, but that they share an impudence of expression. In *The Islanders* (1918), for example, Zamyatin creates an English vicar, Dewly, who is the author of a book called *Precepts of Compulsory Salvation*. Burgess can be equally impudent. He may not construct well-made novels. He sometimes seems to forget what he started out to accomplish, as in *Tremor of Intent*, which begins as super spoof of the James Bond or Eric Ambler sort of story and runs away from him; but he nearly always manages to shock his audience or somehow sting it into wakeful alertness. "It is not always easy," he has said, "to become a great novelist."[14] But when I wrote that he lacked the stature of Zamyatin, Burgess had not written *1985*, *The Napoleon Symphony*, *Earthly Powers* nor *The End of the World News*, to mention only some of the bigger works. I rescind what I said then. If only for their language and techniques these books make him a great novelist.

He is even more so an experimental novelist, more than Zamyatin, more than Robbe-Grillet and the other writers in the school of the *nouveau roman*, more (perhaps because he is so indefatigable) than any other writer in English today. He has sought since his very early book *A Vision of Battlements* (in which, he says, he simply set out to recall his wartime experiences in Gibraltar) to find new ways of expressing devastating truths, not perhaps so subtly as the French novelists but quite as deliberately. His force is language while theirs perhaps is structure. This is the light, then, in which I think his dystopian works should be read. We may fault him on several grounds, primarily for not having always written well-made books, but not for any ambiguity of intention. His dystopian works are not calculated as warnings but rather as expressions of what he considers to be the truth of the human condition. [15]

NOTES

1. Anthony Burgess, *1985* (London: Hutchinson, 1978), fr. Arrow ed. (1980), 51.

1. *The New Novel from Queneau to Pinget* (New York: Farrar, 1971), 4.

3. The young men who formed the school were admirers of E. T. A. Hoffmann, the German romantic writer, one of whose heroes believed that through the power of the imagination one could conquer time and space; he gave up his career, asserting he was Serapion, an Egyptian who lived in Roman times, and became a hermit.

4. Marc Slonim, *Soviet Russia Literature: Writers and Problems 1917–1967* (Oxford: Oxford Univ. Press, 1964), 98.

5. *1985*, 53.

6. Slonim, 88.

7. Anthony Burgess, *Honey for the Bears* (New York: Ballantine, 1965), 207.

8. "Nadsat: The Argot and Its Implications in Anthony Burgess's *A Clockwork Orange*," *Journal of Modern Literature*, 1: 3 (March 1971), 406–410.

9. *Ibid.*

10. *Honey for the Bears*, 134.

11. *1985*, 87.

12. *Ibid.*, 91.

13. *The Novel Now: A Guide to Contemporary Fiction* (New York: Norton, 1967), 213.

14. *Ibid.*, 210.

15. It is perhaps worth adding there are traces of the science-fiction theme, surely related to the dystopian approach Burgess has used, in his latest brief novel, *Enderby's Dark Lady, or,*

No End to Enderby (1984), where the author plays with his audience and the time-space continuum in the first and last chapters. In the first we see Shakespeare and Ben Jonson, in supposedly historical situations, before we move to the present-day scene in which Enderby is writing the script for a play on the life of Shakespeare for production in Terrebasse (Terre Haute), Indiana. In the last chapter Burgess returns to the theme via spaceship to another clone-type planet where Shakespeare is still a young man just approaching his career. This development has little to do with Enderby's Indiana experience, but it is certainly amusing for the reader.

Muriel Spark: The Novelist's Sense of Wonder

JAY L. HALIO

In his Ewing Lectures at the University of California, Los Angeles, some years ago, Angus Wilson spoke on the source, process, and purpose of the novel. He particularly emphasized an aspect of the novel which in these poststructuralist days deserves more attention, that is, the sense of wonder. He did not refer to wonder as such; instead, he spoke of the childhood vision of the novelist, the ability from his or her earlier years to see or imagine life in two different but related ways: first, through a kind of fantasy to reshape bits and pieces of experience into new patterns and thus make games of life; second, through assimilation or identification with many different people to engage in a form of self-dramatization. Both ways are important to the novelist to counteract the tendency acquired through growing up to an "overpurposeful maturity," such as Wilson finds in the novels of Galsworthy, C. P. Snow, or James G. Cozzens. The novelist must touch the reader's emotion and sensibilities, must awaken the imagination, and through this means stimulate the intellect as no other art form (except possibly drama) can do. Other aspects of the novelist's experience also enter into the process of creation, such as inner conflicts that help in the development of drama and suspense, and certain moral or metaphysical preoccupations. But the childhood vision of life—what I have termed the novelist's sense of wonder—is primary, as the work of Dickens (to cite but one example) shows.[1]

From the very first, Muriel Spark seems to have been endowed with all the requisites for successful novel writing. Although she began as a poet, had written both short stories and nonfiction, such as her studies of Mary Shelley and Emily Brontë, and had worked hard as an editor, she soon recognized where her main talent lay. Alan Maclean of Macmillan's must have had some good intuition of this, for it was he who first invited Mrs. Spark to write a novel for his firm, as Derek Stanford recounts in his memoir of his friend and former collaborator.[2] With an advance from her publisher, she sequestered herself in a tiny cottage in Kent owned by the Carmelite Friary at Aylesford and began writing. What emerged was *The Comforters*, a remarkable first novel. One of its salient characteristics and perhaps its most intriguing is its self-reflexiveness, the wonder at—and eventual enjoyment of—the process of composition itself that the chief character, Caroline Rose, experiences. But it is not a novel she is writing, or believes she is writing, at least not at first. She is writing a thesis on the history of the novel. But after a particularly upsetting experience at a Catholic retreat—she is a recent convert—she begins hearing voices to the accompaniment of a typewriter, and the voices distinctly reproduce some of her thoughts and some of the dialogue she engages in with others. She has little control over this phenomenon, and understandably she believes she may be going mad, as others in whom she confides also begin to think.

Caroline, of course, is not going mad. She is experiencing what many writers experience: the formulation in words for a novel or story or poem of bits of experience, if not quite in the manner that Angus Wilson describes as part of the childhood vision, then close enough to it. Caroline, moreover, takes a very objective view of the phenomenon, convinced that some "Typing Ghost" is at work "in a different dimension from ours," who is constructing characters and plots in which she is an unwilling participant. She even determines to obstruct or interfere with his work (she uses the masculine pronoun) wherever and whenever possible so that she will not be organized into his "convenient slick plot." She is a Christian, after all, by which she means, I suppose, that she enjoys free will and self-determination. The pain she feels from injuries suffered in a bad automobile accident convinces her that she is real and not "wholly a fictional character." At the end, when she has finished her book about novels, she goes off on a holiday to write her own novel and after a while sends her fiancé to her flat to fetch her some books. An inveterate snooper, Laurence Manders discovers notes for a novel (her records of the "voices") that she has left behind, and writes Caroline a letter that he finally decides not to send. He tears it up into little pieces and throws it away. The novel concludes with a comment on this act: "he did not then foresee his later wonder, with a curious rejoicing, how the letter had got into the book."

This relationship between fiction and reality has fascinated many novelists but none more, I think, than Muriel Spark from the outset of her career. Caroline's consternation is a reflection in ironic form of this fascination, and her attempts to come to terms with the Typing Ghost, "to see if the novel has any real form apart from this slick artificial plot," as she conceives it, reflect Mrs. Spark's interest in the novel as a form and as an image of experience. In a later novel, *Loitering with Intent*, the principal character, Fleur Talbot, is a fictionalized version of Muriel Spark, as a young poet embarking on her first novel and intrigued with the ways in which life imitates art, sometimes with literally deadly precision. We all recognize, or should recognize, the ways in which the artist creates his or her own reality, believes in it, becomes convinced that it is the *only* reality,[3] to the point where we begin believing it, too, or almost. Mrs. Spark goes a step further in several of her novels to show that the imagination not only can lead us in these ways, but sometimes actually does.

Her second novel, *Robinson*, like her first, begins and ends in wonder and "a curious rejoicing." Although neither is essentially a thriller, this novel also employs elements of mystery and suspense to add to the sense of wonder and fascination of the fiction. A young widow, January Marlow, is one of three surviving victims of a plane wreck on a tiny island in the mid-Atlantic called after its owner, Robinson. It is an odd, man-shaped island, and critics have readily explained the allegorical significances of its various parts, such as the "furnace," the secret caves and tunnels, the pomegranate grove, etc. January has suffered a bad concussion; to help her recover, Robinson has given her a notebook and told her to keep a diary, sticking closely to the "facts." January is not the most conscientious diarist, nor does she keep to the facts; she engages more and more in speculation, especially after Robinson's mysterious disappearance with all the apparent signs that he has been murdered. This diary, as January tells us from the start, almost costs her her life, as one of the other survivors, a blackmailer whom she suspects of the presumed murder, finds out about it. Robinson reappears just in time to prevent further disaster, and all of the survivors are returned to their homes when the pomegranate boat makes its annual visit to the island. Shortly afterwards, January Marlow reads that the island is beginning to sink and disappear, a fact which persuades her to think of the island as, in part, a landscape "of the mind." But then there are her journal, newspaper accounts, and other indicators of its "materiality." Once again, reality and imagination intersect. Here, January's journal has the opposite effect from Caroline's Typing Ghost, and it is the strange lived experience which seems fictional, not the entries in her book. Thinking back over her time on the island and rereading her journal, she recognizes the transforming power of her imagination, so that events undergo a kind of sea change, the island "resembles a locality of childhood, both dangerous and lyrical." She recognizes, too, that there was more in the experience than she has been able to retell, or could tell, had she a "hundred tongues." But she goes on to say—and these are the final words of the novel—"sometimes when I am walking down the King's Road or sipping my espresso in the morning—feeling, not old exactly, but fussy and adult—and chance to remember the island, immediately all things are possible." January, like her creator, thus becomes aware of the childhood vision which lies at the heart of the creative imagination.

The relation between the phenomenal and the noumenal worlds, touched on from time to time in her first two novels, becomes a major focus of the third, *Memento Mori*. A group of elderly people, many of them friends or otherwise in close contact with each other, begins receiving mysterious phone calls reminding them that they will die. The caller is never identified, that is, traced by the police, who are summoned to discover the source of what most believe to be a terrible prank. Only two characters recognize the possibility that the caller may be Death itself, and unlike the others they are neither panic-stricken nor overly casual. One is a retired police inspector, a friend of those who have been receiving the messages and who has been asked by them to look into the situation. The other is the bedridden former servant of one of the principal characters, a well-known novelist. Now living in a nursing home, crippled by arthritis, Jean Taylor is the most devout person in the book. Doubtless it is her religious convictions that not only enable her to contemplate with equanimity this first of the four Last Things, but also bring her to act in ways that imply a rigorous charity for her former employer and her husband. Mrs. Spark was just forty when she wrote this novel, whose cast of characters almost without exception was many years older than she. It is a tribute to her sympathetic understanding of such characters and her ability to project, or "self-dramatize," her perceptions in the way of childhood vision that makes the novel succeed. As she said herself shortly after the publication of the book: "Every theme demands a different sort of commentator, a different intellectual attitude. In order to achieve that, you have to write the narrative from a consistent point of view that's not your own. . . . The narrator of *Memento Mori*, for example, would be an old wise person who knew how these other old people in the story really felt."[4] Mrs. Spark became that narrator for the purposes of this fiction.

From meditation upon Last Things it is only a step to the implications of demonology in the next two novels, *The Ballad of Peckham Rye* and *The Bachelors*. A different sort of wonder, one closer to that which inspired the first two novels, infuses Muriel Spark's most famous book, *The Prime of Miss Jean Brodie*, and characterizes her abiding interest in fiction. As always, the narrator is different from previous narrators, as befits the setting, tone, and theme of this novel; the style, heavily given to very effective repetitions, is also unique. But here, perhaps more than anywhere else in her early fiction, Mrs. Spark's evident delight in her creative abilities shows through and becomes one with her principal character and her theme. For Miss Jean Brodie, that unusual schoolmistress revelling in her prime, takes extreme pleasure in not merely educating her girls, her special "set," to her own ideas, but in directing their careers and their lives. Or so she believes. She fails to reckon adequately with the independent spirit most of the girls retain, despite their apparent devotion to their mentor. Most of all, she fails to reckon adequately with Sandy Stranger, she of the little eyes, who vies with Jean Brodie in great imaginative capability, including self-dramatization, manipulation of experience (especially the experiences of others), and in general a highly charged fantasy life. Miss Brodie and Sandy thus become rivals not only for the affections of Teddy Lloyd, the painter and art master of Marcia Blaine School, but in every other way, although for most of the novel Miss Brodie seems entirely unaware of this rivalry. Nevertheless, it is Jean Brodie who from the first has impressed upon her girls, even somewhat "dull" Jenny the actress, the "hidden possibilities in all things." And it is this sense of the possible that nourishes the creative talents that the others have, most particularly Sandy, as well as her own.[5]

Always fascinated by the novelist's creative control of character and situation, Muriel Spark here shows a virtuoso capability in her handling of time. Eschewing for the most part slick plot devices to build suspense, she frequently anticipates climaxes and undermines them through flashforwards, as for example in the early revelations that it was one of her own girls, and then Sandy, who had "betrayed" Miss Brodie and cost her her job.[6] In a later novel, *The Driver's Seat*, we learn the nature of the catastrophe, Lise's murder, from the beginning of the second chapter. From all of this we gather that Mrs. Spark is more concerned with the how and the why of plot than with simply what happens. She adapts the devices of mystery novels, as in her earliest fiction, but for her own purposes: to delve below them and discern how fiction works and why characters behave as they do. It is only gradually that Sandy's rivalry with Miss Brodie emerges, and it is only at the very end that her motive for betraying her teacher becomes clear: she wanted to stop her from going on as she had done. The vehicle she chooses, which succeeds, is Miss Brodie's predilection to fascism. The political motif, present throughout the novel but never dominant, is but the means to Sandy's end, which is destructive finally, not creative. Whatever may be said of Miss Brodie's teachings—her peculiar definitions and applications of Goodness, Truth, and Beauty—and her "defective sense of self-criticism" notwithstanding, she was keenly aware of the possibilities of living vicariously through her girls. But this was a serious error, reflecting a profound flaw in her nature, and she pays dearly enough for it at the end, alone and bewildered. But her fate is sharply contrasted to Sandy's, now Sister Helena of the Transfiguration, clutching the grille of her cell when visitors come to see her or to discuss her famous book on psychology, *The Transfiguration of the Commonplace*.

In the fate of another of Miss Brodie's girls, Mary Macgregor, killed in a hotel fire in 1944, lies the germ of the catastrophe for Mrs. Spark's next novel, *The Girls of Slender Means*, which again concerns the diverse personalities and careers of a group of young women—a few years older than Miss Brodie's set, and living in the May of Teck Club in London. And again time past, time present, and time future intesect with interesting and illuminating effects. The most arresting aspect of this novel, however, is the way poetry interleaves through it, as it were, highlighting and commenting upon both the characters and the action. Mrs. Spark has always been interested in poetry, is herself a poet, and has used this technique from time to time in her fiction, but never before or since as fully or effectively. The main vehicle for this device is the character Joanna Childe, who teaches elocution in her spare time and has a marvelous gift for reciting verse, which resounds through the corridors of the May of Teck Club from time to time, never more appropriately (from the vantage point of hindsight) than when she recites lines from Hopkins's *The Wreck of the Deutschland*.

From these slender, well-crafted fictions to *The Mandelbaum Gate*, Muriel Spark's eighth novel, is a near-quantum leap. It is the longest by far of any of her books; it is also the most ambitious from almost any point of view. The first to be set almost entirely outside of Britain (if we except *Robinson*, a special case), its location is of the utmost significance for its theme and structure. The

time is 1961, when Jerusalem was still a divided city, part in Israel and part in
Jordan. The title refers to the narrow passageway connecting the two parts. As
many critics have noticed, the divided city is an emblem for other divisions
that concern the novelist: the division within the self, most particularly. As in
The Prime of Miss Jean Brodie, the two main characters parallel each other's
development, though not in deadly rivalry. Barbara Vaughn is an intelligent,
attractive schoolmistress in her mid-thirties engaged to Harry Clegg, an
archaeologist working on the site of the Dead Sea Scrolls. It is to meet him
that she has come to Jerusalem, hoping to pass over from Israeli territory into
Jordan. A recent convert to Catholicism, she has also come on a pilgrimage to
visit the shrines of the Holy Land. But there are complications: as the child of
a Jewish mother and a Gentile father, she is in some danger if her Jewishness is
discovered while she is in Jordan. As a divorced Protestant, Harry Clegg must
have his marriage annulled by the Church before Barbara can marry him. In
addition, Miss Rickward, headmistress at Barbara's school and her best friend
there, is determined to prevent the marriage and pursues Barbara to the Holy
Land with this intention.

   Living at the same hotel in Israel where Barbara has come is fiftyish Freddy
Hamilton, a reserved, very British member of the foreign service attached to
the consulate in Jerusalem. Although at first they do not hit it off with each
other very well, eventually they are drawn closer together, to the point where
they engage in a series of dangerous escapades. After Barbara decides to enter
Jordan despite the risks involved, Freddy comes to her rescue at night and
helps her to escape from a convent which she is using as a hostel. He is
motivated by a recognition of the danger she is in, but it is a very un-
characteristic act of Freddy's. The escape from the convent symbolizes as well
Barbara's shedding of certain nunlike attitudes once and for all. She has
decided to marry Harry regardless of the Church's ruling, which at that point
seems unhopeful, and has determined to fulfill her desire to visit the shrines of
her pilgrimage whatever the risks. Similarly, Freddy discovers in himself the
possibilities for love (not with Barbara, but through her with Suzi, a beautiful
and emancipated Arab woman), an adventure for which he believed he no
longer had any capacity.[7] The catalyst for his transformation—as intense as it
may also be temporary—are the words from the Book of the Apocalypse which
Barbara utters to him, or rather at him, in a kind of reproach early in the
novel: "I know of thy doings, and find thee neither cold nor hot; cold or hot, I
would thou wert one or the other. Being what thou art, lukewarm, neither
cold nor hot, thou wilt make me vomit thee out of my mouth."

The biblical setting, the divided city, the conflicts within and between characters, peoples, races, also help to force the issue: in this Middle Eastern land, cool temperateness is an alien ideal hardly tolerated. Nor are the evasions and accommodations Anglo-Saxons are prone to make in their own climates. One must become commited, or cease to exist as an entity. It is here, then, that Barbara Vaughn finds her commitment as a person in love with her fiancé, a commitment that takes precedence over her commitment—still very strong—as a Catholic, won despite her mixed parentage. She must first undergo various irritations, danger, illness (she falls prey to an epidemic of scarlet fever), and agonized self-searching. But she comes through. Freddy's experience is more sudden. It comes like a blow, and like a blow it causes him a temporary amnesia. But as bits and pieces of the extraordinary two days in Jordan he has lived through with Barbara Vaughn return to him, he recognizes both the joy and the fulfillment he has known. He has even been heroic as well as clever and has uncovered a spy ring run by one of his own colleagues and his wife in a lonely hideaway in Jordan, where he has brought Barbara to recover from the scarlet fever. As usual, Mrs. Spark eschews "vulgar chronology," as a character in one of her later novels, *Not to Disturb*, refers to it, in presenting events. But the time structure is not nearly so fascinating in this novel as in others: by now we are used to this technique and accept it in the same way we accept Faulkner's treatment of time, say, in *Absalom, Absalom*, different though the specific techniques may be. What is compelling here is Muriel Spark's tackling the conventional novel, with all its complexities of plot and subplot, diversity of characters, landscapes, and other settings, and interwoven twin myths of personal quest (Barbara's) and unconscious quest (Freddy's). Compounded with all this are the elements of the thriller and the mystery novel. Freddy's mother is murdered back in Harrowgate—he has a premonition of bloodshed but not in England. Barbara in disguise twice comes into close contact with her pursuer, Miss Rickward, but remains undetected, although the spy, Ruth Gardnor, is not as lucky when Freddy stumbles upon her at "Nasser's post office." And through everything also runs Mrs. Spark's unfailing sense of comedy, as many critics have noticed.[8]

The Mandelbaum Gate thus represents a watershed in Muriel Spark's fiction. Though not everyone was pleased with her accomplishment, most recognized the breakthrough to a freer, fuller form in her art.[9] But this was a freedom Mrs. Spark seems not to relish especially; although she recognized the importance of the work, she became dissatisfied with it and has sworn not to return to the longer form.[10] She prefers the tight, crisp novel or novella, where everything—including the characters—is easier to keep under more complete control. Longer fiction, for all its freedoms, apparently holds less fascination for her, requires more effort and more time and affords fewer opportunities, it would seem, for the controlled play of fancy or for development of her favorite theme, the ways in which life imitates art, or art leads life. Thus in her next two, very short novels, major characters develop a scenario for actions deliberately planned to culminate in their own deaths—so seriously do they take their ability to manipulate people and events. Frederick Christopher in *The Public Image* is an actor turned screenwriter who becomes disillusioned with his career, his marriage, everything, to the point that he decides to play a terrible joke on his wife, Annabel, a less talented (he thinks) but more successful theater professional than he is. The couple and their infant son have recently come to Rome, and on the night they are to move into a new apartment, he invites an unseemly crowd to a housewarming, unknown to his wife. While the party takes place to Annabel's bewilderment, Frederick commits suicide, leaving various notes intended to implicate his wife—she "drove him" to it. The plot is thus designed to cost Annabel her career as well as Frederick his life. It succeeds, though not quite in the way Frederick intends. In the end, it is through an act of free choice that Annabel permits her public image to crash. Other possibilities exist for her in life—as a mother, for example—and she is not as attached to her public image as Frederick and others believed.

In *The Driver's Seat* Lise, too, decides to take charge of her life, but her atttitudes, like her actions, more closely resemble Frederick's than Annabel's. Fed up with her job and her humdrum life, she plans a holiday abroad that will end in her planned murder by a sexually degenerate man, recently released from a mental hospital, whom she persuades to commit the act. She cultivates a public image on her trip that is designed to call the maximum attention to herself: her life of hitherto anonymous passivity will now be vindicated utterly! But surely this is the childhood vision of the "special" providence governing one's life, such as David Storey writes about in *Prodigal Child*, turned inside out, or upside down. The morbid interest in such characters and their destinies may have put Mrs. Spark in the hospital for a time, but it did not prevent the composition of subsequent novels, such as *Not to Disturb*, in which servants carry on a dialogue throughout a whole evening fully aware that their master and mistress in the Swiss household are enacting murder and suicide even as they talk. Or in *The Hothouse by the East River* Mrs.

Spark plays with the idea of a kind of resurrected couple, themselves bedevilled (it would seem) by the return of someone they believe had died years ago in a prison camp in England where they used to live.

These experiments with reality, for that is what they are, reach a focal point in *Loitering with Intent*, a very recent novel in which Muriel Spark returns to the beginning of her career as a novelist and recounts in fictional form the joys and disasters that can befall a young writer. But the emphasis is all on the joys: "How wonderful it feels to be an artist and a woman in the twentieth century," Fleur Talbot says of herself, proclaiming the theme of the book. Writing her novel took up "the sweetest part" of her mind and "the rarest part" of her imagination: "it was like being in love and better." This was her first novel, and Muriel Spark's sixteenth. The joy of composition has clearly returned (if it was ever lost), and the play of Mrs. Spark's imagination, as it treats a writer's looking back on her past, considers the differences between autobiography and fiction. But this autobiography is also fiction. Thus the realities of life lived and imagined once again intersect and, like the poetry in *The Girls of Slender Means*, comment upon each other. The sense of wonder persists: "I wasn't writing poetry and prose so that the reader would think me a nice person," Fleur says, "but in order that my sets of words should convey ideas of truth and wonder, as indeed they did to myself as I was composing them." Fleur thoroughly enjoys writing her novel, *Warrender Chase*, as indeed Mrs. Spark seems quite definitely to have enjoyed writing hers. All the difficulties Fleur encounters in a somewhat bizarre plot (when, for example, every existing copy of her novel is stolen, including her manuscript, as the book is in proofs) only reinforce her determination to succeed. And she does. For not only has she the full commitment of the artist; like Muriel Spark she has the childhood vision, the sense of wonder and joy at the possibilities of creation that provide concomitant experiences for the reader. She recognizes—and we can almost hear Muriel Spark speaking *in propria persona*—that the true novelist is "one who understands the work as a continuous poem, is a myth-maker, and the wonder of the art resides in the endless different ways of telling a story. . . ." Muriel Spark has found endless different ways of telling her stories and, in so doing, conveying the wonder of her art.

NOTES

1. Jay L. Halio, *Angus Wilson* (Edinburgh: Oliver & Boyd, 1964), 93-98.
2. *Muriel Spark: A Biographical and Critical Study* (London: Centaur Press, 1963), 61.
3. *Wilson*, 95.
4. "My Conversion," *Twentieth Century*, 170 (Autumn 1961), 62.
5. See Judy Little, *Comedy and the Woman Writer: Woolf, Spark, and Feminism* (Lincoln: Univ. of Nebraska Press, 1983), 129.
6. See Ruth Whittaker, *The Faith and Fiction of Muriel Spark* (London: Macmillan, 1982), 131-133.
7. See Whittaker, 77.
8. See, for instance, Little, 140-146.
9. Whittaker, 78.
10. "Keeping It Short," *The Listener*, 24 (29 Sept. 1970), 411-413.

"Malformed Treatise" and Prizewinner: Iris Murdoch's *The Black Prince*

PETER WOLFE

T*he Black Prince* (1973) ranks high among the novels of Iris Murdoch's maturity—those long, rich, deeply imagined works that have appeared since *The Nice and the Good* (1968). Writing with feeling, grace, and wit, the Iris Murdoch of *The Black Prince* not only faces two of the chief realities of her life—marriage and novel-writing—but, fending off the threat of special pleading, faces them from an alien standpoint. The main character and narrator of her fifteenth novel is a divorced man who, at fifty-eight, has published only three books (one, according to a long-term friend). "I am a writer," Bradley Pearson exclaims. "I have, I hope and I believe, kept my gift pure. This means, among other things, that . . . I have never tried to please at the expense of truth."[1] Distinguishing inspiration from whim, he derides fluency and fruitfulness in other writers. A prolific, book-a-year writer herself, Iris Murdoch has read many reviews attacking her for quick and careless composition. Would her writing improve if there were less of it? *The Black Prince*, winner of the 1973 James Tait Black Memorial Prize for fiction, marks Iris Murdoch's most sustained look at the question.

The novel looks also at the relationship between sex and art. Are erotic and literary impulses linked? "Men truly manifest themselves in the long patterns of their acts" (xii), says Pearson. The action in which he manifests his own reality is dull and tame. A cautious, timid man, he has had no sex life for many years; his pronouncements about art aren't backed by an artistic career or, perhaps, even artistic talent; he has worked with quiet competence for the Inland Revenue Commission for many years. Accustomed to solving problems by ignoring them, he will enclose words inside inverted commas or parentheses when feeling uneasy or defensive. The first passage quoted below describes a sister he has always secretly and guiltily despised. The second shows him struggling to convey his feelings about a former protégé, Arnold Baffin, who has outstripped him:

> She was smartly dressed in a navy-blue "jersey" coat and skirt. . . . She had retained her looks into middle age, though she had put on weight and looked a good deal less "glossy," now resembling a "career woman": the female counterpart perhaps of Roger's specious "military look." Her well-cut ungaudy clothes, deliberately "classic" . . . looked a bit like a uniform, the effect being counteracted however by the vulgar "costume jewellery" with which she always loaded herself.
>
> (49)

* * *

> I suspect that I have not yet succeeded in purveying the peculiar quality of my relationship with Arnold. . . . I was, as I said, his "discoverer" at first, his patron. . . . I can even remember at that time thinking of him as a pet dog (Arnold resembles a terrier.) There was even a "dog" joke between us. . . . Only gradually did the poison get in, deriving mainly from the fact of his (worldly) success and my (worldly) failure. (How hard it is for the best of us to be genuinely indifferent to the world!)
>
> (153)

Fittingly, Pearson's London flat has a rear view, looking away from the shimmering world and out to the squalor and monotony of dustbins, a fire escape, and a drab brick wall. As can be imagined, his facing the sunny vistas of romantic love dazzles and confuses this familiar of dim alleys, featureless brick, and grim, rusting slabs of iron. On the other hand, Pearson, as an artist, comes to life in imagined as well as material action. And his imagination is wilder than he knows. Despite his dormant sexuality, he has an erotic mind: "Sex . . . reveals itself as the great connective principle whereby we overcome duality" (176), he says. Sex colors his daily life. Weighing against his many disclaimers of Freud are references to the "sunless and cosy womb" (4) of his flat and to "the serene austere erection of the Post Office Tower" (4).

Pearson's scant literary output can't surprise us. Any denier of his basic drives and needs will fall short of his goals; any detractor of the key realities of his life, *viz.*, his parents and sister, won't allow himself the joy of success: you can't suppress nearest things without suppressing yourself. The background of his drama of missed chances and false starts prefigures what will follow: he has retired early from his job in order to write full-time. Despite the description of him in the "Editor's Foreword" as a seeker of truth and wisdom, he runs away not only from truth and wisdom but also from love, beauty, and self-renewal. From start to finish he misjudges the woman he loves, insults her, discounts her feelings. What is more, trouble comes between them only when he puts it there. The list of his failings goes on. The sister who loves him he pushes away. The book he wants to write he drops at the slightest provocation. Finally, the events making up the memoir called "The Black Prince" and comprising all but sixty pages of Iris Murdoch's 432-page text don't come from solitude and repose. He could never have invented the wildness he recounts. Nearly everything that takes place in his memoir happened to him. Unless he had first lived these events, he'd never have set them down. The fame withheld him as a writer does come, but as notoriety; Bradley Pearson becomes front-page news as his best friend's murderer.

I

After some weeks of freedom from work routine fail to produce literary results, Pearson decides to change his life anew. He rents a seaside cottage in order to shut out the distractions of the city. Typically, he doesn't achieve his hopes. Though seeking quiet, he steps straightaway into a storm of domestic clamor. Presaging this ruinous step is the lesson that distraction and interference can wear humble garb. He opens his front door to bedraggled Francis Marloe, an "unfrocked" physician and brother of Pearson's former wife. Marloe has come to say that Christian, now widowed after living some twenty years in Illinois, has returned to London and wants to see Pearson. While hearing this upsetting news, Pearson gets a telephone call from his old friend and fellow writer, Arnold Baffin. Baffin wants Pearson's help right away. Pearson doesn't make the cab ride from North Soho to Ealing alone, because medical training and a sharp eye for the main chance give "coarse, fat, red-faced, pathetic" (7) Marloe the opportunity to be useful and to cadge some free drinks.

He and Pearson find Baffin's wife, Rachel, locked in her room. Opening the door, Rachel displays a swollen lip, a bruised cheek, and eyes red and puffy from crying. The ministrations of Marloe, "still a doctor in the eyes of God" (10), as he insists, calm Rachel enough so that she can be left on her own. But Pearson isn't through with Baffin women. Several blocks from the Baffin home, he sees what looks like a young man flinging white petals under the tires of oncoming cars. The petal-flinger, no young man at all, is the Baffins' twenty-year-old daughter, Julian; the white scraps she throws are torn pieces of some letters written by a suitor she has discarded. Pearson has been watching an exorcism. Disavowing all but "a modest avuncular interest in the fairy-like little girl" (34), the childless Pearson surveys her lackluster career since leaving school four years ago: "Julian had left school at sixteen. She had spent a year in France, more at Arnold's insistence than out of her own sense of adventure . . . . Fledged as a typist she took a job in the 'typing pool' at a Government office. When she was about nineteen she decided that she was a painter, and Arnold eagerly wangled her into an art school, which she left after a year. After that she entered a teachers' training college somewhere in the Midlands" (34). Unlike her past, there is nothing lackluster about Julian's ambitions. Julian wants to write—not like her father, she claims, but like the obscure Pearson. Having pandered to his pet peeve—Baffin's allegedly speed-smudged work—she asks Pearson to compile a reading list for her and to criticize her writing. She has underrated his powers of resistance. The prospect of wasting several hours a week on Julian's misplaced ambition appalls him. "There was little doubt that Julian's fate was to be typist, teacher, housewife, without starring in any role" (37), he forecasts inwardly, while telling her of his plans to leave London.

These plans he repeats in a letter to his ex-wife, Christian, as he orders her not to visit him for any reason. But before he can decide whether his anger ("As my wife you were unpleasant . . . cruel . . . destructive" [44]) will attract rather than repel Christian, his doorbell rings. At his door stands his younger sister, Priscilla, who introduces the novel's second marital crisis: claiming that her husband, Roger Saxe, tried to poison her, Priscilla has left her home in Bristol to stay indefinitely with Pearson. She counters her brother's attempt to send her away by announcing that she has just swallowed her sleeping pills. Another ringing doorbell produces Francis Marloe. This despised drunkard and homosexual, now prized for his medical knowledge, rushes to Priscilla's side, as he had to Rachel's the day before, and helps her vomit up the pills. The arrivals, first, of the Baffin family and, next, of an ambulance, inject fun into the confusion. The presence of the three Baffins also dispels the emergency and dread caused by Priscilla's suicide attempt: the running from room to room by five people in search of the empty sleeping pills bottle and the delay over calling a hospital ("I always said you needed glasses" [54], says Baffin to Pearson while the latter is groping through the phone book) keeps crisis at bay. Less than a fifth done, the novel isn't ready for a death, especially the death of a freshly-introduced character.

Iris Murdoch keeps the tempo crisp and lively, giving Pearson more to deal with than a weepy sister. The next time his doorbell rings it brings back Arnold Baffin, who reports that he has been enjoying himself with Christian, whom he finds "enormously nice" (65) and with whom, it later comes out, he is falling in love. Imposing and insistent, Christian won't wait in the wings. Her bothering Pearson with four phone calls inside a page draws him to her. His visit takes place immediately. This handsome, elegant woman, whom he had remembered as being dumpy and frilly, surprises him afresh by calling him her only friend and, by stages, proposing to him. Another shock follows, again in the zone of sex and marriage. Giving in to Priscilla's wish that he go to Bristol to collect her jewels and mink stole, he finds both the Saxe house and Roger, Priscilla's estranged husband, looking immaculate rather than rundown, as Priscilla had foretold. "Looking healthy and distinguished" (76) amid polished, dustless appointments, Roger explains his plans to divorce Priscilla and marry his pregnant mistress, Marigold, her junior by some twenty-five years.

Instead of recounting this awkward development to Priscilla, Pearson takes it to Rachel Baffin. The upshot of their confidence is a disconcertingly ardent kiss, a letter in which Rachel insists that she needs his love, and a bedroom encounter, which ends when Arnold arrives home unexpectedly. While Rachel averts calamity by dressing quickly and then intercepting Arnold in the garden, a flustered Pearson cowers out of the house, his necktie, socks, and shorts jammed in his pockets. But his escape is flawed. On the next street, he cannons into Julian Baffin. The chance collision leads them to the same shoe store where they had parted less than a week before after another accidental meeting. In an act devised to buy her silence, lest her father ask why he was in Ealing, Pearson offers to treat her to some high purple boots she had been admiring. To his amazement, the sight of Julian's legs and feet gives him what a naked Rachel had failed to rouse less than one hour before—an erection. His announcement on the next page, that he will stay in London, could refer more strictly to this sexual arousal than to his usual practice of finding excuses to avoid writing his book.

But which Baffin is the main target of Pearson's feelings? Are his sexual encounters with Rachel and Julian, however nugatory, red herrings in a game of literary misdirection?

As has been suggested, Pearson and Arnold Baffin are both rivals and foils. Pearson claims to have launched Baffin's writing career by finding a publisher for his first novel and then reviewing it favorably. Baffin has kept busy since that time. Though some fifteen years his ex-mentor's junior, he has outpaced Pearson commercially and perhaps artistically. Pearson, naturally, denies grudging Baffin his wealth and fame, arguing that his ex-protégé, writing too much too quickly, has "achieved success at the expense of merit" (11). Unfazed, Baffin admits that each of his books betrays a perfect idea and that failure haunts him all his days. Yet, a cheerful workman, he enjoys writing for a living; writing less and more slowly wouldn't improve his work. Perhaps this self-acceptance rankles the frustrated non-starter Pearson more than Baffin's large output. At any rate, he seizes every chance to snipe at his friend's career. But his resentment doesn't end here. A divorced man, self-styled "possibly . . . a natural bachelor" (6), he faults Baffin's marriage as often as his books. Do the Baffins believe that they are not only happier but also more moral than Pearson, as he claims? As the family friend who is called first in emergencies, he has seen trouble fouling the Baffin hearth. But the trouble hasn't persisted. Pearson knows little of the texture and depth of the marriage: "A marriage is a very secret place" (23) and "What a mystery a marriage [is]" (32), he muses. If the Baffins' trouble occurs inside and is subsumed by their love, as Rachel says, then Arnold has outshone him once again. No wonder he carps at Arnold's taste in clothes, fondness for music, and living arrangements. No wonder he seizes any chance to harpoon his rival. Whereas an affair with Rachel would exclude him, one with Julian would twist and dwarf him.

Yet the repressed puritan Pearson won't admit either lusting for Julian or wanting to foil Baffin. He receives Julian, who has come for a *Hamlet* tutorial, "with a silent curse" (160). Moments later, he is taking off his jacket and tie and then opening his shirt. The news that in a student production she once played Hamlet, his aesthetic ideal and the sum of his aesthetic hopes, upsets him so much that he dismisses her and, after her departure, lies face down on his sitting-room rug. The aura cast up by Hamlet has made him fall in love with Julian Baffin. This happy change declares itself immediately. He looks younger and more vital; Rachel and Christian both wonder at his rejuvenation. His heart softens and warms. Roger and Marigold, whom he had earlier scorned, he welcomes when they bring some of Priscilla's things to his flat; he both asks for and grants Christian forgiveness. But his radiance dims when Priscilla's announcement that she wants to go back to Roger forces him to explain Roger's new life. The emotional pitch of the novel remains high as Christian comes in with Francis Marloe. The foursome regroups straightaway. While Marloe attends to suffering Priscilla, his sister proposes to Pearson. Rejecting Christian with charm and tact, Pearson goes off to indulge his favorite pastime—thinking about Julian. Love continues to strengthen him. Acting with new boldness, he uses Julian's telephone request that he return her copy of *Hamlet* to ask her to have dinner with him that evening—at the Post Office Tower restaurant.

The dinner date marks one of several appearances of the Post Office Tower. Pearson buys six postcard views of it the day he realizes he loves Julian. Earlier, he had imagined seeing it while kissing Rachel: "Her wet mouth . . . settled on my mouth. . . . As blackness fell for a moment I saw the Post Office Tower . . . looking in at the window. (This was impossible, actually, since the next house blocks any possible view of the tower.)" (112). This vision relates his sexual rebirth to urban renewal and, given the purpose of the Tower, communication; in phase with each other, both London and Londoner are refurbishing themselves by erasing distances. Pearson enjoys the mirroring relationship. Symbolizing his deepest wishes, the Tower fascinates him. He sees it again with Rachel, this time materially as "very hard and clear, glittering, dangerous, martial and urbane" (150), a proud phallic ideal. This splendid column of steel is the modern, non-literary counterpart of Hamlet. In contrast to matronly Rachel, who usually accompanies him when he sees it, and to doughy, drooping Priscilla, the Tower surges implacably upward with leaping radiance and pride.

The soaring Tower needs a dark, cavelike recess to give life to the impulses it sends out. Thus, it isn't till his next date with Julian, at the Covent Garden Opera House the following week, that Pearson confesses his love. So moved is he by the joy of sitting next to her in the dark auditorium that stomach convulsions drive him to a nearby street, where, like a baby, he vomits. Nor does he recover quickly. Finding Julian alongside him in "the filth and muck" (223) of the shut-up vegetable stands near Drury Lane confuses him. He tells her that, though he loves her, he won't see her again; he calls her a liar when she says she loves him, too; after walking away from her several times, he sends her home. Not until the next morning does his lunging comic rage mellow. Instead of phoning him at ten o'clock, as she had said, Julian comes to his flat at nine. She comes with a sense of purpose that shocks him; besides starting to undress him, she announces her plan to tell her parents that she loves and wants to marry him.

That same afternoon, he is visited by a fuming Rachel and Arnold, who accuse him of disorienting Julian. They are determined to stop him. Unless Pearson, whom he calls a "filthy lustful old man" (241), leaves her alone, Baffin will either lock her in her room or take her out of the country. He does neither. Some hours later, she calls Pearson from a phone booth near her parents' home, from which she has run away. The lovers unite and flee in a hired car to Patara, the seaside cottage Pearson had rented in order to write his long-delayed book.

End of novel? The lovers, having foiled the interfering parents, escape to the country where they will blend sexual love and work—Julian learning how to cook and keep house while Pearson, inspired by his ladylove, writes his book. Iris Murdoch's irony and moral complexity rule out such concessions to popular taste; her putting an age difference of thirty-eight years between the lovers stays in our minds. Now that the fairy-tale rescue and flight have been carried out, our memories are jogged. Ambiguity comes forth. Pearson's spotting of a bicyclist pedalling away from Patara introduces moral challenge to the coastal idyll. Without telling Julian, Pearson reads a telegram the cyclist had left on the doormat: Marloe, whom he had left with Priscilla, wants Pearson to call him. With a lie about an empty fuel tank, Pearson drives to the nearest phone booth, leaving Julian behind. What he hears on the phone chills his blood. Blubbering Priscilla, always more of an annoyance than a legitimate claim, has committed suicide. His response to the hard news impresses and disappoints. Putting his loyalty to Julian first, he tells Marloe to have Roger organize the funeral; the living rank higher than the dead. Yet he mistakes badly in not telling Julian what has happened.

His failure to share this deep home truth rocks her faith in him. And with good reason: taking away her chance to comfort and strengthen him betrays her love. But the betrayal doesn't emerge straightaway. As she did amid the vegetable rot of Drury Lane, where Julian and Pearson first declared their love, Iris Murdoch again shows deathliness whetting people's hunger for life. Fusing in Pearson's mind with the sadness of Priscilla's death is the first image confronting him in Patara after talking to Marloe—Julian dressed as Hamlet and holding a sheep's skull. A sudden lust overtakes him, compressing his love for Julian, whom he resents for being young and alive while Priscilla is dead, his guilt over Priscilla's death, and his imaginative identification with Hamlet, whom he had called "the most romantic of all romantic heroes"

(165). He tears at her so wildly that he rips her blouse, snaps the gold chain hanging around her neck, and smashes the sea-whitened sheep's skull symbolizing the sacrificial lamb of innocence. The novel's emotional torque rocks madly. In "a kind of horrified trance of triumph" (282), Pearson feels that he has taken a major step: having possessed Julian wildly, he possesses her forever. The same rush of divine or demonic power, the black Eros, that sacrifices her to his fury sends her back to his bed later that day; the lovers inhabit a spot on the map of love they had never known before.

Then retribution makes its inevitable appearance. Their dark intimacy is destroyed by the arrival of Baffin in the middle of the night. Though coming in darkness, Baffin represents the daylight world of fact, reason, and responsibility. He has come to fetch Julian home. To pry her from Pearson, he mentions Pearson's treachery—his keeping Priscilla's death a secret in order to prolong his sexual idyll and his lying about his age, which he gave as forty-six; secretly, Baffin also slips Julian a letter in which Rachel admits having recently gone to bed with Pearson. Torn between father and lover, Julian acquits herself well. She sends Baffin away, staying in Pearson's home, if not his bed. But Pearson's half-victory vanishes. Turn about is fair play; if Pearson can leave the love nest on his own, so can Julian, who departs from Patara while Pearson is sleeping on the sitting-room couch.

Reeling with misery, Pearson goes back to London to attend Priscilla's funeral and to find Julian. A week of frustration peaks with Rachel's telling him how she lured Julian home with a distorted version of her liaison with him: "you appeared to be in love with me . . . you started kissing me passionately . . . we went to bed together and it wasn't a great success but you swore eternal devotion and so on, and then Arnold came and you ran out" (310).

The bitterness that follows leads to Pearson's asking Rachel if her husband and Christian are in love. Why should he ask such a question? Rachel's denial that Baffin ever took Christian seriously prompts an allegedly confused Pearson to produce a letter Baffin wrote him a week before spelling out his mad, wild love for Christian. In the book's most shameless contrivance, he hands the letter absentmindedly to Rachel as he answers a ringing doorbell. Returning to Rachel, who had just spoken a high-flown encomium on her marriage, he hears himself savaged for having shown her the letter: "You are a destroyer. . . . You are the sort of person who goes around in a dream smashing things. . . . You are one of those wretchedly unhappy people who want to destroy happiness" (313–314). The melodramatic session ends with Rachel stampeding out of the flat and, in a symbolic slaughter, Pearson destroying a complete works of Arnold Baffin, which had come by post only minutes before.

A letter from Julian the next days helps Pearson sustain the heights he had soared to while dismembering Baffin's books. But, as happens so often in the novel, a crisis changes both mood and plot. Rachel, who had just proclaimed herself his foe, now begs Pearson on the telephone to come to her. What he finds on the next page justifies her alarm: Baffin lying on the drawing-room floor, his blood-encircled head dented with the same poker that hurt Rachel at the outset. The presence, near the corpse, of the letter in which Baffin confessed his love for Christian reveals the letter as the cause of the violence. Foolishly, Pearson burns the letter and washes the poker that killed Baffin. His folly reveals itself in his postscript, which shows him being tried for and convicted of murder.

II

How to explain Pearson's self-defeating behavior at the end of the book—his washing and then hiding the weapon that bore Rachel's fingerprints and his burning the proof of Rachel's motive for murder? These suicidal acts chime with his refusal to protect himself during the trial, where he holds back evidence, contradicts himself, and lies. "I . . . acted as guiltily as any man could," he says. "Perhaps at moments I almost believed that I had killed him" (332). Then he admits, "I rolled in my guilt, in the very filth of it. Some newspapers said I seemed to enjoy my trial" (333). Pearson accepts his guilt dramatically, if not literally, because it gives him, self-confessed a "timid incomplete resentful man" (333), a wholeness and a symmetry he couldn't supply from within. A life sentence brings release from his dull, ineffectual routine; no wonder he calls it "not something to be wasted" (333). The chance to create both a self and a scenario in one stroke kindles the god-flame in him. He can rise to a tragic grandeur. The man who wants to be something he can't is a stock figure of comedy—Shakespeare's Bottom and Malvolio. To pose as a murderer without having to murder is to silence his mockers. At the same time, the imposture lets him play both martyr and saint (he calls the prison where he is stowed a monastery). He had also said, apropos of the Post Office Tower, "The beatific vision would be a similar experience if one also *was* what one *saw*" (201). This impulse, expressed by the *was-saw* palindrome, conveys his imaginative self-concept, that of the creator, who, Hegel-like, merges with his creation. As Marloe points out in his postscript, Bradley Pearson's initials are the same as those of his memoir. His feigned fury has lifted Pearson to the radiant maleness of the Post Office Tower and even pushed him toward Hamlet, with whom not only Shakespeare but also nearly everybody who reads or sees the play identifies. In a sense, Pearson's manufactured malice carries him past the Oedipal Hamlet, who never had the nerve to kill either his natural father or stepfather.

The image of Baffin's head ringed by blood evokes John the Baptist; Baffin *is* a precursor. But he ushers in a realm of shadows, not one of living substances. Pearson's life imprisonment vindicates his prediction, made early in the novel, that his end will flow from the beginning; his final, and greatest, opus stems from a harrowing ordeal; his shouldering the blame for a crime he may not have committed makes him actor, dramatist, and director: the others must act *his* script. Finally, his publishing *The Black Prince* after his death gives him the last laugh over these others; his book will outlast and outshine their gossip. But who will care? The completeness that comes with making his life imitate art shuts out contingency. It is a literary, rather than a fully human, sensation. His yearning for perfection has precluded the finite. His draining his ideal of humanity has nullified his creed of salvation through art; unless grounded in human contingency, aesthetic experience runs to waste.

Pearson's cold, mean-spirited actions reflect this drift. He calls himself "conventional, nervous, puritanical" (xvii); Rachel deems him "a sort of parasite, an awful nuisance" (354); Priscilla's disclaimer spells out his imaginative failure: "no wonder you can't write real books—you don't see—the horror" (189). The glory as well as the horror escapes him because he dislikes people. Calling himself "an incorrigible Peeping Tom" (89), Baffin accuses him rightly of being censorious: "you mustn't disapprove of people," he warns, explaining, "It cuts you off" (28). The contrast between the two men can be extended. Whereas Baffin defines curiosity as charity, Pearson calls it malice. So heedless is he of others that, until Baffin tells him, he never knew that Christian, his ex-wife, was Jewish. Pearson can attack his friend for mistaking Sufism as a form of Buddhism and for confusing Mahayana and Theraveda, but the friend has the moral insight to unearth Christian's Jewishness at first meeting, simply by asking.

Pearson's contempt for others springs from self-contempt. As has been said, he has rejected the key realities of his life. He disparages Priscilla constantly, never missing a chance to mention her puffy face, mottled skin, or dry, brittle hair. His father he always disliked for having had the same defects he scorns in himself—timidity, obtuseness, slavery to routine. Yet, like him, he resents having cut short his education, and he mistreats Priscilla as badly as his father mistreated his mother. "My mother filled me with exasperation and shame but I loved her" (xiv), he insists. His love doesn't amount to much. The shame that overshadows it he transfers to Priscilla and punishes her for it. Punish he must. Like the rest of his family, he nurses a grudge against the world. He dreams at least once a week of the stationery shop his parents kept in Croydon—the warm, dark womb they pushed him out of to earn his way. But how? To make up for his father's lack of education, he wanted to write for a living. His subsequent failure as an author hardened him against his father for indirectly prodding him to act beyond his powers in hope of wiping out a family shame. Like Hamlet he kills neither his natural nor surrogate father: Rachel says of him, "His relation to myself and my husband was virtually that of a child to its parents" (355). Nor does he give in to the incest-craving he believes gnaws at Hamlet. But fathers stay on his mind. He defies the father-figure Arnold Baffin by bedding his daughter, and he pays tribute to authority by leaguing with it as a tax inspector.

To reject one's origins is to reject oneself. Thus, Pearson must go outside himself to find the strength he can't supply internally. He works for the Inland Revenue Service, his society's fullest embodiment of the obedience-exacting father. But his job doesn't teach him street sense, heart knowledge, or control. Nothing works out for him as planned. The page after he insists that his love for Julian won't change his movements, he asks her out. Though determined to keep his love a secret, he blurts it out the next time he sees her. Then he dismisses both her and their mutual love with the news that he's leaving London. Pearson lives at a great distance from his feelings. The sentence after he gets the sensation of being in hell, he is told, "You're icy cold" (129). His failure to get an erection with Rachel embarrasses him. Embarrassment grips him again in the next scene, looking at Julian's legs and feet in the shoe store, because he does get an erection. He is sexually maladjusted. In the shoe store, he speaks of "the anti-gravitational aspiration of the male organ" (133). Later he refers to vomiting as "a remarkable drive contrary to the force of gravity" (221). Are vomiting and sex both unnatural to him? Does he see any difference between the two activities?

Despite his faults—laziness, ineffectuality, blurred moral vision—people like him, respect his opinions, and search him out during crises. He doesn't let them down. At the Baffins', where he is sent for when Arnold believes he may have killed Rachel, he acts boldly and decisively. He shoves Arnold away from Rachel's door, pushes him into a chair, and orders him downstairs for drinks. Then Rachel admits him into her heretofore locked room. He attracts women. Priscilla goes straight to him when her marriage cracks; Rachel wants him in her bed; Christian comes to London to propose to him; Julian has loved him from a little girl. The homosexual Marloe loves him, too, as does Arnold Baffin, according to Rachel and Marloe. Are they right? Baffin is probably the main figure in Pearson's drama. The relationship between the two men cuts deeply; to slight their rivalry in the spheres of letters and family life is to bypass much of importance.

This importance hinges on Pearson's ability to sustain the rivalry despite heavy odds. As he does in most of his other personal ties, he holds his own with his more successful colleague. He admits indulging an "obsessive relationship" (304) with Baffin, whom Marloe calls "Bradley's protégé, rival, idol, gadfly, friend, enemy, *alter ego*" (348). Denying any sexual motives, Pearson has defined the love-hate bond himself: "we constantly thought about each other. He was (but of course not in Marloe's sense) the most important man in my life. . . . he sometimes seemed like an emanation of myself, a strayed and alien *alter ego*. He made me laugh deeply. . . . He was . . . always slightly (I cannot avoid the word) flirting with me. He was well aware of being the disappointing and even slightly menacing son-figure" (154). Thus menaced, Pearson warms to Julian's announcement that she wants to model her writing career on his rather than on her father's. Setting horns on his head as Rachel's lover and usurping him as the first man his daughter, an only child, ever loved would gladden him still more. He fears and tries to score off Baffin whenever possible. But Baffin, too, fans the flames of the rivalry. Why? He has succeeded in areas from which Pearson has opted out—marriage and writing. On the face of things, he has beaten his friend in the race for life's prizes by many lengths. But he lacks the pride of the conqueror. "I live . . . with an absolutely continuous sense of failure. I am always defeated, always" (141), he believes. Pearson threatens him. If Pearson plays a sexual charade with Rachel, Baffin reciprocates many times over—having an affair with Christian, telling Pearson about it, and then asking him to run interference with Rachel for him. He goes to these extremes because Pearson hasn't failed; where no attempt exists, there can't be failure. If only by default, Pearson has kept his creative gift unsmirched, or so Baffin believes, experience having taught him that the execution of most ideas betrays their noble conception.

Pearson waits patiently for inspiration; he revises, rewrites, destroys. The popular writer can't afford such fastidiousness because his livelihood depends on a large readership, and he's honest enough to admit it. He also thinks well enough of Pearson to withhold doubt that he meets his own high aesthetic standards. Like his curiosity, Baffin's moral charity undergirds both his art and his humanity.

P. Loxias, the editor of the book, doesn't rank compassion high among an artist's gifts: "Every artist is an unhappy lover. And unhappy lovers want to tell their story" (x), he says in his Foreword. Conceived in sorrow, *The Black Prince* comes to life in the waste of a prison. Pearson, whose low self-esteem keeps him from thinking well of others, is writing to save face, to see where he went wrong, and to stop the pain. Like him, the authors of the five postscripts following his long narrative talk more about themselves than about others. Their defensiveness is surprising: though no dates are given, Pearson died in prison soon after completing his book, the action of which must have taken place about five years before the postscripts were written. Each writer suppresses. Yet each includes either vital new data or a vital new slant on Pearson's omissions and distortions. Julian, Rachel, and Christian each claim that Pearson loved her, but deny requiting his love. Christian calls his narrative "off key" (343). First, it gives a twisted picture of her marriage to Pearson and her conduct with him as a widow. She left *him* and sued for divorce, contrary to the impression he gives. Next, she turned *him* down when he approached her after her return to London. She turned him down because he was mad. Is she lying? Despite our emotional preference for Pearson, we can't take his word over hers. But her omission of any mention of a liaison with Baffin doesn't strengthen her case. The same truth applies to Rachel, who also believes Pearson mad, calling his memoir "a piece of fantastic writing" and "a sort of mad adolescent dream" (352). Writing from the standpoint of an innocent widow, which she could be, she calls Pearson "an unhappy disappointed man" (354) consumed by envy over her husband's success. Yet these disclaimers lose conviction owing to her failure to deal with both her propositioning Pearson and her idle dismissal of his romance with Julian as fantasy.

Julian, who seems to have more reason than either her mother or Christian to scorn Pearson, withholds scorn. She had looked for ways to be with him and to make him feel strong. She had praised him at her father's expense. Throughout, her love showed more maturity and *élan* than his. After the Covent Garden episode, he walked away from her, told her not to touch him, and accused her of talking "lying rubbish" (230) when she said she loved him.

Lying rubbish didn't prompt her to kiss him ardently within minutes of his vomiting. Nor did it make her the sexual aggressor with him, introduce the subject of marriage, or tell her parents about their love. For his part, Pearson cared little about her needs. He lied and held back. Feeling most passionate toward her when she dressed as Hamlet, he used her to bloat his ego. Then he takes her so wildly that he frightens and hurts her. Being Hamlet is his ruling purpose and life drama; the prospect of merging with his narcissistic ideal steals all his control. In the process, though, he has reduced her to an abstraction. He calls his love and his art "ultimately one and the same" (174). In the same scene, he says, "I was . . . creating Julian and supporting her being with my own. . . . I was a god and I was involved with her in some eternal activity" (173–174). He pays heavily for forfeiting a warm, human-centered love. Rachel speaks more wisely than she knows when she says, "Your Julian is a fiction" (307) and then accuses him of living a "sort of literary dream" (308). There are depths of commitment he doesn't know, lacking the nerve to have plumbed them and the imagination to invent them.

Julian doesn't parry this narrowness with rancor. She does disown her love for Pearson. "Centuries separate me from these events" (358), those of the memoir, she asserts, coyly eschewing details. Without refuting anybody's interpretation of the memoir or the memoir's factual truth, she hides behind a wall of perplexity: "A letter . . . is quoted. Did I write this letter. . . . It seems inconceivable. And the things that I said. (Supposedly.) Surely they are the invention of another mind" (358). This feigned perplexity typifies her. In place of the shrillness of her mother, she substitutes a tone of detachment. Most of her postscript consists of aesthetic pronouncements. In a subtle way, she hasn't dodged the question of Bradley Pearson, whose influence shows in most of what she says. Her "art is concealment" and "Art is concerned neither with comfort nor with the possible" (360) resemble his "All art deals with the absurd and aims at the simple" (xi) and "Art comes out of endless restraint and silence" (29) both in voice and vocabulary. She has no reason to hate him. Her stance and the attitude behind her pronouncements show him to be the force behind her career as a poet.

Francis Marloe owes Pearson less and speaks out more angrily. Pearson had thrown him out of his flat, complained that he smelled bad, and belittled him in front of others. "Francis is not important at all," Pearson says of him when he enters the novel. "He is a subsidiary, a sidesman. . . . Poor Francis will never be the hero of anything" (xiv). He perpetrates these insults after Marloe tends to his sister, tries to help him find Julian, and speaks in his favor in court. Marloe, who told an unheeding Pearson that he loved him, feels sold out. His resentment unearths many painful home truths. Iris Murdoch recognized his acuity, and, by placing his postscript in the most obscure slot, second among a roster of five, plays it down lest it outshine the others. Her strategy doesn't mean, though, that she accepts his rigorous psychoanalytic reading of Pearson outright. Rigidly dogmatic, it reflects no warmth of observation, thinking, or phrasing, Marloe making many confident assertions without reservation or irony. Yet the masochism he sees in Pearson is borne out by Pearson's obsession with feet and his acceptance of the underdog's role with Arnold Baffin. The charge that Pearson is homosexual Marloe defends by contrasting Pearson's attitudes toward Priscilla and the Post Office Tower. Marloe's contrast carries the confirmation of his own homosexuality: "The female principle is what is messy, smelly and soft. The male principle is what is clear, clean and hard" (347). An excellent example of how a postscript entry can force us to reinterpret an event we thought we had understood comes in Marloe's reading of Pearson's love for Julian: "When he first (in the story) catches sight of his young lady he mistakes her for a boy. He falls in love with her when he imagines her as a man. He achieves sexual intercourse with her when she has dressed up as a prince. (And who incidentally is Bradley Pearson's favorite author? The greatest homosexual of them all. What sends Bradley Pearson's fantasy soaring as high as the Post Office Tower? The idea of boys pretending to be girls pretending to be boys!)" (348).

Is this fantastic reading valid? Pearson had the answers to nearly everything except the riddle of his own life. The aura of mystery strewn by his Foreword, with its serious, formal tone, recalls Henry James's *The Turn of the Screw*. This tie-in and the book's last word, "nothing" (366), should discourage dogmatic assertions on subjects like Pearson's homosexuality, Oedipal fixation, or murderousness. In the *The Black Prince*, Iris Murdoch deals with materials that defy both control and cognition. Their value comes more from their imaginative power than their literal meaning. Her absorption in them betokens a commitment that goes beyond logical probability. The drama energizing *The Black Prince* cuts to the inner planes of the mind and the secret places of the heart, where it reverberates rather than giving up answers.

III

The vibrations evoke the theater. In *The Black Prince*, Iris Murdoch joins with a recent tradition of fictional experiment that includes novels-in-draft, like

James Merrill's (*Diblos*) *Notebooks* (1965); nonfiction novels, like Capote's *In Cold Blood* (1966); and model-kit novels, like Cortazar's *Hopscotch* (English trans., 1966); works whose protean form invites different readings and interpretations. Without letting dialogue dominate, *The Black Prince* tries to catch the immediacy and compression of the stage play. The book abounds with different stage conventions. For example, the following stage directions precede an important scene: "For the moment . . . behold me sitting with Priscilla and Francis. A domestic interior. It is about ten o'clock in the evening and the curtains are drawn" (119). One fairly long scene is all dialogue, much of it extending only one line. Even though the speakers aren't identified, the tone and matter of their words make them recognizable. The three-page scene (85–87) works smoothly: no speech answers its predecessor; yet all help build the ongoing knockabout, and all address the main issues of the moment. Much of the comedy elsewhere depends on contrivances reminiscent of French farce, like the crucial letter and the coincidence. Baffin arrives home at the very moment Rachel and Pearson are in bed together; he interrupts Pearson and Christian the only time they kiss in the novel. The scene after Priscilla's failed suicide attempt also takes on the busy look of a domestic interior in a French farce. Pearson's flat is crowded with well-meaning people scurrying about; danger has luckily been averted; another fillip to the plot and threat to the hero's tranquillity, *namely*, Christian, who is drinking in a nearby pub, will materialize shortly.

Most of the comic machinery comes in the first half of the book. The attempt of parents to foil their daughter's marriage belongs more strictly to comedy than to tragedy. Pearson escapes from the city with Julian just before Baffin stops them, boarding the same taxi that brought Baffin to his flat. Now that he has won Julian, Pearson has the challenge of keeping her. The contrivances all but drop out. Because the machined plot hasn't flattened her characters, Iris Murdoch lends this challenge weight and meaning. Some of the dignity comes from references to tragedy. Just as French comedy enlivened the actions of Parts One and Two, so does Shakespearean tragedy deepen that of Part Three. As has been seen, *Hamlet* and Hamlet haunt Pearson. He tries to make *The Black Prince* as much of a self-projection as *Hamlet* is a work "about Shakespeare's own identity" (165). "*Hamlet* is words and so is Hamlet. . . . Hamlet is speech" (166), adds this literary non-starter. The sight of Julian dressed as Hamlet excites him so much that he rapes her, yoking himself to the literary ideal that his laziness and mediocrity had always kept out of his reach.

Other Shakespearean echoes drum through the book. Pearson's first name is the same as the last name of one of the greatest Shakespeareans, A. C. Bradley, author of *Shakespearean Tragedy* (1904); the killing of the father of one's beloved hearkens to Richard III; just before she tells Pearson to stop looking like King Lear, Rachel says of Julian, "You haven't lost a pearl of great price" (310). The reference to *Othello* is apt. Pearson had said, echoing Shakespeare's Emilia, "Jealousy is the most dreadfully involuntary of all sins. It is at once one of the ugliest and one of the most pardonable. . . . Jealousy is a cancer, it can kill that which it feeds on" (209). This sermon on jealousy, a fainting fit that later takes him, his blasted love for a much younger woman, and his fascination for the black Eros all put him closer to Othello than to Hamlet. Yet the distance between him and them is huge, Pearson falling far short of both men in nerve, force, and soul.

Iris Murdoch invites comparisons between Pearson and Shakespeare's tragic heroes to keep alive the running analogy between her novel and the theater, to belittle Pearson, and to work in the idea of revenge, a leading theme in Renaissance drama. Exacting the letter of the law was one of the great rewards of his job at Inland Revenue. It made him special. Only the dentist conjures up as much horror and loathing as the taxman. "What makes a man more obsessively miserable than income tax or the toothache?" (xvi) snickers this man who has rarely taxed or challenged himself. The retributive morality of taxation has twisted and darkened his mind. The prospect of getting even with Baffin might have drawn him to Julian as much as Julian's charms did. Though he had faulted Baffin as a writer and a husband, he had never defeated him as a father. Making him stand by as a man fifteen years his senior makes love to his daughter would make Baffin look as ridiculous as Pearson could wish. Further, it would give Pearson his revenge much more quickly and easily than would the chore of writing a better book than Baffin. With Julian and the Prince of Denmark as bonuses, Pearson can't be blamed for grabbing the chance to get even with Baffin.

The novel's broad emotional sweep includes vindictiveness and flaming sexual love. Iris Murdoch also brings to *The Black Prince* an eye for social detail, an ear for philosophical undertones, and a heart attuned to the many nuances of commitment. This sensitivity allows her to narrate and to distill. While she makes things happen to people, she also conveys meanings and consequences. Many of these are funny. The amusing incidents and verbal wit generated by her charming liars keep the book's pace lively. The trim pace, in turn, combines with scenic richness to give a sense of peopled space, apropos

of the city. Many characters fill the scenes; often four of five will appear at
once, all of them actuated by different motives and all claiming center stage.
Yet the novel's texture stays smooth, the God's plenty of character and event
never congesting. In addition, the crises caused by Priscilla delay the development of the love story, and Iris Murdoch tones down the intensity building
from Priscilla's problems by interweaving comic scenes and meditative passages with her cries of pain. Controlling all is the tension resonating between
Pearson's pompous, Victorian-sounding style and the wild, unpredictable
things that happen to him. That the tensional field includes local color,
dramatic movement, and depth of insight confirms the elaborate technique
and critical eminence of Iris Murdoch's most celebrated novel to date.[2]

NOTES

1. *The Black Prince* (New York: Viking, 1973), xii.
2. Iris Murdoch's novels subsequent to *The Black Prince* are: *The Sacred and Profane Love
   Machine* (1974), *A Word Child* (1975), *Henry and Cato* (1976), *The Sea, the Sea* (1978),
   Nuns and Soldiers (1980), and *The Philosopher's Pupil* (1983). [Ed.]

An Interview with Iris Murdoch

JACK I. BILES

The headnote often is of the identifying and introducing sort, frequently enlivened with more or less germane personalia. Such a headnote to an interview with Iris Murdoch seems superfluous. Miss Murdoch clearly is a major novelist. She has been a productive one as well: her nineteenth novel, *The Sea, The Sea* was published on August 24, 1978. On November 22, 1978, she received for this work Britain's prestigious Booker Prize for Fiction. Her twentieth and twenty-first novels are *Nuns and Soldiers* (Viking, 1981), and *The Philosopher's Pupil* (Viking, 1983). The interview took place at Miss Murdoch's home in Oxfordshire.

BILES: I should like to begin by asking a question about Joyce Cary. I have got the impression that at one point you showed the manuscript of *Under the Net* to him. His biographer, Malcolm Foster, refers to this and suggests that Cary was rather negative about the novel. Foster states that you paid no attention to Cary's censures and quotes you as saying "His ways were not my ways." Do you remember that?

MURDOCH: I knew Joyce quite well and I liked him. And I admired him, although I have read only two of his books.

BILES: Which two did you read?

MURDOCH: *The Horse's Mouth* and *Mister Johnson*.

Certainly I didn't show him the manuscript of *Under the Net*. He read the book after it was published.

Joyce had a rather interesting way of working, in that he wrote a great deal

299

of stuff about the characters which wasn't actually part of the novel as published. He did the whole thing in fits and starts—and worked on the end first; I found this particular technique surprising. I suspect I said "His ways are not my ways" in the context of saying that writers have very different techniques of writing. For example, I plan everything in immense detail before I start; the writing is the very last thing which happens. When I've got the story clear, every single word, at that point, matters. The planning stage is just rough notes.

BILES: At one time, Bill Golding told me that writing *Lord of the Flies* was "easy," that it was very like "tracing words already on the page," because he had planned it to "almost the last flick of an eyelid," as he put it.

MURDOCH: Yes, I know. That is what I feel.

BILES: Let me ask you to recall something else. I read in an old *New Yorker* [1961] an item by an unidentified writer who came up to Oxford and talked to several of you in the Philosophy Department of your college.

MURDOCH: Ah, that was the blind Indian, Ved Mehta. A nice man.

BILES: I recognize the name. He asserted it was quite clear to him that you are much more an intuitive person than an analytical person. To be sure, he was describing you as a philosopher and not as a novelist; but I wish to ask how far he is right, considering the analytic turn of mind that seems to me implicit in the careful and detailed planning which you do for a novel.

MURDOCH: Well, this is the sort of thing that people like to say—particularly about women. It's just a bit of journalese. I don't know: most writers are both intuitive and analytical. I happen to be trained as a philosopher, and philosophy, too, is a combination or intuition and analysis. And if you're writing anything important either in philosophy or literature, you can't really do without what people vaguely call "intuition," which I'd call "imagination" perhaps, an ability to fuse together things which are highly dissimilar, to see similarities in their connections, and so on.

BILES: Sounds like Wordsworth.

MURDOCH: Well, it may be. Yes. I think it's something which both in philosophy and writing I am conscious of. To my mind, philosophy is a completely different game, although the intuitive element enters into it. This is quite unlike writing stories, and I play the game according to the rules. It's a separate operation and one's mind is working very differently in philosophy.

BILES: You admire Dostoevsky, for example, and everyone terms him a philosophical novelist. Now, here you are—a philosopher *and* a novelist—and the matter continually arises: but, do you see yourself as a "philosophical novelist," whatever that means?

MURDOCH: No, I don't. Or, if I am, it's in the same sense in which Dostoevsky is and not in the sense in which Simone de Beauvoir is or Sartre is. I have definite philosophical views, but I don't want to promote them in my novels or to give the novel a kind of metaphysical background. Of course, any seriously told story may have metaphysical aspects and will certainly have moral aspects. And morality does connect with metaphysics; so, in this sense, any novelist has got a kind of metaphysic. But, I don't want philosophy, as such, to intrude into the novel world at all and I think it doesn't. I find really no difficulty in separating these activities. I mention philosophy sometimes in the novels because I happen to know about it, just as another writer might talk about coal mining; it happens to come in. No, I wouldn't say I am a philosophical novelist. I wouldn't say Dostoevsky is, either—in the kind of strict sense. Though he is a highly reflective novelist.

BILES: I should like to turn our discussion toward the drama and your own plays. A couple of years ago, in a book about the dramatic in contemporary fiction, a man named Alan Kennedy says near the end that he hasn't talked of your novels because you have a special definition of "dramatic," which is markedly different from the one he uses in his book. Then he does speak about you: he quotes from "The Sublime and the Beautiful Revisited" and declares that you clearly equate the word "dramatic" with the word "self-centered" and that in your novels self-centeredness is the greatest of all evils. Would you accept such a view? Do you equate "dramatic" and "solipsistic"?

MURDOCH: No, I don't think so. It seems a rather odd idea.

BILES: Something to do with Hegel's idea concerning the Spirit's struggling with itself in an internal effort to reach a higher state?

MURDOCH: Yes. I think there is a kind of self-centeredness which takes a dramatic form, but I don't think it is the only kind. What I mean is that it is consoling to feel that you are taking part in an inner drama. In a way, psychoanalysis depends upon this idea, doesn't it? The patient is cheered up by the analyst's picturing a drama in which the patient figures. I think this is a very ambiguous idea.

BILES: He had in mind what he identifies as your "central theme," namely, "the necessity to admit the reality of the other person"; that is, how, if you are completely self-centered, you can't see the otherness, the reality, of other people.

MURDOCH: Well, cetainly in the books I am concerned about egoism. After all, a story is dramatic; one is dealing with drama the whole time as well as using drama as one's medium—in the novel as well as in the theater. But in a way, plays and novels are very different: in the play, the drama has necessarily got a central and poetic function which in the novel it hasn't, I think. In fact, many novels rightly—this is something I also do—fight against the drama. I mean that ordinary life is not dramatic. I think it was the word "tragedy" that your critic may have been playing with; probably, I have said somewhere that I believe novels are comic and not tragic, that tragedy belongs to the theater. Some sort of drama must belong to the theater, where everything is highly significant and rather poetic and where there is a definite shape.

It seems to me that in the novel very often the novelist quite properly is destroying this shape, because ordinary life doesn't have shape. Ordinary life is comic and absurd. It may be terrible, but it is absurd and shapeless, and the novelist very often attempts to convey the shapelessness by having a dramatic shape, which if he is telling a story, he usually has to have. At the same time, he is fighting against it and blurring it—even destroying it. For me, this is a proper proceeding in the novel, but the theater is a very different matter. The theater is more like poetry.

BILES: When you say "absurd," do you mean ridiculous or do you mean absurd in an Existential sense?

MURDOCH: I mean absurd in the sense of being purposeless and senseless.

BILES: Regarding your plays, I have had the good fortune to see one of them performed. In the mid-1960s I saw a production of *A Severed Head* at the Criterion theater in London and found it altogether brilliant. This play came out of a collaboration between you and J. B. Priestley. Will you tell me about the nature of that collaboration?

MURDOCH: Well, I wrote, as it were, the words. Jack contributed very important things in structure. At that time, I knew really very little about the theater. I don't go to theater much; I don't actually *like* the theater very much. But I would like to write for it, which is a paradox. I hadn't got much perception of dramatic theater structure at that time, and Jack helped me a great deal with that. Of course, he is a great craftsman. As far as I can remember, the whole operation took about a week. Jack had a bottle of whiskey, and somehow or other it happened!

BILES: I understand that there is a play version of *The Italian Girl*.

MURDOCH: Yes, there is. I am not pleased with that. I was told that nothing would happen until I was satisfied with the version, but in the end I was hustled and it was a botched job.

BILES: Where was it produced?

MURDOCH: It started off in Bristol. It had quite a long run in London. It was successful in a commercial sense, but I didn't like it. It was imperfect.

BILES: The distinction is one I'd expect you to make.

MURDOCH: I'd never collaborate with anyone again.

BILES: How long did *A Severed Head* run?

MURDOCH: About two years. *The Italian Girl* ran for more than a year. I can't remember precisely.

BILES: These other two plays: *The Servants and the Snow* and *The Three Arrows*?

MURDOCH: They were both put on in the provinces and scheduled for limited runs. They haven't, either of them, been put on in America; so, if you know anybody who is dying to put something on in New York or Washington, I trust they will get into his hands!

The Three Arrows was beautifully done here, with Ian McKellen. I think it is a rather good play.

BILES: Are there any others?

MURDOCH: Well, there is another one. Somebody saw it and didn't like it, and I haven't really tried to sell it to anyone else.

BILES: It hasn't been produced?

MURDOCH: Not yet. But in any case I certainly hope to write more for the theater.

BILES: Here is a matter that I find curious and extremely interesting: I can't remember exactly, but you have written perhaps half a dozen novels with first-person narrators and in every instance that first-person narrator is male.

MURDOCH: I'm writing one at the moment, actually.

BILES: I am sure it is unique in the history of the English novel for any novelist to have written consistently in the opposite sex, when writing first-person narratives. Emily Brontë is an exception of sorts, since she wrote *Wuthering Heights* as a first-person narrative by Mr. Lockwood, but only one novel is involved. And, of course, there are men, like Angus Wilson, who can write excellently and convincingly from the female point of view, as in *The Middle Age of Mrs. Eliot*, though that is not actually a first-person work. But, no one does what you do. I am curious as to why it was that you chose such a narrator in these instances. Was it something in the particular story which dictated a male narrator or what?

MURDOCH: Well, I don't really see there is much difference between men and women. I think perhaps I identify with men more than with women, because the ordinary human condition still seems to belong more to a man than a woman. Writing mainly as a woman may become a bit like writing with a character who is black, or something like that. People then say, "It's about the black predicament." Well, then, if one writes "as a woman," something about the female predicament may be supposed to emerge. And I'm not very much interested in the female predicament. I'm passionately in favor of women's lib, in the general, ordinary, proper sense of women's having equal rights. And, most of all, equal education.

BILES: But not in the stridency?

MURDOCH: I'm not interested in the "woman's world" or the assertion of a "female viewpoint." This is often rather an artificial idea and can in fact injure the promotion of equal rights. We want to join the human race, not invent a new separatism. This self-conscious separation leads to rubbish like "black studies" and "women's studies." Let's just have studies.

BILES: Your mentioning the difficulties inherent in working with a black character reminds me of your charming black girl, Pattie, in *The Time of the Angels*.

MURDOCH: I hope she was successful. Of course, a writer attempts to inhabit all sorts of consciousnesses. My point was that as a main explanatory narrating consciousness, especially in a first-person novel, I find I prefer to be male!

BILES: In "Against Dryness," which I see as absolutely fundamental to the reading of your novels, you talk about one of the major problems today being the absence of a commonly accepted background of views, attitudes, the Victorian "eternal verities." And you say that nowadays all that is fragmented and gone. Will you elaborate a little and indicate what you suppose caused these changes? The failure of Progress and Liberal Humanism and such?

MURDOCH: I don't know; there are many causes. The general disappearance of religion from the background of the human mind is one of the most important things that has happened recently. There are all sorts of causes to do with science and the scientific method and the breaking up of capitalism, and the loss of confidence in a single human world, which came after Hitler. A whole complex of causes.

One is tremendously struck, reading the great Victorian novelists, with how much religion *was* taken for granted. In some way, even when people were skeptical, there was a kind of Christian attitude or morality or something, which was absolutely unshaken. I think all these things *are* shaken, now. The disappearance of prayer from people's lives, the disappearance of any sort of practice of religion, is, in any case, a sad phenomenon.

I am not myself a Christian believer, but I was brought up as a Christian and I feel close to Christianity. I believe in religion, in some sort of non-doctrinal sense—in a Buddhist sense. I think people miss this particular steadying influence, this spiritual home and spiritual center.

BILES: I am reminded that, early on in her writing career, Muriel Spark said of her conversion to Roman Catholicism that she denied being specifically a Catholic novelist but that her conversion gave her a framework. This absence of a framework is what you are talking about, a moral framework which religion gives?

MURDOCH: Yes.

BILES: As I understand it, Existentialism tends to be rather against that.

MURDOCH: Yes. Well, I am against Existentialism! I think it is less fashionable than it used to be: as the assertion of a sort of undirected freedom as being a central human attribute, it is surely wrong. It is psychologically unrealistic, and I think it is morally misleading.

BILES: I want to return to a literary subject we have discussed before. You told me the other day that students should be reading Homer, and last year you said Chaucer and Shakespeare and that they should not be studying contemporary writers. As you know, the novel always has been on its last legs and there always has been a new novel. I am curious as to whether you find no genuinely significant novelists today or how you do see the state of the novel.

MURDOCH: The novel is rather in good shape. A tremendous variety of stuff is coming out in England and America. And in France, too. The thing is that the novel can be practically anything. It is so versatile you can do virtually anything you like with the novel. In the last twenty years, novelists have been realizing this versatility and there is a lot of experiment, which I think is good. Quite honestly, I don't read a great many modern novels, so I'm not an expert on the subject.

BILES: Apropos of experimentation, the strong influence of James Joyce, Virginia Woolf, and others, seems to have slackened somewhat, in the novel. Do you take this slackening to be of the influence of Joyce and Woolf, or do you see it as a going on *from* that influence?

MURDOCH: I would think something going on from that. I feel that the sort of direct impetus of those two is, in a sense, over. This is just my instinctive feeling. I'm not an expert. I've not read enough modern stuff; but I think there is a new atmosphere and a new world and that novelists feel really liberated from the past. A long time has passed since that particular revolution was going on. And novelists learn from poets and the theater. There has been much experiment with narrative techniques, which has been of different kinds, not just of Joyce and Woolf types. I think it is a new phase.

BILES: *The Horse's Mouth* and Golding's novels are examples. On this subject, Angus Wilson said to me years ago that, though there is this experimental aspect of the contemporary novel, also there is a kind of leapfrogging which some writers—he mentioned himself and Snow specifically, at that time—do, rather hopping over the modernist people back to the Victorians. Thus, a traditional kind of social novel is still being written.

MURDOCH: Yes, this is probably true. The great models are still there and, in a way, one is closer to Dickens than one is to Joyce. These great models offer story and reflection and social comment and so on; they are *more live* models. Though in a sense you can't go back. One's consciousness is different; I mean our whole narrative technique is something completely different from that of Dickens. But the model still inspires. I personally feel much closer to Dickens and Dostoevsky than I do to James Joyce and Virginia Woolf.

BILES: In tracing to me his literary forebears, Angus has pointed to George Eliot, to Jane Austen, and, of course, to Samuel Richardson, which seems a very accurate assessment. You have referred to Dickens and Dostoevsky already, but the question remains: which writers do you see as your literary forebears? Besides Henry James.

MURDOCH: Well, Homer and Shakespeare most of all! At least, these are the people I want to be influenced by! As far as novelists go, I suppose Jane Austen, Dickens, Dostoevsky, Tolstoi, James. I think probably not the Turgenev aspect of Russian literature. Not French literature at all, apart from Proust. I can't get on with Stendhal particularly; I don't actually like that aspect of the French genius. Proust I find very congenial and feel very happy with. But, it's mainly Dostoevsky, Dickens, Tolstoi.

BILES: Which is all the more interesting, in the light of Dostoevsky's and Tolstoi's having been influenced most strongly by Dickens.

MURDOCH: Yes.

BILES: Do you mind if I ask some rather impertinent questions?

MURDOCH: No.

BILES: You have published some seventeen novels. Generally, how well content are you with that as a body of work?

MURDOCH: Oh, I am not particularly content. I mean I know what's wrong with the stuff. And one tries to improve it, one does one's best to improve.

BILES: In *The Black Prince*, Arnold tells Bradley Pearson that you can't simply sit and wait forever, trying to make one book perfect, you do the best you can and go on.

MURDOCH: That's right.

BILES: But, in overall terms, you feel you've produced a fairly solid body of work, don't you?

MURDOCH: Well, there it is. Yes, I suppose so. But, all the time, one is terribly conscious of one's limitations as an artist. I think I *have* improved: the later stuff is better than the earlier stuff. However, one's ability to improve is still extraordinarily limited. One's always hoping to do better the next time: to create better characters, to break out of certain patterns. One knows one's mind pretty well after writing for some years and there are certain patterns which show up.

BILES: Perhaps this is an absurd question. Nevertheless, the earlier novels tend to be short and the later ones have come to be quite long. Is there any connection to your trying to work out some of the problems, so that more space simply was required?

MURDOCH: Well, in a way, I have become more relaxed and, in a sense, more confident. There is more reflection in the later novels than in the earlier ones. I think it is true of many writers and, indeed, of many other artists, because there is a parallel in painting, for instance: that the young person is anxious and afraid to ramble round. Then, later on, you don't care if you ramble round. You know what you can do and what you can't do, and you're not frightened of destroying your form by blurring it.

BILES: You wouldn't want to say which of your novels you like best and which least, would you?

MURDOCH: I don't really know. It's not the sort of question I answer for myself. I suppose—just in general—that I like the later ones better than the others, but I haven't any favorites.

BILES: I don't know how far you'll wish to pursue this topic, but I do want to raise the question. In my study of the contemporary British novel and my contacts with novelists, I have been surprised at how some of them assert flatly that they didn't consciously put in certain metaphoric or symbolic elements which are clearly present in the books. Graham Greene is the prime example. If you know *Carving a Statue*, you may recall that Greene wrote a somewhat petulant brief preface for the version of the play published after it had been produced at the Haymarket. He said he was "accused" of encumbering the play with symbols, but "I can detect no symbols in this play." Despite his protests, the fact remains that one can choose many—possibly all—of Greene's fictions and show highly detailed and apparently carefully worked out patterns of metaphor—not to say symbol.

In your novels, there occurs a great deal of interlinked and very important detail. For example, in *A Severed Head* Martin Lynch-Gibbon is called a "violent man" throughout and Martin means "warlike"; and the first part of his surname is that of the man who originated the extralegal practice of lynching. Martin is a military historian and you apparently name him after Edward Gibbon; Gibbon had a number of things wrong in his view of history, and seeing things mistakenly is Martin's stock-in-trade. One can go on and on, and the things seem demonstrable in *A Severed Head*. One could make equally obvious statements to Greene about a book of his and he'd say "No." What do *you* say?

MURDOCH: I am sure that people can go too far in playing these games, for sometimes this can actually be misleading, because somebody can see a pattern which *really* isn't there. I think out matters of symbolism and I'm very careful about names and so on; thus, the chances are, if there is something fairly telling in the book, then, that is something I intended. I feel there is a *small* area of conscious activity of this kind. By the way, there's nothing in that Lynch-Gibbon idea!

BILES: And some of it is unconscious?

MURDOCH: This is possible. I should be surprised, in fact, if anybody pointed out anything of this sort in my own work which I wasn't conscious of, but I wouldn't rule out the possibility of there being an area of this kind. It isn't very profitable to look at.

BILES: The reason I bring up conscious symbolism is the enormous amount of planning you do. Examples: one of Martin's secretaries is named Seelhaft, which means "soulful"; now, that's not an accident. I had a student at one time who investigated the names of the wines mentioned specifically in *A Severed Head* and they all are meaningful; unfortunately, I can't recall at the moment the identifications he made.

MURDOCH: They are all roses. The names of old-fashioned roses.

BILES: I am fascinated by the usefulness of this device, but you are quite right that preoccupation with it can be overdone.

MURDOCH: Henry James is a fruitful subject for this kind of exploration. He was very deliberate; one can find an awful lot of things of this sort in James, things which were put there by James, things which are not necessarily obvious. I think this is a part of the charm of the novels—as a area of subliminal effects, if you see what I mean.

BILES: As I said, I am much struck by the utilization of this indirect means of communication, but some novelists deny making use of it. I don't understand whether it is from some distorted concept of modesty or what. Bill Golding is the only novelist, except you, who has ever acknowledged to me so employing metaphor or symbol; in a discussion comparable to this, he once said to me, "Things just present themselves that way," namely, with a literal meaning and some other kind of meaning.

MURDOCH: Yes, that is true. When you are imagining the whole thing, much of this happens absolutely instinctively. Sometimes, one notices later on various things one has done, things which were done instinctively at the time. The total situation is thoroughly set up and you are thoroughly imagining it; then, many of these effects happen automatically.

BILES: Another question—a specific perhaps not directly relevant to our discussion. When I was reading in *The Black Prince* the long disquisition on *Hamlet*, when Bradley has the girl Julian studying the play, it seemed to me that there were some distortions in *his* arguments about *Hamlet*.

MURDOCH: Oh, yes!

BILES: I took it that you did this deliberately to show us the element of unreliability in Bradley himself. The *Hamlet* incident is most stimulating, for some of Bradley's declarations about the play are self-evidently correct and others are mighty peculiar.

MURDOCH: Yes, yes. Part of this is, in a manner of speaking, the writer entertaining himself. Some of Bradley's observations, I think, are quite acute; others are dotty.

BILES: Exactly the impression! Speaking of the unconscious or the instinctive—and for reasons which I cannot give you, except perhaps the quality of destructiveness on his part—the character's name, Bradley, continually calls to mind Bradley Headstone of *Our Mutual Friend*.

MURDOCH: Yes. Oddly enough, here is another of these things. I love *Our Mutual Friend*, and Bradley Headstone is a marvellous character. There is a connection, although obviously the characters are totally different. Bradley is a good name.

BILES: Bradley seems definitely appropriate.

MURDOCH: The surname Pearson has got a private origin. I once a wrote a philosophical piece—I don't type, so I send all my material in longhand to a typist—and in this piece I constantly used the word "Reason," with a capital *R*. Talking about Kant, I believe. The typist misread this on each occasion as "Pearson"! With extremely comical results, as you can imagine!

BILES: The Alan Kennedy I was referring to earlier offers an ingenious interpretation of the name Pearson. He praises this novel, although he confesses to having had no great sympathy for your novels. He finds that you do go dramatic, according to his definition, in *The Black Prince*, and (what you continually wish for) that your characters do get free of authorial manipulation and control. At any rate, Bradley does.

MURDOCH: Yes.

BILES: Then, Kennedy singles out the name Pearson and proclaims it an "obvious anagram" for persona.

MURDOCH: I think he's going too far, there!

BILES: He also talks about how you are the omniscient narrator directing everything; yet, at the same time, Bradley has got completely away. Bradley is both authorial persona and an independent person.

In my opinion, *The Black Prince* is an excellent book. And a difficult one. A genuine masterstroke in those appendices, in which the other people tell their individual screwy versions of what happened. And there is no way in the world to know what really did happen. Which is what you were aiming for.

MURDOCH: Yes, yes. I should say just one thing about this matter of symbolism: that I certainly don't aim at any kind of, as it were, allegorical method of telling the story. That is, I think the symbols must be very carefully controlled and, very often, the symbolism in a novel is invented by the characters themselves, as happens in real life. We're all constantly inventing symbolic images to express our situations.

BILES: I'm afraid I have about run out of time; so, we'll just break off in mid-career. Thank you so much.

Margaret Drabble and the Journey to the Self

JOAN MANHEIMER

The novels of Margaret Drabble tell an old story, the struggle of the individual toward identity, and her version of the tale is extreme. Her heroines suffer confusions about the self that, at times, border on the pathological. The clarity of a Hopkins—"My selfbeing, my consciousness and feeling of myself, that taste of myself, of *I* and *me* above and in all things . . . is more distinctive than the taste of ale or alum, more distinctive than the smell of walnutleaf or camphor, and is incommunicable by any means to another man (as when I was a child I used to ask myself: What must it be to be someone else?)"[1]—eludes these women. Looking inward, they discover the face of another staring calmly back.

Like children, Drabble's women struggle. Her stories emerge from the anarchy in which Freud locates the origins of human consciousness. Awareness of self develops, according to Freud, as the infant first identifies with the human figures surrounding it. The child wakes into confusion and learns, slowly, of the difference between self and other. Insofar as the problem of her heroine (to separate from the other and achieve a clarity about the self) is the problem of the child, Drabble's novels suggest the extent to which our society has succeeded in infantilizing its female members. Drabble's fictions posit the family as the source of this infantilization: they also posit, as the crucial experience threatening destruction of the self, the fluidity with another which the family offers the female. The author recognizes an intensity in relationships between women which invites a real confusion about the boundaries of the self. She attempts to circumvent the dangers of that intensity with ample respect for attention to the storytellers who have preceded her.

The problem Drabble addresses rests within a rich tradition. Contemporary feminist writers remind us of the frequency with which patriarchal interests subsume female energy in fiction. It is tempting to identify those interests with the male and content oneself with lamenting that Dorothea's story is concluded by marriage or that Miriam's story is obliterated by the egotism of Paul Morel and his creator. A close examination of the novel tradition suggests, however, an equal and perhaps more dangerous threat to female autonomy levelled by other women. Women in the novel frequently suffer a division of the world; they often are paired in an unrelenting complementarity which insists that whatever quality one possesses, the other, by necessity, lacks.

Dickens gives this fierce symmetry humorous expression in the naiveté of Georgiana Podsnap:

> "I'll tell you something *I* know about you, my dear," returned Mrs. Lammle in her winning way, "and that is, you are most unnecessarily shy."
> "Ma ain't," said Miss Podsnap. . . .
> "Dearest Georgiana, pardon me if I scarcely see, my love, why your mamma's not being shy, is a reason you should be."
> "Don't you really see that?" asked Miss Podsnap. . . .[2]

Georgiana's question expresses an innocent hope to which volume after volume gives the lie: Aunt Tabitha lusts after matrimony while Lydia is becomingly modest; Mrs. Selwyn exercises a "masculine" tartness while Evelina displays femininity; Lydia is all rashness as Elizabeth Bennet learns maturity; Celia's gushing frivolity emphasizes Dorothea's solemnity. We appreciate Becky Sharp's pragmatic cleverness in contrast to Amelia's dreary goodness, Zenobia's strong beauty alongside Priscilla's frailty, Edna Pontellier's sensuality against Madame Ratignolle's white crinolines. Mrs. Ramsey and Lily Briscoe; Anna and Molly; the list is extensive.

The most extreme form of this symmetry is suggested by the numbers of motherless literary heroines: that the centrality of women in the novel is often conjoined with the absence of a maternal figure suggests motherlessness as a prerequisite for significance.

When the mother is present in the novel, she is, more often than not,

dangerous. Whether possessed by the silliness of a Mrs. Bennet, the indifference of a Mrs. Jellyby, or the hard anger of a Mrs. Quest, the mother frequently threatens her offspring with destruction. When Neumann describes the
Terrible Mother archetype as devouring all that belongs to it, choking its
offspring with nurture, refusing the offspring independence,[3] he invokes a
beast slumbering in the imaginations of generations of novelists. Freedom
from this beast is a prerequisite for life. And it is the absence of a mother
which gives Evelina and Jane Eyre mobility in their societies; that absence
allows Lizzie Hexam her most effective poses; motherlessness, Thackeray
points out, demands the development and employment of Becky Sharp's
powers.

The novel traditionally presents women as molded into a complementarity
so profound that they are dependent on each other for identity. They are
shackled by an inverse double; and in order to achieve autonomy, they must
discover ways to dissolve that bond. This problem Margaret Drabble sets out
to solve in her novels. Her first four novels approach the problem variously,
but she fails to imagine a solution. In her fifth novel, *The Waterfall,* Drabble
successfully assaults the problem; and her success liberates her from the con-
straints of voice, structure, and imagination evident in her earlier work.

In her first two novels, Drabble explores the dimensions of the problem. *A
Summer Bird-Cage* presents a narrator, Sarah, unable to distinguish clearly
between herself and her older sister, Louise. Sarah makes use of all of her
claims on our attention to tell not her own story, but her sister's; and when the
fact of Louise's adultery is first stated publicly, Sarah reacts as if her life were
in question.

Emma, heroine of *The Garrick Year,* suffers from a similar confusion. At the
beginning of the novel, she chooses to follow her actor husband to Hereford at
the expense of a job as a television newscaster. Emma's choice, the traditional
female choice of the other over the self, implies her initial weakness; and her
defense of that choice indicates the extent of that frailty: "This living thing,
whatever it was, kept us still intertwined, so that at each move I knocked
against him, each breath of his swelled against my own ribcage. We were not
separate at this point: we were part of the same thing still."[4] The marriage is
secured by the fact that Emma has no distinct sense of her own boundaries.
Her "at this point" and "still" promise a story about separation; but her story
documents her increasing inability to constitute the self apart from others.
Emma grasps at identity everywhere: from her husband, an old school friend,
even from her children. Reflecting on a friend's suicide, Emma observes: "I

used to be like Julian myself, but now I have two children, and you will not find me at the bottom of any river. I have grown into the earth, I am terrestrial" (218).

A fantasy of the other who completes the self is a common preoccupation of female characters in novels. Here is Ella of *The Golden Notebook,* dwelling on the image of her lover's wife:

> She thinks a great deal about the invisible woman to whom Paul returns (and to whom he will always return) and it is now not out of triumph, but envy. She envies her. She slowly, involuntarily builds up a picture in her mind of a serene, calm, unjealous, unenvious, undemanding woman, full of resources of happiness inside herself, self-sufficient, yet always ready to give happiness when it is asked for. It occurs to Ella (but much later, about three years on) that this is a remarkable image to have developed, since it does not correspond to anything at all Paul says about his wife. So where does the picture come from? Slowly Ella understands that this is what she would like to be herself, this imagined woman is her own shadow, everything she is not.[5]

Ella desires autonomy, but like Emma and Sarah, can only imagine it taking shape outside herself.

In *A Summer Bird-Cage* Drabble most fully explores the nature of the relationship between the self and the other who is its imagined fulfillment. She pictures the bond between Sarah and Louise as competitive, so intense that it borders on the sexual, and finally enigmatic.

The two sisters are trapped in a world that offers little with which to occupy themselves. With a boring job and an absent lover, Sarah practices the passionate worship of her sister. She fumbles uncomfortably when buttoning the front of Louise's wedding dress; she analyzes an invitation from her sister as if the note were from a lover. She approaches Louise throughout the novel with the subtle eroticism of an acolyte nearing the altar.

Drabble allows Sarah emergence from her slavery to Louise at the end of the novel; but freedom as Sarah claims it is rather disappointing: "She had been an expert at using me and impressing me without my noticing it. And this time I had noticed: I noticed and I genuinely, truly resisted. As I went and sat down by Jackie something very very old snapped in me. It snapped as though it had been a piece of old and rotten string, long useless, long without any power to tie, and yet still wrapped round and confining an ancient parcel spilled apart all over the floor."[6] Sarah's moment of freedom exists in a dimension other than that of the story: what snapped in her is "very very old" and lest we miss the implication of the repetition, the parcel is called "ancient." But if the image elevates the bond between the women into timelessness, it also reduces it to the level of the ordinary: it is like rotten string around a parcel. This conjunction suggests the difficulty of framing an appropriate response to something which invites both veneration and casualness. The bond appears as a riddle that neither Sarah nor, at this point, her creator can solve.

Although *A Summer Bird-Cage* and *The Garrick Year* provide suggestive definitions of the problem, neither imagines a satisfactory resolution. The final elaboration of the image quoted—the "parcel spilled all over the floor"—suggests that for all Sarah's declaration of emancipation, she still is confused about the relationship between inner and outer reality. What begins as a description of an interior—"snapped in me"—concludes as an exterior—"all over the floor." The shapelessness suggested by this final image is emblematic of the difficulty Sarah suffers from. Even at the end she cannot name herself without vagueness, cannot determine the shape of her life. Instead, she awaits her lover's return to give herself definable form: "I am waiting to take up my life again, not indeed where I left off, for I shall only find where it is when I try. But somewhere, and somewhere further on, moreover" (219). Similarly, Emma fails to discover passage out of her confusion.

The Garrick Year records the process by which female identity often is destroyed. The sphere in which Emma is visible shrinks as the novel progresses. Instead of being engaged in television broadcasting—and therefore being everywhere visible—she spends her energies in a clandestine love affair, being everywhere hidden. Unable to consummate the affair, choosing motherhood over sexuality, Emma, at the end, is trapped in absolute privacy, neither seeing herself clearly nor allowing herself to be seen by others:

> . . . but as I passed, walking slowly, supported by David, I looked more closely and I saw curled up and clutching at the sheep's belly a real snake. I did not say anything to David: I did not want to admit that I had seen it, but I did see it. I can see it still. It is the only wild snake that I have ever seen. In my book on Herefordshire it says that that part of the country is notorious for its snakes. But "Oh well, so what," is all that one can say, the Garden of Eden was crawling with them, too, and David and I managed to lie amongst them for one whole pleasant afternoon. One just has to keep on and to pretend, for the sake of the children, not to notice. Otherwise one might just as well stay at home.
>
> (220)

At the end of this rather weak novel, Drabble indicts her heroine for the self-indulgence in her confusion: the image and therefore Emma's pat dismissal of it are disturbing. What Emma sees suggests a perverse and consuming motherhood, precisely what she herself has suffered throughout the novel. Her failure to think seriously about the implications of that image reflects her failure to take seriously the implications of her own life: she has already announced that she is going to repeat the sacrifice of her own interests, represented by the year at Hereford, in a trip to the East Indies. When Emma airily dispenses with the threatening overtones of her vision and justifies the dismissal with that lame saw "for the sake of the children," Drabble implies that the child Emma is protecting is Emma herself.

This snake image, so powerful and so jarring in the mild novel which precedes it, suggests Drabble's frustration at her failure to imagine autonomy for her heroines. If such is indeed the case, it is understandable that she takes an entirely different tack in her next novel. In *Thank You All Very Much* (in England, *The Millstone*), Drabble seeks to avoid the problem by presenting at the outset an autonomous woman who suffers no confusion about her identity.

Various forms of the double represent no threat to Rosamund Stacey's integrity. When Rosamund encounters herself fictionalized in a friend's novel, she is easily able to distinguish herself from her image: "It was nothing more nor less than my life story, with a few minor alterations here and there, and a few interesting false assumptions amongst the alterations. . . . Farfetched as the theory seemed with regard to me who did not know what the word jealousy meant, and indeed suffered from its opposite, if it has one, it certainly explained a possible line of conduct: it amused me to think of Lydia sitting there racking her brains trying to work out why I was having the child, and why I hadn't got rid of it."[7] Likewise, she suffers no confusion of identity with Octavia. She visits her child in the hospital, and her surprise is a measure of the distinction between them: "She had forgiven me for our day of separation, I could see, and such generosity I found amazing, for I am not generous. Fair, but not generous" (113). Unlike Drabble's earlier heroines, Rosamund does not look outside herself for completion; and this clarity of mind is a source both of her strength and weakness.

In *Thank You All Very Much,* Drabble creates a heroine to challenge standard conceptions of female identity. Trying to work, and thinking about her pregnancy, Rosamund dismisses traditional lore about women: "Love is of man's life a thing apart, 'tis woman's whole existence, as Byron mistakenly remarked" (10). Against the background of a dreary catalogue of female characters whose happiness depends on their fortuitous union with the proper man, Rosamund offers a refreshing image of a woman successful and satisfied without one. The presentation of a woman who is not, nor is destined to be, half of some whole represents a significant achievement for a writer who previously had imagined only women with such fluid boundaries that they threatened to lose themselves entirely in union with another.

Still, this achievement signifies not a solution to the problem Drabble addresses, but an evasion of it. The cost of Rosamund's integrity is such that we must finally balk at the expense. Rosamund is a disappointingly asexual creation. Her pregnancy is the result of her having slept with one man once in her life; she herself acknowledges "my suspicion, my fear, my apprehensive terror of the very idea of sex" (17). While we may admire the imaginative energy and courage requisite to create a heroine so blatantly athwart the spirit of our times, we must regret the limitations such a creation implies. When Rosamund treats her fear of sex as a clever literary joke—"I had the additional disadvantage of being unable to approve my own conduct; being a child of the age, I knew how wrong and how misguided it was. I walked around with a scarlet letter embroidered upon my bosom, visible enough in the end, but the A stood for Abstinence, not for Adultery" (18)—her irony protects her from a question that vitally concerns her.

Drabbble suggests that Rosamund continues her life of abstinence not only out of fear, but as a result of motherhood. Because she loves Octavia, Rosamund rejects the possibility of loving Octavia's father: "Love had isolated me more securely than fear, habit or indifference. There was one thing in the world that I knew about, and that one thing was Octavia. I had lost the taste for half-knowledge. George, I could see, knew nothing with such certainty" (143). If the integrity of the self depends on a world in which such choices are not only necessary but viewed as natural,[8] then we can hardly be expected to take simple delight in integrity. Some of us might even prefer Sarah's weakness to Rosamund's cold strength.

Drabble recognizes part of the problem as she indicates her heroine's lack of warmth and spontaneity. While Rosamund may have learned the truth of the heart in relation to Octavia, she is deficient in its lore elsewhere in her life: she persists in analyzing human relationships as if they were amenable to mathematical formulae. Having realized her terror with sex, she "experiments" until she devises "an excellent system, which combined, I considered, fairness to others, with the maximum possible benefit to myself" (18). Rosamund, discussing the fact that her pregnancy taught her about the nature of human bonds, continues to sound like a market analyst: "However, it did occur to me one day, quite early on, that although I recognized the principle of payment, I had some basic deficiency when it came to taking appropriate goods in exchange" (59). She even characterizes her deep love for Octavia as "A bad investment, I knew, this affection, and one that would leave me in the dark and the cold in years to come; but then what warmer passion ever lasted longer than six months?" (143).

It is possible to regard the term "investment" as unexceptional usage, but by this point the persistency with which Rosamund returns to the language of finance to convey the workings of her heart lends her discourse a metallic ring. Rosamund's refusal to entertain any confusion of identity with any other leaves her more calculating than intuitive, more intelligent than emotional. She is deficient, in fact, in all the traditional female graces. An alternativity more profound than the choice of sexuality or motherhood is at work in this novel: the alternativity of the traditionally defined male and female worlds.

At this stage in her career, Drabble's novels describe a dilemma in which intimacy is the cost of identity. In her next novel, she begins to conceive a way out of this dilemma as she returns to her original preoccupation with a woman struggling against a loss of self. Throughout *Jerusalem the Golden*, Mrs. Maugham looms as her daughter Clara's nightmare; like Cronus, she threatens her offspring's autonomy. When Clara hears of her mother's illness, she conceives of herself trapped in an absolute complementarity with the older woman: "let them tell me no more that we are free, we cannot draw a breath without guilt, for my freedom she dies."[9]

The trap is rigid, but Drabble suggests that it can be sprung by further experiences with a double. Clara's response to her reflection in wet floor tile is one of the first indications of her potential independence from a mother who saw her as plain:

> She had been truly moved by herself, by her own watery image, by her grotesquely elongated legs, her tapering waist, and above all by the undersides of her breasts, never before seen. She stood there and stared at herself, seeing herself from that unexpected angle, as though she were another person, as though she were a dim white and blue statue on a tall pillar, a wet statue, a statue in water, a Venus rising from the sea, with veined white marble globes for breasts. She had never expected to be beautiful, and she was startled to see how nearly she approached a kind of beauty.
>
> (57)

By means of repetition and the careful elaboration of the image, Drabble presents this encounter with a double as a process by which Clara begins to learn to name herself. Another double, embraced by Clara when she is a bit older, continues the process and maintains Drabble's suggestion that repeated loss of identity is the means toward a salvation of sorts.

Clelia Denham and her family offer Clara even more confusion of identity than did her mother: the three younger Denhams look alike (and Clara chooses to resemble them, cutting her hair in imitation of Clelia's), and are wrapped in an intensity of love bordering on incest. Their tenacity in clinging to one another suggests the fragility of each and the danger of separation: the only child to break completely with the family goes mad. Clara, in self-deprecating adulation of the family, enters this new symbiosis (she has an affair with Gabriel, Clelia's married brother), and shrugs off the old.

As Clara visits her mother in her final illness, she is awakened by Gabriel from a dream of her own death; it is Gabriel who facilitates Clara's final recognition that she is separate from her mother: "Her mother was dying, but she herself would survive, because she did not have it in her to die. Even the mercy and kindness of destiny she would survive; they would not get her that way, they would not get her at all" (236–237). But Drabble suggests that this separateness is purchased at serious cost; Clara's final declaration of independence resounds with disquieting coldness. Clara has learned something of herself, but not enough. Yet the solution imagined in this novel was obviously a suggestive one, for it appears again, elaborated, in Drabble's pivotal novel, *The Waterfall*.

In *The Waterfall* Drabble finally is able to imagine the potential fruitfulness of a confusion of identity. She creates a heroine who, through her experience of various doubles, discovers the boundaries of the self and achieves a meaningful independence of her varied reflections. *The WaterFall* is a contemporary feminist version of the quest in which the trial of distinguishing between the true and the false Una belongs not to the Redcrosse Knight but to Una herself; and the repeated submergence of the self in the dangerous fluidity of doubleness finally offers the self the safety of determinant identity.

At the beginning of the novel, Jane Gray, enfeebled by a barrage of false doubles, toys listlessly with her life. Born into a family which persists in seeing her as respectable, Jane hides from them with evasion and accepts the burden of a belief in the Medusa-like powers of her own reality: "I felt all the time afraid that any word of mine, any movement, my mere existence, might shatter them all into fragments."[10] Literally conceived as part of a pair (Jane's mother and her cousin Lucy's mother plan their concurrent pregnancies), Jane

names her cousin "my sister, my fate, my example" (114) and wonders if Lucy
is the repository of the control that she, Jane, so obviously lacks: "Sometimes I
think that I married because Lucy married. I got a house because Lucy had a
house. I had a baby because Lucy had a baby. One should not underestimate
the force of example" (129). Malcolm, her husband, offers other falsifying
images: he persists in perceiving his own guilt as accusations from her, his
own latent homosexuality as her frigidity.

These false doubles have crippled Jane until she is a woman afraid to venture down the block, as if she might evaporate outside her house. We see her
initially, blanketed in the moist blue warmth of her room, giving birth,
passively enveloped by the womblike atmosphere. She is almost incapable of
action: "Once married, I gave up; or rather, I began to see activity as evasion,
and inactivity as an obligation" (99). What rescues Jane from the absolute
privacy of the Wonderland inversion of meaning is, ostensibly, an affair with
her cousin's husband, James. What Drabble offers Jane, however, is not
simple romantic escapism, but the experience, via James, of seeing and eventually being able to constitute a true image of herself.

Drabble carefully surrounds her real story, the constitution of the self, with
a story direct from the annals of female fantasy, rescue by the miraculous in-
tervention of a man, in order to testify to the seductive hollowness of the
fantasy without the underpinnings of clarity about the self and, inversely, the
sterility of such clarity without the fantastic capacity to love. The gift of a
handsome prince is the enlightenment of an honest mirror:

> When James looked at me, he saw me, myself. This is no fancy, no con-
> ceit. He redeemed me by knowing me, he corrupted me by sharing my
> knowledge. . . . I thought I could negate myself and wipe myself out.
> But when James looked at me it was my true self he saw: alive, speaking,
> demanding him, despite all my efforts. . . . I had lived in denial for so
> long, had made such virtue of necessity, had built so weighty a case for
> my own actions, that I could hardly bear to see it all destroyed at a touch
> of his hand. And yet I could not resist him: I knew that I could not resist
> recognition.
>
> (51–52)

The experience of James's mirror helps Jane survive repeated ambushes by
false images: images of her cousin, images from the literary tradition, from
her own writings. Hers is the story of a kaleidoscopic reshaping of the self
through the agency of other as mirror; the repetitive nature of her experience
testifies to Drabble's sense of the difficulty of the endeavor.

Even after the beginnings of the affair with James, Lucy poses a threat to Jane not unlike that which Louise represented for Sarah; but Jane emerges from the influence of example. It is typical of Drabble's delight in ironies that when Jane does, in fact, become Lucy in the eyes of the world, she preserves her identity inviolate. When James and Jane on holiday have an atuomobile accident in which James is seriously injured, Jane is assumed to be his wife and, dazed, does not correct the mistake. In the public world she becomes her cousin; and, in a scene reminiscent of Shakespearean comedy, Lucy, hearing of the accident, arrives precipitously and adopts Jane's identity. But Jane insists on her distinctness from Lucy even at the moment when Lucy is in possesion of her name, her address, and her bed. Having previously displayed confusion about where Lucy stops and Jane begins, Jane has by this time earned immunity from the world's confusion.

Doubled by the expectations of her family, by a cousin who partially mirrors her fate, Jane is also doubled by the literary tradition. Herself a poet, she repeatedly measures her story against earlier fictions. By means of this repetition, Drabble both illuminates certain features of the tradition and suggests a critical perspective on the advances enjoyed by women over the last century.

Recognizing the power of the literary tradition in shaping female identity, Jane evokes the works of major nineteenth-century female novelists as potential paradigms for her own story. She recalls Jane Austen only to dismiss "her desperate wit" (57). Austen represents the same social values Jane deplores in her family; and Austen evidences a disregard for passion which Jane bitingly questions: "What can it have been like, in bed with Mr. Knightley?" (58). Jane next considers the world as conceived by Charlotte Brontë and, similarly, finds it lacking: "or I could have maimed James so badly, in this narrative, that I would have been allowed to have him, as Jane Eyre had her blinded Rochester. But I hadn't the heart to do it. I loved him too much, and anyway it wouldn't have been the truth because the truth is that he recovered" (231). The literary tradition is full of restrictions which Jane refuses. Even in Jane's consideration of Eliot's Maggie Tulliver, a literary predecessor more suggestive than those offered by Brontë or Austen, she insists that her mold be more generous. Both Jane and Maggie have cousins named Lucy; both fall in love and go off with their cousins' men; the fates of both involve water (in Maggie's case literally, in Jane's metaphorically); but here the parallelism stops. What Maggie renounces, Jane enjoys. Where Maggie dies by water, water imagery surrounds Jane's giving birth to her daughter, her sexual pleasure, and her creation of an active self. By means of the numerous parallels between the two books, Drabble underscores the contrast in their resolutions. The unconventional structure of her novel implies that Jane's life is different, not just in scope but in kind, from that of her literary ancestors. The old fictional forms do not fit her.

To mistake these changes, however, for evidence of female emancipation, is to invite the shock that while the old forms may be irrelevant some of the old realities are not. That Jane is successful in wresting an identity from an environment of falsifying mirrors is true, but her success is limited. Although Jane enjoys what her literary predecessors were forced to renounce, Drabble presents her gain as tinged with loss. Jane concludes her story not with the magnificent title image but with remarks on her narrow escape from a pulmonary embolism: "The price that modern woman must pay for love. In the past, in old novels, the price of love was death, a price which virtuous women paid in childbirth, and the wicked, like Nana, with the pox. Nowadays it is paid in thrombosis or neuroses: one can take one's pick. I stopped taking those pills, as James lay there unconscious and motionless, but one does not escape decision so easily. I am glad of this. I am glad I cannot swallow pills with immunity. I prefer to suffer, I think" (238–239).

The choice of vulnerability may be moving and the hesitant afterthought appealing; nevertheless, the implications of this conclusion are disturbing. Even when contemporary heroines survive their love, they suffer the slow torture of the mind. In her implied comparison between pox and neurosis, Drabble suggests a loss of physical substantiality in the contemporary world. The suggestion of loss is borne out by the use she makes of *The Mill on the Floss* as a model for her novel: the literal river of Eliot's book becomes a metaphor in Drabble's treatment of similar themes: "In this age, what is to be done? We drown in the first chapter. I worry about the sexual doom of womanhood, its sad inheritance" (153–154). The greater independence of contemporary women merely knells a quicker doom. Women must pay for their pleasure; neither love nor autonomy comes cheap. They often are mutually exclusive: James, coming out of the hospital, is discomfitted by Jane's energy, so she tones it down for him. Drabble's references to the traditional novel suggest that if it has robbed women of autonomy, the instinct about limitation which underlay that theft was and still is, to some extent, wise.

Drabble recognizes that such scarcity visits painful limitations on human lives; she also understands that the proper endurance of its devastation is potentially liberating. In this novel, for the first time, she creates a woman who proceeds from shapelessness to identity without the emotional sacrifice of a Rosamund or a Clara. She discovers in *The Waterfall* a passage to selfhood through the act of repeatedly distinguishing the self from the others who threaten to absorb it.

The potential for self-definition available in the experience of the double is most fully exemplified by the novel's narrative structure. *The Waterfall* consists of an oscillation between two strands of narration: Jane's third-person fiction about her affair and her first-person criticism of her own creation. The story of Jane as "she" begins the novel; the impulse to narrative, like the initial speech of the child ("Jane wants candy. . . . Jane goes for a ride"), is first conceived as an objectification of the self.[11] This objectification allows certain satisfactions: it permits Jane, for example, to exclude her husband and James's wife from her story. But Jane as "I" interrupts the story of Jane as "she" to correct such distortions: "It won't, of course, do: as an account, I mean, of what took place. I tried, I tried for so long to reconcile, to find a style that would express it, to find a system that would excuse me, to construct a new meaning, having kicked the old one out, but I couldn't do it, so here I am, resorting to that old broken medium" (46). The difficult questions raised by the existence of Lucy and Malcolm she confronts in her own person.

The novel's narrative structure implies that the development of identity (story) is a function of a dialectic between the self as object and the self as subject. It also implies that the self as subject arises from the felt necessity to distinguish the self from the other. The counterpoint of the two voices in *The Waterfall* records Jane's increasing maturity as she explicitly claims more and more of her own experience. Jane's first-person narration, which begins with a statement of incapacity, becomes the dominant voice as the novel progresses; and it is the voice of the "I" which concludes the narrative.

With the conclusion of *The Waterfall,* Drabble achieved a cathartic response to the question that has haunted her since the beginning of her career as a novelist. She finally was able to discover in the threats to female identity, which she so acutely perceived and understood, the potential for the construction as well as for the destruction of the self. The discovery was a significantly freeing one for the novelist, endowing her last three novels with a richness and breadth missing in her earlier work.

In a more recent novel, *The Realms of Gold,* Drabble revels in this freedom to the extent that she betrays her insight about the significance of limitations on female identity. The result is a delightful portrait of a powerful woman which finally fails to convince.

Like Drabble's other novels, *The Realms of Gold* makes ample use of the double. The novel is structured as an oscillation between the stories of cousins who, ignorant of each other's existence for much of the book, nonetheless suggest each other throughout: Frances Wingate and her cousin Janet, unknowingly walking down the same street, are inverse reflections of one another. Frances is divorced, mobile, a successful archaeologist, a powerfully energetic woman; Janet is trapped in a dully vicious marriage, unable to even take an evening course, wispy, and passive. The device is a potentially rich one, capable of exploring the distinction between inherited and chosen relationship, capable of illuminating the perverse economy of a world which doles out riches so unjustly, capable of asking serious questions about how women achieve certain shapes to their lives.

But where Drabble uses the double in her other novels to ask such questions, here the double is often merely an occasion for the demonstration of authorial cleverness. She glories in the full use of her power, reeling off coincidences and defying the reader to deny their legitimacy. She teases her reader with narrative intrusions which are, too often, manipulative, self-congratulatory, and condescending. Sometimes her narrative stance is defensive: "So there you are. Invent a more suitable ending if you can."[12] At times, she veers toward self-conscious cuteness: "As for Sir Frank Ollerenshaw and Harold Barnard, who knows what they were thinking? Omniscience has its limits" (336). But, one wonders, on what basis? Once you assume a narrative voice that delights in knowledge barred from your characters, once you create endless parallels between disparate characters to foreshadow the genuine community which the novel's conclusion creates, why limit your voice at all unless you mean those limitations to have some significance, to cast, perhaps, a critical glance at the absence of limitations in the life of your heroine.

Drabble has no such intention. She fails to stint on Frances Wingate at all. Frances has everything: a glamorous career, four spunky, obligingly independent and unobtrusive children, the love of a good man: even her tumor is benign. Such a heroine is a welcome addition to a canon which slays or mutilates so many powerful women; but she is so fortunate that it is hard to believe in her. When Frances and her lover survey the living room wrecked by his wife, reality is given short shrift: "There was earth all over the carpet, as well as wine and blood and glass. . . . They stood there in the wrecked room, holding hands, contemplating the debris of their own confusions. They were both strong and healthy people, able to take a lot more of the same kind of thing. One blow, one row, was nothing. They would tidy up and begin again" (72-73). Drabble quickly shifts our attention from physical to emotional reality. The transition is a neat one, but it reinforces the insubstantiality which plagues Francs throughout the book. It is a fancy bit of housecleaning: emotional stability disposes of carpet stains. Drabble pays dearly for her indulgence of Frances. This novel is sure to delight the dreamer, but as Drabble recognized elsewhere, to realize dreams requires effort.

If *The Realms of Gold* describes a world difficult to credit, it nonetheless suggests the exuberance with which Drabble has cut her Gordian knot; and it reveals freedoms similar to those which characterize its more successful predecessor, *The Needle's Eye*. In many ways Drabble's strongest novel, *The Needle's Eye* suggests the extent of Drabble's achievement in *The Waterfall*: it demonstrates considerable development in her narrative voice, in her skill with structure and characterizaton, and in her imaginative capacities.

In *The Needle's Eye* Drabble first consistently evidences generosity of interest in more than one character's consciousness. Her earlier novels suffer the restrictions of a more limited point of view: we have access to the interior of the heroine but only exterior portraits of everyone else. Drabble's heroine in *A Summer Bird-Cage* might be speaking for her creator: "The thing is I couldn't start to feel them in my terms because I couldn't really feel them in theirs, and one needs the double background. Perhaps it can be learned by long apprenticeship and dedicated exploration: I hope so" (137).

The Needle's Eye reveals the fruits of "the long apprenticeship." In it, Drabble explores the recesses of an interesting variety of figures and modulates between interior and exterior perspective with a flexibility reminiscent of George Eliot: "He stood there and waited. He was good at that. There was no hurry. There was plenty of time. He always had time. He was a punctual and polite person, and that was why he was standing there, buying a gift for his hostess. Politeness was an emotion—could one call it an emotion, he wondered? That was how he regarded it, certainly—an emotion that he both feared and understood."[13]

The confidence implicit in the modulations of Drabble's voice is also suggested by the fact that in *The Needle's Eye* she completely abandons the fictions of the authorless story. In her previous novels, excepting *Jerusalem the Golden*, Drabble ostensibly relinquishes narrative responsibility to her heroine. In *The Needle's Eye* she speaks in her own voice. Even when she reveals the thought of her characters she does so in her own language. In a manner again reminiscent of Eliot, Drabble renders the thinking process of her characters fully coherent, suggesting their substantiality at the same time that she subtly acknowledges her own presence:

> She could no longer imagine herself so rash and foolish—sitting there, at
> the very table, with her dog-eared little cheque book full of meagrely-
> pared electricity payments, writing out with a shilling biro, Pay
> Akisoferi Nyoka twenty thousand pounds—her hand trembling, her
> heart beating loudly in her frightened chest, exhilarated beyond bearing
> by the extremity, the irrevocability of the act, by its irreversible
> determining quality, by its implications, by its very size. (In much the
> same spirit she had married Christopher, trembling, afraid, mad and
> blinkered by a suicidal commitment, haunted by an image that had to be
> made flesh.)
>
> (77)

The voice is authoritative: Drabble, fully responsive to the manner of her
heroine's inner life.

The development in Drabble's narrative skills is accompanied by a significant enlargement in her subject matter. For the first time she creates a male
character who has an existence independent of her heroine's concerns. Where
her earlier novels are insular, largely bounded by one family, one home, this
novel concentrates on the stories of two families and offers brief, penetrating
glances into the workings of several others. Having resolved the problem of
constructing identity, the work of privacy, Drabble is now free to encroach on
the public realm. The professions featured in her previous novels—writing,
acting—provided rich metaphorical indices of private life; the profession at
the center of this novel, the law, offers a metaphor for the relentless, rigid
pressure the social world visits on the life of the individual.

The Needle's Eye enjoys an intricate structure to accommodate the enlarged
scope of its author's concerns. Replacing the sometimes monotone chronology
of an individual life which characterized her earlier plots is a complex interweaving of various stories, unified as much by the verbal echoes (often
allusions to Biblical or legal language) which run through them as by the
passage of time.

The novel's heroine is yet another index of Drabble's maturity. Rose Vassi-
liou is easily the most radical of Drabble's creations. A somewhat wispy
woman, timid, shabby, she has the unconventional creativity of a visionary.
Where Drabble's other heroines make marriages or books, Rose constructs a
world which challenges the existing social order. She persists in loving and
marrying Christopher in opposition to her father and at the expense of a
sizeable portion of her inheritance; she persists in giving away most of her

money and in living quite modestly in opposition to just about everyone's notion of common sense and human nature. Although she loves Simon and is beloved by him and although they live in a society not fazed by divorce, neither is able seriously to contemplate predicating their happiness on the abandonment of his wife and her ex-husband. Finally, her private morality, despite her passionate need for his understanding and approbation, prevents Rose from explaining to Simon her decision to take Christopher back. A woman less clear would never recognize that "She could not acquire his esteem without begging for it, and thereby forfeiting a right to it" (363). A woman less powerfully centered within herself would never have possessed, much less acted on, the knowledge that Christopher had a moral right to the children when she was fortified by a legal ruling which deprived him of that right. Rose honors her own values, substituting the garbage in the gutter for the goddess on the pedestal. She takes friends on walks to an empty lot and her enthusiasm transforms a discarded armchair and an assortment of chickens into a charming scene. In contrast to the marble beasts on the gateposts of her family's estate, she celebrates a chipped plaster lion which, like herself, has "weathered into identity" (369).

The strength of Rose's vision contrasts sharply with the anemic wafflings of her early predecessors; it is fitting that she should enjoy the relationship which signifies the extent of Drabble's development as a writer. Having discovered the potential for growth in female relationships, Drabble realizes that potential in *The Needle's Eye*. Describing a friendship that dates back to girlhood, she writes:

> Life has been so much better, and so much worse, than they had expected: what they had not expected was that they were both happy people, incapable of resisting, incapable of failing to discover the gleams of joy. It was no wonder that Christopher had cited infidelity with Emily in his divorce case, and all the more bitterly because there was no sexual element to create offense. How could one not resent the natural flowing of a resilient, indestructible personal joy? Such things must not be spoken of, they must not be admitted. But why are we alive, at all?
>
> (223)

Such a question represents a radical departure form the novel's standard perspectives on women. Against the context of a tradition rarely able to credit female relationships with even the small benefice of harmlessness, Drabble's celebration of such relatedness is remarkable; for it alone, she deserves our respect.

NOTES

1. Quoted by J. Hillis Miller, "The Creation of the Self in Gerard Manley Hopkins," in *The Practice of Criticism,* ed. Sheldon P. Zitner, James D. Kissane, M. M. Liberman (Chicago: Scott, Foreman, 1966), 146.

2. Charles Dickens, *Our Mutual Friend* (1865; rpt. London: Oxford Univ. Press, 1952), 138–139.

3. Erich Newmann, *The Great Mother: An Analysis of the Archetype,* trans. Ralph Manheim (New York: Pantheon, 1955), 152.

4. *The Garrick Year* (New York: Belmont Books, 1971), 23–24.

5. Doris Lessing, *The Golden Notebook* (New York: Simon and Schuster, 1962), 179.

6. *A Summer Bird-Cage* (New York: Belmont Books, 1971), 203.

7. *Thank You All Very Much* (New York: New American Library, 1969), 78–79.

8. A similar choice is suggested in *The Garrick Year.* Drabble's writing generally suffers from her limited interest in female sexuality.

9. *Jerusalem the Golden* (New York: Belmont Books, 1971), 220.

10. *The Waterfall* (Middlesex, England: Penguin, 1971), 50–51.

11. See Jacques Lacan, "The Mirror-phase as Formation of the Function of the I," trans. Jean Roussel, *New Left Review,* 51 (Sept./Oct. 1968), 72–73.

12. *The Realms of Gold* (New York: Knopf, 1975), 351.

13. *The Needle's Eye* (New York: Knopf, 1972), 3.

Selected Bibliography

CATHERINE SMITH and JACK I. BILES

G iven the limited space available, practicality dictated that this bibliography be strictly selected—at least in most cases. We naturally devoted more of our space to novelists with substantial critical bibliographies (e.g., Conrad, Woolf, Golding) than to novelists who have had little notice (e.g., Sackville-West, Bedford, Manning). And we have striven to achieve a measure of proportion.

Our aim was not to provide a bibliography sufficient for the expert, but rather to offer some aids to the general reader, a useful beginning to the researcher or the critic, and to the interested reader desirous of suggestions as to further reading.

Certain arbitrary limitations controlled our decisions to include or exclude given titles. We excluded theses and dissertations, and published bibliographies for individual writers. We included (in the individual listings) biography and autobiography, collections of essays about a given author and/or special numbers of literary journals, and books established as standard works, as well as newer works of clear merit.

The bibliography consists, first, of a General Section containing works pertinent in most cases to more than one of the novelists treated in *British Novelists since 1900*. The names in brackets following the entries in this section identify those novelists considered in the work in question who also are studied in the present work.

The second part of the bibliography contains listings of criticism and commentary related to each individual novelist.

GENERAL

Adams, Robert Martin. *After Joyce: Studies in Fiction after Ulysses*. Oxford: Oxford Univ. Press, 1977. [Burgess, Woolf]

Alcorn, John. *The Nature Novel from Hardy to Lawrence*. New York: Columbia Univ. Press, 1977. [Wells]

Aldiss, Brian. *Billion Year Spree*. New York: Schocken Books, 1973. [Wells]

Andreach, Robert J. *The Slain and Resurrected God: Conrad, Ford, and the Christian Myth*. New York: New York Univ. Press, 1970. [Conrad, Ford]

Axthelm, Peter M. *The Modern Confessional Novel*. New Haven: Yale Univ. Press, 1967. [Golding]

Batchelor, John. *The Edwardian Novelists*. New York: St. Martin's Press, 1982. [Conrad, Ford, Sackville-West, Wells, Wilson, Woolf]

Benedikz, B. S., ed. *On the Novel: A Present for Walter Allen on His 60th Birthday from His Friends and Colleagues*. London: Dent, 1971. [Golding, Woolf]

Bergonzi, Bernard. *The Situation of the Novel*. London: Macmillan, 1970. [Burgess, Conrad, Drabble, Ford, Golding, Greene, Murdoch, Spark, Wells, Wilson, Woolf]

Berthoff, Warner. *Fictions and Events: Essays in Criticism and Literary History*. New York: Dutton, 1971. [Murdoch, Spark]

Blodgett, Harriet. "Enduring Ties: Daughters and Mothers in Contemporary English Fiction by Women." *South Atlantic Quarterly*, 80 (Autumn 1981), 441–453. [Drabble, Rhys, Woolf]

Boyd, Michael. *The Reflexive Novel: Fiction As Critique*. Lewisburg, Pa.: Bucknell Univ. Press, 1983. [Conrad, Woolf]

Bradbury, Malcolm. *Possibilities: Essays on the State of the Novel*. London: Oxford Univ. Press, 1973. [Murdoch, Spark, Wilson]

Bradbury, Malcolm, and David Palmer, eds. *The Contemporary English Novel*. London: Arnold, 1979. [Burgess, Drabble, Murdoch, Spark, Wilson]

Bruffee, Kenneth A. *Elegiac Romance: Cultural Change and Loss of the Hero in Modern Fiction*. Ithaca, N.Y.: Cornell Univ. Press, 1983. [Conrad, Ford]

Buckley, Jerome Hamilton. *Season of Youth: The Bildungsroman from Dickens to Golding*. Cambridge, Mass.: Harvard Univ. Press, 1974. [Golding, Wells, Woolf]

Burgess, Anthony. *The Novel Now: A Guide to Contemporary Fiction*. New York: Norton, 1967. [Burgess, Compton-Burnett, Golding, Greene, Manning, Murdoch, Spark, Wells, Wilson, Woolf]

Chatman, Seymour, ed. *Literary Style: A Symposium*. London: Oxford Univ. Press, 1971. [Golding]

Clareson, Thomas, ed. *Many Futures, Many Worlds: Theme and Form in Science Fiction*. Kent, Ohio: Kent State Univ. Press, 1977. [Burgess, Wells]

Crawford, Fred D. *Mixing Memory and Desire: The Waste Land and British Novels*. University Park: Pennsylvania State Univ. Press, 1982. [Burgess, Ford, Greene, Murdoch]

Crosland, Margaret. *Beyond the Lighthouse: English Women Novelists in the Twentieth Century*. London: Constable, 1981. [Compton-Burnett, Drabble, Ford, Greene, Manning, Murdoch, Rhys, Sackville-West, Spark, Wells, Woolf]

Daleski, H. M. *The Divided Heroine: A Recurrent Pattern in Six English Novels*. New York: Holmes and Meier, 1984. [Greene, Woolf]

Delbanco, Nicholas. *Group Portrait: Joseph Conrad, Stephen Crane, Ford Madox Ford, Henry James, and H. G. Wells*. New York: Morrow, 1982. [Conrad, Ford, Wells]

Dockerty, Thomas. *Reading (Absent) Character: Towards a Theory of Characterization in Fiction*. Oxford: Clarendon Press, 1983. [Compton-Burnett, Greene, Woolf]

Donovan, Josephine, ed. *Feminist Literary Criticism: Explorations in Theory*. Lexington: Univ. Press of Kentucky, 1976. [Woolf]

Eagleton, Terry. *Exiles and Émigrés: Studies in Modern Literature*. New York: Schocken, 1970. [Conrad, Greene]

Enright, D[ennis] J. *Man Is an Onion: Reviews and Essays*. London: Chatto and Windus, 1972. [Burgess, Greene, Spark]

Fleishman, Avrom. *The English Historical Novel: Walter Scott to Virginia Woolf*. Baltimore: Johns Hopkins Univ. Press, 1971. [Conrad, Woolf]

Fone, Byrne R. S. "Sons and Lovers: Three English Portraits." In *The Gay Academic*, ed. Louie Crew, 200–215. Palm Springs: ETC Publications, 1978. [Sackville-West, Woolf]

Ford, Ford Madox. *Portraits From Life: Memoirs and Criticism*. 1937; rpt. Boston: Houghton Mifflin, 1980. [Conrad, Wells]

Fraser, G. S. *The Modern Writer and His World: Continuity and Innovation in Twentiety-Century English Literature*. Rev. ed. New York: Praeger, 1965. [Compton-Burnett, Conrad, Greene, Wells, Wilson, Woolf]

Friedman, Alan Warren, ed. *Forms of Modern British Fiction*. Austin: Univ. of Texas Press, 1975. [Murdoch, Woolf]

Friedman, Melvin J. *The Vision Obscured: Perceptions of Some Twentieth-Century Catholic Novelists*. New York: Fordham Univ. Press, 1970. [Greene, Spark]

————, and John B. Vickery, eds. *The Shaken Realist: Essays in Modern Literature in Honor of Frederick J. Hoffman*. Baton Rouge: Louisiana State Univ. Press, 1970. [Burgess, Woolf]

Friedman, Norman. *Form and Meaning in Fiction*. Athens: Univ. of Georgia Press, 1975. [Woolf]

Gallagher, Donat, ed. *The Essays, Articles and Reviews of Evelyn Waugh*. London: Methuen, 1983. [Compton-Burnett, Greene, Spark, Wells, Wilson]

Garnett, David. *Great Friends: Portraits of Seventeen Writers*. New York: Atheneum, 1980. [Conrad, Ford, Wells Woolf]

Gill, Richard. *Happy Rural Seat: The English Country House and the Literary Imagination*. New Haven: Yale Univ. Press, 1972. [Ford, Sackville-West, Wells, Wolf]

Gillie, Christopher. *Movements in English Literature 1900–1940*. Cambridge: Cambridge Univ. Press, 1975. [Compton-Burnett, Greene, Wells, Woolf]

Gindin, James. *Harvest of a Quiet Eye: The Novel of Compassion*. Bloomington: Indiana Univ. Press, 1971. [Wilson, Woolf]

————. *Postwar British Fiction: New Accents and Attitudes*. Berkeley: Univ. of California Press, 1962. [Golding, Murdoch, Wilson]

Halio, Jay L., ed. *British Novelists since 1960. Dictionary of Literary Biography*, vol. 14. Detroit: Gale Research Co., 1983. [Burgess, Drabble, Murdoch, Wilson]

Hall, James. *The Lunatic Giant in the Drawing Room: The British and American Novel since 1930.* Bloomington: Indiana Univ. Press, 1968. [Greene, Murdoch]

Hawthorn, Jeremy. *Multiple Personality and the Disintegration of Literary Character: From Oliver Goldsmith to Sylvia Plath.* New York: St. Martin's Press, 1983. [Conrad, Rhys]

Higdon, David Leon. *Time and English Fiction.* Totowa, N.J.: Roman and Littlefield, 1978. [Conrad, Golding, Greene, Woolf]

Hunter, Jefferson. *Edwardian Fiction.* Cambridge, Mass.: Harvard Univ. Press, 1982. [Conrad, Ford, Wells]

Hynes, Samuel. *Edwardian Occasions: Essays on English Writing in the Early Twentieth Century.* Oxford: Oxford Univ. Press, 1972. [Conrad, Ford, Wells, Woolf]

Johnstone, Richard. *The Will to Believe: Novelists of the Nineteen-Thirties.* Oxford: Oxford Univ. Press, 1982. [Greene]

Joseph, Gerhard. "The *Antigone* as Cultural Touchstone: Matthew Arnold, Hegel, George Eliot, Virginia Woolf, and Margaret Drabble." *PMLA*, 96 (January 1981), 22–35. [Drabble, Woolf]

Josipovici, Gabriel. *The World and the Book: A Study of Modern Fiction.* Stanford: Stanford Univ. Press, 1971. [Golding]

Kaplan, Sydney Janet. *Feminine Consciousness in the Modern British Novel.* Urbana: Univ. of Illinois Press, 1975. [Woolf]

Karl, Frederick R. *A Reader's Guide to the Contemporary English Novel.* Rev. ed. New York: Farrar, 1972. [Burgess, Compton-Burnett, Golding, Greene, Murdoch, Wilson]

Kellogg, Gene. *The Vital Tradition: The Catholic Novel in a Period of Convergence.* Chicago: Loyola Univ. Press, 1970. [Greene]

Kennard, Jean E. *Number and Nightmare: Forms of Fantasy in Contemporary Fiction.* Hamden, Conn.: Archon Books, 1975. [Burgess, Golding, Murdoch]

Kennedy, Alan. *The Protean Self: Dramatic Action in Contemporary Fiction.* New York: Columbia Univ. Press, 1974. [Greene, Spark]

Kermode, Frank. *Continuities.* London: Routledge, 1968. [Golding, Spark]

————. *Puzzles and Epiphanies: Essays and Reviews 1958–1961.* London: Routledge, 1962. [Golding, Greene, Wilson]

Kettle, Arnold. *An Introduction to the English Novel.* Vol. II, *Henry James to the Present.* Harper Torchbooks, 1951; rpt. New York: Harper, 1960. [Compton-Burnett, Conrad, Greene, Wells, Woolf]

Kostelanetz, Richard, ed. *On Contemporary Literature.* New York: Avon Books, 1964. [Burgess, Golding, Murdoch, Spark]

Kunkel, Francis L. *Passion and The Passion: Sex and Religion in Modern Literature.* Philadelphia: Westminster Press, 1975. [Golding, Greene]

Little, Judy. *Comedy and the Woman Writer: Woolf, Spark, and Feminism.* Lincoln: Univ. of Nebraska Press, 1983. [Drabble, Rhys, Spark, Woolf]

Lodge, David. *The Novelist at the Crossroads and Other Essays on Fiction and Criticism.* London: Routledge, 1971. [Greene, Spark, Wells]

May, Keith M. *Characters of Women in Narrative Literature.* New York: St. Martin's Press, 1981. [Murdoch, Spark, Woolf]

Miles, Rosalind. *The Fiction of Sex: Themes and Functions of Sex Difference in the Modern Novel*. London: Vision Press, 1974. [Burgess, Compton-Burnett, Conrad, Drabble, Ford, Manning, Murdoch, Rhys, Sackville-West]

Morris, Robert K. *Continuance and Change: The Contemporary British Novel Sequence*. Carbondale: Southern Illinois Univ. Press, 1972. [Burgess, Manning]

————, ed. *Old Lines, New Forces: Essays on the Contemporary English Novel, 1960–1970*. Rutherford, N.J.: Fairleigh Dickinson Univ. Press, 1976. [Burgess, Drabble, Wilson]

O'Connor, William Van, ed. *Forms of Modern Fiction: Essays Collected in Honor of Joseph Warren Beach*. 1948; rpt. Bloomington: Indiana Univ. Press, 1962. [Greene, Woolf]

O'Faolain, Sean. *The Vanishing Hero: Studies of the Hero in the Modern Novel*. The Universal Library. New York: Grosset & Dunlap, 1957. [Greene, Woolf]

Otten, Terry. *After Innocence: Visions of the Fall in Modern Literature*. Pittsburgh: Univ. of Pittsburgh Press, 1982. [Conrad, Golding]

Panichos, George A., ed. *The Politics of Twentieth-Century Novelists*. New York: Hawthorn Books, 1971. [Greene, Wells]

Patterson, John. *The Novel as Faith—The Gospel According to James, Hardy, Conrad, Joyce, Lawrence, and Virginia Woolf*. Boston: Gambit, 1973. [Conrad, Woolf]

Porter, Katherine Anne. *The Collected Essays and Occasional Writings of Katherine Anne Porter*. New York: Delacorte Press, 1970. [Ford, Woolf]

Pritchett, V. S. *The Tale Bearers: Essays on English, American and Other Writers*. New York: Random House, 1980. [Conrad, Greene, Wilson]

Raban, Jonathan. *The Technique of Modern Fiction: Essays in Practical Criticism*. London: Arnold, 1968. [Conrad, Drabble, Ford, Golding, Murdoch, Spark, Wilson]

Rabinovitz, Rubin. *The Reaction against Experiment in the English Novel 1950–1960*. New York: Columbia Univ. Press, 1967. [Burgess, Compton-Burnett, Conrad, Golding, Greene, Murdoch, Spark, Wells, Wilson, Woolf]

Richter, David H. *Fable's End: Completeness and Closure in Rhetorical Fiction*. Chicago: Univ. of Chicago Press, 1975. [Golding]

Rigney, Barbara Hill. *Lilith's Daughters: Women and Religion in Contemporary Fiction*. Madison: Univ. of Wisconsin Press, 1982. [Drabble, Woolf]

Rippier, Joseph S. *Some Postwar English Novelists*. Frankfurt/Main: Diesterweg, 1965. [Golding, Murdoch]

Rule, Jane. *Lesbian Images*. Garden City: Doubleday, 1975. [Compton-Burnett, Sackville-West]

Ruotolo, Lucio P. *Six Existential Heroes: The Politics of Faith*. Cambridge, Mass.: Harvard Univ. Press, 1973. [Golding, Greene, Woolf]

Scholes, Robert. *The Fabulators*. New York: Oxford Univ. Press, 1967. [Murdoch]

Schorer, Mark, ed. *Modern British Fiction*. New York: Oxford Univ. Press, 1961. [Conrad, Ford, Woolf]

Seiler-Franklin, Carol. *Boulder-Pushers: Women in the Fiction of Margaret Drabble, Doris Lessing, and Iris Murdoch*. European University Studies: Series 14, volume 78. Bern: Verlag Peter Lang, 1980. [Drabble, Murdoch]

Shapiro, Charles, ed. *Contemporary British Novelists. Crosscurrents/Modern Critiques*. Carbondale: Southern Illinois Univ. Press, 1965. [Golding, Murdoch, Spark, Wilson]

Sheed, Wilfrid. *The Morning After: Selected Essays and Reviews*. New York: Farrar, 1971. [Golding, Greene, Murdoch]

Showalter, Elaine. *A Literature of Their Own: British Women Novelists from Bronte to Lessing*. Princeton: Princeton Univ. Press, 1977. [Drabble, Rhys, Wells, Woolf]

Sinfield, Alan, ed. *Society and Literature, 1945–1970*. New York: Holmes & Meier, 1983. [Burgess, Compton-Burnett, Conrad, Drabble, Golding, Greene, Murdoch, Spark, Wells, Wilson]

Solotaroff, Theodore. *The Red Hot Vacuum and Other Pieces of Writing on the Sixties*. New York: Atheneum, 1970. [Burgess]

Sparks, Patricia Meyer. *The Adolescent Idea: Myths of Youth and the Adult Imagination*. New York: Basic Books, 1981. [Burgess, Sparks]

————, ed. *Contemporary Women Novelists: A Collection of Critical Essays*. Twentieth Century Views. Englewood Cliffs, N.J.: Prentice-Hall, 1977. [Drabble, Murdoch, Rhys, Spark]

Staley, Thomas F., ed. *Twentieth-Century Women Novelists*. New York: Barnes and Noble, 1982. [Drabble, Manning, Murdoch, Spark]

Stern, J. T. *On Realism*. Concepts of Literature Series. London: Routledge, 1973. [Compton-Burnett, Conrad, Ford, Golding, Murdoch, Woolf]

Stevenson, Lionel. *The History of the English Novel*. Vol. II, *Yesterday and After*. New York: Barnes and Noble, 1967. [Compton-Burnett, Ford, Golding, Greene, Murdoch, Sackville-West, Wells, Wilson, Woolf]

Swinden, Patrick. *Unofficial Selves: Character in the Novel from Dickens to the Present Day*. London: Macmillan, 1973. [Ford, Murdoch, Spark]

Updike, John. *Hugging the Shore: Essays and Criticism*. New York: Knopf, 1983. [Murdoch, Spark]

Walker, Ronald G. *Infernal Paradise: Mexico and the Modern English Novel*. Berkeley: Univ. of California Press, 1978. [Greene]

Webster, Harvey Curtis. *After the Trauma: Representative British Novelists since 1920*. Lexington: Univ. of Kentucky Press, 1970. [Compton-Burnett, Greene]

West, Rebecca. *The Young Rebecca: Writings of Rebecca West 1911–17*. Ed. Jane Marcus. New York: Viking, 1982. [Ford, Wells]

Wilde, Alan. *Horizons of Assent: Modernism, Postmodernism, and the Ironic Imagination*. Baltimore: Johns Hopkins Univ. Press, 1981. [Compton-Burnett]

Wilson, Angus. *Diversity and Depth in Fiction: Selected Critical Writings*. Ed. Kerry McSweeney. New York: Viking, 1984. [Compton-Burnett, Woolf]

————. "Evil in the English Novel." *Books and Bookmen* (June 1963), 3–6, 39–43. [Compton-Burnett, Conrad, Golding, Greene, Wilson, Woolf]

SYBILLE BEDFORD

Furbank, P. N. "John Bull and the German Garden." *Encounter* (April 1964), 85–91.

Malin, Irving. "The Whole Mystery of Form." *Shenandoah*, 14:4 (Summer 1963), 58–61.

Mizener, Arthur. "Spring Fiction." *The Kenyon Review*, 19:3 (Summer 1957), 484–493.

Morse, J. Mitchell. "Brand Names and Others." *Hudson Review*, 22:2 (Summer 1969), 316–329.

Olney, James. "'Most Extraordinary': Sybille Bedford and Aldous Huxley." *South Atlantic Quarterly*, 74 (1975), 376–386.

O'Neill, John. "Sybille Bedford." In *Contemporary Novelists*, ed. James Vinson, 70–71. New York: St. Martin's Press, 1982.

Pritchett, V. S. "Daughter of a Lady." *New Statesman*, 11 January 1963, 46–47.

Sale, Roger. "Huxley and Bennett, Bedford and Drabble." *Hudson Review*, 28:2 (1975), 285–293.

Waugh, Evelyn. "A Remarkable Historical Novel." *Spectator*, 13 April 1956, 498.

ANTHONY BURGESS

Aggeler, Geoffrey. *Anthony Burgess: The Artist as Novelist*. University: Univ. of Alabama Press, 1979.

————. "The Comic Art of Anthony Burgess." *Arizona Quarterly*, 25 (Autumn 1969), 234–251.

"Anthony Burgess Special Number." *Modern Fiction Studies*, 27 (Autumn 1981).

Coale, Samuel. *Anthony Burgess*. Modern Literature Series. New York: Ungar, 1981.

DeVitis, A. A. *Anthony Burgess*. New York: Twayne, 1972.

Evans, Robert O. "Nadsat: The Argot and Its Implications in Anthony Burgess's *A Clockwork Orange*." *Journal of Modern Literature*, 1:3 (March 1971), 406–410.

Hartveit, Lars. *The Art of Persuasion: A Study of Six Novels*. Oslo: Universitetsforlaget, 1977.

McNeil, David. "The Musicalization of Fiction: The 'Virtuosity' of Burgess's *Napoleon Symphony*." *Mosaic*, 16 (Summer 1983), 101–116.

Morris, Robert K. "Anthony Burgess: *The Malayan Trilogy*: The Futility of History." In *Continuance and Change: The Contemporary British Novel Sequence*. Carbondale: Southern Illinois Univ. Press, 1972.

————. *The Consolations of Ambigiuity: An Essay on the Novels of Anthony Burgess*. Columbia: Univ. of Missouri Press, 1971.

Pritchard, W. H. "The Novels of Anthony Burgess." *Massachusetts Review*, 7 (Summer 1966), 525–539.

Sullivan, Walter. "Death without Tears: Anthony Burgess and the Dissolution of the West." *The Hollins Critic*, 6 (April 1969), 1–11.

IVY COMPTON-BURNETT

Burkhart, Charles, ed. "Ivy Compton-Burnett Special Number." *Twentieth Century Literature*, 25 (Summer 1979).

————. *Herman and Nancy and Ivy: Three Lives in Art*. London: Gollancz, 1977.

————, ed. *The Art of I. Compton-Burnett*. Atlantic Highlands, N.J.: Humanities Press, 1973.

Dick, Kay. *Ivy & Stevie: Ivy Compton-Burnett and Stevie Smith*. 1971; rpt. London: Allison & Busby, 1983.

Grylls, R. Glynn. *I. Compton-Burnett*. Writers and Their Work. London: Longman, 1971.

Johnson, Pamela Hansford. "I. Compton-Burnett." In *Important to Me*. New York: Scribner's, 1974.

Kettle, Arnold. "I. Compton-Burnett: *A Family and a Fortune*." In *An Introduction to the English Novel*. Vol. 2, *Henry James to the Present*. Harper Torchbooks. 1951; rpt. New York: Harper, 1960.

MacSween, R. J. "Ivy Compton-Burnett." *Antigonish Review*, 24 (Winter 1976), 24–30.

McCarthy, Mary. "The Inventions of I. Compton-Burnett" and "More on Compton-Burnett." In *The Writing on the Wall and Other Literary Essays*, 112–144, 145–152. New York: Harcourt, 1970.

Sprigge, Elizabeth. *The Life of Ivy Compton-Burnett*. New York: Braziller, 1973.

Spurling, Hilary. *Ivy When Young: The Early Life of Ivy Compton-Burnett 1884-1919*. London: Gollancz, 1974.

Wilde, Alan. "The Epistemology of Late Modernism." In *Horizons of Assent: Modernism, Postmodernism, and the Ironic Imagination*, 106–123. Baltimore: Johns Hopkins Univ. Press, 1981.

————. "Surfacings: Reflections on the Epistemology of Late Modernism." *Boundary 2*, 8:2 (1980), 209–227.

JOSEPH CONRAD

Berman, Jeffrey. *Joseph Conrad: Writing as Rescue*. New York: Astra Books, 1977.

Biles, Jack I. "Winnie Verloc: Agent of Death." *Conradiana*, 13:2 (1981), 101–108.

Bonney, William W. *Thorns and Arabesques: Contexts for Conrad's Fiction*. Baltimore: Johns Hopkins Univ. Press, 1980.

Bruss, Paul. *Conrad's Early Sea Fiction: The Novelist as Navigator*. Lewisburg, Pa.: Bucknell Univ. Press, 1979.

Conrad, Joseph. *A Personal Record*. New York: Harper, 1912; rpt. Marlboro, Vt.: The Marlboro Press, 1983.

"Joseph Conrad Special Number." *Modern Fiction Studies*, 1:1 (February 1955) and 10:1 (Spring 1964).

Geddes, Gary. *Conrad's Later Novels*. Montreal: McGill-Queen's Univ. Press, 1980.

Gillon, Adam, Ludwik Krzyzanowsky, et al., eds. *Joseph Conrad: Commemorative Essays*. New York: Astra Books, 1975.

John D. Gordan. *Joseph Conrad: The Making of a Novelist*. Cambridge, Mass.: Harvard Univ. Press, 1941.

Guerard, Albert. *Conrad the Novelist*. Cambridge, Mass.: Harvard Univ. Press, 1958.

Hewitt, Douglas. *Conrad: A Reassessment*. 3rd ed. Totowa, N.J.: Rowman and Littlefield, 1975.

Jean-Aubry, G. *Joseph Conrad: Life and Letters.* 2 vols. Garden City: Doubleday, Page, 1927.

Johnson, Julie M. "The Damsel and Her Knights: The Goddess and the Grail in Conrad's *Chance.*" *Conradiana,* 13:3 (1981), 221–228.

Karl, Frederick R. *Joseph Conrad: The Three Lives.* New York: Farrar, 1979.

————, ed. *Joseph Conrad: A Collection of Criticism.* New York: McGraw-Hill, 1975.

Mudrick, Marvin, ed. *Conrad: A Collection of Critical Essays.* Twentieth Century Views. Englewood Cliffs, N.J.: Prentice-Hall, 1966.

Najder, Zdzislaw. *Joseph Conrad: A Chronicle.* New Brunswick, N.J.: Rutgers Univ. Press, 1983.

Oates, Joyce Carol. "'The Immense Indifference of Things': The Tragedy of Conrad's *Nostromo.*" *Novel,* 8 (Autumn 1975), 5–22.

Sherry, Norman, ed. *Joseph Conrad: A Commemoration.* New York: Barnes and Noble, 1976.

Stallman, R. W., ed. *The Art of Joseph Conrad: A Critical Symposium.* 1960; rpt. Athens: Ohio Univ. Press, 1982.

Tennant, Roger. *Joseph Conrad: A Biography.* New York: Atheneum, 1981.

Watt, Ian. *Conrad in the Nineteenth Century.* Berkeley: Univ. of California Press, 1979.

Watts, Cedric. *A Preface to Conrad.* London: Longman, 1982.

MARGARET DRABBLE

Harper, Michael F. "Margaret Drabble and the Resurrection of the English Novel." *Contemporary Literature,* 23 (Spring 1982), 145–168.

Lambert, Ellen Z. "Margaret Drabble and the Sense of Possibility." *Univ. of Toronto Quarterly,* 49:3 (1980), 228–251.

Libby, Marion V. "Fate and Feminism in the Novels of Margaret Drabble." *Contemporary Literature,* 16 (Spring 1975), 175–193.

Mannheiser, Monica Lauritzen. "The Search for Identity in Margaret Drabble's *The Needle's Eye.*" *Dutch Quarterly Review,* 5:1 (1975), 24–35. With comment by Margaret Drabble, 35–38.

Moran, Mary H. *Margaret Drabble: Existing within Structures.* Cross-currents/Modern Critiques/New Series. Carbondale: Southern Illinois Univ. Press, 1983.

Murphy, Brenda. "Women, Will, and Survival: The Figure in Margaret Drabble's Carpet." *South Atlantic Quarterly,* 82 (Winter 1983), 38–50.

Myer, Valerie Grosvenor. *Margaret Drabble: Puritanism and Permissiveness.* New York: Barnes & Noble, 1974.

Nicolaisen, W. F. H. "'What a Name, Stephen Halifax': Onomastic Modes in Three Novels by Margaret Drabble." *Literary Onomastics Studies,* 10 (1983), 269–284.

Rigney, Barbara Hill. *Lilith's Daughters: Women and Religion in Contemporary Fiction.* Madison: Univ. of Wisconsin Press, 1982.

Rose, Ellen Cronan. *The Novels of Margaret Drabble: Equivocal Figures.* New York: Barnes & Noble, 1980.

Schmidt, Dorey, ed. *Margaret Drabble: Golden Realms.* Living Authors Series, No. 4. Edinburg, Tx.: Pan American Univ., 1982.

FORD MADOX FORD

Bender, Todd K. "The Sad Tale of Dowell: Ford Madox Ford's *The Good Soldier.*" *Criticism*, 4 (Fall 1962), 353–368.

Bowen, Stella. *Drawn from Life: Reminiscences.* London: Collins, 1941.

Cassell, Richard A., ed. *Ford Madox Ford: Modern Judgements.* London: Macmillan, 1972.

————. *Ford Madox Ford: A Study of His Novels.* Baltimore: Johns Hopkins Univ. Press, 1961.

Donoghue, Denis. "Listening to the Saddest Story." *Sewanee Review*, 88 (Fall 1980), 557–571.

"Ford Madox Ford Special Number." *Modern Fiction Studies*, 9:1 (Spring 1963).

Goldring, Douglas. *The Last Pre-Raphaelite.* London: MacDonald, 1948.

Gordon, Ambrose, Jr. *The Invisible Tent: A Key to the Novels of Ford Madox Ford.* Austin: Univ. of Texas Press, 1964.

Greene, Graham. "Ford Madox Ford." In *Graham Greene Collected Essays.* New York: Viking, 1969.

Hoffmann, Charles G. *Ford Madox Ford.* New York: Twayne, 1967.

Hungiville, Maurice. "'The Last Happy Time': Ford Madox Ford in America." *Journal of Modern Literature*, 6 (April 1977), 209–221.

MacShane, Frank. *The Life and Works of Ford Madox Ford.* New York: Horizon Press, 1965.

Meixner, John A. *Ford Madox Ford's Novels: A Critical Study.* Minneapolis: Univ. of Minnesota Press, 1962.

Mizener, Arthur. *The Saddest Story: A Biography of Ford Madox Ford.* New York: World, 1971.

Moser, Thomas C. *The Life in the Fiction of Ford Madox Ford.* Princeton: Princeton Univ. Press, 1981.

Secor, Robert, and Marie Secor. *The Return of* The Good Soldier: *Ford Madox Ford and Violet Hunt's 1917 Diary.* English Literary Studies, No. 30. Victoria, B.C.: Univ. of Victoria Press, 1983.

Snitow, Ann Barr. *Ford Madox Ford and the Voice of Uncertainty.* Baton Rouge: Louisiana State Univ. Press, 1984.

Stang, Sondra J., ed. *The Presence of Ford Madox Ford: A Memorial Volume of Essays, Poems, and Memoirs.* Philadelphia: Univ. of Pennsylvania Press, 1981.

WILLIAM GOLDING

Anderson, David. *The Tragic Protest: A Christian Study of Some Modern Literature.* Richmond, Va.: John Knox Press, 1969.

Babb, Howard S. *The Novels of William Golding.* Columbus: Ohio State Univ. Press, 1970.

Baker, James R. *William Golding.* New York: St. Martin's Press, 1965.

Biles, Jack I. "Piggy: *Apologia Pro Vita Sua.*" *Studies in the Literary Imagination*, 1 (October 1968), 83–109.

————. *Talk: Conversations with William Golding.* New York: Harcourt, 1970.

————, ed. "A William Golding Miscellany." William Golding Special Number, *Studies in the Literary Imagination*, 2:2 (October 1969).

_____, and Robert O. Evans, eds. *William Golding: Some Critical Considerations*. Lexington: Univ. of Kentucky Press, 1978.

Bufkin, E. C. "The Nobel Prize and *The Paper Men:* The Fixing of William Golding." *The Georgia Review*, 39:1 (Spring 1985), 55–65.

"William Golding Special Number." *Twentieth Century Literature*, 28:2 (Summer 1982).

Kinkead-Weekes, Mark, and Ian Gregor. *William Golding: A Critical Study*. London: Faber, 1967.

Nelson, William, ed. *William Golding's* Lord of the Flies, *A Source Book*. New York: Odyssey Press, 1963.

Oldsey, Bernard S., and Stanley Weintraub. *The Art of William Golding*. New York: Harcourt, 1965.

Peter, John. "The Fables of William Golding." *The Kenyon Review*, 19 (Autumn 1957), 577–592.

Smith, Eric. "Lord of the Flies." In *Some Versions of the Fall: The Myth of the Fall of Man in English Literature*. London: Croom Helm, 1973.

Sullivan, Walter. "The Long Chronicle of Guilt: William Golding's *The Spire*." *Hollins Critic*, 1 (June 1964), 1–12.

Tiger, Virginia. *William Golding: The Dark Fields of Discovery*. London: Calder & Boyars, 1974.

GRAHAM GREENE

Allott, Kenneth, and Miriam Farris. *The Art of Graham Greene*. London: Hamilton, 1951.

Bryden, Ronald. "Graham Greene, Alas." In *The Unfinished Hero and Other Essays*. London: Faber, 1969.

Evans, Robert O., ed. *Graham Greene: Some Critical Considerations*. Lexington: Univ. of Kentucky Press, 1963.

Greene, Graham. *A Sort of Life*. New York: Simon & Schuster, 1971.

_____. *Ways of Escape*. New York: Simon & Schuster, 1980.

"Graham Greene Special Number." *Modern Fiction Studies*, 3 (Autumn 1957).

Hartveit, Lars. *The Art of Persuasion: A Study of Six Novels*. Oslo: Universitetsforlaget, 1977.

Hynes, Samuel, ed. *Graham Greene: A Collection of Critical Essays*. Twentieth-Century Views. Englewood Cliffs, N.J.: Prentice-Hall, 1973.

O'Faolain, Sean. *The Vanishing Hero: Studies of the Hero in the Modern Novel*. The Universal Library. New York: Grosset & Dunlap, 1957.

Sharrock, Roger. *Saints, Sinners, and Comedians: The Novels of Graham Greene*. Notre Dame: Notre Dame Univ. Press, 1984.

Spurling, John. *Graham Greene*. Contemporary Writers. London: Methuen, 1983.

Stratford, Philip. *Faith and Fiction: Creative Process in Greene and Mauriac*. Notre Dame: Notre Dame Univ. Press, 1964.

Wolfe, Peter, ed. *Essays on Graham Greene*. Vol. 1. Greenwood, Fla.: Penkevill Press, 1985.

OLIVIA MANNING

Mooney, Harry J., Jr. "Olivia Manning: Witness to History." In *Twentieth-Century Women Novelists*, ed. Thomas F. Staley, 39–60. Totowa, N.J.: Barnes and Noble, 1982.

Morris, Robert K. "Olivia Manning: *The Balkan Trilogy*: The Quest for Permanence." In *Continuance and Change: The Contemporary British Novel Sequence*. Carbondale: Southern Illinois Univ. Press, 1972.

Willy, Margaret. "Manning, Olivia." In *Great Writers of the English Language: Novelists and Prose Writers*, ed. James Vinson, 802–804. New York: St. Martin's Press, 1979.

IRIS MURDOCH

Baldanza, Frank. *Iris Murdoch*. New York: Twayne, 1974.

————. "Iris Murdoch and the Theory of Personality." *Criticism*, 7 (Spring 1965) 176–189.

Berthoff, Warner. "Fortunes of the Novel: Muriel Spark and Iris Murdoch." *Massachusetts Review*, 8:2 (Spring 1967), 301–332.

Byatt, A. S. *Degrees of Freedom: The Novels of Iris Murdoch*. London: Chatto and Windus, 1965.

Detweiler, Robert. *Iris Murdoch's* The Unicorn: *Introduction and Commentary*. Religious Dimensions in Literature. Gen. ed., Lee A. Belford. New York: Seabury Press, 1969.

Dipple, Elizabeth. *Iris Murdoch: Work for the Spirit*. Chicago: Univ. of Chicago Press, 1982.

Hall, James. *The Lunatic Giant in the Drawing Room: The British and American Novel since 1930*. Bloomington: Indiana Univ. Press, 1968.

Lloyd, Genevieve. "Iris Murdoch on the Ethical Significance of Truth." *Philosophy and Literature*, 6:1 & 2 (1982), 62–75.

Martz, Louis L. "Iris Murdoch: The London Novels." In *Twentieth-Century Literature in Retrospect*, ed. Reuben A. Brower. Cambridge, Mass.: Harvard Univ. Press, 1971.

"Iris Murdoch Special Number." *Modern Fiction Studies*, 15:3 (Autumn 1969).

O'Connor, William Van. *The New University Wits and the End of Modernism*. Carbondale: Southern Illinois Univ. Press, 1963.

Poirier, Richard. "The Politics of Self-Parody." *Partisan Review*, 35 (Summer 1968), 339–353.

Randall, Julia. "Against Consolation: Some Novels of Iris Murdoch." *Hollins Critic*, 13 (February 1976), 1–15.

Rippier, Joseph S. *Some Postwar English Novelists*. Frankfurt/Main: Diesterweg, 1965.

Todd, Richard. *Iris Murdoch: The Shakespearian Interest*. New York: Barnes and Noble, 1979.

Weatherhead, A. K. "Backgrounds with Figures in Iris Murdoch." *Texas Studies in Literature and Language*, 10 (Winter 1969), 635–648.

Wolfe, Peter. *The Disciplined Heart: Iris Murdoch and Her Novels*. Columbia: Univ. of Missouri Press, 1966.

JEAN RHYS

Abel, Elizabeth. "Women and Schizophrenia: The Fiction of Jean Rhys." *Contemporary Literature*, 20 (Spring 1979), 155–177.

Alvarez, A[lfred]. "The Best Living English Novelist." *The New York Times Book Review*, 17 March 1974, 6–8.

Davidson, Arnold E. "The Dark Is Light Enough: Affirmation from Despair in Jean Rhys's *Good Morning, Midnight*." *Contemporary Literature*, 24 (Fall 1983), 349–364.

Delany, Paul. "Jean Rhys and Ford Madox Ford: What 'Really' Happened?" *Mosaic*, 16 (Fall 1983), 15–24.

de Nève, Edward. *Barred*. London: Harmsworth, 1932.

Ford, Ford Madox. *When the Wicked Man*. New York: Liveright, 1931.

Gardiner, Judith K. "'The Grave,' 'On Not Shooting Sitting Birds,' and the Female Esthetic." *Studies in Short Fiction*, 20 (Fall 1983), 265–270.

Lai, Wally Look. "The Road to Thornfield Hall: An Analysis of Jean Rhys's *Wide Sargasso Sea* (Andre Deutsch, 1966)." *New Beacon Reviews, Collection One*. Ed. John La Rose. London: New Beacon Books Ltd., 1968, 38–52.

Mellown, Elgin W. "Character and Themes in the Novels of Jean Rhys." *Contemporary Literature*, 13 (Autumn 1972), 458–475.

Nebeker, Helen. *Jean Rhys, Woman in Passage: A Critical Study of the Novels of Jean Rhys*. Montreal: Eden Press Women's Publishers, 1981.

Plante, David. "Jean Rhys: A Remembrance." *Paris Review*, 76 (Fall 1979), 238–284. Rpt. Plante, David. *Difficult Women: A Memoir of Three*. New York: Atheneum, 1983.

Pool, Gail. "Jean Rhys: Life's Unfinished Form." *Chicago Review*, 32:4 (Spring 1981), 68–74.

Porter, Dennis. "Of Heroines and Victims: Jean Rhys and *Jane Eyre*." *Massachusetts Review*, 17:3 (Autumn 1976), 540–552.

Rhys, Jean. *Smile Please: An Unfinished Autobiography*. London: Deutsch, 1979.

Staley, Thomas F. *Jean Rhys: A Critical Study*. Austin: Univ. of Texas Press, 1979.

Thompson, Irene. "The Left Bank Apéritifs of Jean Rhys and Ernest Hemingway." *The Georgia Review*, 35:1 (Spring 1981), 94–106.

Thorpe, Michael. "'The Other Side': *Wide Sargasso Sea* and *Jane Eyre*." *Ariel*, 8:3 (July 1977), 99–110.

Tiffin, Helen. "Mirror and Mask: Colonial Motifs in the Novels of Jean Rhys." *World Literature Written in English*, 17 (April 1978), 328–341.

Wolfe, Peter. *Jean Rhys*. New York: Twayne, 1980.

Wyndham, Francis. "An Inconvenient Novelist." *Tribune*, 15 December 1950, 16, 18.

VITA SACKVILLE-WEST

Bell, Anne Olivier, ed. *The Diary of Virginia Woolf*. Vols. 2–5. New York: Harcourt, 1978–1984.

DeSalvo, Louise A. "Lighting the Cave: The Relationship between Vita Sackville-West and Virginia Woolf." *Signs*, 8:2 (1982), 195–214.

Glendinning, Victoria. *Vita: The Life of V. Sackville-West*. London: Weidenfield and Nicolson, 1983.

Julian, Phillippe, and John Phillips. *The Other Woman: A Life of Violet Trefusis Including Previously Unpublished Correspondence with Vita Sackville-West*. Boston: Houghton Mifflin, 1977.

Love, Jean O. "*Orlando* and Its Genesis: Venturing and Experimenting in Art, Love, and Sex." In *Virginia Woolf: Revaluation and Continuity*, ed. Ralph Freedman. Berkeley: Univ. of California Press, 1980.

MacKnight, Nancy, ed. *Dearest Andrew: Letters from V. Sackville-West to Andrew Reiber 1951–1962*. London: Michael Joseph, 1980.

Nicolson, Nigel. *Portrait of a Marriage*. New York: Atheneum, 1973.

Nicolson, Nigel, and Joanne Trautmann, eds. *The Letters of Virginia Woolf*. Vols. 2–6. New York: Harcourt, 1976–1980.

Olson, Stanley, ed. *Harold Nicolson: Diaries and Letters 1930–1964*. New York: Atheneum, 1980.

Pomeroy, Elizabeth W. "Within Living Memory: Vita Sackville-West's Poems of Land and Garden." *Twentieth Century Literature*, 18 (Fall 1982), 269–289.

Stevens, Michael. *V. Sackville-West: A Critical Biography*. London: Joseph, 1973.

Trautmann, Joanne. *The Jessamy Brides: The Friendship of Virginia Woolf and Vita Sackville-West*. Univ. Park: Pennsylvania State Univ. Press, 1973.

Walpole, Hugh. "V. Sackville-West." *Bookman* (New York), (September 1930), 21–26.

Watson, Sara Ruth. *V. Sackville-West*. New York: Twayne, 1972.

MURIEL SPARK

Adler, Renata. "Muriel Spark." In *On Contemporary Literature*, ed. Richard Kostelanetz. New York: Avon Books, 1964.

Baldanza, Frank. "Muriel Spark and the Occult." *Wisconsin Studies in Contemporary Literature*, 6:2 (Summer 1965), 190–203.

Bedford, Sybille. "Fantasy without Whimsy." *Saturday Review*, 19 November 1960, 28–29.

Berthoff, Warner. "Fortunes of the Novel: Muriel Spark and Iris Murdoch." *Massachusetts Review*, 8:2 (Spring 1967), 301–332.

Bradbury, Malcolm. "Muriel Spark's Fingernails." In *Possibilities: Essays on the State of the Novel*. London: Oxford Univ. Press, 1973.

Dobie, Ann B. "Muriel Spark's Definition of Reality." *Critique: Studies in Modern Fiction*, 12 (December 1970), 20–27.

Evans, Robert O. "A Perspective for American Novelists." *Topic: A Journal in the Liberal Arts*, 6 (Fall 1966), 58–66.

Grosskurth, Phyllis. "The World of Muriel Spark: Spirits or Spooks?" *Tamarack Review*, 39 (Spring 1966), 62–67.

Harrison, Bernard. "Muriel Spark and Jane Austen." In *The Modern English Novel: The Reader, the Writer, and the Work*, ed. Gabriel Josipovici. London: Open Books, 1976.

Hoyt, Charles Alva. "Muriel Spark: The Surrealist Jane Austen." In *Contemporary British Novelists*, ed. Charles Shapiro, 125–143. Carbondale: Southern Illinois Univ. Press, 1965.

Kemp, Peter. *Muriel Spark: Novelists and their World*. London: Paul Elek, 1974.

Lodge, David. "The Uses and Abuses of Omniscience: Method and Meaning in Muriel Spark's *The Prime of Miss Jean Brodie*." In *The Novelist at the Crossroads and Other Essays on Fiction and Criticism*. London: Routledge, 1971.

Malkoff, Karl. "Demonology and Dualism: The Supernatural in Isaac Singer and Muriel

Spark." In *Critical Views of Isaac Bashevis Singer*, ed. Irvin Malin, 149–168. New York: New York Univ. Press, 1969.

Massie, Alan. *Muriel Spark*. Edinburgh: Ramsey Head Press, 1979.

Parrinder, Patrick. "Muriel Spark and Her Critics." *Critical Quarterly*, 25 (Summer 1983), 23–31.

Richmond, Velma Bourgeois. "The Darkening Vision of Muriel Spark." *Critique: Studies in Modern Fiction*, 15 (1973), 71–85.

Stanford, Derek. *Muriel Spark: A Biographical and Critical Study*. London: Centaur Press, 1963.

Whittaker, Ruth. *The Faith and Fiction of Muriel Spark*. New York: St. Martin's Press, 1982.

H. G. WELLS

Bellamy, William. *The Novels of Wells, Bennett, and Galsworthy*. London: Routledge, 1971.

Bergonzi, Bernard. *The Early H. G. Wells: A Study of the Scientific Romances*. Manchester: Manchester Univ. Press, 1961.

————, ed. *H. G. Wells: A Collection of Critical Essays*. Twentieth Century Views. Englewood Cliffs, N.J.: Prentice-Hall, 1976.

Brooks, Van Wyck. *The World of H. G. Wells*. 1915; rpt. St. Clair Shores, Mich.: Scholarly Press, 1970.

Dickson, Lovat. *H. G. Wells: His Turbulent Life and Times*. New York: Atheneum, 1969.

Hammond, J. R. *An H. G. Wells Companion*. New York: Barnes and Noble, 1979.

Haynes, R. D. *H. G. Wells Discovers the Future: The Influence of Science on His Thought*. New York: New York Univ. Press, 1980.

Hillegas, Mark R. *The Future as Nightmare: H. G. Wells and the Anti-Utopians*. New York: Oxford Univ. Press, 1967.

Hynes, Samuel. "The Fabians: Mrs. Webb and Mr. Wells." In *The Edwardian Turn of Mind*, 87–131. Princeton: Princeton Univ. Press, 1968.

Kemp, Peter. *H. G. Wells and the Culminating Ape*. New York: St. Martin's Press, 1982.

Mackenzie, Norman, and Jeanne Mackenzie. *H. G. Wells: A Biography*. New York: Simon and Schuster, 1973.

McConnell, Frank. *The Science Fiction of H. G. Wells*. Oxford: Oxford Univ. Press, 1981.

Parrinder, Patrick. *H. G. Wells*. New York: Putnam, 1977.

Philmus, Robert M. *Into the Unknown: The Evolution of Science Fiction from Francis Godwin to H. G. Wells*. Berkeley: Univ. of California Press, 1970.

————. "Revisions of His Past: H. G. Wells's Anatomy of Frustration." *Texas Studies in Literature and Language*, 20:2 (Summer 1978), 249–266.

Ray, Gordon N. *H. G. Wells and Rebecca West*. London: Macmillan, 1974.

Suvin, Darko, and Robert M. Philmus, eds. *H. G. Wells and Modern Science Fiction*. Lewisburg, Pa.: Bucknell Univ. Press, 1977.

Wagar, W. Warren. *H. G. Wells and the World State*. New Haven: Yale Univ. Press, 1961.

Wells, H. G. *Experiment in Autobiography: Discoveries and Conclusions of a Very Ordinary Brain (since 1866)*. New York: Macmillan, 1934.

————. *H. G. Wells in Love. Postscript to an Experiment in Autobiography.* Ed. G. P. Wells. Boston: Little, Brown, 1984.

West, Anthony. *H. G. Wells: Aspects of a Life.* New York: Random House, 1984.

West, Geoffrey. *H. G. Wells: A Sketch for a Portrait.* London: Howe, 1930.

Williamson, Jack. *H. G. Wells: Critic of Progress.* Baltimore: Mirage Press, 1973.

ANGUS WILSON

Bergonzi, Bernard. "Between Nostalgia and Nightmare." In *The Situation of the Novel*, 149–187. London: Macmillan, 1970.

Cox, C. B. "Angus Wilson: Studies in Depression." In *The Free Spirit: A Study of Liberal Humanism in the Novels of George Eliot, Henry James, E. M. Forster, Virginia Woolf, Angus Wilson*, 117–153. London: Oxford Univ. Press, 1963.

Gindin, James. *Harvest of a Quiet Eye: The Novel of Compassion.* Bloomington: Indiana Univ. Press, 1971.

————. "Angus Wilson's Qualified Nationalism." In *Postwar British Fiction: New Accents and Attitudes*. Berkeley: Univ. of California Press, 1962.

Halio, Jay L. *Angus Wilson.* Writers and Critics. Edinburgh: Oliver and Boyd, 1964.

Haule, James M. "*Setting the World on Fire*: Angus Wilson and Problem of Evil." *Twentieth Century Literature*, 28 (Winter 1982), 453–466.

Kissane, Joseph, ed. "Angus Wilson Special Number." *Twentieth Century Literature*, 29 (Summer 1983).

McSweeney, Kerry. "Angus Wilson: Diversity, Depth, and Obsessive Energy." In *Four Contemporary Novelists: Angus Wilson, Brian Moore, John Fowles, V. S. Naipaul*. Montreal: McGill-Queen's Univ. Press, 1983.

Rabinovitz, Rubin. "Angus Wilson." In *The Reaction against Experiment in the English Novel, 1950–1960*, 64–96. New York: Columbia Univ. Press, 1967.

Waugh, Evelyn. *A Little Order: A Selection from His Journalism.* Ed. Donat Gallagher. New York: Little, Brown, 1981.

Wilson, Angus. "As If by Magic: Angus Wilson on His Own Novel." *Dutch Quarterly Review*, 6:4 (1976), 259–278.

————. *The Wild Garden, or Speaking of Writing.* London: Secker & Warburg, 1963.

VIRGINIA WOOLF

Annan, Noel. *Leslie Stephen: The Godless Victorian.* New York: Randon House, 1984.

Bell, Anne Olivier, ed. *The Diary of Virginia Woolf.* 5 vols. New York: Harcourt, 1977–84.

Bell, Quentin. *Virginia Woolf: A Biography.* New York: Harcourt, 1972.

Bennett, Joan. *Virginia Woolf: Her Art as a Novelist.* 2nd ed. Cambridge: Cambridge Univ. Press, 1964.

Blackstone, Bernard. *Virginia Woolf: A Commentary*. New York: Harcourt, 1949.

Brewster, Dorothy. *Virginia Woolf*. New York: New York Univ. Press, 1962.

Clements, Patricia, and Isobel Grundy, eds. *Virginia Woolf: New Critical Essays*. Totowa, N.J.: Barnes and Noble, 1984.

Dahl, Christopher C. "Virginia Woolf's *Moments of Being* and Autobiographical Tradition in the Stephen Family." *Journal of Modern Literature*, 10 (June 1983), 175–196.

Fleishman, Avrom. *Virginia Woolf: A Critical Reading*. Baltimore: Johns Hopkins Univ. Press, 1975.

Forster, E. M. "Virginia Woolf." In *The Bloomsbury Group: A Collection of Memoirs, Commentary and Criticism*, ed. S. P. Rosenbaum, 1975; rpt. Toronto: Univ. of Toronto Press, 1977.

Freedman, Ralph, ed. *Virginia Woolf: Revaluation and Continuity*. Berkeley: Univ. of California, 1980.

Ginsberg, Elaine. *Virginia Woolf: Centennial Papers*. Ed. Laura Moss Gottlieb. Troy, N.Y.: Whitston, 1983.

Richter, Harvena. *Virginia Woolf: The Inward Voyage*. Princeton: Princeton Univ. Press, 1970.

Rose, Phyllis. *Woman of Letters: A Life of Virginia Woolf*. New York: Oxford Univ. Press, 1978.

Spilka, Mark. *Virginia Woolf's Quarrel with Grieving*. Lincoln: Univ. of Nebraska Press, 1980.

Sprague, Claire, ed. *Virginia Woolf: A Collection of Critical Essays*. Twentieth Century Views. Englewood Cliffs, N. J.: Prentice-Hall, 1971.

"Virginia Woolf Special Number." The 25th Anniversary Number of *Twentieth Century Literature*, 25:3–4 (Fall-Winter 1979).

"Virginia Woolf Special Number." *Modern Fiction Studies*, 2 (1956) and 18 (1972).

Woolf, Virginia. *Moments of Being*. Ed. Jeanne Schulkind. New York: Harcourt, 1976.

Notes on Contributors

CAROL AMES, formerly Assistant Professor of English at the State University of New York College at Plattsburgh, is now a writer living in Santa Monica, California. In addition to short stories and book reviews, she has published critical articles on Goethe, Jane Austen, and Shirley Jackson. She recently researched unsung American heroes for the CBS documentary series "An American Portrait."

JOHN ATKINS, an English writer of force and range, is the author of three novels: *Cat on Hot Bricks* (1948), *Rain and the River* (1954), *A Land Fit for Eros* (with J. B. Pick, 1956); a three-volume literary history, *Sex in Literature;* and, besides critical essays, numerous books of literary commentary and criticism, including studies of Hemingway, Orwell, Koestler, Huxley, Greene, and *Tomorrow Revealed: A History of the Future* and *Six Novelists Look at Society*.

FRANK BALDANZA was Professor of English at Bowling Green State University. The author of many scholarly articles, he published books of criticism and commentary on Mark Twain, Ivy Compton-Burnett, and Iris Murdoch. Professor Baldanza passed away in 1985.

TODD K. BENDER is Professor of English at the University of Wisconsin at Madison. Besides critical articles, he has published *Gerard Manley Hopkins: The Critical Reception and Classical Background of His Work,* is coauthor of *A Hopkins Concordance,* and editor of the series of concordances to Joseph Conrad's complete works. Expert in the subject, he is the principal editor of *Modernism in Literature* and the motivating force behind the MLA seminars on Impressionism over the past several years.

JACK I. BILES was Professor Emeritus of English at Georgia State University. His work appeared in various scholarly journals; other publications include *Talk: Conversations with William Golding* and *William Golding: Some Critical Considerations* (with Robert O. Evans), as well as four special numbers of *Studies in the Literary Imagination,* including issues on twentieth-century novelists of Great Britain. Forthcoming are three contributions to books: two on Sir Angus Wilson and one on Graham Greene. Jack I. Biles died in the spring of 1986.

RICHARD BRADFORD holds the Doctor of Philosophy degree from Oxford University and is currently the University of Wales Research Fellow in the Department of English, Saint David's University College, Lampeter, Dyfed. His publications include articles on poetics and versification. At present, he is at work on a book concerning post-Renaissance poetic form.

CECIL DAVIES is senior Staff Tutor in Literature and Resident Tutor in Cheshire (Macclesfield District) for the Department of Extra-Mural Studies of the University of Manchester, England. Author of the first essay on William Golding's poetry *(English,* Autumn 1968) and

347

other critical articles, he has written "the first full account in any language of the history, productions, and significance of the Volksbühne" in *Theatre for the People: The Story of the Volksbühne* (1978).

MARGARET DRABBLE is a penetrating and impressive British writer, the author of numerous remarkable novels. Additionally, she has written a massive biography of Arnold Bennett, studies of William Wordsworth and of the Victorian Age, *A Writer's Britain*, and has edited *The Genius of Thomas Hardy* and *The Oxford Companion to English Literature*.

ROBERT O. EVANS is Professor of English and Director of the General Honors Program at the University of New Mexico. Besides numerous articles, he has written or edited many books, including *A Study of Milton's Elision; The Osier Cage: Rhetorical Devices in Romeo and Juliet; Style, Rhetoric, & Rhythm* (with J. Max Patrick et al.); *Graham Greene: Some Critical Considerations;* and a novel. Among recent publications are an edition-translation of both *An Introduction to American Literature* and *An Introduction to English Literature* by Jorge Luis Borges (with L. Clark Keating), as well as *William Golding: Some Critical Considerations* (with Jack I. Biles).

AVROM FLEISHMAN is Professor of English at The Johns Hopkins University and a former Guggenheim Fellow. His publications include, besides numerous articles in journals, *A Reading of Mansfield Park, Conrad's Politics, The English Historical Novel, Virginia Woolf: A Critical Reading, Fiction and the Ways of Knowing,* and *Figures of Autobiography.*

JAY L. HALIO, Professor of English at the University of Delaware, is the author of a book on Angus Wilson and the editor of volume 14, *British Novelists since 1960,* of the *Dictionary of Literary Biography.* He also has written extensively on Shakespeare and the Elizabethans and continues to work in his field of major interest.

JOAN MANHEIMER is Assistant Professor of English at Vassar College. Her primary interests are in American literature and Women's Studies. Publications include articles on Edwin Arlington Robinson's poetry and on Maxine Hong Kingston's autobiography. She is presently working on the theme of "murderous mothers" in Victorian fiction.

ROBERT K. MORRIS is Professor of English at the City College of the City University of New York. He is the author of *The Novels of Anthony Powell, The Consolations of Ambiguity: An Essay on the Novels of Anthony Burgess, Continuance and Change: The Contemporary British Novel Sequence,* and *Paradoxes of Order: Some Perspectives on the Fiction of V. S. Naipaul,* as well as of a number of reviews and articles on contemporary British and American literature. He also has edited *Old Lines, New Forces: Essays on the Contemporary British Novel, 1960–1970,* and is the principal editor of the original and revised editions of *The Achievement of William Styron.*

NORMAN PAGE is Professor of English at the University of Alberta and a former Guggenheim Fellow. His books include *Speech in the English Novel* (1973), studies of Jane Austen, Wilkie Collins, Thomas Hardy, and E. M. Forster, and editions of novels by Dickens and Hardy. He has edited the two-volume *D. H. Lawrence: Interviews & Recollections* (1981), *Nabokov: The Critical Heritage* (1982), and *Tennyson: Interviews & Recollections* (1983). His most recent work is a critical biography of A. E. Housman (1983).

WILLIAM J. SCHEICK is Professor of English at the University of Texas, Austin, where he also serves as editor of *Texas Studies in Literature and Language.* His wide-ranging work has appeared in numerous journals, and his books include *The Will and the Word: The Poetry of Edward Taylor; The Writings of Jonathan Edwards: Theme, Motif and Style; The Slender Human Word: Emerson's Artistry in Prose; The Half-Blood: A Cultural Symbol in Nineteenth-Century American Fiction;* and *The Splintering Frame: The Later Fiction of H. G. Wells.*

CATHERINE SMITH, Assistant Professor at the Georgia Institute of Technology, teaches technical writing and public speaking. She has written laboratory books for freshman composition courses and has published an article on Alan Sillitoe. Currently, she is working on a study of the fantasy element in the works of Sir Angus Wilson.

PHILIPPA TRISTRAM, a graduate of Oxford University, a Lecturer in English literature at the University of York, and former Visiting Associate Professor at Vassar College (1976–77), has published on the nineteenth- and twentieth-century novel. Her book *Figures of Life and Death in Medieval Literature* appeared in 1976.

ANGUS WILSON, a most distinguished British man of letters, has written stories, novels, plays, and biographical-critical studies. An inveterate commentator, he has produced many brief critical articles, innumerable reviews, and a variety of miscellaneous writings. His most recent work includes the editing of *East Anglia in Verse* (1983) and *The Portable Charles Dickens* (1983).

PETER WOLFE is Professor of English at the University of Missouri at St. Louis. The author of many articles and reviews, he has published critical books on Iris Murdoch, Mary Renault, Rebecca West, Graham Greene, Ross Macdonald, Jean Rhys, Dashiel Hammett, Patrick White, and Raymond Chandler.

INDEX

350